SWALEDALE AND WHARFEDALE REMEMBERED

Tan Hill Coal Mine, Arkengarthdale, 1931

Muker street scene, outside Peacock's shop

Cover pictures.

Front:

Top row, left to right: John Thomas Ideson, wife Lilian and two of his children, of Barden, near Bolton Abbey. He would die during the Great War;
Haymaking on the Grassington to Conistone Road c1905.
Bottom row, left to right: Tan Hill Coalmine, Arkengarthdale;
Caravans on Reeth Green during agricultural show time 1907.

Back:

Top row, left to right: First Chapman motor charabanc, Grassington;
Bales of cotton from Linton Cotton Mill pre-Great War.
Next row, left to right: Crossing the stepping stones at Bolton Priory (Bolton Abbey) c1900;
The Calvert family (blacksmiths), of Gunnerside, pre-Great War.
Bottom row: Judging sheep, Muker Show, Swaledale, 1920's.

SWALEDALE AND WHARFEDALE REMEMBERED

KEITH TAYLOR

The Smithy, Buckden, c1911

ASHRIDGE PRESS
COUNTRY BOOKS

Published by Ashridge Press/Country Books
Courtyard Cottage, Little Longstone, Bakewell, Derbyshire DE45 1NN
Tel/Fax: 01629 640670
e-mail: dickrichardson@country-books.co.uk

ISBN 1 901214 66 4

British Library Cataloguing in Publication Data.
A catalogue record for this book is available from the British Library.

By the same author:
DARLEY DALE REMEMBERED:
THROUGH 50 YEARS OF WAR AND PEACE

WENSLEYDALE REMEMBERED: THE SACRIFICE MADE BY THE
FAMILIES OF A NORTHERN DALE 1914-1918 AND 1939-1945

TANSLEY REMEMBERED:
ASPECTS OF VILLAGE LIFE THROUGH PEACE AND WAR

By the same author in conjunction with Trevor Brown:
A DERBYSHIRE PARISH AT WAR:
SOUTH DARLEY AND THE GREAT WAR 1914 – 1919

A DERBYSHIRE PARISH AT PEACE AND WAR
SOUTH DARLEY 1925 – 1955

Printed and bound by The Gutenberg Press Ltd.

CONTENTS

ACKNOWLEDGEMENTS

A special thanks to Dick Richardson at Country Books for all his help in getting the manuscript and photographs into book form.

Another very special thank you to Joyce Sunter of Downholme Manor for her hard work and support in helping me with the project.

Clive Torrens for allowing me the use of a large number of picture postcards of places in the dales.

Frank Dickens and Duncan Rhodes for help with computer work.

Curators of 30 Regimental Museums.

Staff of the Darlington Local Studies Library, Darlington and Stockton Times Library, Richmond Library, Skipton Local Studies Library and Matlock Local Studies Library.

Fiona Rosher and Debbie Allen at The Dales Countryside Museum, Hawes, Jane Hatcher at the Richmondshire Museum (Wenham Collection), Helen Bainbridge at the Swaledale Folk Museum, Reeth, and Mrs. Astell-Burt at the Upper Wharfedale Museum, Grassington.

Chris Foster, Trevor Croucher and John Richardson of The Craven Community Projects Group.

Editors of various parish magazines and publications.

Special thanks for their time, information, memories and loan of photographs to the following people (please accept my apology if I have left out any name by mistake):

Trevor Brown, James Sunter, Margaret Cody, R. Lingard, Duncan Bythell, Nan Kettlewell, Beryl Simpson, Barbara Weatherald, V. Chandler, Cynthia Rymer, Kathleen Carlisle, Mrs Caygill, Shirley Bainbridge, Dorothy and Ken Guy, David Guy, Marina Whitehead, Barbara Buckingham, Cicely Bailey, David Cherry, Jack Alderson, Walter Appleton, John Rukin, Jennie Rukin, Matt Spensley, Alan Spensley, Jim Calvert, Robert Clarkson, Agnes Beswick, Jim Russell, Doris West, Clifford Clarkson, Rosa Laurie, Elsie Thornborrow, Mr. and Mrs. D. Mudd, Mr. and Mrs. Richard Sunter, Tracy Little, Lawrence Barker, Arthur Beresford, Peter Beresford, Barbara Slater, Joan Daggett, Brian Metcalfe, Alan Akers, Raymond Rutter, John Cockett, John Blenkiron, Elvie Squires, Joe Morgan, Sylvia Clemminson, Ann Kilburn, Mrs Parkin, Derek Parkin, Thomas and Hilda Wellock, Mary Sanderson, John Martin, Dennis Daykin, Tom Peacock, Harry and Andoline Petty, Avril Richardson, Mrs. Carter, Maurice Hutchinson, James Reed, Hilda Harker, Malcolm Ingleby, James and Jennifer Kendall, Lorraine Hartley, Annette Wetherell, Dr. Harrison, Ric Halsall, Derek Tennant, Tommy Metcalfe, Charlie Hall, James Cooper, Betty Balderstone, Roma Brass, William Dinsdale, Tommy Ingleby, Ronnie Brown, Patricia and Chris Procter, Simon Barningham, Margaret McGill, Muriel Hargraves, Janet Stockdale, Colin and Rita Maxfield, Mary Smith, Mavis Dyson, Margaret Alderson, John Goat, Pauline Lewis, Frank Horner, Chris Best, Lawrence Hathaway, Lance Robinson, Pat Carlin, Bob Cheyney, Brian Robinson, Constance West, Elizabeth Calvert, Philip Hartley, Pamela Hall, Laura Simpson, Sheila Lofthouse, Caroline Cunningham, E.M. Child, Ian Eccles, Stuart Leslie, Andrew Seeger, Allan Blackburn, Freda Smith, Enid Briggs, G. Alderson, Norman Simpson, Herbert Holmes, Richard Gill, Mrs. Wallbank, W. Dickinson, Anne Luxmoore, Richard Dalrymple-Smith, Mr. Hodgson, P. Wyness. B. Cuthbertson, V. Worthington, Eva Parker, Anthony Petyt, T.J. Walter, Heather Swires, Dorothy Newall, Mr. Lund, Mr. Merlane, D. Holdsworth, David Kirkley, Eric Rowley, Margaret Lister, Mary Spink, Allan Akers, Jim Stubbs, P. Kipling, John Pickles, Neville Little, Brian Todd, Keith Todd, Jean Sherratt, Peter Hughes, George Lundberg, Julie Dodd, Steve Howarth, Tom Carr, David Squires, J. Reinsch, Sheila Charlton, William Kendall, Mr. Salvin, Bill Kendall, Maurice Hall, E.A. Moralee, Ramsay Hutchinson, Simon Barningham, Jim Stubbs, George Calvert, Dennis Daykin, Laura Simpson, Susan and Colin Hird, Dick Metcalfe, Colin Easterby, Graham Binns, Brian Parker, J. Turner, Norah Bratley, E. Stubbs, Mrs. R. Warhurst, Jack Swales, Norman Reeday, George Fielden, Basil Spensley, Ralph Clarke, John Lovell, Sheila Pedley, Jean Murdoch, Winnie Delf.

BIBLIOGRAPHY AND SOURCES

Craven's Part in the Great War Editor John T. Clayton
Squadron Histories by Peter Lewis, Putnam and Company
Fighter Squadrons of the RAF by John Rawlins, Macdonald and Janes
Bomber Squadrons of the RAF by Philip Mojes, Macdonald and Janes
Battalion war diaries and Regimental histories
World War Two, Orbis Publications
Pen and Sword publications
The Face of Battle by John Keegan, Jonathan Cape
History of the First World War by Liddell Hart
Passchendaele in Perspective – The Third Battle of Ypres, Pen and Sword
Messines Ridge, Ypres, Pen and Sword
The Grenadier Guards in the Great War by Sir Frederick Ponsonby, Macmillan and Company
The Second World War – Winston Churchill
History of the Green Howards 1914 - 1919
Census for 1881, 1891 and 1901
Various newspapers, including :
The Darlington and Stockton Times, The Northern Echo, The Craven Herald and The Yorkshire Post
The Compostellan (Richmond Grammar School)
Commonwealth War Graves Commission web site
CD Rom of *The Soldiers Died in the Great War*

The most valuable sources of information and many accompanying photographs have been generously provided by people connected to the dales.

INTRODUCTION

In October 2004 I published "Wensleydale Remembered", telling the stories of all the servicemen whose names are enshrined on that dale's war memorials.

As I travelled through Wharfedale in May 2005, on one of my frequent visits to West Witton in Wensleydale, it occurred to me that I would like to accomplish something similar for Wensleydale's northern neighbour, Swaledale, and Wharfedale to the south.

As I passed through Wharfedale on my return home a week later, I called at St. Michael and All Angel's Church, Hubberholme, St. Oswald's Church, Arncliffe and Linton Church, in order to take down the names of all the servicemen who died in uniform whilst serving their country during the two world wars.

A decision had been made, and for me there was no turning back. During further visits to the Yorkshire Dales I was able to add the names of servicemen from the war memorials in Bolton Abbey, Burnsall, Hebden, Rylstone, Hetton, Cracoe, Conistone and Kettlewell, as well as from the settlements in Swaledale and Arkengarthdale, from Keld in the west to Richmond in the east.

In writing the book I have attempted to reveal the background to these men of the dales, as well as show what happened to them when they went off to war. However, I have also set these men back into the dales' villages, towns and landscapes they would have been familiar with, either before the Great War or during the inter-war years of the 1920's and 1930's.

Through words and photographs, a picture emerges of life in the relative backwaters of Swaledale, Arkengarthdale, Wharfedale, Langstrothdale and Littondale, before events on the world scene were to rudely intervene and take these dalesmen away from their families and to their deaths during the two world-wide conflicts of the 20th century.

War memorials are sited in virtually every parish, but who now remembers the "Pals" of 1914 - 1918? Thirty seven thousand war memorials were built throughout Britain, naming over 750,000 men who lost their lives in the Great War. They grew out of the grief generated by this loss, and through the fact that the British Government decided that those who died on the battlefield would be buried near where they fell. The families of those who fell required their names to be commemorated closer to home and so the local war memorial sprang from this collective grief during the early 1920's.

The First World War is passing from human memory into history, whilst many of those who survived the Second World War have passed away. 236 men from these dales gave their lives for "King and Country" between 1914 and 1918, whilst the supreme sacrifice was again asked of 103 men during the years 1939 to 1945.

It is the aim of "Swaledale and Wharfedale Remembered" to celebrate the lives of these lost generations (and their colleagues who were fortunate to survive these conflicts). On the following pages I have attempted therefore to rekindle memories of these gallant dalesmen, by finding out, wherever possible, about their lives and deaths. In doing so I have felt privileged, as always, to be delving into their histories, and hope that it will help others to appreciate their supreme sacrifices.

Keith Taylor
2006

Unveiling Richmond War Memorial

Haymaking near Low Row

CHAPTER ONE

A VIEW OF SWALEDALE AND WHARFEDALE

Many of the men whose names are carved on the war memorials, though by no means all, came from families long associated with the dales. Those who came from elsewhere to live and work would still have been very familiar with the landscape and history of these beautiful dales.

The unique Dale's landscape is one of sweeping fells and raging becks, crisp limestone escarpments or the dark crags of gritstone. A calmness pervades the landscape and yet there is always the lapwing's lament, the curlew's cry or the harsh rasp of the grouse to keep one company.

The major part of the Dales lies on a platform of ancient rock, chiefly granite, known as the Askrigg Block. However, most of this base platform lies covered by strata of more recently formed rocks, with limestone mainly dominating. The Great Scar Limestone is up to 400 feet thick in parts of the Dales and is magnificently exposed in Wharfedale, Malhamdale and Ribblesdale.

Wharfedale is wooded white limestone in Craven Country, with dry stone walls forming geometric patterns on the valley floors and leading ever upwards on the sides of the fells. The headwaters of the river, named after the Celtic goddess Verbena, are to be found at Cam Beck and Oughtershaw Beck, in the upper valley of the Wharfe, above Buckden, known as Langstrothdale.

Formed by a huge glacier in the later stages of the Ice Age, Wharfedale is dominated by the Great Scar Limestone, the most dramatic feature of which is Kilnsey Crag, four miles north of Grassington. The glacier that formed the dale came up against the huge mass of the fells of Buckden Pike and Great Whernside, forcing it to turn southwards. The dale's landscape has been greatly affected by the Craven Fault, which thrust huge sections of great slab limestone to the surface, the greatest example being the crag at Kilnsey.

Towering 170 feet above the valley floor, this gigantic thrust of the Great Scar Limestone has a remarkable 40 feet overhang at the top, which today provides rock climbers with a stiff challenge. The base of the cliff was scoured back by the Wharfedale glacier and a spring gushes out of the base to form a beck.

Swaledale, together with its tributary dale, Arkengarthdale, is the most northerly of Yorkshire's major dales. It runs 30 miles from the source of the Swale among the peat haggs, 2000 feet up on the uplands of Birkdale Common, to Richmond in the east.

In Swaledale, the Great Scar Limestone lies hidden beneath layers of rock strata known as the Yoredale Series. Formed in an alternate succession of sandstone, shale

Kilnsey Crag, in Wharfedale

The pattern of field barns in the haymeadows of 'Gunnerside Bottoms', Swaledale

and limestone, the Yoredales have weathered to produce hillsides with a distinctive stepped profile. In both Swaledale and Wharfedale, though, the higher fells are capped by beds of millstone grit.

Man has contributed greatly in this narrow, beautiful dale, from the hanging woods between Reeth and Richmond, to the stone walls, field barns, villages and the remains of lead mining activity to be found in the upper dale.

Swaledale is famous for its spring meadows and the wonderful array of field barns. Gunnerside Bottoms, in particular, a fertile stretch of old glacial flood plain, was turned into a patchwork quilt of fields, separated by dry stone walls. From small quarries in the hills, local grey brown sandstone was hewed to provide stone for the villages, hamlets, farms and barns.

In Wharfedale in particular, New Stone Age settlements existed on the lower slopes and "henge" sites at Yarnbury, above Grassington, are evidence of Bronze Age usage in 2000 BC, while Middle Bronze Age stone circles can be seen at Appletreewick, Bordley, Embsay and Yockenthwaite.

By 100 BC an Iron Age culture of pastoral farming was established on the well-drained limestone soils of the Craven uplands.

Today's pattern of settlement was mainly established through successive waves of colonisation by Angles, Danes and Norsemen between 700 and 1100 AD. Whilst Danish settlers kept stock, cultivated the land and lived in communities, the Norse settlers favoured pastoral farming, grazing the valley pastures in spring and autumn and moving to higher land during the summer months. The village greens at Arncliffe and Linton originated as central areas in Anglian villages where the live-stock could be safely kept should danger threaten.

As Norman power increased after the invasion of 1066, Reeth in Swaledale and Starbotton in Wharfedale were forest-edge villages, whilst a century later the next settlements were built as foresters' villages (Healaugh in Swaledale and Buckden in Wharfedale). Forest land was set aside for hunting. The Norman lords hunted Arkengarthdale Forest and Bishopdale Chase, whilst Langstrothdale Chase in Upper Wharfedale was hunted by first the de Romilles and then the Cliffords of Skipton Castle.

Langstrothdale Chase was a hunting preserve for deer and game. Forest courts prevailed, with their laws, privileges and harsh punishments. However, the area had originally been settled by the Norsemen and their sheep farms became lodges in this forest environment, forming the small hamlet settlements we see today in this beautiful dale – Oughtershaw, Beckermonds, Deepdale, Yokenthwaite, Raisgill, Hubberholme and Cray. It is just beyond Yockenthwaite that we find even earlier evidence of human settlement, with 20 stones forming a Bronze Age circle, hidden behind a wall in a field across the river.

The minor road through the dale from Buckden to Hawes, in Wensleydale, is the highest road in North Yorkshire, reaching a height of 1934 feet at the watershed on Fleet Moss. It is also, without doubt, one of the most beautiful.

Beyond Yokenthwaite, the woodland diminishes as the valley narrows, whilst the river follows a course over limestone beds and ledges, forming natural weirs and pools of water. The former stone packhorse bridge at Deepdale was replaced by an iron structure in 1907, whilst at Beckermonds (called Beggarmuns by the locals) the road splits into two, the main arm twisting and turning to Oughtershaw at 1200 feet and the lesser arm taking the traveller westwards to High Greenfield. In Medieval times this narrow road was a more important route, used by packhorses on their way from Lancaster to Richmond, and Greenfield was an important grange, worked on behalf of the monks from Fountains Abbey.

A profound influence on the Dales' landscape was that of the Monasteries. Members of the Augustinian order settled at Bolton Priory in Wharfedale in 1155 AD. Huge areas of uplands throughout the dales were owned by the monasteries, bringing farming and sheep-breeding skills to their vast estates and organising a pastoral economy from their series of granges, worked by lay brothers and local labour.

They were largely responsible for founding the hill farming life style and the present network of roads and tracks. Increasingly, they enclosed small fields by stone walls to exclude other animals.

The greatest number of farmhouses and yeomen's houses date from the waves of rebuilding that took place between 1670 and 1700 and 1720 to 1750. Local stone, usually sandstone, was used, and these buildings have therefore grown from the landscape. From 1720 the Georgian style became fashionable through the influence of such buildings as Fountaine Hospital (Almshouses) at Linton.

It was during the period 1760 to 1840 that the valley bottoms and lower hillsides were enclosed by hundreds of miles of dry stone walls, providing the view of the landscape we value so much today. Barns were built and the rectangular enclosed pastures enabled the land to be managed more efficiently.

Without doubt, the grazing of sheep has had a great influence on the landscape. The Dales are renowned for sheep and years of careful breeding has produced animals ideally suited to the landscape and weather, such as the black faced Swaledale. Indeed, the Yorkshire Dales National Park Authority chose the Swaledale tup as its symbol, for sheep grazing has had a profound effect on the natural vegetation of the dales. The dalesman's way of life was regulated by the natural rhythm of the seasons. Lambing took place in April, shearing at the beginning of July, hay cutting in late July, November witnessing tupping and always the twice daily routine of milking.

From 1700 to 1900 the droving trade of Scottish cattle to the Midlands and the South flourished. Along quiet, un-turnpiked roads and avoiding towns and villages, the drover and his dogs walked upwards of 200 beasts to the great English markets. They travelled rough and slept rough, occasionally sleeping at a drover's inn.

Drovers' roads entered the Yorkshire Dales at Tan Hill and continued southwards down Arkengarthdale, crossing Reeth Moor into Swaledale at Feetham and thence to Askrigg. The journey continued over the Stake Pass to Buckden in Wharfedale, to Littondale and Malham.

By 1745 as many as 10,000 cattle were moving along the drove roads at any one time. An enormous field of 732 acres on Malham Moor, called Great Close, north-east of Malham Tarn, was used for pasturing Scottish cattle and 20,000 beasts are recorded as grazing there during one summer. By 1900 however, the trade was almost dieing out with the decrease in demand for Scottish cattle and the development of the railway system making such transportation over long distances obsolete (although, throughout the first thirty years of the 20th century it was a common sight to see local dales farmers driving their flocks or herds along the roads and from one dale into the next).

Farming predominated as the principal occupation in both Swaledale and Wharfedale but up until even the late 19th century lead mining was of great importance in Upper Swaledale and Arkengarthdale, as well as in the Grassington and Kettlewell areas of Wharfedale. A local Swaledale poet, Mr. Ford, confirmed this when he wrote:

> "Among the mines we may relate,
> Surrender, Kinning and Blakethwaite;
> With Bunting, Blind Gill, Beldi Hill,
> And celebrated Swinnergill:
> The ancient fields have long supplied
> The metal for a soldier's pride;
> And doubtless Russian soldiers know
> Full well its force to lay them low."

In the northern dales shallow bell pits formed the early workings, before horizontal adits (tunnels) were driven into the hillsides to follow the vein of ore. These veins were revealed by a process of scouring a hillside with water released from a temporary dam built on the hillside above. This process, known as "hushing", has left huge gashes in the landscape in areas such as Gunnerside Gill, Swaledale, and above Langthwaite in Arkengarthdale.

There was a constant need for water to separate the ore after crushing and for powering water-wheels to operate bellows that forced air across the ore-hearth in small furnaces where ore was smelted to produce pure lead. Fuel was provided by local peat or coal from the coal mines near Tan Hill, in Arkengarthdale, such as the Moulds Gill Colliery or Punchard Colliery.

Only the ruins of the smelt mills, furnaces and peat stores, together with the courses of the flues that took away poisonous gases to the chimneys, now remain in these lonely side valleys. Impressive examples of such ruins can be seen on the slopes of Arkengarthdale, on Cogden Moor above Grinton, at the Sir Francis Level in Gunnerside Gill and at the Old Gang Mine on the moors above Kearton and north of Reeth. On these last two sites were two smelt mills, Lownathwaite and Blakethwaite.

On the moors above Grassington was a network of flue tunnels leading to high chimney stacks. The gases from the smelting process passed up the tunnels to cool and deposit the lead on the tunnel walls. Children with brushes were then sent along the tunnels to recover the metal.

During the 12th century, Swaledale and Wharfedale lead roofed French Abbeys and the castle at Windsor. Foreign cathedrals, including those in Rome, had lead from these Yorkshire dales.

Lead mining in the dales possibly went back to the Bronze Age but the Romans were certainly involved in the trade. The ore was carried to smelting mills and then by pack horse to their fort at Bainbridge in Wensleydale, and on to Richmond and Barnard Castle. After the defeat of the Brigantes by the 9th Roman Legion in 74 AD, many of the defeated warriors were taken by the Romans as slaves to work the lead mines at Hurst in Swaledale and Greenhow Hill in Wharfedale.

In later years, Swaledale and Arkengarthdale between them produced 6000 tons of lead annually. During the mid to late 19th century, however, competition from the continent and Spain in particular, caused a depression, when many northern dales families moved to the Durham area to work in the collieries or to the Lancashire textile mills, whilst some emigrated abroad, especially to America and Canada. By around the 1880's the lead mining industry in Swaledale and Arkengarthdale was coming towards an end and all mines had closed by the early years of the 20th century.

Yorkshire's most northerly Pennine dale, **Arkengarthdale**, with the Arkle Beck's course running from near Tan Hill to its meeting with the River Swale at Grinton, 11 miles away, was settled by Norsemen, as we can see from the names of their settlements – Arkle Town, Langthwaite, Whaw (meaning an enclosure for cows) and Booze (meaning a house by the bend in the river). Though the valley bottom is pastoral and well wooded, the upper fell sides are still slashed by the scars caused by "hushing". On the bleak moors behind High Faggergill Farm was Faggergill mine, one of the largest lead mines in the area.

The Stang and Faggergill Mines, with associated mines such as Sloate Hole and Nut Hole, in a valley perched high above Arkengarthdale, witnessed the final years of lead mining in the dale. The Sloate Hole Level continued throughout 1909 and for a few years longer. A 600 yard tramline was built across the moor to the Faggergill dressing floors, which were renovated in 1909 when a 14 foot diameter waterwheel at the Surrender Smelt Mill was purchased to drive the crushers.

Arkle Town once boasted a parish church, an inn and a workhouse, but with the decline in lead mining, it lost all three. The only remains of the church site are the ruins of the graveyard. The main focus in the dale is **Langthwaite**, with its inn, chapel and "Waterloo" church, erected in 1818 and consecrated in 1820. The church was built with money provided by Parliament to counteract the spread of atheism and free thinking that seemed to threaten the Established Church after the French Revolution and also as a thanksgiving for Wellington's victory over Napolean at Waterloo in 1815.

Charles Bathurst, grandson of Oliver Cromwell's physician, bought the manor of Arkengarthdale in 1656 and developed the lead mines, the family connection lasting until 1912. Just above Langthwaite is CB, the only place name in England composed of initials, named after Charles. Nearby, in a field by the road that turns off to cross the wooded Stang on the way to Barnard Castle, is the hexagonal powder house built in 1807 to store black gunpowder for use in the lead mines, before the use of dynamite. Isolated at the head of the dale is **Tan Hill Inn**, England's highest public house, at 1732 feet. Children born at Tan Hill had to walk to school at Keld, at the head of Swaledale. In bad weather they were found lodgings in Keld during the week.

In the 1930's, 87 year old James Rukin of Keld recalled in a BBC wireless (radio) broadcast his life in the Tan Hill coal mines. He started work in the mines at the age of nine years, first at the William Gill pit, Swaledale, before going to the Tan Hill pit.

He recalled when coal was sold at the pit head for "fippence" (five pence) a corf (2 cwt). "I remember seeing as many as 30 carts waiting at the mine for coal. A man we called the banker used to jot down on a slate the names of the buyers and the number of corves they had. The usual cart load was five corfs at 2sh. 1d. The pit was about 30 fathoms deep and the men were let down by a rope. At William Gill the pulleys were worked by a horse, so that when a full corf was hauled up an empty one would be let down.

"I have known ten men and lads and two horses working at Tan Hill mine and then we could not cope with the demand. Often the carts went away empty because they would have had to wait too long to be loaded.

"I never saw daylight from one Sunday to another during the winter months. I would go down before daybreak and not come up again until after dark and then I had to walk four and a half miles to Keld. We were paid 3 shillings for a full day's work, but during a slack period we would make only 7sh. 6d a week."

Near Punchard House, Arkengarthdale, was Punchard Colliery. In 1902 Joseph Caygill of Whaw worked the pit until 1907, when William Caygill took over. William (Willem) Scott of Whaw, brother of John Alderson Scott, who we shall see was killed in the Great War, became manager of the mine and leased the pit in June 1922 for £5 a month. He employed his brother, Harry Scott, as the manager, with George William Stubbs and George Hird employed as workers, together with Thomas Peacock, brother of Michael Peacock, landlord of the Tan Hill Inn.

They used a pit pony to pull the tubs that ran on rails, which entered the pit by an entrance into the level. Horses and carts from Swaledale came to collect the coal, including transport belonging to Ned Hammond, who arrived to take coal for Reeth workhouse (his son William would be killed on active service in the London Blitz).

During the General Strike of 1926 there was much activity at Punchard Colliery, with horses and carts lining up in queues because of a shortage of coal. William's other brother, James Scott, a miner from County Durham, arrived to help at Punchard.

William would test the quality of the coal by bringing samples back home in his pockets and trying them on the fire. If they "caked" the coal was of reasonable quality.

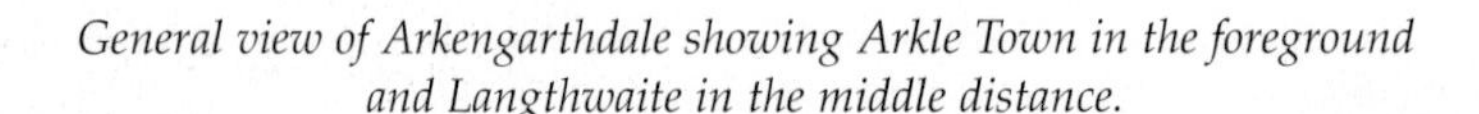

General view of Arkengarthdale showing Arkle Town in the foreground and Langthwaite in the middle distance.

View of Langthwaite village, Arkengarthdale 1913

The shop belonging to the Stubbs family at Langthwaite c1914
Left to right: ? Stubbs, John Robert Stubbs, George William Stubbs, Margaret Lizzie Hillary

Arkengarthdale Band c1907, left to right
Back row: Robert Harker, Weldon Calvert, Frank Mudd, Tom Carter, Fred Hutchinson, Jim Scott, George Barningham, Albert Mudd
Front row: Tom Mudd, John W. Mudd, Michael Hall, John Woodward, Bobby Whitehead, Ben Hall

A view of the bridge into Langthwaite, in Arkengarthdale

The old hexagonal gunpowder store for the leadmines in Arkengarthdale. It is situated above the CB Inn, Langthwaite, as one turns onto the Barnard Castle Road across the Stang

Lead miners at the Nut Hole Incline Mine (Faggergill area, Arkengarthdale) c1906 (the last gasp effort at this formerly rich mine). The entrance to the mine was at the bottom of a shakehole called Nut Hole and ore was hauled up in the waggon. In 1908 a horse level was made into the mine so that full-sized waggons could be used, with the entrance sited near Sloate Hole.
Standing: Ashton Stones, Pratt Demain
Seated: Ralph Harker, John W. Hird, George Harker (manager in the waggon), Jimmy Waller, William Longstaffe, Ben Hall, Jack Alsop, Mark Alsop, Robert Longstaffe
At the front: George Hird
Clive Torrens Collection

The horse-drawn waggons are about to enter Stang Level, near Faggergill Lead Mine c1908. In the background can be seen the Barnard Castle road and also Stang House

Clive Torrens Collection

Miners at the dressing floor at Nut Hole/Sloate Hole, Faggergill Lead Mine c1908/1909.
The wooden launder was used for washing (buddling) the lead ore.
Top row, left to right: Ralph Harker, Pratt Demain, Ben Hall, William Longstaffe, George Harker, Robert Hird, Ashton Stones
Bottom row, left to right: Jimmy Waller, Mark Alsop, John W. Hird, Robert Longstaffe, Jack Alsop

Tan Hill coal mine, on the road between Tan Hill Inn and Keld, c1910

Another view of activity at Tan Hill coal mine, in June 1931

Punchard coal mine, Arkengarthdale, just above Langthwaite, c1914

View of the hamlet of Whaw, in Arkengarthdale 1936
Clive Torrens Collection

Tan Hill Inn, the highest public house in England

The colliery was closed in 1927 and was abandoned in 1929.

Swaledale, the grandest of the dales, with a rugged beauty of its own, is a dale of fast flowing streams and tumbling waterfalls. It is of course famous for its sheep, named after the dale, a hardy black-faced breed that survives the winters well and crosses well with other breeds. One important trait is that they keep to their own area of fell and don't wander.

At the head of Swaledale and surrounded by soaring green fells, lies the grey stoned village of **Keld**, its cottages clustering around a tiny square, whose most imposing buildings are two chapels, a former school and the gaunt youth hostel, sited just above the village. The Cat Hole Inn, the only pub in the village, was closed in the 1950's.

The village derived its name from the Norse word Kelda, meaning a spring or stream and Keld's situation, hidden in a fold and hollow in the fells, provided a sheltered retreat and a refuge from enemies. Dominated by the bulk of Kisdon Hill, it is the last and highest village in the dale.

It was in Medieval times that funeral processions made their way along a track over the top of Kisdon Hill, known as the Corpse Way, as they carried the wicker coffin to the nearest consecrated ground at Grinton Church, near Reeth, 14 miles away (before the church at Muker was built in 1580). Stone slabs were placed along the route to enable the coffin to be rested and one of these large rectangular slabs

A view of Keld village, Swaledale, c1914. The church and school can be seen
Clive Torrens Collection

Cat Hole Inn at Keld between the wars
Clive Torrens Collection

Cat Hole Inn, Keld, in the 1920's. It was run by the Hutchinson family

Keld Band c1910
Back row: Jack Metcalfe, Christopher Metcalfe, James Alderson, Simon Scott, Robert Rukin, Richard Alderson, John Rukin, Cooper Metcalfe
Front row: Ralph Alderson, Waller Hutchinson, James Rukin, James Iveson
We shall find that a quarter of Keld Band would be killed during the First World War, whilst serving in the army (Robert Rukin, Richard Alderson, Waller Hutchinson)

The village, Keld

Keld School c1905

Keld School
Back row: Jim Whitehead, George Alderson, Nellie Alderson, Will Alderson, Nellie Alderson (Harker), Alice Whitehead, Sarah Scott, Ella Harker, Lizzie Scott, Amelia Alderson, John Alderson (Harker), John Whitehead, John Alderson (Pat)
Second row: Willie Whitehead, George Appleton, Joe Sinclair, Dick Metcalfe, Annie Clarkson, Lizzie Clarkson, Jennie Scott, Mary Ellen Fawcett, Isabelle Alderson, Laurie Rukin, Lizzie Metcalfe, Amy Nunn, George Alderson, Lizzie Appleton, Tommy Dinsdale
Front row: Maggie Appleton, George Fawcett, Lizzie Calvert, Kitty Peacock, John Alderson (Stone House), George Metcalfe

Ivelet Bridge, between Muker and Gunnerside, Swaledale.
Built in 1699, it is one of the finest examples of a pack horse bridge in the dales

The sun shines on the coffin stone, set into the ground near Ivelet Bridge.
On its journey along the old Corpse Way, the coffin was rested on the stone

can be found set into the ground on the northern side of Ivelet Bridge (the present bridge was built in 1699 and is one of the finest examples of a packhorse bridge in the Dales).

The Queen's Inn at Muker (no longer a public house) and the Punch Bowl Inn at Feetham were once stops for the coffin bearers and at the former establishment they kept special tankards for their use. The pallbearers sometimes took two days and one night to make the journey, leaving the corpse overnight in the "Deadhouse" at Blades, near Long Row and Feetham (it is a ruin nowadays). When the corpse arrived in Grinton churchyard it was buried without a coffin, dressed in a linen shroud.

The River Swale at Keld provides superb riverside scenery as it flows into a wooded limestone gorge below the village, with fine examples of waterfalls and cascades at Catrake and Kisdon Falls, while a mile above Keld, near Park Bridge, in the austere grandeur of the high Pennine fells, the Swale tumbles over a series of ledges at Wain Wath Force. On the other side of the road from here, are the remains of Keldside Lead Smelting Mill, its flue still traceable up the fellside to the stump of a chimney.

On the footpath from Keld that heads towards Swinner Gill, on the northern bank of the Swale, lies the ruins of Crackpot Hall (Norse for "pothole of the crows"), built originally as a deer stalking lodge for Lord Wharton to hunt the deer which roamed this part of Swaledale. The present buildings were erected in the late 17th century , becoming a farm, which would have been known to all the lads from the upper dale who went off to war between 1914 and 1918. In its last few years it was farmed by Percy and Mary Metcalfe, helped by their farm man, William Calvert, before it was abandoned in 1953. Now it is a sad but imposing ruin on the hillside, its walls brought down by subsidence due to the presence of old lead mines below ground.

Behind the hall and to the west can be seen the spoil heaps left by the miners. Large groups of miners worked the lead mines here in Swinner Gill, both at Lord Pomfret's Smelt Mill and the Beldi Hill Smelt Mill. In those days the present day quietness would have been shattered by the noise of picks, crowbars, barrows, water wheels and crushing hammers. The nearby hillside was the scene of a pitched battle in the 1770's between rival groups of lead miners, when the workings were flooded and blame was placed on one group by the other. The ruined smelt mill at Swinner Gill used to contain two rooms when it was in use from 1769 to 1820. In one room were the smelting hearths, whilst in the other room were the bellows, driven by a water wheel.

A little further down the dale lie the hamlet of **Thwaite** and the village of **Muker** (a Norse name meaning small cultivated field). Muker church, built in 1580, was a chapel of ease, offering a respite for the coffin carriers, who we have seen had previously carried the corpse to Grinton Church (Muker was one of the few churches built during the reign of Elizabeth I). A chapel and Institute were added during the lead mining days of the 19th century (Muker is proud of its band, formed in 1879. Brass bands were a feature of these old lead mining villages and were encouraged by the lead companies).

The largest of the Upper Swaledale settlements, Muker is situated at the southern

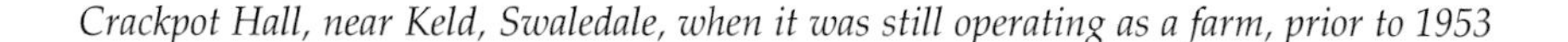

Crackpot Hall, near Keld, Swaledale, when it was still operating as a farm, prior to 1953

The ruins of Crackpot Hall, near Keld, in April 2006

Lord Pomfret's lead smelt mill at East Grain, Swinner Gill, Swaledale, near Keld. Note the flue near the bottom left hand corner

The Beldi Hill Lead Smelt Mill at Swinner Gill, Swaledale, near Keld

foot of Kisdon, a hill over 1600 feet high. Some of the finest hay and flower meadows in the Dales lie behind the village. Purple cranesbill, buttercups, clover and sweet cecily make these hay meadows a feast for the eye during May and June. Of course, for the servicemen from the dales who we will be dealing with later, such a sight would be much more commonplace in 1914 than today. Nowadays, because of changing methods of farming, it is only in certain sections of Swaledale, Wharfedale and Littondale that such a riot of Spring colours grace the scene.

Probably Thwaite's most famous native born inhabitants were the Kearton brothers. Richard (1862 – 1928) was a naturalist, author and lecturer, whilst Cherry Kearton (1871 – 1940) was, in addition, an explorer and pioneer of wild life photography. As lads, they both were scholars at Muker School and are commemorated on plaques on the wall of Muker Chapel. Cherry went on to become a popular radio broadcaster and was killed in 1940 when leaving Broadcasting House during a German air raid.

Tragedy hit the village of Thwaite in 1899 when the waters of Thwaite Beck swept down from Stock Dale in the west and resulted in a loss of life in this isolated Swaledale community. Reports of the time mentioned that flowers washed from Thwaite cottage gardens were later found growing in Muker.

The village of Thwaite in 1904

Clive Torrens Collection

Thwaite c1914

Clive Torrens Collection

The village of Muker in Swaledale c1912

Clive Torrens Collection

Building the new bridge at Muker, Swaledale, in 1906/1907

Muker c1913. The pair in the doorway are William and Dinah Peacock (nee Whitfield). It was a grocers and drapers shop (today it is a house called 'Bramble Bottom'). Most of the people are wearing clogs. The clog maker for Muker was Tom Parrington whilst John Robert Whitell was to be found at Gunnerside.

Clive Torrens Collection

Muker Show c1905

A gathering of people in Muker on the Annual Show Day c1905.
The shop in the foreground is William Peacock's draper's shop

Muker Main Street c1905

Muker Band c1908

Muker, showing the Literary Institute and Church
Clive Torrens Collection

Until the first few decades of the 20th century many Dales farmers practised a method of husbandry still common in parts of the Alps or Norway. A subsidiary house further up the dale was occupied during the summer, with sheep and cattle grazing on the high fells, while valley fields produced the hay, essential for the winter feed.

To store this hay, barns or laithes were built and Swaledale, possibly more than anywhere else in Britain, displays a pattern of dispersed barns, especially in the area of pasture west of Gunnerside, known as Gunnerside Bottoms. Here, where there is a fertile stretch of old glacial flood plain, it has been turned into a patchwork quilt of fields, each with its own barn.

These functional stone barns were for storing hay in the upper storey, and housing cattle below, from November to May. Most barns stored hay gathered from one or two fields and accommodated four cattle below, together with a small area for foddering, milking and "mucking out" during the long, severe winter months.

Before the Great War, most Upper Swaledale family farms consisted of between 100 to 200 sheep and 5 to 15 cows, with pigs and hens also being kept. Being self sufficient in milk, they also produced butter and cheese, with members of the family sometimes standing at Richmond Market to sell the produce.

Sheep provided the main income and the yearly farming cycle started in October with the tup (male) sales at Hawes or Kirkby Stephen, selecting tups to use for the next year's lamb crop. By early November, the tups were put to the ewes.

The sheep remained on the "in-bye" land (pasture) around the farmhouse until mid-December, when they were taken onto the fells for the winter. These hardy Swaledales received very little extra fodder in pre-war years, unless the weather was extremely bad, when bales of hay were carried in "creels" on either side of a pony, or on the farmer's back.

Christmas was a busy time for the women folk on the farm, with the preparation of geese and chickens for the seasonal trade. In late March and early April the sheep were brought back onto the in-bye land and lambing took place (it continued into mid-May, but mainly occurred in April). During lambing time the lambs were castrated and tailed and then marked up. Some sheep stayed for awhile on the in-bye land if they had twins, but the remainder were released onto the fells for the summer, where the lambs got "hefted" (heughed) by their mothers (learning by instinct their own patch of moorland so that they would not stray into another flock's territory). It was always the case that heughed sheep had to be sold with the farm.

They remained on the fells until clipping (shearing) time in July, and were brought down in July and August. Clipping took place 10 days after washing and was a festive occasion, to which relations, friends and their children came. In early September the sheep were gathered back in and the lambs were "spained" (taken off their mothers), whilst after sorting, the "weathers" (castrated males) and the "shut gimmers" (lower quality females) were sold at the sheep sales or autumn fairs. The "gimmers" (females) were retained for breeding.

Cattle were grazed on the in-bye land and lower commons. After lambing time, the pastures were shut up to grow a crop of hay. The gathering of this crop took place between late June and the end of August and a considerable amount was cut by hand due to the steepness of the valley sides.

The process of winning the hay consisted of mowing, haymaking and leading. In earlier days, scythes (leas) were used for cutting, and an acre was considered an average day's mowing. They started early while the dew was on the grass and the sun not up, with the best mower leading the others in an echelon across the field.

A good crop of hay was vital, to provide fodder for cattle in bad winters, and farmers would hope to still retain half their store in barns by mid-February, for it was not until May that the cattle were turned out to graze. Some farmers sledded (sledged) their hay to the barns, others used sweeps, whilst horses and carts could be used. In periods of inclement weather, it was necessary to secure the hay against the rain, by making small, well packed heaps, the tops of which would turn the weather (they were called cocks or jockeys). A much larger heap was called a pike, and secured it for a longer period.

Gunnerside was an old Norse settlement, originally called Gunnars Seatre, or the pasture of Gunnar, a Norse chieften, attracted by its sheltered location at the confluence of Gunnerside Gill and the River Swale. Many of the stone cottages are the previous homes of lead miners working the Sir Francis Level and Blakethwaite mines or the Old Gang Mine on Brownsey Moor, above Kearton and Blades, during the 18th and 19th centuries (the word "gang" derives from the Old English word

Another view of the haymeadows and field barns at Gunnerside, Swaledale in the year 2005

Preparing the sheep ready for shearing in the dales, c1900
By permission of the D.C.M.

Sheep shearing in the dales c1900
By permission of the D.C.M.

Clipping sheep at Raisgill Farm, Yockenthwaite, in Langstrothdale

Haymaking near Low Row, Swaledale c1910
Clive Torrens Collection

Jim Sunter and young neighbour, near Bank Heads, Swaledale (in the Gunnerside area), pulling a sled used to carry hay to the barn at haymaking time 1930's

Haymaking at Haverdale, Low Row c1920
Clive Torrens Collection

James Rukin (senior) and son James at haymaking time, Keld, in the late 1930's

James Rukin (senior) and Mr. Pryer haymaking at Keld, August 1938

The Allan family haymaking near Reeth. Ronald Allan, one of the family, died whilst on service in the Great War

Haymaking at Grassington, on the Conistone road

On top of the two carts: X X X X X Horace Maxfield X
Norah Maxfield X
Next row standing:
Beatrice Maxfield, Fred Maxfield, John Woodhouse, X X *Jim Bownas, George Easterby, Bob Chapman*
Seated: X X

Haymaking at Arkle Beck, near Langthwaite, Arkengarthdale

In the hayfield at Arkle Town, Arkengarthdale 1962. (Robert Hird and Lizzie Stubbs)

Haymaking time at Scottie Corner, Low Row, near Bell Isle, Swaledale 1951. Colin Hird stands by the hay sweep, whilst his father, George William Hird is forking the hay into the barn

Taking the hay home, on the Oughtershaw road, Langstrothdale 1911

A gathering at High Frith farmhouse at hay time c1900. It is situated on the hillside on the road between Keld and Tan Hill. The tenants, Mr. and Mrs. Scott, are standing, 3rd and 5th from the left, at the front

meaning a road).

The heart of the Swaledale mining field was a vein called the Friarfold Vein, running from the neighbourhood of Keld across to Arkengarthdale.

Gunnerside Gill was the site of two of the most important lead mines in Swaledale. A short distance into the Gill are the remains of the Sir Francis Level, one of the last and most mechanised mines in the dale. Opened in 1864 and closed in 1882, the mine produced ore worth £16 million at today's prices.

Further upstream, at Friars Hush and Bunton Hush, are the old levels, tailings of spoil and the ruined buildings of further workings. At the head of Gunnerside Gill are the fine ruins of Blakethwaite Mine and the dams that served it. It was from this mine alone that lead worth more than £112,000 (worth £48 million today) was extracted in the early 19th century.

Eastwards, across Friarfold Moor, towards Arkengarthdale, through a desert landscape of lead mine spoil, lie the ruins of the Old Gang and Old Surrender Smelt Mills. They provide the most complete collection of buildings still standing in this mining field. Their chimneys, dressing floors, flues and smelting hearths are clustered together in a valley, the sides of which are covered in heaps of spoil. One of the most impressive ruins is that of the Peat Store. Many thousands of tons of peat were cut each year to burn in the ore hearths. The 391 foot long store was heather thatched, the open sides allowing the wind to dry the peat thoroughly.

The 1831 Census for Melbecks show that out of a population of 1455 people, 223 were miners. But by 1850, men were beginning to work at both mining and farming.

Several miners used to make an agreement (bargain) among themselves to work a certain number of yards. The "pick men" dug out the ore, the "dead men" sank shafts or tunnelled the "levels" where the veins of ore were whilst boys and women "dressed" the ore ready for smelting.

At hay time or lamb sales, or during the snows, when "fothering" the stock was a full time job, the miners would revert to farming. They were independent of masters or companies; they made working agreements with them, but were not employees. Gunnerside miners were sturdy-natured people who arranged their own work, and showed qualities of independence and trust.

The peak of production was in the early 1870's and people living along the Swale valley could tell how busy the mines were by the nature of the river. When the Bunting and Sir Francis Levels were productive, the washings turned the water the colour of clay as far as Richmond.

After 1872, Limited Liability Companies formed, with ownership of the mines passing to shareholders. The old mining partnerships would tighten their belts to tide them over a bad period but shareholders would quickly remove their money from a non-paying concern.

Beyond Low Row, Feetham, Kearton and Healaugh, the village of **Reeth** occupies a commanding position on the lower slopes of Calver (Calva) Hill and Reeth Low Moor, whilst to the north-east it is overlooked by the limestone scars of Fremington Edge. Situated at the junction of roads leading deep into Swaledale and Arkengarthdale, its importance led to it being granted a market charter in 1695, becoming a centre for industry and agriculture, with hand-knitting and lead mining providing prosperity.

Hand knitting was a cottage industry which dated back to 1590, when a school

A general view of Gunnerside, Swaledale, from the road leading to Winterings c1914
Clive Torrens Collection

Gunnerside, with the Kings Head Inn sign showing on the right 1908
Clive Torrens Collection

Lead mining in Gunnerside Gill. The ruined building was once used for storing the ore that came out of the mine in waggons. They belonged to the Old Gang Partnership of the Sir Francis Mine, downstream of the Sir Francis Level

The Bunting Level crushing plant and the ruins for storing the ore. The 'hushes' are showing above the ruins

The Blakethwaite Mine peat store, Gunnerside Gill

The Old Gang Lead Smelting Mill ruins. Situated betwen Swaledale and Arkengarthdale it shows the smelt mill in the foreground, a flue on the near hillside and the ruins of the peat drying store on the skyline of the far hillside

The flue and ruins of the peat drying store at the Old Gang Lead Mine

Ruins of the peat drying store at the Old Gang Lead Mine. It once had a thatched roof

Feetham, Low Row, Swaledale in 1907, showing the Punch Bowl Hotel
Clive Torrens Collection

Low Row School, near Reeth, Swaledale 1908
Back row: Master Gill, Lizzie Pearson, Lizzie Agnes Sunter, John Appleton
Next row: Bill Coates, Fred Pearson, Joseph Sunter, Jimmy Pratt, Dora Reynoldson, Louise Brown, Polly Wilkinson, Rose Bell, Willie Appleton, Tommy Appleton, Wesley Calvert, Jim Petty
Next row: Miss Gill (teacher), Master Gill, Hannah Appleton, Elsie Calvert, William Thompson, Ethel Gill, Bella Wiseman, Bessie Appleton, Rose Brown, Winnie Petty, Agnes Appleton, Lizzie Wiseman, Lizzie Calvert, Iris Newcastle
Next row: Nellie Thompson, Lizzie Calvert, Albert Calvert, Isabel Pearson, Esther Pearson, Esther Calvert, Lora Gill, Margaret Hannah Scott, Hilary Brown, Mabel Bell, Lizzie Guy, Bessie Coates, Edmund Coates
Front row: Bob Brown, Tom Scott, Bob Thompson

The sawmill at Haverdale, near Feetham, Low Row, Swaledale in 1916. Timber was cut, ready to be used in the trenches on the Western Front

Sports at Rowleth Bottoms, near High Row, Swaledale
Clive Torrens Collection

Street scene at Healaugh, in Swaledale 1912
Clive Torrens Collection

was set up in York to teach the children of the poor how to knit in order to provide them with the means of earning a meagre living. In the 17th century the project was moved out to the rural area around Richmond and hand knitting began to spread throughout the Dales. Men, women and children toiled away in dimly lit cottages knitting stockings, top garments and latterly gloves, while singing songs relieved the monotony.

Seven fairs a year and a weekly Friday market were held and the village expanded at its height to 1300 inhabitants (since the decline of lead mining, its population has dwindled to a quarter of that size). Its former prosperity and growth is indicated by the fine 3-storey houses and inns around the huge village green, especially along High Row, but it was also helped by the introduction of the turnpike to Tan Hill in Arkengarthdale in 1741.

Quarrying for chert (a quartz like mineral, similar to flint in its brittleness) was undertaken along Fremington Edge between 1905 and 1953 and employed a number of local men. A second mine was begun in 1922 at Moulds Side, near Langthwaite, in Arkengarthdale (later known as Hungry Hushes Chert Quarry), which closed in September 1950. Levels were driven into the hillside, with as much separation and dressing done underground to avoid unnecessary carrying. Much of the chert was taken to the Potteries and ground down to be used in glazing fine quality china.

In 1910, Reeth became the first settlement in Swaledale to receive electric lighting, thanks to the vision of the Burton family of Askrigg in Wensleydale. The family, strong Methodists, owned West Mill on Mill Lane, Askrigg. William Handley Burton, a millwright, joiner, builder and maker of hand rakes, had seen the possibilities of producing hydro-electric power by harnessing the force of the water tumbling over the 70 feet falls at Mill Gill. The former corn mill of West Mill was set up for operation and in 1908, the Burton home, Mill Gill House, was the first house in Wensleydale to be lit by electric light.

The old mill near the present day Arkle Hotel, Reeth, was operated by Willie Burton and produced electric lighting for Reeth, using water power from a sluice operated dam on the Arkle Beck to work a water wheel. Lower down the beck, the same water operated another water wheel at Reeth saw mill and lead storage yard, whilst at Fremington it powered a third water wheel at the corn mill.

The power of the Arkle Beck had been harnessed 100 years earlier by the building of a large slanting stone weir to provide, via a long leat (mill run), the water to drive the wheel of a corn mill. The disused mill was purchased by Mr. Burton in 1910 and the inside was gutted to house a turbine, generating plant and distribution board. The leat was strengthened by forming the side and base in concrete to form a deep channel. A sluice gate was erected where the leat joined the weir, to control the water supply when the river was in flood. Electricity was mostly supplied through the village on overhead poles.

By 1912 there were 25 street lamps, each of 50 candle power, used only during winter time. Private houses that were wired to the supply were permitted to use the electricity only at night. During the day the supply was necessary to charge up batteries or accumulators. Until 1936 the local postman was responsible for maintaining the turbines, in his off-duty hours.

By this stage, each house was allowed one electrical iron, hotels were allowed electric fires, whilst in 1935 electric cookers were permitted. By 1936 there were 160 customers. Just before 1933 the business changed its name from W. H. Burton and Sons to The Askrigg and Reeth Electric Supply Company, Limited. In 1936, the village of Grinton received an electric supply from the Company.

It was not until 1949, when electricity was nationalised, that the company was taken over and Bainbridge was the first of the villages to be connected to the national grid; the others soon followed.

In nearby **Grinton**, at the bridging point over the River Swale, most of the village's stone houses line the road to the south of the church or up the steep hill road that climbs to the moors and over into Wensleydale. Grinton Lodge, nowadays a youth hostel, lies on the moor's edge, a 19th century battlemented shooting lodge of Colonel Charlesworth.

St. Andrews Church, the "Cathedral of the Dale", was founded in the 12th century. For 120 years it acted as an outlying mission of the Augustinian Priory at Bridlington and was the mother church for the whole of Upper Swaledale until Tudor times. In the south wall is a "leper's squint" or hagioscope, through which people with contagious diseases could watch the service. Scratches on the stonework around the porch are said to show where retainers sharpened their arrows while their lords were at service.

A distant view of Reeth, in Swaledale, from Fremington Edge, showing the village green and High Row. A small fairground is in occupation

All that remains of Fremington Edge Chert Quarry, near Reeth, Swaledale

A load of chert is transported from Fremington to Richmond in 1905
Clive Torrens Collection

*Transporting timber at Reeth saw mill, near Arkle Bridge, Reeth c1911.
A steam traction engine is also being used*

A trader stands in front of Langthorne House, High Row, Reeth c1910

The Buck Hotel and Silver Street, Reeth c1910
Clive Torrens Collection

The showground for Reeth Agricultural Show 1906.
In the far distance can be seen Grinton Church and Bridge
Clive Torrens Collection

Caravans on Reeth Green during Reeth Agricultural Show 1907. High Row is on the left
Clive Torrens Collection

The showground for Reeth Agricultural Show 1906. On the right can be seen Arkle Bridge
Clive Torrens Collection

The Green Howard's Band resting after performing at Reeth Show in 1907. Seven years later, some of these men would be fighting in the Great War
Clive Torrens Collection

The army at Reeth (6th NE Battery Sergeants) in 1910
Clive Torrens Collection

At Cogden Beck, above Grinton, a smelt mill was built in the early 1700's. Between 1820 and 1822 this mill was rebuilt and the flue extended onto nearby Sharrow Hill.

A 330 metre long ground level flue carried the lead-rich smoke (fume) from the mill to the chimney. The main reservoir nearby was fed from Cogden Gill, an adjacent spring. A wooden launder or leat carried water to a large wheel inside the smelt mill building. Below the dam the beck passed through a stone-lined channel, covered over where it ran beside the smelt mill.

The main fuel for the mill was peat, gathered from the surrounding moors and brought by horse and cart to the Peat House, where it was stored and dried. The arched openings in this building helped air to circulate and dry the peat.

In the smelt mill were two ore hearths, a slag hearth and a furnace, as well as bellows, a water-wheel and other equipment. Smelting ceased at Grinton in December 1895, when Grinton Mining and Smelting Company went bankrupt.

From Grinton, the main road continues its course to Richmond along the valley bottom, but a more interesting and rewarding journey is to be found on the higher level route from Fremington via Marske.

A short distance from Fremington lies Marrick village, with Marrick Priory nearby. The Priory, now a residential field study centre for the Diocese of Ripon, was

Grinton Bridge across the River Swale and St. Andrew's Church, Grinton, near Reeth, Swaledale

Grinton Youth Hostel, near Reeth, Swaledale. Until the Second World War period, it was the shooting lodge for the Grinton Estate of the Charlesworth family

Grinton Lodge, near Reeth, the hunting lodge of the Charlesworth family, 1911.
The Charlesworths had made their money as colliery owners at Wakefield
Clive Torrens Collection

Grinton Lead Smelting Mill, Swaledale, in the foreground, with the peat house and flue leading to a chimney that was sited on nearby Sharrow Hill

The peat house at Grinton lead smelting mill, near Reeth.
All of the archways used to be open, to allow the air to dry the peat

originally founded about 1165 AD as a house for the black-robed nuns of the Benedictine Order, with the surrounding pasture land and **Marrick** village belonging to the Priory. The track from the Priory to the village, via the wood by means of an ancient stone-paved, stepped path, is known as the "Nuns' Steps", as it passes through Steps Wood. In the early years of the 16th century the Priory was closed during the Dissolution of the Monasteries. The prioress and the 16 nuns were granted pensions and thrown out to fend for themselves.

Marrick was always mainly an agricultural centre, but owing to its proximity to the smelt mills of the lead mines at nearby Hurst, smelters also resided here, as well as at Hurst. The 1871 Census shows five of them still living at Marrick, two of them named Longstaffe.

In 1971 the population for the whole of Marrick was 86, whereas in 1841, at the peak of the mining boom, the hamlets of Hurst, Washfold and Shaw contained 415 people, not counting those in Marrick itself. By 1881 this figure for the hamlets fell to 152 as the industry declined and whole families began to move away in search of work. Those miners remaining supported their families by farming as well. Shaw and Washfold are no longer hamlets, whilst Hurst nowadays consists of mainly holiday homes.

Opposite **Hurst**, the two engine chimneys and the vast spoil heaps are all that remain to remind one of this lead mining history. It was in this area that the major veins which form the backbone of the North Swaledae mining field die out.

The surface topology at Hurst, with its gently sloping hillsides and scarce supply of surface water, meant that it was not suitable to the kind of "hushing" that was used to advantage elsewhere in Swaledale.

The rectangular shaped engine house chimney at Hurst, built in 1883, was called Cat Shaft Chimney and was used for pumping and winding purposes. The circular Brown's New Engine House Chimney and shaft was built in October 1887. Transporting the boiler from Richmond to Hurst caused some problems, with 18 horses pulling the boiler and extra horses required to get up the steep climb out of Marske.

In 1887, 44 men were employed in stoping, 22 in driving the levels and 8 more in clearing water and helping to ventilate the workings. By 1888 the Hurst mines and the Arkengarthdale mines were the only large producers of lead left in Swaledale, all the other mines either shut down or merely "ticking over". By 1891, even these mines had come to the end of their workings.

The only other village on this particular route to Richmond is **Marske**. Beautifully situated in a hollow in the landscape, it is purely agricultural and surrounded by wooded hills beneath wild moors. Its church, of Norman origin, has 13th and 17th century additions.

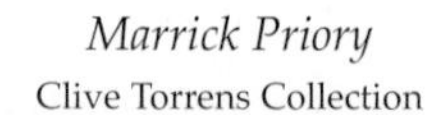

Marrick Priory
Clive Torrens Collection

Marrick Priory, home of the black-robed Benedictine nuns, until the early years of the 16th century. In the foreground stands the remains of the original priory

The paved 'Nuns' steps rising through 'Steps Wood' at Marrick in Swaledale

The village of Marrick in 1910
Clive Torrens Collection

The village of Marrick in 1910
Clive Torrens Collection

The remains of the spoil heaps in the old lead-mining village of Hurst. Nowadays, many of the dwellings are holiday homes. In earlier days it was larger and had its own school

Brown's New Engine House Chimney at Hurst, Swaledale, built 1887, was used for pumping and winding purposes in the lead mines

A view over the roofs of the village of Marske, Swaledale, showing a glimpse of the Hall amongst the trees

View over the village of Marske, showing the hall in the foreground
Clive Torrens Collection

The main street of Hudswell village, near Richmond, Swaledale 1908

At the gateway to the dale lies the market town of **Richmond** (a market granted in 1155). Its hill-top position above the Swale gave Richmond an importance and prominence, resulting in its growth. The Norman castle commands the scene, especially when viewed from the Catterick road and dominates the town. Earl Alan Rufus built his massive castle soon after the Norman Conquest and roofed it with Swaledale lead.

The massive keep, built in the late 12th century, gives the finest prospect of Richmond from its 100 feet high battlements. At its south-east corner, Scolland's Hall is probably the oldest hall in England, dating from the 11th century.

The lines of shops surrounding the Market Place follow the line of walls of the Castle's outer bailey. The medieval town walls were about 50 yards beyond them, but only the gateways on Cornforth Hill and in Friar's Wynd survive. The upkeep of the town walls was paid for by lead coming out of the dale, on a toll of two old pence a mule load.

St. Mary's Parish Church lay outside the town walls, whilst Holy Trinity Church in the Market Place was little more than a Chapel. It was built around 1150 but was allowed to fall into ruin in the mid 14th century and later was used to shelter victims of the great plague of the late 16th century.

Registered as a church in 1745, it was at this stage that shops were built into it. It has been a court, a town hall, a school and a warehouse in its time, but is now the Regimental Museum of the Green Howards.

The curfew bell which sounds automatically daily from the church's clock-tower at 8a.m. and 8p.m. is also known as the "Prentice Bell". Besides it sounding the curfew, it marked the start and end of the apprentice's working day. The Town Crier rang the bell from his house at the foot of the bell tower. It is said that the use of a rope meant that he could ring the bell at 8a.m. without getting out of bed.

The market town of Richmond, with its cobbled wynds (alleys) twisting their ways in all directions among the houses, roofed with pink pantiles, stone slates or Welsh slates, and its beautiful small Georgian theatre dating from 1788 and restored to theatrical use in 1963, is certainly an appropriate place to leave Swaledale behind, as we visit instead the villages and towns of **Wharfedale in Craven** to the south.

Buckden was originally a foresters' village, for it is to be found at the junction of Langstrothdale with Wharfedale and Langstrothdale Chase was a hunting preserve of the aristocracy. We have already seen that monastic sheep granges were established throughout Langstrothdale and at one time the inn at Buckden doubled as a wool sale room (with some of the old weighing equipment surviving here).

However, it is in the tiny hamlet of **Hubberholme**, a little way further up

Richmond Castle and Bridge
Clive Torrens Collection

Richmond Market Place with carriers' carts drawn up c1910

Traffic on the road at Skeeby, near Richmond in 1912
Clive Torrens Collection

Bridge Street, Richmond 1920's
Clive Torrens Collection

The Market Place, Richmond c1905, showing Holy Trinity Church and the Castle

Ready to depart the Market Hall, Richmond Market Square c1910

Langstrothdale, that the parish church for the Upper Dale is to be found. St. Michael and All Angels originated as forest chapel and chapel of ease to the main church at Arncliffe, in Littondale. Originally known as St. Oswalds, it is set in a superb riverside setting, with wooded hillsides and bare fells in the background. The old vicarage was converted into the present day George Inn, but still remained church property until 1965. Hubberholme Bridge, linking the inn and the church, was part of the old and important route between Lancaster and Newcastle and was rebuilt in 1734 after lying in ruins in 1709.

The interior of the church has a medieval feel with unplastered walls of local stone and an exquisite rood loft dated 1558, carved in oak and painted red, black and gold (one of only two in Yorkshire, the other being at Flamborough). Most of the woodwork in the church is modern oak, made by the "Mouseman of Kilburn", Robert Thompson, in 1934, who left his signature, a tiny church mouse, hidden on many of the pieces.

Thomas Lindley was for many years in the first half of the 19th century the minister and also teacher at the little church and school at Halton Gill, at the head of Littondale, as well as incumbent at Hubberholme. He would ride over Horse Head Moor from Halton Gill in all weathers to take the service at St. Michael's. It is said that the sexton would stand on top of the tower looking up the dale until he caught sight of Thomas Lindley before ringing the church bell to summon the parishioners to worship.

A track near to the church leads up to Scar House, a 17th century farmhouse, which was once a meeting place for local Quakers during the time of religious persecution. Many were imprisoned and died for their faith in York jail and one local man, James Tennant, was buried in a small enclosure at the side of the house.

At the George Inn (the former vicarage) on New Years Day, a one thousand year old custom takes place with the letting of the "Poor Pasture" at the "Hubberholme Parliament". Local farmers bid for the annual tenancy of a 16 acre field behind the inn which has been left in trust for the sick and the poor of the parish.

The public bar is the Commons, where the farmers sit and the lounge bar, the Lords, where the churchwardens sit with the vicar, who acts as auctioneer. It is a candle auction, lasting for as long as a candle, lit at 8p.m., will burn. The auction usually lasts until midnight, when the bidding becomes serious.

Near the head of **Langstrothdale** lies **Oughtershaw**. Oughtershaw Hall was built towards the end of the 18th century and it was the various members of the Woodd family who lived there who were responsible for the Victoriana found in Oughtershaw (the Memorial Chapel, later to become the village school, the memorial fountain for Queen Victoria's Diamond Jubilee and, on leaving the hamlet, the cross commemorating the monarch's Golden Jubilee in 1887).

The Buck Inn, Buckden, in Wharfedale

The Smithy, Buckden in Wharfedale c1911
Clive Torrens Collection

Shooting party in front of the Buck Inn, Buckden 1912. Thomas Cambage, the gamekeeper, stands with his gun under his arm, next to Tom Gill, smoking a pipe on the left. Sitting on the front row are Matthias Dixon 1st left, and Frank Kendall 3rd from left. Both would be killed in action during the Great War

Buckden, Upper Wharfedale, showing the Buck Inn
Clive Torrens Collection

A view of Hubberholme Bridge and the George Inn, Hubberholme, Langstrothdale.
In far earlier days, the Inn was the Rectory for nearby Hubberholme Church

Hubberholme Church, Langstrothdale, near Buckden

The Rood Loft in Hubberholme Church, Langstrothdale, Upper Wharfedale
Clive Torrens Collection

Farmhouses at Yockenthwaite, Langstrothdale, with only a trickle of water in this section of the River Wharfe

The hamlet of Beckermonds, in Langstrothdale
Clive Torrens Collection

In the main dale of the River Wharfe, just below Buckden, lies the hamlet of **Starbotton**, in Kettlewell parish. Developed by the Saxons, it grew with the discovery of lead on nearby Cam Head Moor. On June 8th 1686 the worst recorded flood in Wharfedale's history wiped out practically the whole hamlet, with only a handful of houses prior to that date remaining, when a terrible storm turned Cam Gill Beck, behind the village, into a raging torrent.

During the 12th century the manor of **Kettlewell** had been granted to Coverham Abbey, in Coverdale, whilst Fountains Abbey and Bolton Priory had estates here. As a result of its importance, a market was established here in the 13th century and by this time the settlement was thriving.

Kettlewell's appearance today mainly resulted from activities taking place during the previous 250 years, for the village was revitalised in its prosperity by the manufacture of textiles and especially by the development of lead mining during the late 18th and early 19th centuries. The ruins of a lead smelting mill that was used between 1700 and 1886 are to be found half a mile above the village, where the Cam and Dowber Becks meet. Redeveloped in 1861, the mill was still roofed until it was demolished as an exercise during World War Two.

A number of fine 17th and 18th century houses can be found in Kettlewell's narrow lanes, including the vicarage, although St. Mary's Church is of late Victorian origin, standing on the site of an early 12th century church.

On the minor road running south from Kettlewell is the tiny settlement of **Conistone**. Settled by the Angles in the 8th century AD (called Cunestune by the time of the Domesday Book), they used the meadow lands by the river for farming as well as using strip lynchets (a series of terraces on the hillside) along the lower slopes of the hills to grow arable, whilst grazing their animals on the common pastures above the high limestone scars (these areas are called "Old Pasture" and "New Close Allotments").

Conistone's farmhouses and barns are grouped around a tiny village green, and mainly date from the late 17th century. By this time the land had been enclosed, the older dry-stone enclosure walls being uneven and curling, whilst the planned 18th century enclosure walls run straight and true.

The Church of St. Mary is considered to be one of the oldest buildings in Craven district, with parts believed to date from Saxon times, although it is largely Norman and was restored in 1846.

Four miles from Grassington and separated from neighbouring Conistone by green meadows that were once a large post-glacial lake, is the hamlet of **Kilnsey**, with Wharfedale's outstanding landscape feature, **Kilnsey Crag**, close by.

Kilnsey consists of a few houses and farms, together with the Tennant Arms Hotel. The Old Hall at Kilnsey, built in 1648, was on the site of a monastic grange belonging to Fountains Abbey, whilst Mastiles Lane, a monastic track and drovers' road, led from Kilnsey to monastic estates on Malham Moor and beyond the River Ribble to the Lake District. It was to Kilnsey Grange that the sheep were brought to be sheared. Merchants travelled from as far away as Venice to inspect and buy the fleeces. Provisions were taken along Mastiles Lane to Malham for the shepherds, whilst sheep, milk and cheese came back to the monks, via Kilnsey.

One present day feature of the hamlet, however, that would not have been recognised by those departing to fight in the Great War or Second World War, is

Kilnsey Park. It has been developed as a visitor centre for those interested in fresh water fish. Trout fishing lakes, a trout feeding pond and a river life museum have been developed, together with farm shops, where fish and game can be bought.

However, those same servicemen would have been familiar with an important event in the Dale's farming social calendar, taking place annually at Kilnsey on August Bank Holiday Tuesday. One of Wharfedale's most popular annual events is still the Kilnsey Show, first held in 1897. Many competitive events take place at this agricultural show, including livestock displays, sheepdog trials, rural crafts, horse trotting, sports and a fell race around Kilnsey Crag.

A few hundred yards from Kilnsey Crag is the entrance to **Littondale**. The dale provides a wonderful limestone landscape of white scars along green hillsides and an intricate patterning of dry stone walls and barns on the flat valley floor. Drained by the River Skirfare, main tributary to the Wharfe, it provides a wonderful example of a valley carved by ancient glaciers from the Ice Age (and one of the few dales not affected by the ravages of lead mining).

The pastures of the dale attracted man since early times. Anglian settlers built their villages on the well-drained gravel sites – Halton Gill, Litton and Hawkswick on the north of the river and **Arncliffe** on the south. Though used as a hunting forest by the Normans, the pattern of farming has changed little since Medieval times. Then, it was a sheep rearing estate of Fountains Abbey, but after the Dissolution of the Monasteries, sheep were still kept on the hills and the cattle in the

Street scene at Starbotton c1915
Clive Torrens Collection

View of Kettlewell, Wharfedale, from Moor End
Clive Torrens Collection

General view of Conistone, looking towards Kilnsey Crag
Clive Torrens Collection

Kilnsey Crag in Wharfedale. Today, its overhangs provide a test of the skills of climbers

Kilnsey Old Hall, built in 1648, is on the site of a monastic grange belonging to Fountains Abbey

Mastiles Lane, heading towards Malham, from Kilnsey. It was a medieval monastic route connecting the monastic grange with the sheep grazing areas. Later, it became a drovers' route

The hamlet of Kilnsey and the fishing lakes (ponds) of Kilnsey Park, in Wharfedale

riverside meadows.

The barns of Littondale are splendid, many of them having covered porches dating back to times when corn was brought from the fields to be stored and the carts were brought under shelter for unloading it. The large double doors enabled air to be brought to the stone flagged threshing floor. Nowadays, a number of these barns have been converted into cottages at Litton and Hawkswick.

Halton Gill, a hamlet at the head of the dale, consists of a cluster of 17th century farms and cottages at the foot of Horse Head Pass, an ancient packhorse route that traced its way over the fells to Raisgill in Langstrothdale, whilst the modern road leads off sharply uphill to Stainforth and Ribblesdale.

The imposing hall, with its two storey porch and mullioned windows, was built in 1641. Church House was once a church and school under one roof and the inscription W.F. 1626 above the old school door refers to its founder, William Fawcett, a wealthy wool merchant.

Arncliffe is the largest settlement in the dale, situated on a well-drained gravel delta above the flood plain of the River Skirfare. Most of the village's farms, houses, cottages and barns face inwards to a spacious green and outwards to the long limestone scars cutting into the green hillsides and fells.

The most decorative doorheads are to be found in the Craven district of Wharfedale, Littondale and Ribblesdale. A datestone on one of the barns around Arncliffe village green reads 1677, whilst small crofts (fields) lie behind each of the dwellings.

Close to the River Skirfare lies St. Oswald's Church. Built in 1100 AD, the church was partially demolished in 1500 AD and rebuilt, with just the 15th century tower remaining. Further rebuilding took place in 1796 and 1841. On its wall is a list of Littondale men who fought on the Scottish border under Lord Henry Clifford against the Scots at the Battle of Flodden in 1513.

The hamlet of Hawkswick in Littondale, in the 1930's
Clive Torrens Collection

A view of Arncliife, Littondale. The church is in the middle foreground, Bridge House lies to the right hand bottom corner and the winding uphill road leads over to Malham
Clive Torrens Collection

Transportation through the village of Arncliffe

Litton post-office, Littondale, before the Great War. H. Battersby stands by the door. He was also a tailor, holding a licence to sell tobacco

Halton Gill, in Littondale 1908
Clive Torrens Collection

Church House, Halton Gill, was once a church and school under one roof, built in 1626.
The hamlet lies at the foot of Horse Head Pass

Near the bridge over the Skirfare, lies "Bridge End", where Charles Kingsley stayed and gained inspiration for his book "The Water Babies", naming the dale "Vendale". Close by is "Old Cotes", a farmhouse dating from 1650, whose gabled porch has a three-light window typical of the late 17th century Dales houses (Arncliffe was the first setting for the soap opera "Emmerdale Farm", with the Falcon Inn being the original "Woolpack").

Four miles further down the dale from Kilnsey lies Wharfedale's largest settlement, **Grassington**, serving as a "metropolis" for the dale. It was at the junction of a number of important routes and close to the crossing point of the River Wharfe. The monastic route from Fountains Abbey to Malham also passed through Grassington. The present settlement is Anglian in origin and the lords of the manor included the Percys, Plumptons and Cliffords, before passing to the Dukes of Devonshire.

Until the 19th century, Grassington held a weekly market, the Charter granted in 1282, and also an annual fair. Real prosperity came to the village in the early 17th century when lead mining became important.

We have seen that lead was mined under Grassington Moor until the late 19th century. In 1604 the Earl of Cumberland had built a smelt mill near Linton Church and lead mining began in earnest. The mines prospered in the 18th century but most had reached the water table by the late 1760's.

By now in the ownership of the Duke of Devonshire, an adit was needed to drain the deeper mines. Begun in 1796, it started at Hebden Gill and reached Yarnbury, on the moors above Grassington, in the 1820's.

The mines were very poor during the first two decades of the 19th century, but John Taylor, the Duke's new mineral agent, built dams on the moor and brought water to a 15 metre diameter water-wheel, which drove pumps in the mines.

New shafts were sunk, accessed by ropes, wound by horse-powered winding machines (whims). Mechanised dressing mills were established, where ore was crushed and separated before going on to be smelted.

During the next 50 years, a network of water courses and reservoirs was extended for over 11 kilometres to Yarnbury and on to Grassington Moor and served eleven water wheels.

The Cupola Smelting Mill, built for the Duke of Devonshire, had two reverbertory (cupola) furnaces which burnt coal. In order to extract maximum lead from the ore, a long flue and chimney was added in 1849. Tiny particles of lead, carried off in the waste gases from the furnaces, condensed out on the walls of this flue and were then washed off and collected at regular intervals. By 1855 the total length of the flue was 1.8 kilometres.

The most prosperous phase was between 1821 and 1861. Throughout this period 20,273 tons of lead were mined (averaging 965 tons a year) and employed about 170 people. By the early 1800's, Grassington was noted for the drunken and violent nature of its lead miners, but the arrival of Methodism did much to improve matters, with two Georgian style chapels being built (one becoming a Congregational Church).

After 1861, output fell steadily and the mines became exhausted. By 1881 the population of Grassington had fallen by 400. Most mines had stopped production by 1880, although the smelt mill kept going a little longer.

The building of the turnpike roads led to even greater prosperity and the building of fine dwellings (Grassington Hall 1760, with wonderful symmetry and full sash windows and the Town Hall, built in 1885 as the Mechanics Institute and now functioning as the Devonshire Institute).

Grassington became the headquarters for Chapmans, the largest coaching firm and Royal Mail contractors in Upper Wharfedale. Christopher Chapman, or "Old Kit Chapman", as he was known among the Dales folk, had become a carrier at Buckden in the mid-1850's, acting as a means of transport to Skipton and Leyburn. The villages in the district were full of carriers and competition was fierce but Kit had energy and enterprise.

In 1883 the Royal Mail contract became his when he bought the old mail coach belonging to Tom Airey. The posting horn had to be used when travelling through the villages and in snowy conditions, when the mail was delivered on horseback, a bugle was used instead. Other coaches were added and the business moved its headquarters to Grassington, when the Chapman family took over the running of the Temperance Hotel (now called Church House), with the many horses being kept in stables next door to the Hotel.

The business flourished, and in addition to the usual carrying services, an enormous number of parties were taken by horse-drawn waggonettes for day trips to various beauty spots. Another part of the business was the provision of hearses for funerals. One day, in the middle of winter, Kit's eldest son, Bob, had to take the hearse, with coffin and corpse, to Aysgarth. The road above Buckden was impassable and they were forced to remain in Buckden for five days, before they could deliver the body for internment.

At one time there were 50 horses stabled at Grassington but by 1905 the firm began its process of mechanisation, when a 36 h.p. Commer charabanc, seating 28 passengers, was purchased. It ran three times daily between Grassington and Buckden and another regular service was introduced to Bolton Abbey. Over the next few years, other motor vehicles were added to the fleet, with much work being undertaken in carrying pleasure parties.

Sadly, some other businesses in Grassington were not doing as well. From around 1790 water powered former corn mills were taken over as the local textile industry expanded but during the late 19th century the mills closed as steam power replaced water power. A decline also set in at this time in the lead mining industry, but the village received a boost in July 1902 with the opening of the Yorkshire Dales Railway from Skipton to Grassington. The station, however, was at nearby Threshfield. It brought in new dwellers who worked in Skipton or in the developing limestone quarries in the Cracoe area (Swinden Quarry) and Delaney's Quarry at Skirethorns. In 1908 the Railway carried 52,000 passengers to Grassington. The passenger service was withdrawn in September 1930 and today the line operates for mineral traffic from Skipton to Swinden Quarry at Cracoe.

Smelting House Chimney for the lead mines on Grassington Moor, Wharfedale

Leadmining flue and chimney on Grassington Moor, Wharfedale

Christopher Chapman of Grassington was a coach and Royal Mail proprietor.
By 1914 the firm was also using motor vehicles

Chapmans cab proprietors, next to Church House, at the lower end of Grassington Square c1910

Royal Mail contractor proprietor Christopher (Kit) Chapman, family and drivers, in front of the firm's headquarters at the Temperance Hotel (nowadays Church House), Grassington. Christopher stands on the extreme left

Headquarters of Chapman's coaching firm, the Temperance Hotel, Grassington. Robert Chapman, who took over the firm when Christopher, his father, died in 1914, stands with his sister Nancy

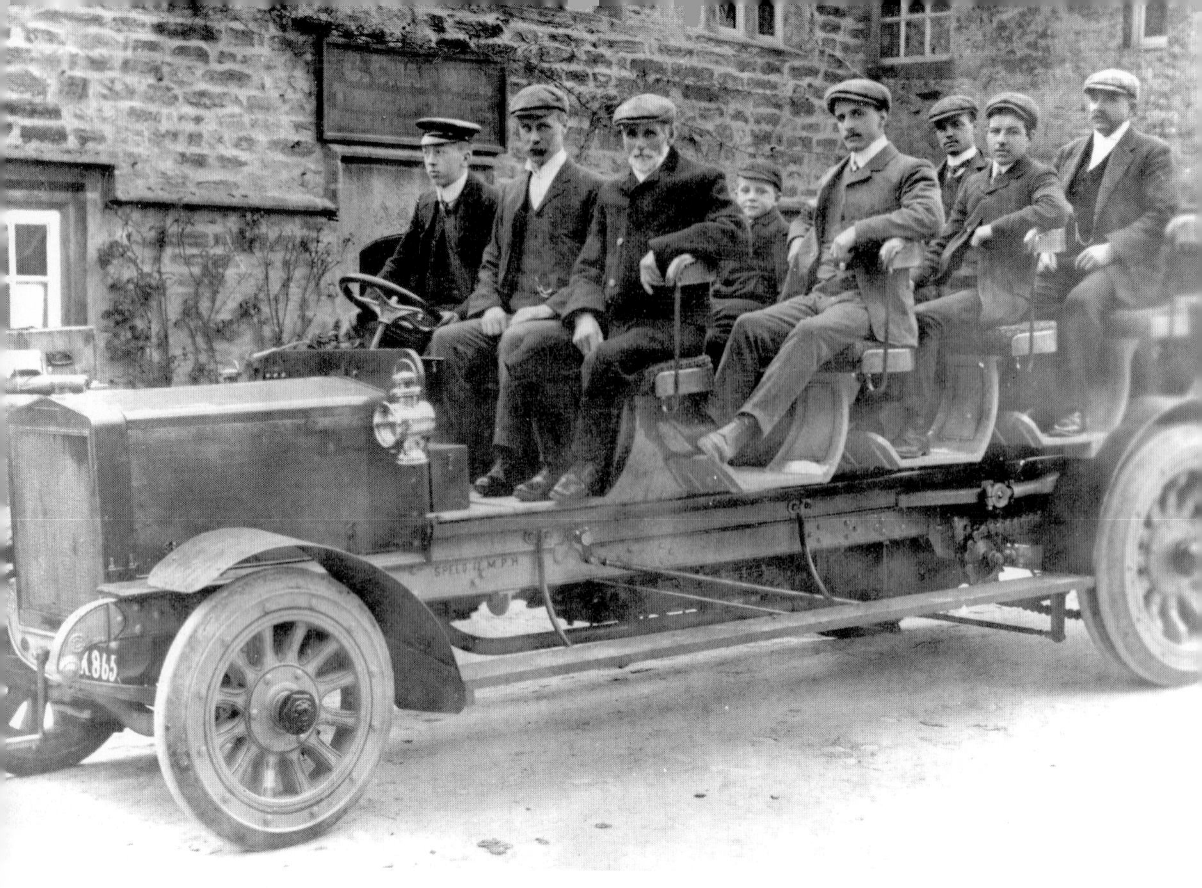

A Commer chain driven charabanc belonging to Chapmans, outside the firm's headquarters, the Temperance Hotel 1907. It was one of their first motor vehicles, Christopher Chapman (senior) sits nearest the camera on the front seat.

Chapmans of Grassington. A Congregational choir trip to Southport, September 24th, 1911. The driver is Dick Hawley

Grassington Town Hall and Chapel
Clive Torrens Collection

Parade and procession through Grassington c1905

A gathering in Market Square, Grassington c1905

Market Square, Grassington c1905. The shop now houses the Upper Wharfedale Museum

Activity in Grassington Square c1908

View of Grassington Hospital, between Grassington and Hebden. For many years it was a Sanatorium for those suffering from TB (tuberculosis or consumption)

The opening of the Yorkshire Dales Railway, July 29th 1902. The first train to arrive at Grassington Station (at Threshfield). Walter Morrison, M.P., addresses the crowd

Crowd and dignitaries on the platform of Threshfield Station, Grassington, at the opening of the Yorkshire Dales Railway, July 19th 1902

Grassington and Threshfield Signal Box at the terminus of the Yorkshire Dales Railway, July 29th 1902

Threshfield itself has a number of 17th century houses and barns, with date panels of 1640 and 1661, including Park Grange, the Manor House and a three-doorway barn, or shippon. Threshfield Free Grammar School, founded in 1674 by the Reverend Matthew Hewitt, rector of Linton, is still in use as the primary school, whilst opposite the shippon is Old Hall Inn, 19th century at the front and Georgian at the back. A narrow road, west of the village, leads to the hamlet of **Skirethorns** and its associated limestone quarries and on to Malham Moor, continuing as a green lane to join Mastiles Lane, the droving lane from Medieval times to the end of the 19th century. One industry that was of importance in Threshfield, but no longer exists, was that of besom (broom) making, using heather (ling) from the nearby moors and fells.

Although Grassington is the largest village in the area, it is at **Linton** that the church was built that served Linton, Grassington, Threshfield and **Hebden**, with each village having footpaths leading to it.

Standing by the bank of the River Wharfe, half a mile away from Linton itself, the church of St. Michael and All Angels dates from the 12th century but was largely rebuilt and extended during the 15th century (it still retains its handsome bell-cote) Until 1866 Linton had two rectors since there were two lords of the manor. 19th century Hebden was larger than it is today, due to the activity of the lead mines. In the 1830's a decision was made to raise, largely by public subscription, sufficient funds (£745) to build their own place of worship. St. Peters was consecrated in 1841.

Sited on well-drained moraine gravels, Linton attracted the Anglian settlers who built their houses around a large irregular green. Flowing down the middle of the village, Linton Beck was crossed by a packhorse bridge, a clapper bridge, road bridge, a ford and by stepping stones.

The grey stone houses are mainly from the 17th and 18th centuries, with Fountaine Hospital (almshouses) founded in 1721 by Richard Fountaine, for six poor men and women. He was a timber merchant for Sir John Vanbrugh, who may have designed the building, which introduced the classical style of building to the dale. "White Abbey" is a typical 17th century yeoman's house, whilst "Beckside" has a decorated lintel and datestone of 1642.

By the river, near the church, was Linton textile mill (closed in 1959) dating from 1901, when it replaced an earlier one for spinning worsteds and after 1840, cotton. A group of mill workers' cottages stand opposite the old mill, given the name "Botony", which is a West Riding name for houses adjacent to a textile mill. A corn mill had also earlier used the waters of the Wharfe above Linton Falls.

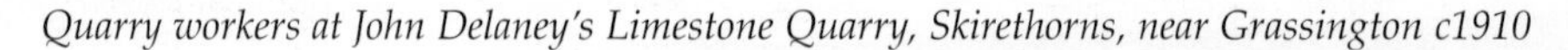
Quarry workers at John Delaney's Limestone Quarry, Skirethorns, near Grassington c1910

Another view of Delaney's quarry, Skirethorns, near Grassington c1910

Swinden Quarry, near Cracoe, c1910, showing the steam shovel in operation

Threshfield Free Grammar School, founded in 1674 by Reverend Matthew Hewitt, is now in use as the primary school

St. Michael and All Angels Church, Linton. Built half a mile away from the village, alongside the River Wharfe, it still retains its handsome bell-cote

One of the numerous crossing points of the beck running through Linton in Wharfedale. (packhorse bridge, clapper bridge, road bridge, stepping stones and ford)

Fountaine Hospital (almshouses and church) in Linton, Wharfedale. Founded in 1721 by Richard Fountaine, for habitation by six poor men or women

Bales of cotton from Linton mill, by the side of the River Wharfe, and close to Linton Church c1910. It had previously been a worsted mill

Linton Falls, on the River Wharfe, near Grassington. The water powered a corn mill in earlier days and a mill for making worsted and later, cotton

The old Linton Cotton Mill, nowadays converted into residential housing

Hebden School c1905

Hebden village near Grassington
Clive Torrens Collection

Before arriving downstream at Burnsall, the hamlet of **Thorpe**, hidden away from the river in a fold of the hills, was once the scene of a thriving boot and shoe-making industry, though one would never guess so today. Burnsall itself is at the crossroads between the gritstone, south of the village, and limestone to the north.

The mellow stone houses of **Burnsall** are mainly of the 17th and 18th centuries, many with fine mullioned windows. The church of St. Wilfreds, near the top of the street, was mainly built in Henry VIII's reign and is approached through a 17th century tapsel gate (a lychgate with a revolving "turnstile" entrance).

In 1612, Sir William Craven "repaired and butified" the church and rebuilt the five arched Burnsall Bridge and the grammar school, which he had founded in 1602. Continuing as a grammar school until 1876, it became a primary school and continues in this use to the present day, its appearance being that of a manor house with its two-storey gabled porch, mullioned windows and leaded lights.

Two miles below Burnsall, on the eastern side of the River Wharfe, lies **Appletreewick** (Aptrick to the locals). In 1300 AD Bolton Priory had acquired its manor and extensive sheep ranges, together with valuable lead mines, and the village prospered.

It was granted a market charter in 1311 and held an annual fair, known as the

"Onion Fair", that continued until the mid 19th century.

Amongst the most imposing buildings are High Hall and Low Hall at either end of the linear village, whilst a pair of cottages was converted into the church of St. John the Baptist in 1898, as a chapel-of-ease to Burnsall. Lower down the main street is Mock Beggars Hall (originally known as Monks Hall), rebuilt in 1697 on the site of Bolton Priory's grange.

Three miles from Bolton Priory (Abbey) is the ruin of **Barden Tower**, a three-storey tower house built in 1485 by Lord Henry Clifford and restored in 1658-1659 by Lady Anne Clifford. When it was first built, the threats from beyond the Scottish border were sufficiently real to merit the building of these fortified houses.

Bolton Priory (in the village of Bolton Abbey) was founded at nearby Embsay in 1120, before moving to its present site in 1154, where it was mainly completed by 1220. The West Tower, started in 1520, was not finished because of the Dissolution of the Monasteries in 1539. However, during the 20th century the tower had its windows glazed, the first time since the Dissolution, and a roof with laminated timbers was raised. The 13th century west front of the church is Early English and the nave was allowed to remain in use as the parish church, called the Priory Church of St. Mary and St. Cuthbert.

The Priory ruins lie in a superb riverside setting, with riverside meadows and moors and woodland in the background. From 1748 to the present time the Bolton Abbey estates have been in the hands of the Dukes of Devonshire, who have created a beautiful park land setting to this area of Wharfedale.

The river Wharfe flows between the arches of Burnsall Bridge.
The five arched bridge was rebuilt by Sir William Craven in 1612

View of Burnsall village and bridge, Wharfedale, taken from the Fell Road in the late 1920's
Clive Torrens Collection

Main Street, Burnsall 1912

Church of St. Wilfred, Burnsall, built in the 16th century but repaired in 1612 by Sir William Craven

Burnsall Grammar School, founded in 1602 by Sir William Craven as a grammar school until 1876, it is now in use as the primary school

Mock Beggars Hall, Appletreewick, originally known as Monk's Hall
Clive Torrens Collection

High Hall, Appletreewick. A minstrel gallery is to be found in the main room

Church of St. John the Baptist, Appletreewick, near Burnsall.
It was built in 1898, when a pair of cottages was converted

Barden Tower, three miles from Bolton Abbey, built in 1485 by Lord Henry Clifford.
These fortified houses were built to ward off the threats from beyond the Scottish borders

Stepping stones across the River Wharfe, with Bolton Priory in the background

Crossing the stepping stones across the River Wharfe at Bolton Abbey c1900

The ruins of Bolton Priory at Bolton Abbey, in Wharfedale. The building was begun in 1154 and mainly completed in 1220. The west tower, started in 1530, was not finished because of the Dissolution of the Monasteries, 1539

Our arrival at Bolton Abbey brings our journey to its southern most boundary. The men whose lives are told within the following pages of this book were connected in one way or another with the dales' villages, towns and landscapes portrayed by words and photographs in Chapter One. As the momentous events of July and early August 1914 unfolded in Europe, leading to war, the lives of many of the men from these dales would be lost and those of their families shattered.

Part of the village of Bolton Abbey in 1907

Clive Torrens Collection

CHAPTER TWO

1914 – THERE IS NO TURNING BACK

Who were these men of the dales who would serve their country in the Great War of 1914-1918 and would lose their lives whilst doing so? A few were regular servicemen, some volunteers, whilst others were conscripts. 236 men would pay the supreme sacrifice and they are remembered on the war memorials that still stand in the parishes running between Tan Hill in the north and Bolton Abbey to the south and from Richmond in the east to Rylstone and Cracoe in the west.

A large number worked locally, in the stone quarries or on the land, farming the fertile bottoms of the Rivers Swale, Wharfe and Skirfare, or looking after the sheep on the higher moors and fells. A sturdy, independent type of person evolved in these dales communities, which were often occupied for generations by the same families. Such communities provided a welcome anchorage for these people in a troubled world. Between June and early August 1914 these "troubles" intruded into their lives in a catastrophic manner.

Many dales folk were out in the fields and on the fell sides, gathering in the flocks and helping in the task of clipping the sheep during the sunny weekend of June 27th/28th 1914. On that same gloriously sunny morning of Sunday 28th June, two pistol shots rang out on a street in the far away provincial Serbian town of Sarajevo, shots which would irretrievably affect the lives of these families.

They were fired from the gun of a Bosnian/Serbian student nationalist, Gavrilo Princip, and his assassination of the heir to the Austro-Hungarian Empire, Archduke Franz Ferdinand and his wife, the Duchess of Hohenberg, would result in the dales' inhabitants finding their lives changed dramatically as Britain and the European Powers became embroiled in a power struggle that would lead to open conflict on August 4th.

The fates of 236 dalesmen would be sealed and the lives of many others affected by hardship and sadness. France, Belgium, Italy, Gallipoli, Egypt, Salonika or Mesopotamia became the destinations for many servicemen from the dales during the Great War and sadly, many of these men would perish in these foreign lands, their names to be inscribed later on the parish war memorials erected throughout the Yorkshire Dales.

The bullets fired by Gavrilo Princip, from a distance of two feet, had found their targets. The Archduke and his wife were carried to a room in the nearby Government building in Sarajevo, next to the one in which the champagne was cooling for their lunch. Within fifteen minutes, however, both were declared dead.

Enthusiasm for war was high amongst the populations of the belligerent nations as the march towards hostilities began throughout the long hot days of July. Vast crowds swept onto the streets of the European capitals, each supporting vociferously their country's hostile stance.

Austria presented Serbia with impossible conditions to avoid annexation; Russia immediately mobilised in support of her fellow Slavs, Germany responded at once and France followed suit.

As the German and French armies moved inexorably towards each other on Tuesday 4th August, hopes that Great Britain could somehow stay out of the conflict were dashed when, following the long prepared Schlieffen Plan, German forces entered neutral Belgium, en route to Northern France.

Monday 3rd August had been a Bank Holiday in Britain, with the weather beautiful, ideal for a visit to the seaside. As thousands flocked to the railway stations to catch special trains bound for the coast, they discovered their exertions had been in vain, for the British fleet had been mobilised and all excursion trains had been commandeered for use by naval reservists returning to their ships.

In Swaledale and Wharfedale the weather was less favourable and many dales folk from the farming communities were involved in gathering in the hay harvest, after a period of inclement weather over the previous fortnight. As the scythes glinted in the intermittent sunshine and the harvest of hay was transported by horse drawn sledge or cart to the field barns that dotted the valley floors, little did the dales' communities realise that Armageddon was looming.

Ready for harvesting the hay c1908
Photograph by permission of the D.C.M.

At 4p.m. on August 5th the British Army was mobilised. Britain demanded that the German Army be withdrawn from Belgium by midnight 5th August or a state of war would exist between the British Empire and Germany. The ultimatum was ignored and war was declared at 11p.m. The Great War had begun.

In 1914 Britain was essentially a maritime power with only a small, if highly trained and professional army. Only 120,000 men would initially make up the British Expeditionary Force that embarked for France, compared with some four million Frenchmen and four and a half million Germans.

Lord Kitchener shocked a meeting of the War Council on August 6th by predicting a long war; countering the popular cry of, "It will be all over by Christmas." On August 7th Kitchener publicly called for 100,000 volunteers. By September 12th, an amazing total of 480,000 men had enlisted as volunteers.

The majority were from urban areas, where large numbers of work mates and neighbours joined together into the famous "Pals" Battalions such as the "Leeds Pals". In more scattered, isolated rural districts, such as Swaledale and Wharfedale, the rush to enlist was not quite so pronounced, but at various recruitment meetings the local dignitaries soon did their best to alter this situation.

Throughout these districts during the first week of August it was noticeable that the price of provisions shot up because of panic buying, with the grocers' shops besieged by the local population. Meanwhile, the Reserves had been called out and the Territorial Battalions embodied and sent to the Front. Horses were being bought up wholesale by the military authorities in these rural areas. However, many farmers and coaching proprietors did not fully cooperate with the authorities, for quite understandable reasons. At Grassington, the Royal Mail and coaching firm of Chapmans had their newest motor vehicles commandeered by the Army. However, the best horses, earmarked by the Military, were quickly concealed by the

The Calvert family of Gunnerside were blacksmiths. Many horses belonging to the dales' farmers were commandeered by the Army in 1914/1915, especially for use by the artillery

Chapmans, for fear of being put out of business. Their patriotism was not to be questioned, however, for during the Great War the Chapman family lost a son, Christopher, his nephews, John Chapman and Robert Bownas, and his brother-in-law, John Easterby.

On July 26th, the 6th Battalion West Riding Regiment (Territorials) went into camp near the little village of Marske-by-the-Sea (on the peaceful moor land of the Yorkshire coast) for its annual training. The camp suddenly broke up and the various companies returned home to Skipton on that fateful first Monday of August 3rd. At 6p.m. the following day the orders for mobilisation were issued from Skipton Drill Hall, and the Skipton men at once began to stream in.

At noon the next day the completed Battalion entrained for Immingham Dock. After a week they moved into billets at the village of Healing, near Grimsby, spending a month until September 15th, when they moved to Riby Park, four miles inland. By the end of October they were in Doncaster, settling down for the winter, before crossing the Channel in mid-April 1915, en route for action on the Western Front.

Meanwhile, in Swaledale, excitement was great in and around Richmond on Tuesday August 4th 1914, with officers and men arriving and departing by train. At 2-30p.m. a striking and enthusiastic demonstration took place in the market square when the respective regiments formed square and the proclamation was read by the mayor, William Walton. All the officers and men were armed and gave three ringing cheers for the King, with the large crowd joining in singing the National Anthem, played by the local Prize Silver Band. The bulk of the soldiers took part in a route march into the surrounding countryside, whilst local and district Territorials were dispatched to other quarters in the afternoon.

William Walton, Mayor of Richmond, reading out the proclamation of war in August 1914
Wenham Collection

The Yorkshire Regiment Territorials marching over Richmond Bridge in 1910.
Scenes like this would have been witnessed in early August 1914
Wenham Collection

The 3rd Yorkshire Special Reserve returned from camp at Barnard Castle on Wednesday August 5th and were billeted in the town. Cooking trenches were made opposite the Town Hall and market place and the cooks were busily employed all day On Thursday August 6th, following a long route march, the colours of the Battalion were deposited in the church during the evening. With fixed bayonets, the troops formed up in Frenchgate, opposite the entrance to the church.

In the Grassington District there was enthusiastic recruiting by local ladies and gentlemen to raise a company for Lord Kitchener's Army to be called The Upper Wharfedale Company. It resulted in 20 local men obeying the nation's call. Each recruit was presented by the local committee with a shirt and a pair of socks and each received a pipe, tobacco and cigarettes on their departure for training from Grassington Station on September 21st. A large number went to the station to bid them "good-bye" and they were photographed by Messrs. Crowther and Grimshaw.

The professional and territorial units of the British Expeditionary Force (BEF) had crossed the English Channel on declaration of war and moved into Belgium. Near the town of Mons the British were struck by the full weight of the aggressive German First Army Group. Outnumbered, the British fought back stoutly, their rifle fire discipline taking heavy toll of the close German formations, but they were forced back onto a long retreat during August.

According to one historian; "During the thirteen days of the retreat, five of the seven German armies scythed down towards Paris, on a 75 mile front. For the troops

Soldiers in Richmond Market Place 1914

Wenham Collection

Recruits from Wharfedale off to join the 10th Battalion West Riding Regiment in 1914. Benjamin Beaumont, Tom Swales, William Burley and Walter Limmer, all shown on the photograph, would be killed in the War

Volunteers from Upper Wharfedale leaving Grassington Station for Skipton, September 21st 1914. The armband reads 'Kitchener's Man' and they each have the gift of a shirt, pair of socks, pipe, tobacco and cigarettes, presented to them on the day

on both sides they were days of endless marching under a scorching sun, marching until nearly every man seemed to have nails through the soles of his boots into his blistered feet, and the horses had worn their shoes wafer thin. Every movement was hampered by refugees. Order and counter order plagued both sides.

"In the days between Mons and the Battle of the Marne, the BEF, smallest of the Allied armies, played a vital role for it found itself at the outset right across the axis of advance of Kluck's army, the most powerful of all the German armies, 320,000 strong."

An important holding action took place at the Battle of Le Cateau, August 26th, when the BEF earned its place in history for the desperate and dogged resistance that took place when no one on either side could possibly have expected it. Again, the disciplined fire power of the professional British Army amazed the oncoming German soldiers as the British rifleman pumped out bullets at the rate of 16 to the minute.

At the Battle of the Marne, September 5th to the 10th, the German advance was brought to a halt, and then turned back, with the BEF, severely mauled but showing great powers of recuperation, playing a vital role. Now came the "Race to the Sea", between September 15th and November 24th, as each side tried to outflank the other in a bid to take the Channel ports.

The final action of the "Race to the Sea" was the bloody "First Battle of Ypres", October 30th to November 24th, in which the BEF was nearly wiped out in a successful, gallant defence against a heavily reinforced German drive that was expected by them to capture the Channel ports (there would be three further major battles here during the war).

Men from Swaledale and Wharfedale participted in the desperate fighting of 1914, both as regulars and territorials, and eight men would die. All came from Swaledale (one from Reeth and the others with Richmond connections), and the first of these deaths took place in the aftermath of the Battle of the Marne, as the Allies began their pursuit of the German Armies.

PRIVATE GEORGE MARTIN
NO. 8409 1ST BATTALION WEST YORKSHIRE REGIMENT
DIED SEPTEMBER 20TH 1914

In 1901, George's parents were George Martin, a native of Watlington, near Oxford, and Alice, who originated from Crakehill, 6 miles south of Thirsk. They were living in Waterloo Street, Richmond, where George senior was employed as a mason's labourer. Eventually they moved to 5 Bank Yard. George, junior, who had been born in Darlington, was a regular soldier serving with the 1st Battalion West Yorkshire Regiment and had gone with the BEF to France at the outset of war.

By early September 1914 the exhausted 1st Battalion and the rest of the BEF, having been on the retreat since August, arrived south of Chateau-Thierry and crossed to the southern bank of the River Marne, 80 kilometres east of Paris.

At the Battle of the Marne, September 5th to 10th, the Germans advanced across the river in pursuit of the BEF and the French Fifth Army. A French counter-attack was launched towards Chateau-Thierry and the German Army pulled back to the northern bank and changed the direction of attack to stop the French. They succeeded in halting the French but left a gap in their front, into which the BEF advanced and threatened the German left and rear. The German advance was halted and they began their withdrawal on September 9th.

Within five days, the Germans, having disengaged without serious interference from the exhausted Allies, were organising their new defensive positions. But Paris and France were saved. Between September 15th and 20th, at the First Battle of the Aisne, the Allies, slow in their pursuit, were rebuffed from the hastily prepared German field fortifications.

It was in this fighting on September 20th 1914 that George Martin was killed in action, the first serviceman from these dales to pay the supreme sacrifice. His body was never recovered from the battlefield and his name is honoured on the La Ferte-Sous-Jouarre Memorial, 66 kilometres east of Paris.

The second death occurred two days later when another serviceman from Richmond was killed, but this time in the murky, oil-stained waters of the North Sea. In fact he was not a man but just a young boy, fifteen years of age.

MIDSHIPMAN HERBERT LAWSON RILEY
HMS "ABOUKIR" ROYAL NAVY
DIED SEPTEMBER 22ND 1914 AGED 15 YEARS

Herbert Riley was the grandson of Sir John Lawson, a Catholic Baronet, of Brough Park, near Richmond. Sir John's daughter, Edith, married John Herbert Riley, a gentleman of means, and the family, consisting of Eileen, Herbert and Rowena, was raised at 59 Frenchgate, Richmond (today the Frenchgate Hotel). John Herbert Riley was also a gentleman of leisure who took great pleasure in hunting, shooting and fishing, and was an avid collector of books.

Young Herbert was sent to St. Anthony's School, Eastbourne, where he excelled in boxing, cricket, athletics and rugby, and he remained there until 1912. His chosen career was to be the Royal Navy and in July 1912 he entered Osborne House, before transferring to Dartmouth Royal Naval College by July 1914.

Herbert Lawson Riley of Richmond

Between the 18th and 21st July 1914 Cadet Riley was on board the battleship "Prince of Wales", taking part in the test mobilisation of the Home Fleet. However, on August 3rd he finally joined the cruiser HMS "Aboukir" as a 15 year old Midshipman.

Herbert was on board the cruiser "Aboukir" on September 22nd 1914, patrolling off the Dutch coast with her sister cruisers, "Hogue" and "Cressy". The German U-boat U-9 sank all three cruisers with torpedoes in quick succession, with the loss of 1400 lives.

When the "Aboukir" was struck, the midshipmen were nearly all below asleep and came on deck immediately, with the exception of Herbert Riley. Stubbs, who was senior midshipman, ran below to the Captain's cabin, where the midshipmen slept, and brought him up on deck. After the "Aboukir" sank, Herbert was alone in the water and clung to a piece of wood, before being picked up by a boat and taken on board the cruiser "Cressy". Herbert, Stubbs and another midshipman obtained dry clothing and drank hot cocoa.

When the "Cressy" was struck by the first torpedo, they went on deck and sat there with the others rescued from the "Aboukir". When the "Cressy" was struck by a second torpedo, they found themselves in the water once again. Herbert and Midshipman Stubbs were seen together, clinging to a piece of wreckage. At this stage the third cruiser, HMS "Hogue", was torpedoed. The two boys clinging to the plank came close to a sailor struggling in the water and crying out for help and they swam towards him in an effort to save him. However, as they came within his reach, the man seized them, a short struggle ensued, and all three disappeared and were drowned.

Herbert is commemorated on the Chatham Naval Memorial, Kent, whilst a plaque and photograph were placed in Richmond Roman Catholic Church.

PRIVATE THOMAS JAMSON
NO. 7013 2ND BATTALION DURHAM LIGHT INFANTRY
DIED 13TH OCTOBER 1914 AGED 33

Thomas was born in Richmond, the son of Thomas and Susannah Jamson. His father was a Richmond hairdresser, his mother came from Hurst, near Reeth, and together they raised a family of seven children. Thomas's brother, Arthur, would be killed later in the war, in 1917, during the Third Battle of Ypres. By 1914, Thomas, junior, was living in Darlington and, as a Territorial soldier, he enlisted at nearby Stockton. He quickly found himself in France with his Battalion, involved with the attempt to stem the German onslaught and later, in the "Race to the Sea".

By October 10th the 2nd Battalion was near St. Omer, before moving by French motor lorries to Hazebrouck on the 12th. Casualties from September 21st to October 12th had been 3 killed and 36 wounded. At 2p.m. on October 13th they marched to Vieux Berquin, a village 8 kilometres east of Hazebrouck and went into the attack on the enemy positions there. Though successful, over 60 casualties resulted, with Thomas being killed by shell fire. His name is commemorated on Panel 8 and 9 of the Ploegsteert Memorial.

SECOND LIEUTENANT FREDERICK CHARLES HATTON
2ND BATTALION YORKSHIRE REGIMENT
DIED 30TH OCTOBER 1914 AGED 36

Frederick was the son of Alfred and Louisa Frances Minetta Hatton and husband of Mrs. E.A.M. Hatton of West Terrace, Richmond. He was a regular soldier who had fought in the South African Campaign (Boer War) and when war was declared in August 1914 the 2nd Battalion, Yorkshire Regiment, with Regimental Sergeant Major Hatton, was quartered in the Channel Islands and not immediately with the B.E.F. in France. It returned to Southampton in late August and on October 5th embarked for France.

By October 14th the Battalion had marched to the Belgian town of Ypres and on the 16th an outpost line was taken up at Gheluvelt, covering the town. While in Ypres, Frederick was granted his commission and promoted to Second Lieutenant. A fortnight later he would be killed in action.

The 18th October was the eve of the First Battle of Ypres. On the morning of October 20th German artillery shelled their positions, and so began a period of attack and counter-attack. This was their first experience of shell fire. The following day the Germans came in wave after wave and managed for a moment to break in between two battalions, but they were repulsed. These attacks and further shelling continued incessantly on the 22nd.

Between October 23rd and 26th, the Yorkshire Regiment were subjected to tremendous shell fire, night and day without a break. As dawn broke on October 30th, the Battalion took up a position which formed a salient. They were fired at fairly regularly during the morning but this caused no casualties. It was, however, through the deadly accuracy of a few snipers, who never seemed to miss, that the Battalion lost their Commanding Officer, Colonel King, as well as officers Brown and Frederick Hatton. Again, the Swaledale man's body was never recovered and his name is now commemorated on Panel 33 of the Menin Gate, in Ypres.

PRIVATE HARRY PEACOCK
NO. 9360 1ST BATTALION EAST LANCASHIRE REGIMENT
DIED NOVEMBER 15TH 1914

By 1871 the Peacock family was living near Haverdale Mill, below High Row, in

Swaledale. Simon Peacock had married Hannah Harker, a girl from Greenses, near Keld. He worked in the lead mines of Swaledale and carted lead to Richmond station, via Marske, bringing back grain for the mills at Fremington, Grinton and Reeth. When the lead mining industry declined he became a shepherd at High End, Ellerton. By 1901, though, he had died and the family was living at Grinton.

Harry Peacock of Grinton, near Reeth, Swaledale

Amongst Simon and Hannah's children were Margaret and Alice and both girls had sons who were born out of wedlock. Alice was the mother of Harry but she left the dale and her son was brought up by his widowed grandmother, Hannah, with Alice helping to pay for his keep at home and at school. When she suddenly stopped making the payments, Harry was sadly sent away into a Home to be looked after. Disliking his time there, he ran away at the age of 14 and joined the regular army, telling them that he was 16 years of age.

So it was that as war was declared in 1914, Harry was serving in the 1st Battalion East Lancashire Regiment and became part of the British Expeditionary force in France and Belgium. He was to die as the result of wounds received while fighting in the First Battle of Ypres. (October 30th to November 24th).

This battle proved to be the graveyard of the old regular British Army. The Germans threw huge numbers of barely trained conscripts, many of them students, at the defending British and so terrible were the German casualties that the battle would be known to the Germans as the "Slaughter of the Innocents".

Just before dawn on October 31st, with the Kaiser himself present to direct operations, Germans of the 119 Grenadier and 125 Infantry Regiments, cheering and blowing horns, made a sudden attack and captured some of the British line. Further attacks were made but the Germans were forced back.It was during the desperate fighting to the south of Ypres in November that Harry Peacock was severely wounded.

The Battalion had sailed from Southampton to Le Havre on the "Braemar Castle" on August 22nd and for the next few weeks was involved in the long retreat, the battles of Le Cateau and The Marne and in "The Race For The Sea".

By October 18th Harry was at Armentieres, where they halted and had lunch in the grounds of the Lunatic Asylum. By October 21st they were at Ploegsteert and were ordered to counter-attack German positions at Le Gheer, through the wood, and had to resist many counter-attacks themselves.

On October 8th they attacked through the wood but the advance was held up by the enemy in a "kink" in the wood. Two Companies attacked but were repulsed with heavy losses and they dug in (with 16 killed and 31 wounded). On the 9th the enemy heavily shelled the position, resulting in 21 casualties, but at 11p.m. two companies again attacked the "kink" in the wood, capturing a German trench.

Throughout the next five days the Battalion positions were heavily shelled, with casualties over that period being 20 killed and 51 wounded. One of the wounded was Harry Peacock and he was taken to a large casualty clearing station set up at Bailleul, just over the Belgian border, in France, where he succumbed to his wounds on November 15th. Harry Peacock was buried in grave C. 21 in Bailleul Communal Cemetery.

Seventeen months later we will find that Harry's cousin, James, would also die whilst serving his country.

PRIVATE WILLIAM ROBINSON
NO. 8913 2ND BATTALION DURHAM LIGHT INFANTRY
DIED NOVEMBER 19TH 1914

Born in Richmond in 1888, William was the eldest child of William and Jane Elizabeth Robinson, with brother John and sister Hannah making up the rest of the family. William, senior, born in Ripon and a groom by occupation, had married Jane, a Middlesbrough girl. William, junior, was a Territorial soldier living in Ripon in 1914, but he travelled to Durham to enlist in the 2nd Battalion Durham Light Infantry and he too soon found himself involved in the fighting to the south of Ypres.

By the end of October the BEF were at their last gasp. Then, for no apparent reason, the German attack seemed to run out of steam. A British counter-attack succeeded in recapturing the vital village of Gheluvelt, only a few miles from the gates of Ypres. Other British units which had been sliding to defeat, rallied, and even started to counter-attack. Even the intervention of the Prussian Guards failed to break the stiffening resistance.

On November 11th and 12th the Germans attacked again from all directions, but, behind the first permanent defence lines constructed by the British (bunkers lined with barbed wire) the soldiers of the BEF poured forth a withering rifle fire that stopped the Germans in their tracks. The BEF as a whole had lost over 50,000 men, but at the cost of these losses Ypres had been saved. The crisis had passed. The "immortal Ypres Salient" had been created.

By November 14th William was just outside Armentieres, the Battalion taking over the trenches from the Shropshires at Rue de Bois. The enemy trenches were very close, in some places as little as 25 yards away. Rifle grenades were used by both sides and mining was resorted to. Rations were brought up at night to a nearby farm and then transported to a railway truck and run down the line. During this period, William Robinson was killed by a rifle grenade. His body was not recovered and instead, his name is honoured on Panel 8 and 9 of the Ploegsteert Memorial, in Belgium. Sadly for the family, we will find that his brother John perished nearby in the Ypres Salient during the Battle of Passchendaele in 1917.

PRIVATE JOB CLARKE
NO. 5989 2ND BATTALION YORKSHIRE REGIMENT
DIED DECEMBER 8TH 1914 AGED 33

Born in Leicester, Job was a 20 year old engineer fitter living with his brother-in-law in that city in 1901, but by 1914 he was residing at Richmond. He was also a

Territorial, and was mobilised at the start of the war. His Battalion, the 2nd Battalion Yorkshire Regiment, took part in the retreat from Mons and subsequent actions, and in late October took part in the bloody action at Ypres.

They showed a tenacious defence, suffering severe losses as a consequence, and were withdrawn from the front line on November 5th. Their losses were so great that in late November they received two new drafts from England, totalling 600 men, to make up the Battalion strength.

One of these losses had been Job Clarke, who had been wounded and taken prisoner by the Germans. Transported to Germany, he sadly died in a POW camp on December 8th and is buried in grave III. B. 3 in Hamburg Cemetery.

PRIVATE SIDNEY ATKINSON
NO. T/S/2871 ROYAL ARMY SERVICE CORPS
(BASE REMOUNT DEPOT) DIED DECEMBER 30TH 1914 AGED 30

Born at Kirby Ravensworth, near Richmond, he was the eldest son of Homer and Annie Atkinson. His father was born at Aysgarth, but by 1901 the family, including siblings Thomas and Ethel, had left Kirby Ravensworth and was living at Barden Dykes, near Bellerby, where Homer was a farmer and 17 year old Sidney worked on the farm. By 1914 Sidney was married, and as a Territorial soldier, he enlisted at Richmond as war was declared. Due to his knowledge of, and ability in working with horses, he was posted to the Base Remount Depot (Royal Army Service Corps) of the BEF in France. He left behind his wife, Mary Isabelle, in the nearby village of Hudswell.

In France, Sidney was involved in supplying horses and transportation to the front line troops, and would see some action during the mobile warfare of August, September and October. However, he was struck down with illness during December 1914 and became a patient at the important hospital centre of Le Havre, on the French coast. He did not recover and Sidney Atkinson was buried in grave 14. I. 3 at Ste. Marie Cemetery, Le Havre.

His death was the last one for the year 1914. During these five months of war, eight men with Swaledale connections had died whilst serving in the forces. Unfortunately, this was just a portent of what was to come.

In France and Belgium throughout December 1914 an Allied offensive beat unsuccessfully for ten bloody days against the rapidly growing German system of field fortifications. The era of stabilised trench warfare from the North Sea to the Swiss border had begun; the spade, the machine-gun and barbed wire rang down the curtain on battlefield manoeuvre.

As 1914 drew to a close and Swaledale mourned the loss of eight of its men, the enormity of the conflict became apparent to everyone as casualty lists were posted. By this time, operations on the Western Front had already cost the Allies nearly one million casualties, with German losses almost as great. The Germans had not won a quick victory and now the Western Front would settle down to four years of bloody attrition. Swaledale, and now Wharfedale, would not be spared its share of the nation's heartache.

CHAPTER THREE

1915 – THE CASUALTIES MOUNT

The eyes of the British public had been rudely opened by the widening of the conflict to new theatres of war and by the vast casualties resulting from the early campaigns. All thoughts of an early end to the conflict had been dispelled. Nevertheless, the feeling persisted that once Kitchener's New Army of volunteers was ready in 1915, the combined efforts of the Allies would then soon defeat the enemy.

On the Home Front, several families of Belgian refugees, fleeing from their occupied homeland, had arrived in Wharfedale by late January 1915. Two families had found shelter at Grassington, three families at Hebden, three at Kettlewell, two at Buckden and one at Burnsall. The families at Buckden were kept by Miss Stansfield of Buckden House and by Tom Smith, who provided a cottage, whilst George Holdsworth of Scargill House, Kettlewell, placed Mile House at a family's disposal. The other families were being maintained by the local Belgian Relief Funds. In early February 1915 there was a whist drive and dance on a Friday evening, put on by the Committee of the Reading Room, in aid of the Fund.

Swaledale had also provided a refuge and in late 1916 it was reported that Joseph Van de Couter, his wife and two children had left Reeth, after two years in the village, to move to Skipton, where he had secured work as assistant gardener. At nearby Hudswell, a wounded Belgian soldier, Joseph Brohee, arrived and did not return to his native country. He eventually married a girl working at the vicarage, where he was employed as the gardener, and they settled in the village to raise a family.

By March 1917 there began the winding up of the Refugee Fund in parts of Wharfedale. Two families (each of four members), one from France and one from Belgium, had received hospitality at Burnsall, in houses provided rent free by Mrs. Green of Woodbine Cottage and Mr. Bauer of Bridge House. During their stay, £182 was raised for their keep and maintenance by Burnsall, Appletreewick, Skyreholme and Hartlington. The two families had now left England for suitable employment, one in Spain and one in Russia.

All communities within the dales, especially the women, were eager to play their part in the war effort by forming Comfort Funds. Money was raised and knitting circles made clothes so that gift parcels could be sent to the servicemen fighting in the war or to those who had been wounded, in order to keep their morale high.

To Colonel Phillips of the 2nd Battalion West Yorkshire Regiment at the Front, the members of the Rylstone, Burnsall and Conistone Comfort Funds sent 2 blankets, 6 shirts, 7 socks, 3 pairs of cuffs, 3 belts, 10 scarves and 1 helmet. Mrs. Phillips wrote back, "I do wish you could see the grateful pleasure the gifts give. Please tell the kind hands who made them, how truly they are appreciated by our Yorkshire men. My husband wrote saying, "The men behaved excellently during the 48 hours in the trenches, so steady and firm they repelled three night attacks."

In July 1915 the same ladies received from Nurse Willis on the hospital ship "Gallika", stationed at Alexandria, a post card saying, "I feel I should like to tell you how very useful the kit bags you so kindly sent have been on this ship. I had several officers and men back from Gallipoli who had lost nearly everything and were most grateful for your kind gifts."

On December 22nd 1915, at Grassington, the school gave an entertainment at the Town Hall. The play was called Dick Whittington, the object being to give the Grassington recruits, who were home on furlough, a pleasant evening and buy them some comforts before going to the Front.

At Rylstone, in October 1916, an urgent appeal was received from Colonel Gordon, who was formerly at Skipton Camp with the 21st West Yorks, for comforts (socks, shirts, warm clothing) for his men, all of whom had been to the Front, and would have to return there as soon as they were fit. Many of them had only partly recovered from wounds and illness and felt the cold and damp acutely and would be most grateful for warm things.

A house to house collection in Rylstone, Cracoe and Bordley Moor raised the sum of £7-9sh-8p in December 1916 and 15 parcels were sent to men serving in the Army and Navy. Each parcel contained fruit cakes, biscuits, chocolate, dates, sweets, cigarettes, soap, candles and handkerchiefs. The Committee had a few shillings in hand and hoped to send cigarettes to the men abroad later. A similar collection at Arncliffe raised £14 by the Littondale folk for the benefit of the dale's soldiers. £1 was to be sent to those abroad and 14 shillings to those in training, as a Christmas present.

The following is an extract from a letter of thanks received by the rector at Bolton Abbey for parcels sent out at Christmas;

"The Germans have made another big gas attack but have suffered very heavily. It is the first time we have been gassed and I hope it is the last. It is awful to see men suffering from gas. Our Battalion has lost a lot of men in this last attack. Nobody wants to get it into their heads that the Germans are short of shells. If they do, they want to come out here round about where we are. We have got a fresh Colonel, but he has got wounded and all the officers in our Company are also wounded but we have got a good name from the General. They will never break through the line where we are, try as they like."

During the third week of February 1917, the small Swaledale village of Keld held a week of action to raise money to provide comforts and money to local servicemen. House to house collections were undertaken, whilst on Friday evening a whist drive was held in the Cat Hole Inn Assembly Room, followed by supper in a room kindly lent by Mrs. Wilson of Keld Lodge, before 70 people attended a dance in the Assembly Room (the waitresses at the supper were the Misses E.A. Alderson, B. Raine, M.A. Peacock, N. Rukin, M. Thornborrow and E. Metcalfe). A total of £11 was raised.

In 1915 a national movement was begun for a constant supply of fresh eggs for the wounded and sick soldiers in hospital Something like 200,000 a week were required and throughout the dales each village school became the collection point. In late February 1915 Mr. A.M. Crabtree of Threshfield, near Grassington, organised a collection of eggs for the National Egg Collection Movement and since January had despatched 2737 eggs to headquarters. (Threshfield and Skirethorns 454, Conistone-with-Kilnsey 264, Cracoe 258, Hetton 187, Rylstone 172, Grassington 152, Linton 101 and Upper Dale 30. The number collected for April rose to 4032 and we can see from information in the Rylstone Parish Magazine that such collections were continuing in March 1919, with the total number of eggs collected by scholars and forwarded to Skipton Hospital for wounded soldiers by Miss Smith being 413.

During the last week before Christmas 1915, a collection of money to send comforts for those from the neighbourhood serving their country realised over £12. The scholars of Arncliffe School were bringing eggs or money to school every week to be sent to the hospital for the wounded, and for the last month, though eggs were scarce, over 30, together with money, had been forwarded to London.

Miss Ashton of Cockerham Farm, Thorpe, near Burnsall, had received acknowledgements in January 1916 of parcels sent to soldiers serving overseas at the Front. Lieutenant J.N. Procter of the 6th West Ridings thanked the subscribers, as did Private Tom Swales of the 10th Battalion. Both said that the weather in the trenches was terrible, with much rain causing problems (sadly, both men would be lost in the war).

During that same month, the women of the Buckden area were hard at work making comforts. 12 pairs of socks, 13 mufflers, 106 vests, 6 pairs of mittens, 6 feather pillows, 27 pillow cases and 20 pairs of slippers were despatched. The parcel from the Oughtershaw district contained 29 mufflers and 22 pairs of mittens. New Year presents of smokes and chocolates had also been sent to everyone connected with the townships at the front and in training.

Empire Day, May 24th, was always a special occasion in British schools, and during the war years was used to encourage school children to contribute to the "Soldiers' and Sailors' Fund", each child receiving in return an attractive souvenir of the day. On Empire Day, 1916, the children of Appletreewick Council School, near Burnsall, collected £1-7sh-8d for the comfort fund.

Everyone could play their part in making a contribution to the war effort. It was reported in the "Darlington and Stockton Times" that 8 year old Jennie Bradbury of Wham Farm, had, during several weeks of wintry weather made the full weeks' attendance at Hurst School, near Marrick, Swaledale, walking forty miles a week across the bleak moors. Jennie and other local children often spent their long winter nights knitting socks, scarves and mittens for the soldiers.

J.T. Clayton, editor of the "Craven Herald", was instrumental in founding an organisation to help stranded soldiers at Skipton Station when they came home on leave and were unable to get back to remote areas of the Dales. Under his direction a volunteer "motor corps" took soldiers home at all times of the night.

Meanwhile, during late 1914 and early 1915, the demand for increased numbers of volunteers for the fighting services became insatiable as casualties overseas increased and the conflict branched out into other theatres of war. At recruitment meetings held throughout the many dales communities, attempts were made to encourage more local men to leave their loved ones and join the Colours. During

1914, eight men from Swaledale had lost their lives but when 1915 drew to a close, we will find that a further twenty men had perished, six from Wharfedale and fourteen from the Swaledale area.

A recruitment meeting was held in the Arncliffe School Room, Littondale, in late January 1915. The Reverend Canon Shuffrey presided and the meeting was addressed by Colonel Dawson. At the close, three volunteers came forward to take the oath (Joseph Simpson of Arncliffe and Gilbert Reynard and Thomas Ingleby of Hawkswick, both being Territorials. Sadly, Tom Ingleby would not survive the war). A similar meeting was held at Halton Gill, the speaker being Mr. Dyson, but the result was fruitless.

A "Flying Column" of soldiers came to the Craven district in late September 1915 for a week, camping at Burley in Wharfedale. They marched through Ilkley and Addingham, before reaching Skipton and held meetings throughout the whole district.

A detachment of men, along with the band of the 6th Battalion West Riding Regiment, journeyed to Grassington by train, then marched round the village to the strains of martial airs. A meeting was held in the Market Place, over which William Clough, MP, presided. He congratulated the dales, relating that Ingleton had sent 145 men, Settle 228 and he understood that 40 had gone from Grassington. He appealed especially to the farmers and other employers to allow further men to be released. The "Flying Column" then left the Skipton district at the end of the week for the Barnoldswick area.

Raising money during War Weapons Week in Richmond. The town mayor is standing next to a captured German gun
Wenham Collection

Burning an effigy of the German Kaiser in Richmond Market Square
Wenham Collection

The Recruitment march in Bradley, near Skipton, late September 1915

Many of the men who volunteered in 1914 or early 1915 were destined for service overseas and 1915 saw continued British involvement on the Western Front and in other theatres of war. Turkey's entrance into the war on Germany's side in October 1914 had changed the war's complexion. Russia, already shaken by the reverses of 1914, was now virtually cut-off from Franco-British war supplies. In an attempt to help Russia, a naval expedition was mounted to clear the Dardanelles for Russian ships in the Black Sea. When this venture stalled, an attack was planned on a little known peninsula called Gallipoli.

On the Western Front during 1915 the BEF extended its front southwards across the wet levels of the River Lys into the dreary coal fields east of Lille, where, during 1915, it fought a series of murderous trench to trench battles (Neuve Chapelle in March, Festubert May to June, and Givenchy) and also mounted one major, miscarried offensive at Loos in September to October.

British casualties mounted as these attacks were launched during 1915 and increased again when the Germans launched their own major assault at the Second Battle of Ypres (April to May), this latter assault seeing poison gas being used by the Germans for the first time in the west.

Increase of lethal fire-power had given the advantage to the defence, for a continuous battle line prevented classical offensive manoeuvres. The Germans had adopted an elastic defence, in two or more lines, highly organised with entrenchments and barbed wire, heavy in machine-guns and supported by artillery. Assaulting troops broke through the first line only to be decimated by the fire from the succeeding lines. As a consequence of these facts we find that the number of Swaledale and Wharfedale men who died on the field of battle or succumbed to their wounds throughout 1915 rose dramatically to twenty.

However, the first casualty of 1915 was a Royal Navy Petty Officer from Richmond.

PETTY OFFICER STOKER JOHN FRANCIS ALLAN
NO. K/89 HMS "FORMIDABLE" ROYAL NAVY
DIED JANUARY 1ST 1915 AGED 27

John was the son of Leonard and Mary Allan of Richmond and husband of Anna. He had been born at Dinnington, a village just north of Newcastle, but in 1901, fifteen year old John was residing at Mason in Northumberland and was working in a coal mine. By 1914, his parents were living in Richmond but John had left the mining industry before the start of the war and was a member of the Royal Navy. He had risen to the rank of Petty Officer, Stoker, by the end of 1914, on board the battleship HMS "Formidable". It would prove to be the first British battleship to be sunk in the Great War.

Commanded by Captain A.N. Loxley, the 15,000 ton pre-Dreadnought battleship was the flagship of Vice Admiral Sir Lewis Bayly's 5th Battle Squadron. On December 31st 1914 HMS "Formidable" was leading the eight battleships of the Squadron down the English Channel, screened by two light cruisers.

The destroyer escort had been sent back to Harwich when the ships passed Folkestone. Unfortunately, the Squadron had been spotted by U-boat U.24,

HMS 'Formidable', the 15,250 ton pre-Dreadnought battleship on which Petty-Officer Stoker John Francis Allan went down on January 1st 1915

commanded by Rudolph Schneider, but he had been unable to manoeuvre into an attacking position and had to watch as the ships sailed by. Shortly after 1900 hours the British ships made a 16-point turn in accordance with orders that course should be altered after dark in areas where submarines were known to be operating.

Again, at 0200 hours on January 1st 1915, a second 16-point turn was made so that HMS "Formidable" and her consorts were steaming back along their course and towards U-24, twenty five miles off Portland. This time Schneider was in a perfect position and at 0225 hours fired a torpedo against HMS "Formidable", the last ship in the line. It hit her on the starboard side by the fore funnel. Her machinery spaces began to flood and she assumed a list to starboard. At 0315 hours Schneider fired a second torpedo which hit "Formidable" on the port side. On board the battleship the dynamos failed, although the crew maintained perfect discipline in the listing and darkened ship (someone even played ragtime music on the piano, whilst others sang). At 0445 hours she capsized and then sank.

Many of the boats were smashed as they were lowered into the gale lashed waters, killing all occupants. One pinnace with 70 men on board was picked up by the trawler "Provident", 15 miles off Berry Head. A second pinnace took off another 70 men, but by the time it arrived in Lyme harbour, 14 had died and had been buried at sea, 6 were dead in the boat and 3 died after landing.

547 members of the crew perished in the waters of the English Channel, including John Allan, with 233 crew being rescued. John's body was not recovered and he is commemorated on the Chatham Naval Memorial, Kent. As with so many families, we shall again find that another member of the family would be killed in the war. Septimus Allan lost his life in November 1917.

LANCE CORPORAL CHARLES WHEELER
NO. 6583 "C" COMPANY 2ND BATTALION YORKSHIRE REGIMENT
DIED MARCH 18TH 1915 AGED 38

Charles was an incomer to Swaledale, having been born in the Eastbourne area of Sussex, but was living in Richmond when the Great War began. A member of the Territorial Army, he went to France with the 2nd Battalion, Yorkshire Regiment, and in early 1915 was preparing to take part in the forthcoming Battle of Neuve Chapelle.

On March 10th, Haig's First Army unleashed nearly 50 battalions against the village of Neuve Chapelle, preceded by a half hour artillery barrage. The German defences consisted of only six companies, supported by just twelve machine-guns. The German front lines were therefore quickly overrun, Neuve Chapelle village being taken within 45 minutes. The British then paused for a fatal five hours, giving the Germans time to recover from the shock and organise a further line of defence.

Too late, Haig gave the order to press on with the attack, "regardless of loss" and, sadly, loss was all that was achieved. On a narrow front of 4000 yards the British gained just 1200 yards, with the loss of 583 officers and more than 12,000 other ranks. Finding that they were running short of artillery ammunition, Haig gave the order to break off the battle on March 13th.

March 10th found the 2nd Battalion moving forward to take over captured German trenches, with the enemy in some places only 30 yards away. On the 11th many casualties were caused by their own artillery. Shortly before dawn on March 12th the Germans counter-attacked but were completely stopped by rifle and machine gun fire and fell back, leaving many dead behind. After a British bombardment, one company went forward to fill a gap and losses were experienced from German cross-fire from a redoubt still in enemy hands and from shelling. Relieved on March 14th, the Battalion had suffered 311 casualties. While leading a bombing party that helped capture 62 Germans, a Corporal was killed and awarded the VC.

Wounded during the battle, Charles Wheeler was taken to the hospital centre at Merville, 15 kilometres north of Bethune, where he died on March 18th. He was buried in grave II. J.5 at Merville Communal Cemetery.

PRIVATE ROBERT JACKMAN
NO. 6704 2ND BATTALION WEST RIDING REGIMENT
DIED APRIL 18TH 1915 AGED 36

Robert's father, John Jackman, had been born at Langcliffe, near Settle, and worked in the local limestone quarries. He married Annie, a London born girl, and brought up their family in the Settle area, living at times at Langcliffe and Giggleswick. Robert, who was born at Giggleswick and was the second eldest son, did not follow his father and brothers into the limestone quarries, but worked instead on the local railway as a navvy. By 1901, the Jackman family, including 22 year old railway navvy Robert, were living close to the quarries at Embsay with Eastby. At some time between then and the start of the Great War, John and Annie Jackman went to live in Ivy Cottage at Linton, near Grassington and the local limestone quarries, whilst their son Robert left the family home to continue his work on the railway at Todmorden.

A member of the Territorial Army, Robert went out to France with the West

Riding Regiment at the beginning of the war and was at the retreat from Mons. However, by early April 1915 the Battalion was in Divisional Reserve in the Ypres Salient, Belgium.

On April 16th they moved into dugouts on the Railway Embankment near Zillebeke and at 6a.m. on the 18th moved out to relieve another battalion who had attacked and captured Hill 60 the previous night, but had been bombed out of the advanced trenches and were holding three craters caused by the explosion of British mines. "A" Company took over these craters but were bombed with hand grenades and lost heavily.

At 4-30p.m. the Battalion was ordered up to the craters ready for an attack on the hill at 6p.m. With supporting artillery fire they charged with bayonets fixed. "B" Company reached the enemy trenches with relatively few casualties, but "C" Company charged over 50 yards of open ground and suffered heavily. Captain Barton and eleven men reached the enemy trench and killed, captured or put to flight the garrison. "D" Company also charged across open ground and lost all their officers, but captured their section of German trenches, having suffered very heavily.

Robert's body was never found and instead his name is honoured on Panel 20 of the Menin Gate, Ypres. His brother John, who went out to France in December 1916 with the West Ridings, was awarded the Military Medal in 1917 and thankfully survived the war.

Four days later, on April 22nd, the Germans launched the Second Battle of Ypres, against the same Salient that Robert Jackman had died defending. A surprise German attack was preceded by a cloud of chlorine gas emitted from some 5,000 cylinders. This was the first use of poison gas in the west. Two German corps drove through two terrorised French divisions and bit deeply into British lines, creating a gap. It was three days into this battle that a soldier from Richmond was killed.

SERGEANT HENRY (HARRY) KINCHIN
4TH BATTALION YORKSHIRE REGIMENT
DIED APRIL 25TH 1915 AGED 34

John James Kinchin and his wife Martha were Richmond folk, living with their seven children at 11 Castle Hill, Richmond. John James was a joiner and under-taker, with a work shop at the bottom of the garden, and Harry worked for his father as a carpenter (when the Spanish Flu pandemic caused such misery around the world in 1918 and 1919, John James was kept extremely busy making coffins for the Richmond area). Harry was married to Priscilla and they lived at 48 Bargate, Richmond.

Harry, his father and three brothers were in the Volunteers and in the Territorial Army and when war broke out, Harry and his brother, Allison Clarke Kinchin, went straight into the 4th Battalion Yorkshire Regiment, travelling with the BEF to France on August 15th 1914 and being involved in most of the fighting during the following desperate months. By April 1915 the Battalion was serving in the notorious Ypres Salient and were in the path of the planned German assault.

On April 25th, Harry's brother Allison was fighting in the vanguard of the Battalion, whilst Harry was at the rear, but it was he and the men around him who

The Kinchin family of Richmond, serving in the pre-war Volunteers.
Harry Kinchin was killed in action in the Great War.
Back row: John Kinchin, Allison Kinchin
Front row: John James Kinchin, Jimmy Kinchin, Harry Kinchin

were affected by chlorine gas. As Allison withdrew, he came across his brother Harry and helped to bury him in a make-shift grave. However, in the fighting over the next few weeks, the area fought over was devastated by shell fire and any graves and their bodies disappeared. There is no official grave for Harry Kinchin and his name is commemorated on Panel 33 of the Menin Gate at Ypres.

Allison Kinchin was badly wounded in the leg in early 1918 and was invalided out of the army. We shall find that Allison's son, also called Harry, would be killed during the Second World War.

Another man with Richmond connections also died as a result of the German offensive, from wounds that he received.

SAPPER WALTER ERNEST BRAND
NO. 18041 56TH FIELD COMPANY ROYAL ENGINEERS
DIED MAY 6TH 1915

Walter was born at Caterham, Surrey, the son of James and Margaret Brand. I have no information on his later connection with Richmond, but in April 1915 he was in the Ypres Salient with the Royal Engineers and was wounded during the German offensive. He did not recover and his body was laid to rest in grave D.22. Dickebusch New Military Cemetery.

DRIVER JACK CHAPMAN NO. T2/12877
29TH RESERVE PARK, ROYAL ARMY SERVICE CORPS
DIED MAY 14TH 1915 AGED 27

Robert (Bob) Chapman, the Grassington "Bus Proprietor", received news from Gallipoli on Wednesday May 26th 1915, confirming the death of his nephew John (Jack) Chapman, from illness.

Jack Chapman of Grassington
Courtesy of The Craven Herald

Jack, who was born at Settle, was 27 years of age and grandson of the late Christopher (Kit) Chapman, bus proprietor. He was quite a public character, being well known and respected in the dales and in the Skipton district as a careful driver of both bus and motor. He was one of the first recruits from Grassington, enlisting at Skipton soon after the war broke out.

He was with the Royal Army Service Corps and attached to the Mediterranean Expeditionary Force at the Dardanelles, in the capacity of driver. After the unsuccessful Allied naval assault on the Dardanelles fortresses between February 19th and March 18th, the first landings took place at Cape Helles on April 25th 1915 in a welter of mismanagement, incurring murderous losses. Failing to take the high ground occupied by the Turkish forces, the landings were doomed to failure and the British soon found themselves involved in the same kind of trench warfare they had known on the Western Front, but with even less room for manoeuvre.

Jack was one of many servicemen who went down with illness during this period and by early May was in hospital in Alexandria, Egypt. He died on May 14th and was buried in grave A149 Alexandria (Chatby) Military and War Memorial Cemetery, Egypt.

On the last day of the Second Battle of Ypres, the main German offensive of 1915, another Dales serviceman was killed, this time from the town of Richmond.

PRIVATE HENRY GEORGE MATTHEW BENSON
NO. 2143 4TH BATTALION YORKSHIRE REGIMENT
DIED MAY 27TH 1915 AGED 26

Henry was born in 1892 at Victoria Place, Richmond, his parents being George James and Mary Isabel Benson (nee Greathead). His father was a master grocer in the town.

Henry, who worked with his father in the shop, was a Territorial soldier and was with the 4th Battalion at their training camp in Wales in late July 1914, when they were ordered to return to Northallerton, before moving to Darlington and then Newcastle. They disembarked at Boulogne, France, on April 18th 1915, before arriving in the Ypres Salient by the 20th.

One of Henry's officers was Lieutenant Percy Orde-Powlett from Bolton Hall, Wensley. Two days later, on the 22nd, the Germans began the Second Battle of Ypres with their deadly gas attack.

In the next few days they were involved in their first actions as they counter-attacked to force the Germans out of the village of Fortuin and back to St. Julien, but they came under severe shelling and machine gun fire, resulting in 15 men killed and 61 wounded.

On May 15th, the Battalion marched to the Railway Embankment and stayed there until May 21st and it was during this period that Lieutenant Percy Orde-Powlett (who would have become the future Lord Bolton) was hit in the neck by a German sniper on May 17th and died of his wounds.

On May 23rd, the Battalion moved to trenches astride the Menin Road at Hooge and here, on the early morning of May 24th the second great German gas attack fell upon the 4th Yorkshire Regiment. From trench to trench they fought gallantly and stuck to their trenches, but at great cost, especially from the gas. By the time they were relieved on May 25th, 30 men had been killed, 70 wounded and 79 were missing. Henry Benson was one of those missing and his name is commemorated on Panel 33 Menin Gate Memorial.

The next three servicemen from the dales, two from Rylstone and one from Richmond, died in day to day action in the dangerous confines of the Ypres Salient, those from Wharfedale serving in the same battalion.

PRIVATE HORACE MARSHALL
NO. 3718 6TH BATTALION
WEST RIDING REGIMENT
DIED JULY 15TH 1915 AGED 24

In 1901, 33 year old Arthur Marshall, a widower and slate quarryman of Greenhow Hill, near Pateley Bridge, lived with his son Horace and daughters Alice and Florrie, all born at that windswept village.

By the start of the Great War, Arthur had remarried and gone to live at Bramley in Leeds, whilst his son, Horace, came to Hetton, near Rylstone, as a farm labourer for Bernard Tennant of Thorntree Farm, situated next to Hetton Chapel.

Horace Marshall from Hetton
Courtesy of The Craven Herald

AND
PRIVATE RHODES SPENCE
NO. 3702 6TH BATTALION WEST RIDING REGIMENT
DIED JULY 17TH 1915 AGED 20

Rhodes' father, Robert Bell Spence, a farmer, was born at Carlton in Coverdale. With his wife Annie, he came to Rylstone, where his eldest son Walter was born. The twins, Martha and Rhodes, were born at Goldshaw Booth in Lancashire, whilst the youngest daughter, Ada, was born at Padiham, near Burnley. By the time Rhodes was 6 years old, however, the family was living on a farm at the Ashes, Burton-cum-Walden, near West Burton.

Rhodes Spence from Hetton and Silsden
Courtesy of The Craven Herald

At some stage before the war began, the Spence family was to be found at Millbanks, Keighley Road, Silsden, where Rhodes attended the Wesleyan Sunday School and found employment as a weaver at Messrs. John Knox, Airedale Shed, Silsden.

Rhodes eventually came to work as a farm labourer for Harry Reeday of Fell View Farm, Hetton, near Rylstone. The Reeday family thought a great deal of Rhodes and were very sad when he had to go off to war.

Horace Marshall and Rhodes Spence were friends, working on neighbouring farms, and in December 1914 they both travelled to enlist in the army at Skipton, joining the same Battalion of the West Riding Regiment. In April 1915 they crossed the Channel and by July were stationed in the Ypres Salient.

RIFLEMAN ALBERT EDWARD KEARTON
NO. 9639 3RD BATTALION RIFLE BRIGADE
DIED JULY 18TH 1915 AGED 31

Born at Richmond, Albert was the son of Frank and Elizabeth Kearton of 1 Castle Terrace, Richmond. Living at Richmond in 1914 he enlisted in his home town and eventually joined the Rifle Brigade. In mid July 1915, he too was serving in the vicinity of Ypres.

Between April 22nd and May 25th the Second Battle of Ypres took place, when a surprise German attack was preceded by a cloud of chlorine gas emitted from some 5000 cylinders, the first use of poison gas in the west. Local counter-attacks by the British Second Army finally stemmed the German advance after bitter fighting. German losses were some 35,000 men, with the British losing 60,000.

However, it was not to be in the cut and thrust of attack and counter-attack that

Horace, Rhodes and Albert would be killed two months later, but in the more mundane day to day actions in the Salient. Mundane is perhaps the wrong word to use for serving in the infamous Salient, for, with the Germans occupying most of the high ground, they could see much of the activity taking place in the British front line and could pour forth an accurate and deadly fire on the defenders, both from artillery positions and by use of snipers.

Horace Marshall's sister at Wakefield received a letter from Second Lieutenant Buxton stating that he had been hit at 2p.m. on July 15th, the bullet having passed through his head. He died about 2-20p.m., having never recovered consciousness and was buried in grave D.12, Colne Valley Cemetery, north of Ypres.

Sometime later, Rhodes Spence received a fractured femur and crushed pelvis due to enemy shell-fire and was taken to the 10th Casualty Clearing Station, based at Lijssenthoek, 12 kilometres west of Ypres. He passed away at 5-45a.m. on July 17th and was buried in the afternoon in the adjacent cemetery (grave III.B.12). Working side by side in the dales village of Hetton in peacetime, the two friends had perished side by side in the hell-hole that was Ypres.

One day later, on July 18th, Albert Edward Kearton of Richmond and the Rifle Brigade, was also killed by shell fire, but his body was never recovered and he is commemorated on Panels 46-48 and 50 of the Menin Gate. By the end of the war, we shall find that three more Keartons from Richmond fell on the battlefield, two of them in the Ypres Salient.

In December 1914, Albert's Battalion had gone into new trenches at Armentieres for 34 days without being relieved. Christmas in the trenches was remembered by the Battalion as a day of perfect peace during which a truce was held. A German juggler drew a large crowd of Riflemen and Germans in the middle of No Man's Land. Yet, just four days later, the Battalion's Commanding Officer was hit and died from his wounds.

At the end of May, 1915, the Battalion left Armentieres, arriving in the Ypres Salient on June 4th. The next two months were spent in the trenches at La Brique, going out occasionally in billets in the woods near Poperinghe. The Battalion diaries report that no one who had ever been to Ypres wanted to go there again and the Battalion had its fair share of this unpleasant spot, receiving more shelling than most of them cared about. They would all have been glad of a change to any other part of the line. On July 18th a shell destroyed the life of Albert Kearton.

The month of August and the first week in September witnessed a total of four Richmond fatalities, with the first being:

LANCE CORPORAL JOHN FRANCIS BENBOW NO. 17881 "D" COMPANY 10TH BATTALION DURHAM LIGHT INFANTRY DIED AUGUST 13TH 1915 AGED 30

John was the son of Mrs. Winifred Benbow of Richmond. Living in the town, he enlisted early in the war at Darlington and was drafted into the 10th Battalion Durham Light Infantry. During the fighting in June he was wounded and was taken eventually to Le Treport, one of the large military hospital complexes, 30 kilometres NE of Dieppe. John died from his wounds on August 13th and is buried in grave 1.J.1 Le Treport Military Cemetery.

It was to be many miles away from the Western Front, in the Turkish theatre of war, that the next two casualties, both with Richmond connections, were to fall in battle. Both men served in the same Battalion and died within the space of 24 hours of each other.

LANCE SERGEANT JOHN HENRY METCALFE NO. 3/8473 6TH BATTALION YORKSHIRE REGIMENT DIED AUGUST 21ST 1915 AGED 32

Born at Crakehall, near Bedale, the son of John Metcalfe, he was a regular soldier who served in the South African campaign with the Coldstream Guards. He later married his wife Emma and lived at Darlington. When war began John enlisted at Richmond and was drafted into the 6th Battalion Yorkshire Regiment.

AND LANCE CORPORAL ALFRED THOMAS WOODHAMS NO. 15629 6TH BATTALION YORKSHIRE REGIMENT DIED AUGUST 22ND 1915 AGED 20

Born at Kilkenny, in the south of Ireland, to parents William and Eliza Woodhams, the family was living at Skeeby Terrace, Richmond, in 1914, when Alfred enlisted in the market town.

In January, 1915, approval was given for a naval expedition to be mounted to clear the Dardanelles for Russian ships in the Black Sea. When this venture stalled, an amphibious operation, led by General Ian Hamilton, was planned on a little known peninsula called Gallipoli.

The plan provided for two daylight assaults on April 25th, one at Cape Helles on the tip of the Peninsula, the other by the Anzacs (Australian and New Zealand Army Corps) on the western side. At Cape Helles the British landed on five beaches in a welter of mismanagement, incurring murderous losses. The Anzacs were beaten back by a vicious Turkish counter-attack, with a loss of 5000 men.

Between August 6th and 8th, following months of the bitterest fighting on the rocky slopes of the Peninsula, General Hamilton attempted a co-ordinated assault. The Anzacs were to make the main effort with a night attack. The newly arrived British Divisions, including the 6th Battalion, landing at Suvla Bay to the north, were to make a secondary attack. The Anzac attack bogged down in the darkness and only the Suvla Bay landing, made without serious opposition, promised success. Sadly, the Corps Commander lacked vigour and drive, the advance lagged until Turkish reinforcements had time to come up, and again it was too late. The entire operation had failed. It was to be in the fighting at Suvla Bay that the two Richmond men would lose their lives.

The Battalion had reached the main base on the Adriatic island of Lemnos on July 10th, aboard HMTS "Aquitania". A fortnight was spent practising night attacks, including night landings from small boats, as they prepared for the Suvla Bay attack. At 10-30p.m. on August 6th the men were loaded into two lighters towed by destroyers, also packed with troops, and landed in pitch darkness on the beach, ready to attack the hilly area inland. Bursts of rifle fire greeted them as they charged up the slopes and took the hill. In the darkness confusion reigned, with battalions getting hopelessly mixed up.

The 6th Battalion had received heavy losses with 16 officers and 250 men killed and wounded. However, they remained in action over the next three days, but withdrew on the night of August 11th. On August 21st they moved forward to the fire trenches on Hill 50 whilst a fresh attack was being planned, They suffered dreadfully from the heat, want of water, the flies and dry rations. Turkish snipers trained their rifles on the few remaining wells.

Their objective was a nearby hill, 300 feet high. At 3p.m. the bombardment opened up, but the flat trajectory of the naval guns had done no damage to the Turkish trenches. There was a lack of direction in the attack, the shrapnel fire was heavy and Turkish machine gunners were provided with a clear target. There could be no movement over the flat plain and the final attack was over by 4p.m.

The remnants of the Battalion stayed out until the next day but came back on the morning of the 22nd. When they reached the beach to go into reserve, the decimated Battalion was only 285 strong, from a complement of 900. John Metcalfe had been killed on the afternoon of August 21st, whilst Alfred Woodhams lost his life on the morning of the 22nd. Their bodies were never recovered and they are commemorated on Panel 55 to 58 of the Helles Memorial, Turkey.

John and Alfred had died far away from home, but the next serviceman to die, also from Richmond, died within the precincts of the market town and was buried in the local graveyard.

PRIVATE HERBERT BROWN NO. 2274 CORPS OF LANCERS, 1ST LANARKSHIRE YEOMANRY, HOUSEHOLD CAVALRY DIED SEPTEMBER 8TH 1915 AGED 22

Herbert was born in Richmond, the 3rd eldest of the nine children of Potts and Margaret Brown, who lived on Cornforth Hill. His parents were born and bred in Richmond and Potts was employed as a Richmond cab driver and groom. With his knowledge of horses, derived from his father's occupation, it is not surprising to find that Herbert joined the cavalry. However, he was taken ill and died at home, being buried in grave C.80 in Richmond Cemetery.

Rumours abounded in September 1915 of a great Franco-British offensive which would shatter the German front. Kitchener's New Armies and Territorials were set to play a prominent role in the proceedings.

The British planned an assault on German positions near the village of Loos, in the bleak coal mining region between Bethune and Lens. The ground was unfavourable, swept by machine gun fire from the enemy trenches and numerous fortified villages behind them. Many of those taking part on the British side were untried members of the New Army, with inadequate heavy artillery backing and shells. The omens were not good.

The Battle of Loos opened on September 25th 1915 with an artillery bombardment and the release of chlorine gas from over 5000 cylinders. The gas carried fairly well over the German trenches on the right, but on the left was a failure, in some places drifting back and poisoning the British soldiers. Those who were able to advance were soon stopped and slaughtered by the surviving German machine gunners.

When gaps did appear in the German defences, the British reserves were held too far back and could not exploit the opportunity. The Battle petered out on October 14th with the minor gains made being out of proportion to the casualties suffered (over 100,000 French, 60,000 British and 65,000 Germans).

One dalesman from Wharfedale and two with Richmond connections would lose their lives during the Battle of Loos.

QUARTER MASTER SERGEANT ROMILLE HARKER NO. 23708 "B" COMPANY 1ST BATTALION THE KINGS (LIVERPOOL REGIMENT) DIED SEPTEMBER 25TH 1915 AGED 36

Romille's parents, Reverend Bailey J. Harker and Ann Harker lived at Grassington, where Bailey was the minister at the Congregational Church. He was also well known in the area for his efforts in bringing tourism to Grassington, writing guide books and seeking to make the settlement as popular as Buckden. Born in Grassington, Bailey Harker had lived at Guisley, then Shrewsbury, before moving to Eccleshall, Staffordshire, where Romille was born. His wife, Anne, was a Shropshire girl, but by 1901 the family, including 21 year old Romille, was living at Deane Church Lane, Bolton, where Bailey Harker was the minister.

Romille Harker, from Grassington and Bolton
Courtesy of The Craven Herald

Romille, their eldest son, had been educated at Caterham Congregational College, but when the family moved to Bolton he was employed for 16 years as clerk and cashier at a Bolton factory. In 1915 his way of life changed when he obtained a position as foreign correspondent to the Central Argentine Railway at Rosario de Santa Fe.

While at Bolton he was a member of the Territorial Battalion, and on declaration of war was one of half a dozen employees of the railway company who answered the call. He made the 7000 mile voyage to England in a tramp steamer, taking five weeks, the greatest vigilance having to be exercised in avoiding German commerce raiders.

Romille enlisted at Wigan as a private in the 1st Battalion King's Liverpool Regiment and was soon promoted to sergeant. He left for France on his birthday, June 1st, and was appointed sergeant of the bomb throwers in "B" Company.

In early July 1915 Reverend Harker received two letters from his son. In one of them was a pressed poppy flower from the trenches. "Since I wrote last we have had another spell of four days in the firing line; my platoon has no lieutenant over it so I am in complete charge and continually employed with one duty or another. We (my platoon) came out short of 4 men wounded – head, arm and hand – but I myself was again among the fortunate ones.

"You may be curious to know my feelings when under fire, but really I have experienced no marked change when in action, except that it be I feel more satisfied with myself, and become aware of a certain exhilaration such as I have felt in a football or cricket match."

The second letter was dated 2/7/15: "We finished our last spell in the trenches on Monday morning, and have since had four days in billet in a small town some four miles away from here. Our last spell cost us 25 casualties in the Battalion, these being the victims of mine explosions and shell fire principally. On one occasion, a "Jack Johnson" burst in the midst of a ration party of 14, only three being left without a souvenir of some kind, and one of the men had his head blown completely away. My platoon came out without anything more than a bullet graze. We saw a copy of the "Craven Herald" last week. Private Maudsley, of Giggleswick origin, received it from home."

On September 25th 1915 the 1st Battalion went "over the top" on the first day of the Battle of Loos and were met by a withering rate of fire from machine guns and rifles. Romille Harker was first wounded in the leg and was heard to call for the stretcher bearers. Immediately afterwards he was shot in the head, and as he fell received three more shots in the body. He was never recovered from the battlefield but his name is honoured on Panel 27 to 30 of the Loos Memorial.

Romille Harker had been an artist, a literary critic, wrote much poetry and was a keen naturalist. He was a frequent visitor to Grassington when resident in the country and was very popular in the neighbourhood. Since receiving the sad news, his father had found the following verses written by Romille on the fly leaf of a book:

"Mid the busy toil and rush
Some poor souls are sighing;
Here amidst a holy hush
Lies a good man dying.

Why those useless, welling tears?
Why that trembling finger?
Death for good men has no fears –
Save for those who linger.

Selfish still we 'gin to mourn,
For our circle broken;
Garb of grief is meekly worn,
Or some death-like token.

But our brother hears the songs
Happier saints are singing;
To that home that knows no wrongs
His free soul is winging.

Constant for his Master here,
In his course diurnal;
Christ will lead him gently there
Into peace eternal.

During the next five days of battle at Loos, two more Richmond men from the same Battalion were killed in action.

LIEUTENANT COLONEL BERTRAM HENRY LEATHAM
2ND BATTALION YORKSHIRE REGIMENT
(BUT SECONDED TO THE WILTSHIRE REGIMENT)
DIED SEPTEMBER 26TH 1915 AGED 34

Bertram was a regular army officer and the third son of Samuel Gurney Leatham and Alice Leatham of Hemsworth Hall, in the large village of Hemsworth, between Wakefield and Doncaster, West Yorkshire. He loved to play the organ at services in the village church and in 1913, Captain Leatham, as he was then, married Everil, the daughter of Canon Robinson, Rector of the neighbouring village of Badsworth.

He then continued his career in the Army at Bombay, in India, and it was from there that he returned as war broke out. Bertram went to France in an early draft of the Expeditionary Force, with the 2nd Battalion Yorkshire Regiment. His wife, Everil, settled down to life in the market town of Richmond, at 30 Frenchgate.

AND
CAPTAIN MARMADUKE THWAITES
"A" COMPANY 2ND BATTALION YORKSHIRE REGIMENT
DIED SEPTEMBER 30TH 1915 AGED 34

Marmaduke was born at Richmond, the eldest son of Marmaduke and Elizabeth Thwaites. By 1901 his father had died and he and his younger brother Arthur were serving in the regular army with the 2nd Battalion Yorkshire Regiment, in the Sheffield area, with Marmaduke having the rank of Corporal. In early 1914 he was Quartermaster sergeant in the 3rd Battalion (Territorials) but when war broke out he was promoted to Second Lieutenant and went out with the British Expeditionary Force to France. Wounded in the fighting around Ypres on October 14th 1914, we find that by February 1915 he had been promoted to Lieutenant and by June 28th he was with the 2nd Battalion as a Temporary Captain, with his Commanding Officer being Lieutenant Colonel Bertram Leatham.

As the Battle of Loos was about to begin, the 2nd Battalion Yorkshire Regiment were positioned in the line next to the 2nd Battalion Wiltshire Regiment. It was at this stage that Bertram Leatham, recently awarded the DSO and promoted to the rank of Major, was temporarily made Lieutenant Colonel and became the Commanding Officer of the neighbouring Wiltshire Battalion. The two Richmond men would still be fighting side by side.

September 25th witnessed an intense artillery bombardment for 40 minutes before they advanced, and, at 10a.m., with the Wiltshires to the right, the Battalions attacked the cross roads on the NE corner of Hulloch village. The Germans held the village in strength, holding a trench running along the edge of Hulloch, with many machine guns positioned in the houses. Casualties mounted and the companies began to dig in., making a good trench.

They were attacked in the area of some quarries the following morning, the 26th. "B", "C" and "D" Companies now held the line throughout the 26th September, together with the Wiltshire Regiment and were the whole time subjected to heavy sniping. It was on this day that Lieutenant Colonel Bertram Leatham was shot and killed while leading his men.

During September 29th there was a heavy and sustained bombardment by both sides and many heavy shells fell near the Yorkshire Battalion, doing little harm. At night, "A" Company was sent forward into the front line on the right of the Scots Fusiliers and on the south of Hulloch Road. It was here that Captain Marmaduke Thwaites was killed by a shell just after the move of the Company was completed in the early hours of September 30th. Between September 25th and 30th the Battalion had received 326 casualties.

Bertram Leatham was buried in grave V1.D.13 Vermelles British Cemetery, 10 km. NW of Lens, whilst Marmaduke Thwaites is commemorated on Panel 44 and 45 Loos Memorial. It is interesting to note that several other sons of Samuel and Alice Leatham made careers for themselves in the armed forces and served in the Great War. Ralph rose to the rank of Admiral and in 1943 he acted as Deputy Governor of Malta at a crucial time in the Second World War. Eustace was also in the navy. He was the Commander of the Royal Naval College, Dartmouth and served at the Battle of Jutland, 1916. Rising to the rank of Vice-Admiral he became an Aide-de-Camp to the King in 1919-1920.

On the same day that Captain Thwaites was killed, a Wharfedale man died in a Cambridge hospital from wounds he had received in earlier action on the Western Front.

PRIVATE WILLIAM BURLEY
NO. 13655 10TH BATTALION WEST RIDING REGIMENT
DIED SEPTEMBER 30TH 1915 AGED 19

Information was received by the Reverend Stavert, Rector of Burnsall, that Private Willie Burley of the 10th West Riding Regiment had died in hospital at Cambridge from wounds received in action. He was wounded by shrapnel early one morning and an hour later another Grassington recruit, A. Stubbs, was also wounded by shrapnel and both were taken together in an ambulance to hospital. Willie Burley's wounds were serious and he was brought back to England, receiving treatment at Cambridge Hospital. He succumbed to his wounds on September 30th.

William Burley of Burnsall

Born in London, one of three children of George and Elizabeth Burley, he was brought to Burnsall a few years before the start of the Great War by the rector, in whose service he continued until he left to live at Skirethorns, where he worked in the quarries of John Delaney. He enlisted from the parish of Grassington.

The deceased was a member of the Golden Fleece Lodge of Oddfellows at Appletreewick. Willie had a brother in the army and an unmarried sister living at Deal in Kent. His body was taken to Kent and buried in grave 157 St. Mary's Old Churchyard, Walmer, Kent. When news of his death was received at Skirethorns and Grassington, the flag on the maypole was put at half mast as a mark of respect. William Burley's name is honoured on both the Linton and Burnsall war memorials.

Before 1915 came to a close, two more servicemen from these dales would die abroad, both as a result of disease brought on by the terrible conditions confronting the troops at Gallipoli.

PRIVATE RICHARD THORNHILL
NO. 3/7959 6TH BATTALION YORKSHIRE REGIMENT
DIED OCTOBER 27TH 1915 AGED 31

Richard and his twin brother Arthur were born at Richmond. By 1901, seventeen year old Richard was stationed in the Sheffield area, where he was a private in the Yorkshire Regiment. When war broke out in 1914 Richard enlisted at Richmond and joined the 6th Battalion, together with Alfred Woodhams and John Metcalfe from Richmond (we have already seen that these two soldiers perished in August 1915).

Fighting side by side with these men, Richard was more fortunate and survived the horrendous losses of Suvla Bay. A draft of 788 men arrived as reinforcements in September and took their share of the trench duties in the vicinity of the Karakol Dagh. Battalion war diaries state for September and October "Nothing to report" but in fact casualties went on steadily mounting, especially from illness.

Anyone who could walk to the trenches was considered fit. The heat was terrific, water scarce and the sanitary conditions appalling. Helles and Suvla Bay were described as middens and smelt like an opened cemetery.

Richard Thornhill went down with dysentery and was one of thousands evacuated to Egypt, being cared for in a hospital in Cairo. He died on October 27th 1915 and was buried in grave D.164 Cairo War Memorial Cemetery. This would not be the final loss for his family. Two years later, in October 1917, his twin brother Arthur would be killed in action at the Battle of Passchendaele.

The final fatality for the year 1915 also died of dysentery after serving in the Dardanelles.

PRIVATE JOHN APPLETON RAW
NO. 18174 6TH BATTALION BORDER REGIMENT
DIED DECEMBER 8TH 1915 AGED 21

John was the eldest child of John Raw, a farm worker, and wife Jane, with the family living at Riddings, in the hills between Reeth and Healaugh. The other children were Annie and sons Lockie and Richard.

John was living with his family at High Fremington, Reeth, when he travelled to Kirkby Stephen to enlist in the 6th Battalion Border Regiment. They were involved in the actions at Gallipoli, relieving the Devon Yeomanry in the firing line trenches on November 11th. Heavy shelling occurred on the 12th, with 5 men hit, and similar activity took place each day until they were relieved on the 25th (one shell wounded three cooks and two stretcher bearers). All the time it was reported that men were falling sick (5 a day was normal) and it was during this period that John was wounded and fell victim to disease. He was transported by ship to the hospital base on the island of Malta, where he died on December 8th 1915. From the spring of 1915 to January 1916 Maltese hospitals and convalescent depots dealt with over 135,000 sick and wounded from the Gallipoli and Salonika campaigns.

John was buried in grave D.X1.2 Pieta Military Cemetery, near Valletta, Malta. He had been an old scholar, chorister and member of Reeth Congregational Church and at the end of the evening service in February 1917 Jane Raw unveiled a marble memorial tablet in honour of her son.

On December 28th the 6th Border Regiment embarked at Mudros Bay on the SS "Tunesian", destination Egypt. When Gallipoli was finally evacuated on January 19th 1916, the eight and a half month campaign had lost the Allies some 215,000 men, of whom 145,000 were due to sickness, 50,000 from dysentery.

As 1915 came to its sad conclusion, appalling losses had been suffered by both sides on the Western Front throughout the year. 612,000 Germans, 1,292,000 French and 279,000 British became casualties. The year ended with no appreciable shift in the hostile battle lines scarring the land from the North Sea to the Swiss Alps. In 1916 it would prove to be the Germans who profited more heavily from the offensive and defensive lesson learned during 1915. Twenty men from these dales had lost their lives during 1915 but the sacrifice made in 1916 would prove even greater, with the loss of 36 dalesmen.

Much of the timber from Reeth Saw Mill went to the Western Front trenches during the Great War

CHAPTER FOUR

1916 – THE SLAUGHTER CONTINUES

The year 1916 will always be remembered by the British and the French for its association with the names **SOMME** and **VERDUN**. The Battle of the Somme (July to November) and the Siege of Verdun (February to December) cost the British and French upwards of one million casualties for very little gain, especially on the Somme.

General Von Falkenhayn, German Chief of Staff, chose to attack Verdun in order to "bleed France white", in the certain knowledge that the French would defend the city to the last man. By June 1916 the French situation was desperate and General Petain begged his Commander-in-Chief, Joffre, to hasten a relieving action on the Somme.

General Haig would have much preferred to use his new armies in Flanders but political necessity demanded otherwise. The Somme area was chosen simply because here the British and French armies met, and even though the Allies knew the German defences were very strong, the offensive was set for July 1st. From that date, no fresh German divisions would be sent to Verdun; the German attack slowly stalled, then failed. The Somme battles contributed to save Verdun but at a terrible cost

MILITARY SERVICE ACT
1916
EVERY UNMARRIED MAN
of
MILITARY AGE
Not excepted or exempted under this Act
CAN CHOOSE
ONE OF TWO COURSES:
(1) He can ENLIST AT ONCE and join the Colours without delay:
(2) He can ATTEST AT ONCE UNDER THE GROUP SYSTEM and be called up in due course with his Group.
If he does neither, a third course awaits him:
HE WILL BE DEEMED TO HAVE ENLISTED
under the Military Service Act
ON THURSDAY, MARCH 2nd, 1916.
HE WILL BE PLACED IN THE RESERVE.
AND BE CALLED UP IN HIS CLASS,
as the Military Authorities may determine.

Recruiting poster explaining the Military Service Act of 1916 (Conscription)

to Britain's citizen army.

By the end of 1915 most people shared an optimistic view of how the war would progress, despite an increasing casualty list, but this view was shattered by the unfolding events of 1916. Thirty six dalesmen died in 1916 and twenty six of these lost their lives during the four and a half months of the Battle of the Somme.

Voluntary enlistment was now no longer an option for Britain and even before the Somme, casualties on the Western Front demanded replacements that could only be filled by conscription. In January 1916, by the Military Service Act, the voluntary system was abandoned and compulsory enlistment came into being. As a result of these actions, all families were now deeply affected by the Great War.

Despite the overwhelming significance of the Somme battles for 1916, we find that eight men from these dales had already perished throughout the months leading up to July 1st. Six of these men died in February, four of them (3 from Richmond and 1 from Marske) on the very same day, February 14th, as they were serving in the same battalion of the Yorkshire Regiment.

PRIVATE JAMES PATRICK BENBOW
NO. 3/8867 10TH BATTALION YORKSHIRE REGIMENT
DIED FEBRUARY 9TH 1916

James was born in Richmond, the son of Patrick and Winifred Benbow. His father, a general labourer, was born in Ireland and married Winifred, a Richmond girl, and by 1914 they were living at 7 The Green, Richmond, where they raised a large family.

We have seen that Patrick and Winifred had already lost one son, John Francis, in the war when he succumbed to his wounds in August 1915. James had enlisted early in the war and was serving with the 10th Yorkshires in February 1916.

Since Christmas they had been in and out of the line in the Armentieres sector, doing their best to keep their parapets intact and their trenches drained, whilst losing small numbers of men almost daily from the enemy artillery and snipers. James lost his life in this day to day activity in the trenches and he was buried in grave 1X.E.12 Cite Bonjean Military Cemetery, Armentieres.

February 14th 1916 was to prove a sad day for the eastern part of Swaledale, for on that day four men from the area were killed as they stood together, side by side in the same trench

PRIVATE JACOB HODGSON
NO. 2861 "Z" COMPANY 4TH BATTALION YORKSHIRE REGIMENT
DIED FEBRUARY 14TH 1916 AGED 22.

In 1901 the Hodgson family was living in part of Marske Hall, with Jacob senior, born at Richmond, working on the estate as a woodsman and his wife, Agnes, born in Staffordshire, acting as the caretaker at the Hall. Jacob, junior, was the third of six children in the family and had spent practically his whole life in the district prior to the war.

Educated at Marske Church of England Enclosed School, he was within a few weeks of completing his apprenticeship as a joiner on the estate of Mr. J.T. D'Arcy Hutton, from whom he received permission to join the Territorial Force, being the first in the parish to volunteer for service abroad. He went out to France in April 1915 and had been twice in hospital, the first time being for a wound to the face. Shortly before Christmas he was home on leave for a few days and had many interesting accounts to tell of the months he had spent in the trenches. By this time his parents were living in part of nearby Skelton Hall, whilst his older brother, Lance Corporal John Hodgson, was also in France, having joined Kitchener's Army in September 1914.

AND
PRIVATE JOHN STANLEY HAW
NO. 1838 "Z" COMPANY 4TH BATTALION YORKSHIRE REGIMENT
DIED FEBRURY 14TH 1916 AGED 18

John Haw was born in the Micklegate area of York in 1898. His father, also called John, had been born at nearby Easingwold and married Ellen, a girl from York. In 1901 John, senior, was working as the steward at the Phoenix Club in York but by 1914 the family was living at 30 Maison Dieu, Richmond. Though John was living at home, it was at Redcar that he enlisted, joining the 4th Battalion.

AND
PRIVATE GILBERT RUMBELLOW
NO. 3520 "Z" COMPANY 4TH BATTALION YORKSHIRE REGIMENT
DIED FEBRUARY 14TH 1916 AGED 25

When Gilbert joined the 4th Battalion he was living in the Richmond area, though his parents were living at North Ferriby, on the Humber Estuary, just west of Kingston upon Hull. Gilbert had been a member of the Territorial Army and enlisted early in the war.

AND
PRIVATE FREDERICK HART TOPHAM
NO. 1533 "Z" COMPANY 4TH BATTALION YORKSHIRE REGIMENT
DIED FEBRUARY 14TH 1916 AGED 20

Frederick was the middle child of three, in the family of Thomas and Margaret Topham. Thomas was a Manchester man who had married Margaret, a Darlington girl and in 1901 he was working as a labourer at the paper mill in Richmond. Though all three children were born at Richmond, we find that soon after Frederick's death his parents had moved to Darlington. Frederick, meanwhile, had enlisted early in the war at Catterick.

On December 17th 1915 the 4th Battalion entrained from their training area in France, travelling to Poperinghe and then to Dickebusch in the Ypres Salient. They went into the trenches in Armagh Wood, repairing and draining the trenches under shell fire. On February 12th 1916 the Battalion for the first time occupied the trenches round the infamous Hill 60. The relief passed off quietly.

On February 14th the Dump was shelled at intervals during the day, but everything was comparatively quiet until 3p.m. when the Germans began to bombard them. At 5p.m. the enemy exploded a mine under a bombing sap (trench) but did not attempt to occupy the crater. The bombardment lasted until 8p.m., when it slackened slightly. Thirteen men had been killed and five wounded by the explosion of the mine. Two men were dug out alive from the trench near the crater and one man picked up alive after being blown 40 yards, but he died soon afterwards. Jacob, John, Gilbert and Frederick were four of the thirteen killed in the explosion of the mine.

At a meeting held at the Rectory in Marske on February 23rd it was decided to have a brass cross inscribed to Jacob Hodgson's memory and placed on the altar on Easter Day, whilst the evening service on February 27th would be a memorial service. John Haw, Gilbert Rumbellow and Frederick Topham were all buried in the Railway Dugouts Burial Ground, 2 kilometres SE of Ypres, but Jacob's body was not recovered from the blast and he is commemorated on Panel 33 Menin Gate Memorial.

Six days later a Wharfedale man, the only son of the Rector of Kettlewell, was killed just over the Belgian border, in France.

Subscriptions raised by the parishioners of Marske were used to buy a cross in honour of Jacob Hodgson, who died whilst serving his country in the Great War. The inscription reads "In Memoriam. Jacob Hodgson killed in action February 15th 1916"

SERGEANT JOHN COCKERILL
NO. 545 ROYAL CANADIAN DRAGOONS
DIED FEBRUARY 20TH 1916 AGED 31

John was born at Mickleton, near Middleton-in-Teesdale, in 1885, where his father James was the Church of England minister. James Walter Cockerill was a Wolverhampton man and his wife Jane also came from that town. By 1901 James was ministering to the spiritual needs of the parishioners of Kettlewell and Starbotton, in Wharfedale, whilst sixteen year old John was a boarder at Skipton Grammar School. He was also educated at Leeds Grammar School.

A very good draftsman, John was trained as an engineer in the Leeds Municipal offices, but in 1912 he went out to Canada and engaged in survey work for the

Canadian Pacific Railway Company. At the outbreak of war he volunteered for service and joined the Canadian Royal Dragoons. He came over to England with the first contingent, going over to France early in 1915, where he was involved in a great deal of action in the trenches.

John Cockerill from Kettlewell and Canada
Courtesy of The Craven Herald

Around September 1915 he was ordered to Canadian Army Corps Headquarters at Bailleul, as a draftsman, an honour that followed his sending up plans of fort constructions which were highly commended by the C.O. John was employed in the Intelligence Branch (Bailleul was an important railhead, air depot and hospital centre). He was home on leave just after Christmas 1915.

John's death on Sunday February 20th 1916 was the result of wounds received from an aerial bomb dropped from a German aeroplane. Sergeant Cockerill left the office at HQ just before noon on Sunday to go down to his billet near the railway station, and while passing down the street, at that time crowded with soldiers and waggons, two bombs were thrown by an enemy plane, whose object was to hit the railway station, an attempt to do so having been made the previous night. John, together with several other soldiers and women civilians, were fatally injured and John died a few minutes later.

A few weeks later, on April 5th, came the death of his mother, Jane Elizabeth Cockerill, in a nursing home, aged 57. She had been in failing health for some time but the death of her son proved a shock that lowered her vitality and hastened the end.

John Cockerill is buried in grave 11.C.158 Bailleul Communal Cemetery Extension, whilst in St. Mary's Church, Kettlewell, is a stained glass window dedicated "To the Glory of God and in loving memory of Jane Elizabeth Cockerill and her only son John, killed in the Great War 1916"

Early the following month, during this winter period of routine front line duties, a Sapper from Richmond was killed.

SAPPER THOMAS BRITTON MYERS
NO. 58533 90TH FIELD COMPANY ROYAL ENGINEERS
DIED MARCH 2ND 1916 AGED 31

Thomas's parents, Samuel and Elizabeth, were born in Richmond, where Samuel worked as a self employed tailor. Thomas, his elder sister Mary and younger brother William were born in Richmond and in 1901 seventeen year old Thomas was working for his father as an apprentice tailor.

Enlisting at Richmond, Thomas joined the Royal Engineers and during the winter of 1915 – 1916 was employed in constructing gun platforms, bringing railway lines up to the front and in improving the trench system. Even when working just behind the front line there was always the danger of enemy shells targeting the back areas. In February and the beginning of March the 90th Field Company was in the Ypres Salient and on March 2nd Thomas Myers was hit by shrapnel and was killed. He is buried in grave 11. B.9 London Rifle Brigade Cemetery, 15 km. south of Ypres.

Some ten weeks later, a native of Grinton and Reeth died, far away in India.

PRIVATE JIM PEACOCK NO. 17432
6TH BATTALION KING'S OWN (ROYAL LANCASTER REGIMENT)
DIED MAY 22ND 1916 AGED 27

Jim was the cousin of Harry Peacock, a regular soldier, who had died from his wounds in November 1914 (see Chapter 2). Jim lived at Grinton with his mother Margaret, a single woman, and his grandmother, Hannah, but he eventually went to work in Liverpool and it was when he heard of Harry's death in 1914 that he volunteered for service in Liverpool, joining the Royal Lancaster Regiment.

Jim Peacock from Grinton, Swaledale, near Reeth

Jim first served with the 2nd Battalion, going out with them to France on July 29th 1915 but later that year he travelled to Egypt to join the 6th Battalion, which had just returned from Gallipoli and was recuperating.

In early 1915 the British had begun fighting the Turks on a different front, in Mesopotamia, where an Expeditionary Force under Major General Charles Townsend travelled from Basra along the River Tigris and in September 1915 defeated the Turks at Kut-el-Amara. He pressed on but the arrival of Turkish reinforcements caused him to retire to Kut, where he was besieged by the Turkish forces. A relief force was sent from India to save Townsend and additional army units, including Jim Peacock's 6th Battalion, were sent from Egypt in late January 1916. They arrived at Basra and, with the Relief Force, battered futilely against the Turks, failing in their efforts to get through. On April 29th 1916 Townsend surrendered his force of 8000 men.

Meanwhile, the Relief Force suffered 21,000 casualties, many of them from disease. One of these casualties was Jim Peacock, who was wounded and was transported by ship to India, where, after succumbing to his wounds and disease, he was buried. Jim Peacock's name is on Face 3 Kirkee 1914-1918 Memorial, adjoining the university town of Poona, India, commemorating 1800 servicemen who died in India during the Great War, and who are buried in civil cemeteries, where their graves can no longer be properly maintained.

The next two dales' casualties for 1916 fell on the battlefield synonymous with that fateful year – the Somme – on the first day. The River Somme meanders through a flat, wide and marshy valley. In the areas where the battle was to be fought, the only geographical feature of any note was the high ground running south-east from Thiepval to Guillemont. This lay in German hands and was the principal tactical objective for Rawlinson's 4th Army. The British, therefore, would everywhere be fighting uphill. The Germans had superb observation points gazing down on the British lines, their excellence matched only by the depth of their fortifications, cut deep into the chalk and safe from all but the heaviest British shell.

Pre-warned of the offensive by British security indiscretion, the German defenders had practised rushing up their machine guns from the dug outs, perfected to a three minute drill, giving them an ample margin on "Z" Day between the lifting of the British barrage and the arrival of the attacking infantry.

The Battle of the Somme was launched on July 1st after a five day barrage by 1,573 artillery guns along a 16 mile front. 120,000 British and Empire troops dashed themselves against highly organised German defensive positions. The men had been told that the enemy lines had ceased to exist after such a bombardment and all they would have to do would be to stroll across No Man's Land, occupy the blasted positions and wait for the three Cavalry Divisions to sweep forward into the open countryside around Bapaume.

However, the Germans were by now the masters in the arts of fortification and the shellfire had not fatally damaged the enemy. From the safety of their dugouts and redoubts, the German machine gun teams emerged after the conclusion of the barrage, ready to pour a withering, murderous hail of bullets into the oncoming mass of Allied soldiers. On that first day, casualties were 50%, with 19,240 killed, 2152 missing, 35,493 wounded and 585 taken prisoner. These were the worst casualties in the history of the British Army. The men who suffered this appalling tragedy were mainly those of Kitchener's New Armies, the cream of the country's youth, who had volunteered in droves in 1914, many forming into "Pals'" Battalions, and had been two years in training for this morning and this very hour (indeed, Wharfedale's first casualty on the Somme was in the Leeds Pals).

Despite the appalling losses of the first day, the British continued to push ahead in a series of small, limited attacks, with the Allied offensive deteriorating into a succession of minor but costly small actions. General Haig launched another major offensive in the Somme battle on September 15th, SW of Bapaume. Tanks had been secretly shipped to the front and spearheaded the attack but were too few in numbers to gain a decisive victory. Gains were made but a breakthrough eluded them. Nevertheless, the British and French continued attacking, gaining small areas of ground through mid November.

British losses in this campaign were 420,000; French 195,000 and Germany 650,000. The battles represented a watershed, for the last traces of the "early carefree spirit" of the war had gone for good. From now on the men who moved into the trenches to replace the fallen would not see the war as a wonderful crusade, but as a bloody, deadly chore, to be slogged through, and if possible, survived.

PRIVATE MAURICE ROBINSON CROWTHER NO. 15/252
15TH BATTALION WEST YORKSHIRE REGIMENT (LEEDS PALS)
DIED JULY 1ST 1916 AGED 24

Maurice's father, John Crowther, had been born at Eccleshill in the northern suburbs of Bradford and married Elizabeth Robinson, a Yorkshire girl. By the late 1880's they had arrived in Grassington, taking over a shop in the village and eventually living at Ridley House. John (Jack) Crowther was the local pharmacist, specialising in cattle medicines and it was here that he and his wife raised their three children, John, Maurice and Arnold. Their father became known as "The Grassington Antiquarian and Botonist" due to the hobbies he indulged in.

Maurice Robinson Crowther from Grassington
Courtesy of The Craven Herald

The eighteen men from the Grassington area who lost their lives during the Great War. Until recent years, this tribute to them was on display in Grassington Town Hall
Devonshire Institute

Maurice joined the Leeds Pals on September 12th 1914, training first at their Colsterdale Camp, moving on to Ripon in the spring of 1915 and Salisbury in September. The Battalion sailed from Liverpool for Egypt in December 1915. However, a few weeks after their arrival they were ordered to France to prepare for the Battle of the Somme.

By the end of June 1916 the "Pals" were in billets at Bus-les-Artois, near Bertrancourt, facing the village of Gommecourt across the enemy lines.

This was to be their objective on the first day of the battle. Gommecourt and its near neighbour Serre were amongst the strongest defended villages on the whole front line and were not necessarily expected to be taken, since this part of the attack was simply a diversion, whilst the main attack went in further south.. Yet it was to result in terrible casualties for the Battalion.

On June 30th, while marching to the assembly trenches, two bombs exploded, killing one man and wounding 14 others. At 7-30a.m. on July 1st the Battalion went over No Man's Land in successive waves, every wave being met by very severe machine gun fire. There had been an hours intense artillery bombardment but the enemy front line was still thick with men. Large numbers of the 15th Battalion, including Maurice Crowther, were casualties before reaching the wire. Out of 900 men in the Battalion, 24 officers and 504 men became casualties on that first day and Maurice was one of 19,240 British men to die on July 1st.

As with so many other soldiers that day, his body was never recovered and his name is inscribed on Pier and Face 2A, 2C and 2D Thiepval Memorial. By this time his mother had died and Jack Crowther was deeply affected by the death of his son. He erected a cenotaph in honour of Maurice in Conistone churchyard.and in 1930 published his book "Silva Gars – A Guide to Grassington and Upper Wharfedale", reverently dedicated to the 18 Grassington youths who made the supreme sacrifice in the Great War.

(*** I believe the 18th man, Alan McDonald, whose name is not to be found on the Linton Memorial, could be Corporal Allan McDonald No. S/11928 2nd Battalion Gordon Highlanders, who was born in the Settle area and enlisted in Aberdeen. He was killed in action on May 7th 1917 and his name is commemorated on the Arras Memorial).

PRIVATE CHARLES PERCY TEMPEST
NO. 23433 2ND BATTALION YORKSHIRE REGIMENT
DIED JULY 1ST 1916 AGED 16

Charles's parents, Thomas and Emily, lived at 17 Mill Lane, Richmond. Thomas, who had been born in Bradford, was a draper's commercial traveller at Richmond. Although Charles was only 15, he lied about his age and was posted to the 3rd Training Battalion Yorkshire Regiment in September 1915. From there he joined the 2nd Battalion and went out to France.

On July 1st 1916 the 18th Kings and 19th Manchesters were the assaulting battalions attacking the village of Montauban, just to the east of Albert and Fricourt, with the 2nd Battalion Yorkshire Regiment in support, responsible for occupying and consolidating the German front and support lines. "A" Company came under heavy machine gun fire and suffered severely, with only 30 men reaching the enemy trenches under a corporal. The whole Battalion suffered 200 casualties whilst crossing No Mans Land. Of the two "cleaning up" platoons, one had been practically "wiped out".

Charles was one of those killed in action and since his body was never recovered from the battlefield, his name is found on Memorial 35 Dantzig Alley British Cemetery at the nearby village of Mametz.

PRIVATE HENRY (HARRY) BIRCH
NO. 4847 "C" COMPANY 6TH BATTALION WEST RIDING REGIMENT
DIED JULY 7TH 1916 AGED 32

In 1901 Harry Birch, aged 17, was living at Holly Cottage, The Green, Burnsall, with his mother Mary and step father, Christopher Inman. Harry was a grandson of John Pickersgill Birch, the well known Burnsall carrier, who operated between Burnsall and Skipton on Wednesdays and Saturdays (when people wanted him to stop for them they would stick a broom in the wall of their garden or house, as a sign).

Henry (Harry) Birch from Burnsall
Courtesy of The Craven Herald

Harry became an apprentice joiner and carpenter, although by 1914 he was employed as a roadman. By this stage he was married to Molly and was raising a family of four children in Burnsall. His entire life had been spent in his native village, where, as boy and man, he had sung for many years in Burnsall Church, being one of four generations who were in the choir there together.

When war broke out, though a married man with family, he was one of the first from the village to respond to the call of his country and enlisted on September 2nd 1914. He was a born soldier but came down with a serious illness and hovered between life and death, being eventually discharged from the Army in December 1915. However, he re-enlisted on January 21st 1916 and went to France in March. Harry was seriously wounded in the leg on July 5th and died in the Canadian Hospital at Etaples, south of Boulogne, on July 7th. A letter from Lieutenant Jacques informed them, "The Company was in the front line at the time, quite close to the enemy and we had several casualties that day. It was difficult work getting the wounded to safety and I could not help admiring the patience with which he bore his injuries." Harry Birch is buried in grave 11.B.64 Etaples Military Cemetery.

CAPTAIN R. H. MURRAY
11TH BATTALION YORKSHIRE REGIMENT
DIED JULY 7TH 1916

Robert, or Bobby as he was known, was the son of Robert and Ann Murray (nee Brand) and lived at West Cottage, Richmond, together with his three sisters. His father was a jeweller in King Street, Richmond. Bobby, an organ scholar at Richmond Parish Church, eventually went to study at Selwyn College, Cambridge, where he was a fine oarsman for the rowing club. He volunteered at the start of the war and on December 3rd 1914 was made temporary Second Lieutenant in the 11th Battalion Yorkshire Regiment. By July 1915 he had been promoted to Captain and in that same month was posted to another battalion in France (I have been unable to find the details). Captain Murray was killed on July 7th 1916, during the Battle of the Somme, and was buried in grave 1.J.37. Philosophe British Cemetary, Mazingarbe, between Bethune and Lens.

SECOND LIEUTENANT EDGAR OSWALD HART
13TH BATTALION YORKSHIRE REGIMENT
(ATTACHED TO 9TH BATTALION)
DIED JULY 10TH 1916 AGED 22

Edgar's father, Edgar senior, was a Church of England minister, who, with his wife Rosamond and children Edgar, Reginald and Rosamond, were living in Leeds in 1901. In 1907 the vicar and his family came to live at the Vicarage at Downholme, near Richmond.

Young Edgar was educated at Leeds and Ripon Grammar Schools and at Pannal Ash College, Harrogate. He enlisted as a driver in the Howitzer Battery of the 4th West Yorks, in September 1914, receiving a commission in the 13th Yorkshires on October 1st 1915 and went to the front in April 1916.

Reverend Curlen at Downholme Rectory 1907. In that year the Reverend Hart arrived to become the vicar for the parish. One of Reverend Hart's sons would be killed in the Great War.

At the Battle of the Somme, Edgar was attached to the 9th Battalion and on July 10th they were ordered to assault the heavily defended village of Contalmaison. The main assault went in at 4-50p.m, with enemy shells bursting amongst them and a deadly fire coming from machine gunners. The 9th Battalion, with bayonets fixed, reached the enemy trench and, bursting through the wire, entered the village. 3 officers and 13 men were killed, 11 officers and 192 men were wounded, whilst 24 men were missing. Edgar's body was not recovered and he is commemorated on Pier and Face 3A and 3D Thiepval Memorial.

On a Sunday afternoon a crowded congregation filled the tiny church of Downholme to honour the memory of the vicar's son. The Rector of Marske officiated and read out the letter received from the Commanding Officer ; "Your son had done excellent work on July 5th, when the Battalion attacked and captured a German position. It was particularly brought to my notice how well he had behaved. On the 10th, we, with another battalion, again attacked and captured a village, taking prisoners and some machine guns. This attack was made over the open ground and it was during the advance that your son was killed whilst gallantly leading his men."

SERGEANT JOHN THOMAS LIMMER
NO. 11491 "A" COMPANY 8TH BATTALION YORKSHIRE REGIMENT
DIED JULY 10TH 1916 AGED 33

John was born in 1883 at Cleveland Street, Normanby, on the southern outskirts of Middlesborough. His father Robert, an iron stone miner, had married Mary King and raised a family which included sons John and Walter, both of whom would be killed during the Great War. By 1903, Robert and Mary were living at Grassington, with Robert employed as a brick layer, but by 1914 John was married and he and his wife Rose were raising their own family.

John Thomas Limmer of Grassington
Courtesy of The Craven Herald

John Thomas Limmer, a Territorial soldier, enlisted at Guisborough, near Middlesbrough, and joined the 8th Battalion Yorkshire Regiment, where he rose to the rank of sergeant by 1916. Sergeant Limmer's Battalion took part in the attack on Contalmaison, side by side with Edgar Hart's 9th Battalion, and he was to fall close to where the vicar's son was killed. At 4-50p.m. on July 10th they advanced on Horseshoe Trench and came under shrapnel fire from Contalmaison Wood. The wire was found to be intact and proved a serious obstacle and 50% of the casualties occurred between this trench and a hedge.

The enemy was now retreating, but at this point, machine gun fire from the rear caused further casualties and only 4 officers and 150 men reached the village. At 7-30p.m. a small party of Germans appeared but were dispersed by machine gun fire. However, in the earlier action John Limmer had been killed and his name is found on the same Pier and Face 3A and 3D of the Thiepval Memorial as Edgar Hart. John left a widow, child and widowed mother and sadly we shall find that brother Walter Limmer was killed in 1918.

LANCE CORPORAL WILLIAM WELSH
NO. 24159 2ND BATTALION YORKSHIRE REGIMENT
DIED JULY 23RD 1916 AGED 19

Timothy Welsh, William's father, was an Irishman from Galway, who was working in Richmond as a bricklayer's labourer and married Mary, a girl from Wallbottle, Newcastle. William was the second youngest of five children, all born in Richmond.

William enlisted in November 1915 and was posted to the 3rd Training Battalion, before joining the 2nd Battalion Yorkshire Regiment, together with another Richmond man, Charles Tempest. On the first day of the Somme Battle William had seen his Richmond colleague killed in action and sadly his turn came on July 23rd. The assault was to be upon the village of Guillemont and the Battalion moved into position at 9-30p.m on the 22nd., north of Trones Wood, ready for zero hour the next day.

Some platoons found the wire uncut and were obliged to retire owing to rifle and machine gun fire. Others managed to struggle into the trench north of Guillemont, beat off two counter-attacks and consolidate their gains. 250 casualties were incurred and one of these was William Welsh, whose grave, V1.F.11. is to be found in Serre Road Cemetery No. 2, eleven kilometres. NNE of Albert.

PRIVATE RICHARD HIRD
NO. 1549 19TH BATTALION AUSTRALIAN INFANTRY, AUSTRALIAN IMPERIAL FORCE, DIED JULY 27TH 1916 AGED 28

Richard was born at Fremington, near Reeth, in 1889, and in 1901 he was living there in the home of his 79 year old grandfather, widower Christopher (Kit) Hird, who was a farmer. In the same household were numerous other grandchildren, including William, who was a coal miner. It was a difficult time, for lead mining in the dale had virtually come to an end, and farming was suffering too. Richard decided to try and seek a better life abroad and sailed for Australia.

Sadly, the war intervened and Richard answered the call of the Motherland and enlisted in the Australian Infantry, arriving in France with the Anzac force and ready to form part of General Haig's reserves in the Battle of the Somme.

By mid July the Anzac Corps (Australian and New Zealand Army Corps) had been moved to the Somme, where Haig's aim was now to enlarge his lodgement on the main ridge. General Gough was given this Corps to attempt to gain the Pozieres – Thiepval end of the ridge. On July 23rd he launched part of it against Pozieres, in which they gained a footing, but the main assault was a failure and yet over the next few days and months the attacks still went on, the Anzac infantry serving as compressed cannon fodder for the artillery. 23,000 men were expended in the process and after six weeks the only gain was a tiny tongue of ground just over a mile deep.

On July 27th, four days after the first attack went in on the ridge, Richard Hird was cut down on the field of battle. His body was never found, but his name is on the Villers-Bretonneux Memorial, just east of Amiens. It commemorates all Australia's soldiers who fought on the Western Front.

LANCE CORPORAL BARTHOLOMEW RUSSELL
NO. 14581 2ND INDIAN FIELD COMPANY ROYAL ENGINEERS DIED JULY 31ST 1916 AGED 29

Bartholomew, together with his siblings Frederick, Thomas, Ruth, Edward, William, Arthur and Harry, were born in Richmond. Their father, Bartholomew Russell, had married Sarah Hodgson, a girl from Marrick, and by 1891 the family was living at Bridge Street. Bartholomew, senior, an Alderman on the Town Council, worked for 40 years as a locomotive driver for North Eastern Railways, on the Richmond to Darlington branch line. His father had been one of the first plate layers helping in the construction of that line. Bartholomew, senior, conducted the town's brass band, whilst in 1909 and 1910, Alderman Russell served as Mayor of Richmond for two successive terms. His wife, Sarah, who ran a noted cafe and bakery in Richmond Market Place, sadly died in 1910.

Bartholomew Russell of Richmond

When Bartholomew, junior, enlisted, he was living at New Brancepeth, four miles west of Durham, where he worked as a superior joiner and carpenter at the local colliery. He was married to Lilian Rose Shields, born at Leeds, but whose parents lived at Middlesbrough, and they had three children, Bert, Stanley and Leslie.

Bartholomew first joined the Durham Light Infantry, but his skills as a carpenter meant that he inevitably joined the Royal Engineers. On the Somme, the work of the Engineers was vital to the operational well being of the army as it attempted to press forward in its attacks on the enemy lines. Working parties operated near the front line, co-ordinating their duties with both the artillery and infantry and even in the support and back areas there was always the risk of being targeted from afar by enemy gunners. Bartholomew Russell was wounded whilst performing such duties in an area close to where Richard Hird and the Australians had launched their attack and he was taken to the casualty clearing station at Mericourt, SW of Albert. There he died and was buried in grave 11.E.60 at Heilly Station Cemetery, Mericourt. His father was spared the anguish of hearing of his son's death, for, back in Richmond, he had passed away on June 12th. If he had survived the year he would have received further devastating news of the loss of another son, Thomas, in November 1916.

The next casualty was also from Richmond, but he was killed far away from the Somme, at Salonika, in northern Greece. In 1915, both sides had pressured Bulgaria to join the war and the Bulgars decided to side with the Central Powers when they saw how badly the Allied Powers were performing at Gallipoli. The Central Powers, with Bulgaria now "on board", at once prepared to renew the attack on Serbia. That nation's call for assistance was answered by the Greeks, who requested Allied troops to aid her in assisting Serbia. A French and British expeditionary force soon disembarked at Salonika, with the Richmond serviceman part of the contingent.

CORPORAL WILLIAM RUHIALL BROWN
NO. M2/183871 705TH COMPANY ARMY SERVICE CORPS
DIED AUGUST 18TH 1916 AGED 36

William's father was William Brown senior, born at South Collingham, near Newark-on-Trent, Nottinghamshire, who married Elizabeth Watson, a girl from Retford in Nottinghamshire.

By 1881 William Brown senior had moved to Matlock Green, Matlock, in Derbyshire, where he was a skilled worker at the corn mill, helping with the horses and transportation. However, a few months later he and Elizabeth began a fresh life together with their four children at Eastinor, near Caistor in Lincolnshire, where William Ruhiall Brown was born in June 1881. His father was working as a groom in the locality.

By 1901, William and Elizabeth were living at Ordsall, in Retford, Nottinghamshire, where William senior was working as a labourer with the Corporation, but 21 year old William junior had left the family home to join the regular army and was to be found fighting in the South African War (Boer War).

By 1914 he was married to his wife, Frances Mary and they were living at 7 Skeeby Road, Richmond, and it was from there that he was recalled to the colours and joined the Army Service Corps. Having served in Egypt and at Gallipoli, his Company, the 705th, became part of the Salonika Expeditionary Force.

By 1916 the Allied forces held a defensive position – the "Bird Cage" – around Salonika. In August 1916 the Allies decided on an offensive up the Vardar Valley. But the Bulgarians struck first. On August 17th a Bulgar-German attack drove the Allied forces to the Struma River line and on the second day of the attack, William Brown was killed in action. He was buried in grave 1613 Mikra British Cemetery, Kalamaria, 8 kilometres south of Salonika (Thessalonika).

Returning to the Somme, we find that in the space of the first three weeks of September, nine more dalesmen were to die as the unrelenting slaughter continued.

PRIVATE JOHN TURNBULL
NO. 4282 "A" COMPANY 6TH BATTALION WEST RIDING REGIMENT
DIED SEPTEMBER 3RD 1916 AGED 23

The Turnbull family lived at Hazel Bank Farm, Oughtershaw, in Langstrothdale. John Turnbull senior had married Elizabeth, a Bainbridge girl, and they raised George, Hannah, Deborah, John, Isabella, Margaret and Matthew. John was a farmer and gamekeeper on the estate of Mr. Wood of Oughtershaw Hall and sons George and Matthew both became gamekeepers.

John Turnbull from Oughtershaw, Langstrothdale

John, junior, worked on the farm with his father but on May 20th 1915 he travelled to Skipton to enlist, joining the West Riding Regiment. Whenever he came home on leave he was always sad to leave the beautiful dale he knew so well and, as he rounded the final bend, he would never look back to the old homestead. He finally arrived in France on February 12th 1916 but was in hospital at Rouen for six weeks with a throat infection and only entered the trenches on June 1st, where he joined his Lewis gun team. There, the Battalion prepared for the forthcoming battle.

Throughout August they were in the line facing Thiepval, where the trenches had been obliterated and one of their jobs was to recover the many bodies during the hours of darkness and bury them. On September 3rd the 49th Division made an assault against Thiepval in which John's Battalion was in support, but they still suffered over 60 casualties from shell fire. A dugout occupied by part of "A" Company was destroyed by an exploding shell and amongst the fatalities was John Turnbull. He was laid to rest by the side of his other comrades that were killed at the same time, whilst the survivors of the Lewis gun team stood by and paid their last respects to him at the graveside. John is buried in grave X11.D.9. in Connaught Cemetery, Thiepval.

SECOND LIEUTENANT ROBERT PULLEINE
"D" BATTERY 18TH BRIGADE ROYAL FIELD ARTILLERY
DIED SEPTEMBER 4TH 1916 AGED 19

The Pulleine family lived at Sandford House, at Easby, near Richmond. A well-to-do family, with coachman, two nurses, a cook, parlour maid, housemaid and kitchen maid, they were related to the Curzon-Howe family at Clifton Castle, near Bedale, and had a strong military tradition. Robert and his sister Violet's grandfather, Colonel H. B. Pulleine, had been killed in the Zulu War of 1879, whilst their father, Henry Percy, was a Captain in the army by 1901, and would serve in Egypt and the Mediterranean during the Great War (he would also be involved with Lord Baden Powell in the beginning of the Scout Movement). Their mother, Alice, had been born in Sydney, Australia.

A British battery of 8 inch howitzers in action on the Western Front during the Great War

Robert was the only son in the family and was educated at Wellington Public School in Somerset. He was in the Officer Training Corps at the school and eventually enlisted, joining the Royal Field Artillery. As the attack by the 49th Division went in against Thiepval on September 3rd, Robert's Battery was involved in the supporting artillery bombardments and received a great deal of shelling itself in the enemy counter-bombardment. He was relaying telephone wires under heavy shell fire, doing himself what he felt he could not ask his men to do, when he was killed by shrapnel. The shell fire was so intense that comrades could not go out to fetch him in for three days. Robert Pulleine is buried in grave 1.W.5. Becourt Military Cemetery, 2km. east of Albert.

PRIVATE GEORGE EDWARD USHER NO. 6547
4TH (HALLAMSHIRE) TF BATTALION
YORK AND LANCASTER REGIMENT
DIED SEPTEMBER 7TH 1916 AGED 19

George's father, Robert Usher, was a gamekeeper and moved between the different large estates in the Richmond area. Robert had been born at Williamswick, a small hamlet near Bellingham in Northumberland and came to North Yorkshire, seeking work as a gamekeeper. By 1901 he was working on the estate at Rokeby Hall, on the way to Barnard Castle. He had married Mary Ann Close, a girl from Hurst, near Reeth, and at Dairy Cottage, Rokeby, they were bringing up 4 year old George Edward (born Downholme) and his 2 year old sister, Isabella, or Cis as she was called (born Marske). Thomas, Robert and Margaret (Peggy) were further additions to the family. During the years leading up to the war, Robert would work on the Marske estate of Mr Hutton, with he and his family living at nearby Hurst.

George Edward Usher
of Marske and Hurst, Swaledale

George Edward Usher, known to everyone as Ted, was training to be a gamekeeper like his father, but in 1914, at the age of 17, he volunteered for the army and joined the Yorkshire Regiment. During August, the 4th Battalion York and Lancaster Regiment, had been severely depleted due to previous actions on the Somme and on August 19th they received drafts of 210 men, including 120 men from the Yorkshire Regiment, one of these being Ted Usher.

An attack was made on Thiepval on September 3rd but it failed under the enemy's terribly severe enfilade machine gun fire. Moving forward, the 4th Battalion took over portions of the line on the River Ancre. 30 casualties resulted, even though they were not fully involved in the action. Within a few days, however, many more became casualties under the very heavy and continuous shelling by High Explosive and gas shells to which the trenches were subjected. Ted Usher was killed by shrapnel on September 7th, but his body was never found and his name is inscribed on Pier and Face 14A and 14B Thiepval.

PRIVATE THOMPSON ALLINSON
NO. 2394 5TH BATTALION YORKSHIRE REGIMENT
DIED SEPTEMBER 13TH 1916 AGED 27

In 1901 the Allinson family were living at Grinton, near Reeth, where their father, Robert, worked as a stone-mason on the Charlesworth's Grinton Estate. He had married Mary, a local Whitaside girl and their children were Robert, Thompson, Matthew, John, James and Frederick. A few years later, Robert senior, died and Mary was left to raise a large family.

Thompson Allinson from Grinton, near Reeth

During the war, four of Mary's sons joined the Army. Thompson found himself with the 5th Battalion on the Somme in 1916. On July 10th three officers and 33 men discarded their helmets and blackened their faces so as to avoid detection as they made a raid on an enemy mine crater, killing 15 enemy and taking one prisoner, for the loss of 12 men wounded. In September they were at Millencourt, ready for a further attack on the Somme, between High Wood and Martinpuich, on September 15th. On September 10th they moved up into the trenches but, during the next few days, before the attack began, shelling took place and the CO of the Battalion, Lieutenant Colonel Mortimer was killed by a shell on the 13th while on his way to the assembly trenches, as was Thompson Allinson. Thompson was buried close by in grave V11.H.3. Flatiron Copse Cemetery, Mametz. In September 1917 his younger brother James would be awarded the Military Medal, while in October 1917 his older brother, Robert, was killed.

PRIVATE THOMAS HILLARY
NO. 19546 6TH BATTALION YORKSHIRE REGIMENT
DIED SEPTEMBER 14TH 1916 AGED 23

Thomas Hillary from Arkengarthdale

The Hillary family came from Arkengarthdale and in 1901 was living at Hillside, near Scar House. 46 year old Stephen Hillary was a lead miner, living with his wife, Hannah, and of their two sons and two daughters, Thomas was their third child. By the start of the war, lead mining had declined in the dale, with many people needing to find work elsewhere, and when Thomas went to enlist in Durham we find that he was living at Esh Winning, a village just to the west of Durham, where he was working in a local coal mine.

The 6th Battalion took no part in the first two months of the Somme battles but on September 8th it arrived in the reserve trenches and went into the front line. Ahead of them was a German stronghold known as the "Wonderwerk", near the southern end of the spur on the higher slopes of which Thiepval stood. On the night of September 14th the Battalion was detailed to carry out a bombing attack on the enemy position, the "Wonderwerk" being the final objective.

At 6-30p.m. "D" Company assailed the enemy trenches and were met by heavy rifle and grenade fire but nevertheless some of them reached the objective and the trenches were gained by a bombing attack about midnight. The enemy counter-attacked violently with bombs at least three times during the night but each time was repulsed. The casualties amounted to 5 officers and 130 men, with one of those killed being Thomas Hillary. His grave is 1X.F.7. in Lonsdale Cemetery, Authuile, 4km. north of Albert.

On that same day, September 14th, a Richmond man was killed and three days later, his friend, also from Richmond and in the same battalion, fell in battle.

PRIVATE HARRY PICKERSGILL
NO. 1714 4TH BATTALION YORKSHIRE REGIMENT
DIED SEPTEMBER 14TH 1916

Harry was born in Richmond and it was there that he enlisted to join the local regiment.

AND
PRIVATE HAROLD C. FAWCETT
NO. 2369 "Y" COMPANY 4TH BATTALION YORKSHIRE REGIMENT
DIED SEPTEMBER 17TH 1916 AGED 22

George Fawcett, a general labourer and his wife, Isabella, were living at 46 Bargate, Richmond, in 1901,with their children, including 7 year old Harold.

Both Harry and Harold enlisted in their home town and joined the same Battalion of their local regiment.

In September 1916 they were stationed in the vicinity of Millencourt, just to the west of Albert, and on the evening of September 14th they moved to the assembly trenches, going over the open ground, where they were fired on by the Germans. There were 40 casualties and one of those killed was Harry Pickersgill. At 6-30a.m. the infantry assault commenced and the objectives were carried in succession, but there was severe resistance in the capture of High Wood. The line was held that day, though there was heavy enemy shell fire throughout the 16th and 17th September, causing many casualties. It was on the 17th that a shell took the life of Harry's colleague, Harold Fawcett. His body was not recovered and Pier and Face 3A and 3D Thiepval Memorial bear witness to his name. Harry's body was brought back and he is buried in grave X.F.9. Flatiron Copse Cemetery, Mametz, 10km. east of Albert.

PRIVATE ARTHUR THWAITES
NO. 2695 8TH BATTALION DURHAM LIGHT INFANTRY
DIED SEPTEMBER 17TH 1916 AGED 31

Born at Richmond, Arthur was the son of Marmaduke and Elizabeth Thwaites. We have already seen that in 1901 his older brother, Marmaduke junior, was a Corporal in the Yorkshire Regiment in the Sheffield area and 16 year old Arthur was also stationed there, as a drummer in the Regiment. On September 30th 1915 Arthur's brother had been killed at the Battle of Loos.

By 1914 Arthur was living at Stanley, County Durham, between Consett and Chester le Street, and he enlisted at nearby Durham, joining the 8th Battalion, Durham Light Infantry.

The battle for the 8th Battalion began at 6-20a.m. on September 15th, between High Wood and the village of Martinpuich, as "C" and "D" Companies made their way past the skeleton trees of Bazentin Wood, through countless shell holes and shapeless trenches into a shallow valley beyond. In crossing the valley they came under fire, for it was being shelled blindly by the Germans, and machine gun fire came from High Wood, on the ridge. The artillery fire of both sides was extremely heavy. "A" and "C" Companies withdrew into the old German lines at midnight, after suffering heavy casualties

Arthur had been severely wounded and was taken for treatment to a casualty clearing station near Amiens but did not recover and died on September 17th. He was buried in grave 111.C.2. St. Pierre Cemetery, Amiens.

GUNNER JOHN ELLIS LAMBERT
NO. 104890 72ND BATTERY ROYAL FIELD ARTILLERY
DIED SEPTEMBER 25TH 1916 AGED 21

John was the only son of John and Elizabeth Lambert of 9 Strawberry Road, Pendleton, Salford, where John was born. His father originated from Settle and his mother (nee Ellis) came from Burnsall. John, senior, was a butcher and cattle dealer, and had land at Threshfield, near Grassington, where he kept animals for his business in Salford. John, junior, spent a good deal of his youth at Threshfield, attending the local school, and loved the area.

John Ellis Lambert of Threshfield, near Grassington, and Salford, Manchester
Courtesy of The Craven Herald

When war began, he was working in the Salford area and by this time his father had died. John enlisted at Manchester and joined the Royal Field Artillery as a gunner, eventually finding himself with 72nd Battery.

Throughout the Somme battles the Battery was involved in supporting the infantry in many of their actions. The Battery's six guns were of 6 inch calibre and were involved in bombardment and counter-bombardment. As they pushed forward from the rear areas, the exchange of artillery fire between the opposing batteries brought great danger to all members of the gun teams. John Lambert was killed by shell fire on September 25th, whilst supporting another big attack which, in conjunction with the French, compelled the Germans to evacuate Combles. Next day Thiepval at last fell. There was no grave and John is remembered on Pier and Face 1A and 8A, Thiepval Memorial. It left his widowed mother to mourn the loss of her only son.

PRIVATE EDGAR WHITAKER
NO. 18379 10TH BATTALION WEST RIDING REGIMENT
DIED OCTOBER 4TH 1916 AGED 21

The Whitakers were living at Mill Lane, Grassington, in 1901, though by 1914 they had moved to 11 Brooklyn Terrace. Father, William, was born at Burnsall and mother, Alice, at Kettlewell, but their children, Clara, Edgar and Sydney were all born at Grassington. Their father was employed as a woodsman and after leaving school, Edgar became a joiner by trade.

Edgar Whitaker from Grassington
Courtesy of The Craven Herald

The story is told that after the Recruitment Drive throughout the Craven District in September 1915, mentioned in Chapter 3, Alice Whitaker locked her two sons in the coal house until the recruiting sergeant had left the area, because she did not want them to go off to war. Eventually, Edgar enlisted at Keighley on January 21st and went to France in May 1916 with the West Riding Regiment. At the time of Edgar's death, his younger brother Sydney had been in training in England for six months. Sadly, he too would pay the supreme sacrifice in 1917 and so their mother's worst fears came to pass.

News arrived in Grassington that Edgar had been killed by high explosive shell on October 4th, with there being no possibility of a burial. Instead, after the war, his name was placed on Pier and Face 6A and 6B Thiepval Memorial.

PRIVATE FRANCIS (FRANK) BATTISON WEBSTER NO. 425471
45TH BATTALION KING'S ROYAL RIFLES, ROYAL CANADIAN REGIMENT,
DIED OCTOBER 8TH 1916 AGED 23

Frank's father, Francis Webster, farmed at Walden Head, near West Burton, having married Elizabeth Wilkinson, a local girl who had been born at Northallerton. A son, Michael, was born in 1890 but shortly afterwards, Francis sold up and took his family to Huyton with Roby, on the eastern fringes of Liverpool, where, in 1901,

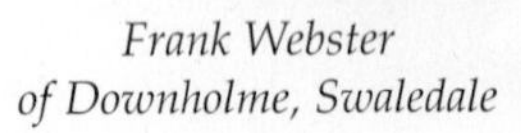

*Frank Webster
of Downholme, Swaledale*

*The Webster family at Huyton, Liverpool
Frank Webster, Francis Webster, Elizabeth with Edward, Michael Webster*

Francis was employed as a farm labourer. It was here that Frank was born in 1893 and the other additions to the family were Edward and Bessie.

By around 1906, Francis Webster brought his family to Swaledale and farmed on the Ellerton Abbey estate, near Downholme. Frank began work as a farm man for the Routh family on Field Gate Farm, Borwins, Bainbridge, in Wensleydale, and "lived in". It was at Bainbridge that he met and fell in love with Florence Bushby.

Frank Webster from Downholme and the girl he was engaged to, Florence Bushby of Bainbridge, Wensleydale

Florence's mother, Emma Jane, was a weaver from Nelson in Lancashire, who married Jim Bushby and at Nelson they raised their children, Florence and Robert. When Jim Bushby died at 32 years of age, Emma Jane began taking her children to stay with her aunty, Elizabeth Walker (nee Metcalfe), the landlady of the Crown Inn, Askrigg. There, she met George Greenbank Atkinson, a local post-man, and they married in 1909, moving to nearby Bainbridge to set up home.

Frank Webster was friendly with George Atkinson and went with him to Bainbridge Show, where he saw Florence from a distance. He enquired of George who she was and George replied, "That's our Florrie." Florence and Frank eventually became engaged but needed money and better prospects for them to be able to marry. Even though it would mean parting from Florence, Frank, together with his older brother Michael, decided to emigrate to Canada for a few years, to earn money from farming. They both travelled to Manitoba, where Frank got work on a farm outside the town of Brandon, Manitoba, 140 miles west of Winnipeg, in one of the most richly cultivated parts of Canada.

When war broke out, the two lads stayed for awhile in Canada, but Michael returned to England and joined the Northumberland Fusiliers, whilst Frank enlisted in Brandon on June 2nd 1915 and was posted to the 45th Battalion King's Royal Rifles, Royal Canadian Regiment. At this stage his parents back in England were still working at Ellerton Abbey.

The Bushby family from Bainbridge c1915. Bob Bushby, their mother, Emma Jane Atkinson and Florence Bushby

Frank Webster's platoon

Frank sailed from Halifax, Canada, on March 13th 1916 on the SS "Baltic", arriving in Liverpool, the place of his birth, on March 25th. The Canadian Expeditionary Force continued its training in England and Frank was able to spend his leave with Florence. His parents had just departed Ellerton Abbey and were farming at Hungary Hall, Middleton-in-Teesdale. He stayed with Florence and, knowing that he was due to embark for France shortly, they decided to get married on his first home leave from France. Sadly, it was not to be.

On June 8th 1916 Frank landed in France and the Battalion began training for fothcoming action in the Battle of the Somme. It was to be in the later stages of the battle that he would be killed. By the first week in October 1916 the Germans were in their last completed line of defences. The early onset of the autumn rains combined with the bombardments to make the ground a morass in which guns and transport were bogged, whilst the infantry could barely struggle forward.

On October 1st 1916 a Canadian Brigade had captured for awhile a strong German earthwork called Regina Trench, near Grandcourt, and on October 8th the Canadian 1st and 3rd Divisions attacked again. Frank was wounded during this attack, but was able to walk to the dressing station. Whilst he was being treated, a shell exploded and Frank was killed. Although at the time the body was not recovered and he was reported as missing, presumed dead, in later times his "dog tags" and other signs of identification were recovered and now his grave is numbered II.G.27. Regina Trench Cemetery, Grandcourt, 9 kilometres NE of Albert.

Frank's brother, Michael Webster, survived the war and came back to live at Downholme and raise a family, whilst Florence Bushby found happiness when later she married and had her own family. However, she never forgot Frank Webster.

PRIVATE PERCY HODGSON
NO. 13771 10TH BATTALION WEST RIDING REGIMENT
DIED OCTOBER 13TH 1916 AGED 31

Percy Hodgson of Littondale and Tosside, near Settle
Courtesy of The Craven Herald

Percy was the eldest of the eight children of Thomas and Mary Jane (Polly) Hodgson. In 1891 Thomas was a farmer living at Dickinson Height, just outside Tosside, near Settle. He had been born at nearby Gisburn Forest and married Polly, a girl from Bolton by Bowland. Their son, Percy, had also been born at Gisburn Forest, but in 1901, aged 15, Percy was "living in" and working as a cowman at the farm of Robert William Paley, at nearby Dale Head in the parish of Easington. The Hodgson family moved around from farm to farm in the Tosside area but by 1914 were farming at Stephen Moor Lodge, between Tosside and Slaidburn. Percy was still not at home because he had gone to work on a farm in Littondale, but when war was declared he came back to Stephen Moor Lodge and went to enlist at Settle, joining the West Riding Regiment. His farming exploits in Littondale before the war explains why his name is to be found on the war memorial plaque in Arncliffe Church.

Serving with the 10th Battalion West Riding Regiment, he was on the Somme front in September, at Melincourt. The 21st September saw much aeroplane activity, whilst the enemy sent over a few shells into their positions, causing 4 casualties. The Battalion also supplied a burying party for the burial of 2 British and 21 German soldiers. September 25th saw arrangements made for the whole Battalion to bathe and the men were served with clean underwear. During the early evening the enemy shelled the vicinity of Battalion HQ, including one close to the HQ mess, with the result that one man was killed and Percy Hodgson wounded. He was taken to the hospital complex at Le Havre, on the French coast, but he did not survive and died on October 13th. Percy was buried in grave 3.L.6. Ste. Marie Cemetery, Le Havre.

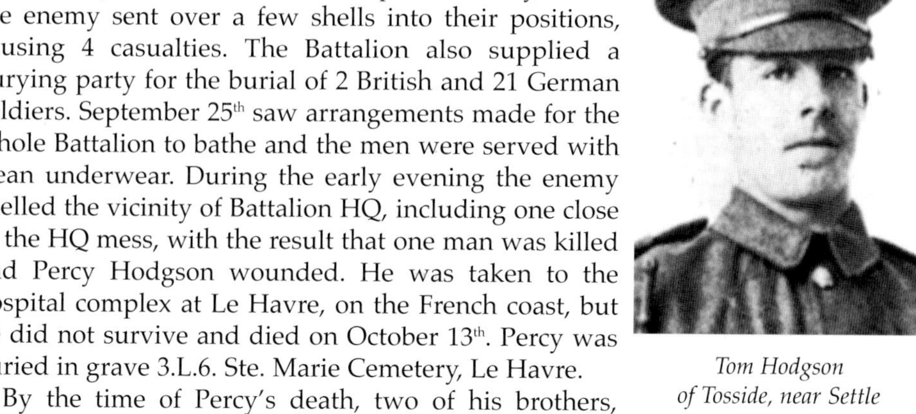

Tom Hodgson of Tosside, near Settle
Courtesy of The Craven Herald

By the time of Percy's death, two of his brothers, Joshua and Thomas were also serving in the army. Sadly, just nine months later, their parents would receive further shattering news that another son had been killed. Percy's younger brother Tom, serving in the Grenadier Guards, was killed when hit above the hip by a piece of shell on the first day of the Battle of Passchendaele, July 31st 1917.

CORPORAL ALBERT EDWARD WILTSHIRE
NO. 5897 2ND BATTALION WEST YORKSHIRE REGIMENT
DIED OCTOBER 28TH 1916 AGED 39

Albert was born in 1876 in the Suffolk village of Kirtling, near Newmarket, the son of Sarah Wiltshire, a single woman. She later married and Albert lived with his mother and step father. Albert married and he and his wife, Mary Jane, were living in Downholme parish, near Richmond, by the time war broke out.

Albert travelled to York to enlist and was serving with the 2nd Battalion West Yorkshire Regiment on the Somme as the action ground to a conclusion at the end of October and beginning of November.

October 25th found them in support near Les Boeufs front line. During the afternoon "B" and "D" Companies were heavily shelled and suffered 20 casualties. At night a small patrol was instrumental in capturing 16 prisoners. On the 26th there were 30 casualties, mainly to the carrying parties but also due to the shelling of the trenches. Patrolling proceeded each night, often under sharp fire from the enemy's snipers. The 28th October saw another patrol going out and during this action Corporal Albert Wiltshire was killed. His body was not retrieved because of the shelling and he is honoured on Pier and Face 2A, 2C and 2D Thiepval Memorial.

PRIVATE FRANCIS GEORGE KENDALL
NO. 7273 9TH BATTALION DURHAM LIGHT INFANTRY
DIED NOVEMBER 5TH 1916 AGED 26

In 1891, Francis, aged one, was living with his father, Thomas Hutchinson Kendall and mother, Jane Ann, on the farm at Riddings, near Reeth, the third child of seven in the family. By 1901 the family had moved to Low Whita farm, between Healaugh and Low Row.

Up to 1911, Francis worked as a farm labourer (hind) at Haverdale Farm, Low Row, and had married Mary Metcalfe from Nettlebed, near Bank Heads and Crackpot. In 1912 they moved to work at Polam Dairy, Darlington, where their daughter, Mary, was born. Their next move was to Major Craddock's farm and estate at Hartforth, near Gilling West, where Thomas was born.

When war broke out, Major Craddock told Francis that as he was the last labourer onto the farm, he would have to be the first to enlist. He served first with the Yorkshire Regiment, but by the time of his death he was serving with the 9th Battalion, Durham Light Infantry.

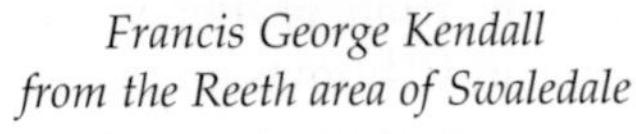

Francis George Kendall from the Reeth area of Swaledale

Mary and the children had to leave the tied cottage and move back to near Low Row, Swaledale. By this time, Francis's older brother, Mark, was also in the army and was to suffer from gassing. Mary gave birth to another son, Francis, in January 1917, months after his father was posted as missing, presumed dead.

One of Francis's colleagues in the 9th Battalion was another Swaledale man, William Appleton, a farmer's son from Dyke Heads, Gunnerside. On November 5th 1916 the Battalion was on the Somme, near Warlencourt village, ready to attack the Butte de Warlencourt, a 40 foot high conical shaped hill and the quarry in front of it.

Initially they found success as they moved over and round the Butte and broke into the German lines beyond. The heavily reinforced enemy began a counter-attack after 3p.m. and the Battalion was gradually forced back. Desperate hand to hand fighting took place during the afternoon, resulting in heavy losses on both sides.

After four hours of sustained bombardment, a final counter-attack was launched against the Durhams at 11p.m. The men of the 9th Battalion were overwhelmed. Many died fighting. Others were compelled to surrender and only a handful of men found their way back. 42 men were killed, 230 wounded and 157 were missing. Francis George Kendall was one of those killed whilst his Swaledale pal, William Appleton was one of those wounded and taken prisoner, later to die as a Prisoner of War.

As with so many other dalesmen killed on the Somme in 1916, his body was never found and Francis is therefore commemorated on Pier and Face 14A and 15C, Thiepval Memorial.

ABLE SEAMAN THOMAS RUSSELL
NO. KX/513 HOOD BATTALION ROYAL NAVAL DIVISION, RNVR, DIED NOVEMBER 13TH 1916 AGED 27

Thomas was the son of Alderman Bartholomew Russell, the former Mayor of Richmond. We have already seen that his brother, Bartholomew, junior, was killed on the Somme on July 31st 1916 and now, some two months later, he too would fall in that same bloody area.

When he enlisted, Thomas, a single man, joined the Hood Battalion of the Royal Naval Division and although receiving the rank of Able Seaman, he fought as a soldier on the Western Front. The Royal Naval Division, consisting of one Royal Marine and two Royal Naval Brigades of 3500 men each, was formed in 1914 and was intended to assist home defence in the early stages of the war. The Division, however, saw service in the defence of Antwerp in 1914, Gallipoli 1915-1916 and on the Western Front. It particularly distinguished itself for its tenacity and courage at Beaucourt, when, on November 13th, the last attack of the Battle of the Somme saw Beaucourt and neighbouring Beaumont-Hamel captured. The Hood Battalion was instrumental in gaining Beaucourt, but sadly, Thomas Russell was lost whilst accomplishing that feat.

Thomas Russell from Richmond

The Battalion certainly had a considerable number of well-known faces serving with it during the war. The poet Rupert Brooke had died in 1915 whilst serving with it in the Gallipoli Campaign, Edmund Blunden, another poet, was with the Battalion just before Thomas Russell was killed, whilst Arthur Asquith, son of the Liberal Prime Minister, Herbert Asquith (1908 – 1916), was an officer. Arthur was injured slightly just before the attack and General Haig pulled him out of the line because the Prime Minister's eldest son, Raymond, had recently been killed in action. It was a bitter blow to Arthur and the Battalion.

On the far right of the attack in the front line on November 13th were the Hood and Drake Battalions of the Naval Division. Hood led the way, followed by Drake, with its objective the German third line, when they would be leap frogged by Drake Battalion. Because of the thick mist, some men passed their objective and found themselves near Beaucourt Station at 6-15a.m. and a battle for the station ensued. Eventually it was captured and 400 prisoners taken. The outskirts of Beaucourt were reached. Other Hood troops, further to the left, encountered resistance in the German front line. Fighting was intense, many prisoners were taken, but casualties were also heavy. Some of the British artillery fired short, resulting in the death of their own men, whilst a German redoubt failed to be subdued and caused carnage to the attackers. As darkness fell, the Hood Battalion consolidated their position and settled down for the night, ready to continue the attack on Beaucourt the following morning.

The sodden November days had soaked the battleground and the artillery bombardments on the previous days had churned up No Mans Land and the German front line into a morass. It is not surprising to find, therefore, that when he lost his life attacking Beaucourt, Thomas Russell was yet another serviceman whose name came to be placed on the Thiepval Memorial, on Pier and Face 1A.

PRIVATE HUBERT WOOD
NO. 4455 7TH BATTALION WEST RIDING REGIMENT
DIED NOVEMBER 14TH 1916 AGED 22

The Wood family was living in Water Lane, Grassington, in 1901. Hubert Wood, senior, a stonemason from Grassington, had married Jane, a Redmire girl, and they lived with their children, Bertie, Elizabeth, Hubert, Jenny, Alice and Charlie. By 1914 the family was living at Laburnum House, Grassington.

Hubert Wood from Grassington
Courtesy of The Craven Herald

Hubert, junior, enlisted at Skipton, and was sent in a draft of men to replace the casualties incurred by the 7th Battalion, West Riding Regiment, during its part in the Battle of the Somme. He had only been in France five weeks when he was killed.

As the British Army made its final push on November 13th, the 7th Battalion was close to where the Hood Battalion and Richmond man, Thomas Russell, were stationed, SW of Arras. At 5-45a.m. on November 13th a smoke barrage was raised for two hours, as smoke and phosphorous bombs, together with smoke candles were used. The line was thinned in case of enemy artillery retaliation. Four platoons were withdrawn to the support trenches. Four squads of Battalion bombers were sent up and the support and reserves were ready for counter attacks, if they were required. German trench mortars and rifle grenades fell chiefly in the trenches and the Company HQ on the right was shelled at 3p.m., with one officer being killed. November 14th saw intermittent shelling during the day, with two casualties in the Lincoln Lane area. One of these was Hubert Wood, who was killed instantly. He was taken to be buried in grave 1.H.4 Foncquevillers Military Cemetery, 18km. SW of Arras. We shall see that his brother Charlie died whilst still in uniform, five months after the war ended, due partly to his experiences in the war.

PRIVATE WILFRED EWART HOLMES
NO. 6056 5TH BATTALION DURHAM LIGHT INFANTRY
DIED NOVEMBER 16TH 1916 AGED 18

Batley was the home town of the Holmes family and in 1901, 2 year old Wilfred was living with his father William, a Holmfirth man and his mother, Amy Gertrude Holmes, a girl from Batley. William was a worker in the rag and woollen trade, and by 1916 he had risen to be one of the managers at the mill of Messrs. Holdsworth, Carter and Co. They now resided at 15 Osborne Terrace, Field Hill, Batley. However, their son, Wilfred, had gone to work on the farm of John Tennant, Manor House,

Buckden. He was at home in Batley when he travelled to Pontefract to enlist in the army.

He joined up with the King's Own Yorkshire Light Infantry in June 1916, training at the Rugeley Camp in Staffordshire, and proceeded to the front with the Northumberland Fusiliers. However, he was with the DLI when he was wounded in the face, chest and right hand in action on the Somme front on November 8th. He was taken to the large hospital complex at Rouen but passed away in the military hospital on November 16th. Wilfred was buried in grave 0.11.C.10 St. Sever Cemetery Extension, Rouen. Soon afterwards, the vicar, Reverend Anderton, conducted a well attended memorial service in Hubberholme Church. (We shall also discover that in September 1917, Wilfred's employer, John Tennant of the Manor House, would lose his own son in this dreadful war).

Wilfred Ewart Holmes of Buckden, Wharfedale and Batby
Courtesy of The Craven Herald

The last casualty from these dales for the year 1916 and the last to result from action on the Somme, was a man with strong connections to Kettlewell.

LIEUTENANT GODFREY CHARLES HAGGAS CUTCLIFFE HYNE 2ND BATTALION IRISH GUARDS DIED NOVEMBER 21ST 1916 AGED 18

Godfrey Charles Cutcliffe Hyne from Kettlewell and Bradford
Courtesy of The Craven Herald

Godfrey Cutcliffe Hyne's father was C.J. Cutcliffe Hyne of Heaton Lodge, Bradford and Kettlewell. He was a confirmed rover, who, after leaving Cambridge University, travelled over 10,000 miles a year in earlier times, to all continents. For example, as a young man, he tramped from Norway to the Gulf of Bothnia, a distance of 850 miles. He was also a well known novelist of the time, but possibly his best known creation was "Captain Kettle", for whom he had to keep inventing stories and adventures.

When war broke out, his son, Godfrey, was at Rugby School and joined the Officer Training Corps there. Aged 18, he was granted a commission in the Irish Guards, and joined his regiment at the front in April 1916. Godfrey was promoted to the trench mortar battery and figured in a notable deed of gallantry which resulted in the saving of all his guns and in the capture of 17 out of 25 of the enemy. He was wounded in a charge by the Guards on September 15th, the opening day of one of the major offensives on the Somme.

Passing through the system of casualty clearing stations and hospitals, he was eventually conveyed to London and nursed at the house of the Honourable Mrs. Guest. Three weeks before his death it was found necessary to amputate his right leg to hopefully save his life, but poison had got such a hold of the system that he succumbed on November 21st. Internment took place with military honours at Kettlewell on Saturday November 26th 1916, with the Reverend Cockerill officiating (Reverend Cockerill's own son, John, had been killed with the Canadian forces on February 20th)

In the atrociously wet days of late October and early November, the last major attack on the Somme in 1916, on November 13th, had succeeded in capturing the shattered village of Beaumont Hamel. Having won the blood soaked disputed high ground, the British were now fighting their way down into the valley beyond – condemning themselves to spend a winter in flooded trenches. Nothing of any strategic value had been attained. The "Big Push" was over and it had cost 26 out of the 36 lives of servicemen from these dales who were killed in 1916. The sadness would be great for each of the families concerned.

1916 had shown that the British armies could not stand up to machine gun fire interlacing a defensive zone, stretching in depth for miles. In four and a half months of almost continuous attack, they were able to advance only a little more than eight miles. The casualty figures had been horrific, for on the first day of the offensive alone (July 1st) the losses easily exceeded the battle casualties sustained in the Crimean, Boer and Korean Wars, combined.

The German defensive role had been magnificent, but repeated German counter-attacks proved even more costly than Allied assaults. The German Army would never be quite the same force again.

Even remote villages such as Thwaite and Keld would suffer the loss of soldiers, either killed or wounded

CHAPTER 5

1917 – THE DARKEST HOUR

As the year 1917 dawned, the families back home would surely find it hard to imagine that it could bring a far greater degree of sadness to the Yorkshire Dales than that experienced in the previous year. 36 men connected to these dales had lost their lives in 1916. Yet, by the end of 1917 another 79 service men would become fatalities in this dreadful war, mainly as a result of the gloomiest drama in British military history, the Third Battle of Ypres, more commonly known by the name "Passchendaele" (July 31st to November 10th). It achieved little except horrendous loss of life, whilst the seemingly inexhaustible powers of endurance and sacrifice shown by the soldiers in the hellish battlefield conditions was amazing and made even more poignant by the futility of the purpose and result. Out of the 79 dales men lost during 1917, 24 of them died in this three month period, fighting in the quagmire conditions of Passchendaele. Another 3 men died in the Battle for Messines Ridge, the preliminary preparation for the larger battle.

The German General, Von Ludendorff, aware of Allied preparations for an offensive later in the year, and fearful of over-extending German lines in the west, deliberately chose a defensive attitude. During the early Spring, between February 23rd and April 5th, the Germans withdrew to a specially prepared, much shorter, highly organised defensive zone – the Hindenburg Line, some 20 miles behind the over-extended line from Arras to Soissons.

Behind a lightly held outpost line, heavily manned by machine gun posts, lay two successive, defensive positions, highly fortified. Behind these again lay the German reserves, concentrated and prepared for counter-attack. Behind the Germans' with-drawal, they left a scene of utter devastation, as they destroyed the crops, killed the animals, poisoned the wells, demolished the villages and blew up the bridges. We will discover that it was in the Allied advance to the Hindenburg Line on the heels of the retreating German forces that 2 dales service men would be killed.

General Nivelle, the French hero of Verdun in 1916, now had command of Anglo-French forces and planned the Nivelle Offensive on the Aisne and in Champagne (April 16th to 20th). The British preliminary to this French offensive was the Battle of Arras, April 9th to 15th, a tactical victory, but without a breakthrough and with eleven men from the dales falling on this battlefield.

For the French and British, the Hindenburg Line had thus proved too great a defensive barrier to break through and more significantly, the French offensive under Nivelle had proved an expensive disaster. Elements of the French Army mutinied and large numbers of soldiers stated that, although willing to defend their position, they would refuse any order to attack. Great pressure was therefore placed upon the British to take the fight to the enemy, and so draw German forces away from the French.

General Haig, the British Commander, had long held the aim to break out of the Ypres Salient on to the Flanders Plain and on to take the Channel ports used by the German U-boats. Sanction was given for a limited offensive to ease the pressure on the French. It would come, though, at a terrible cost.

The first part of the operation was, however, a complete success. On June 7th, after 17 days of general bombardment, nineteen huge mines were exploded under German positions in the southern end of the Salient and the British 2nd Army swept the enemy off the Messines – Wijtschate Ridge between June 7th and 14th.

Tragically, the following six weeks of dry weather passed before the main assault was launched on the Gheluvelt – Passchendaele Ridge. This infamous battle began on July 31st and the rains began immediately. Empire troops were expected to advance through swamp-like terrain in full view of the defending Germans on the higher ground. 80,000 Empire troops were killed and twice that number wounded before Passchendaele was taken and the Battle halted on November 10th 1917, with the Salient deepened by about five miles.

But Haig, still determined to keep pressure on the Germans to permit the French armies to recover from the mutiny, played his final card between November 20th and December 3rd, with a surprise attack on positions in front of Cambrai. The world witnessed the first mass attack of tanks, as 381 metal monsters crashed into the German lines, but once again there were further fatalities amongst the dales men participating.

It was, however, at the start of the year, in January, that the first Dales fatality of 1917 was reported, far away from the Western Front, in the Sinai Peninsula of Egypt.

PRIVATE PHILIP GORDON HOLMES NO. 524
32ND BATTALION AUSTRALIAN INFANTRY AND CAMEL CORPS
DIED JANUARY 9TH 1917 AGED 28

Philip's father, Fieldhouse Holmes, was from an old Addingham family, who came to Grassington at the age of 21 in the days when the lead mines were in full swing. He set up on his own account as grocer and draper in the Market Square and when he died in 1918, at the age of 89, he was the oldest and longest serving trader in Grassington. Sarah, his wife from Newhouse, a farm in Langstrothdale, was 23 years younger than him, and they raised a family of seven children.

In 1910, Philip, the third youngest child, emigrated to Australia, where he gained a good position, before joining the Australian Imperial Forces, after enlisting at Adelaide, and serving in the Sudan with the Camel Corps. His Regiment moved from there at the beginning of December 1916 and he had his first action against the Turks, close to El Arish, on December 23rd.

Throughout 1916 the large British garrison of Egypt remained passive, whilst the few thousand Turks in the Sinai Peninsula created trouble on both flanks. By the end of 1916, however, it was decided to clear the Sinai, ready for an advance into Palestine in late March 1917. A major raid was prepared against the Turkish forces at Rafa (Rafah), with the Australian and New Zealand forces well to the fore.

Phillip Gordon Holmes from Grassington
Courtesy of The Craven Herald

On the evening of January 8th 1917 the Anzac Mounted Division, British 5th (Yeomanry) Brigade and 3 battalions of the Imperial Camel Corps Brigade rode out of El Arish towards Rafa, where a 2000 strong Turkish garrison was based. By 7a.m. on the 9th January they were facing the Turkish positions at El Magruntein, dominated by a bare hill, on which the Turks had constructed four Redoubts.

British horse artillery batteries fired on the strong points but the dismounted troops came to a halt in their advance because of the Turkish fire-power, and because the artillery and British machine gunners began to run out of ammunition. However, final assaults were made upon the Redoubts, with the New Zealand Brigade sweeping up the slope towards the main Redoubt with bayonets fixed, whilst the Camel Brigade charged from the south against another strong-hold. When the attackers reached the Turkish trenches, the defenders quickly surrendered and by nightfall the entire position had been captured. The British and Empire troops had suffered 71 killed and 415 wounded while the Turks lost about 200 killed, 168 wounded and 1434 prisoners. With victory at Rafa, the Allies were now in a position to advance into Palestine and towards Jerusalem, but to do so would require the capture of the Turkish fortress of Gaza.

One of those killed in the battle was Philip Gordon Holmes and he was buried in grave F.298 Kantara War Memorial Cemetery, on the eastern side of the Suez Canal. His Captain sent the following letter to his parents: "Philip was a great man, and thought ever so much of by his comrades – a good, straight forward, honest out and out Yorkshireman of the best type, and you should be proud of your sturdy lad who did his "bit" for dear old England and home."

PRIVATE JAMES BANKS
NO. 13189 8TH BATTALION WEST RIDING REGIMENT
DIED JANUARY 11TH 1917 AGED 38

James was born into a farming family in Nidderdale, in 1878. By 1901, James, aged 22, was working as a cowman at Brough Hill, Bainbridge, in Wensleydale, on the farm of Francis Lambert, but by 1914 he was employed by Mr. Dinsdale, a farmer at Scar House, Hubberholme. James enlisted at Skipton in early September 1914 and went out to the Dardanelles in September 1915. Afterwards, he went with his Regiment to Egypt and from there to France in July 1916, where he fought on the Somme battlefield and was wounded in action on September 14th 1916. After spending some time in a French hospital he returned back to the line in November 1916.

By December 15th the 8th Battalion was holding the front line in Bois d'Hollande but by December 22nd were in reserve at Arqueves, NW of Albert, using this day to celebrate Christmas. Between December 29th and 31st they were in the front line trenches, receiving 3 casualties in the normal day to day shelling of these areas.

Arriving back at Arqueves on January 1st, the following nine days were spent on fatigue parties and training, before returning by bus on January 10th for front line action in the Bois d' Hollande. During their stay they suffered one casualty, when James Banks was killed during "routine" shelling of the lines by the Germans on January 11th. He was buried in grave 1V.A.47 Ancre British Cemetery, near Beaumont Hamel.

James Banks from Buckden, Wharfedale
Courtesy of The Craven Herald

PRIVATE WILLIAM APPLETON
NO. 7227 9TH BATTALION DURHAM LIGHT INFANTRY
DIED JANUARY 25TH 1917 AGED 21

William, the son of George Appleton and Margaret, a woman from Grinton, was born on a farm at Dyke Heads, situated on the small road running between Gunnerside and Ivelet, in Swaledale. The second youngest of five sons and one daughter, William had to find work elsewhere and went to seek employment in Wensleydale, on a farm in Askrigg parish. It was from there that he went to Leyburn to enlist and join the 9th Battalion Durham Light Infantry (Gateshead Gurkhas). Joining him, eventually, was another Swaledale farmer, Francis George Kendall.

We have already seen in the previous chapter how, on November 5th 1916, Francis Kendall was killed and William wounded and taken prisoner during the 9th Battalion's attempt to capture the Butte de Warlencourt, SW of Bapaume, during the Battle of the Somme. It was only in late December 1916 that his parents were informed that he was a POW and one month later they learned that he had died. Nursed by the Germans behind their lines, he died from his wounds on January 25th 1917 and was buried by the Germans in grave 1V.C.9. in Valenciennes (St. Roch) Communal Cemetery, France. The cemetery was in German hands throughout the war, using it to bury their own dead, but William is one of 348 British soldiers buried there by the Germans.

PRIVATE WILLIAM CLEMINSON
NO. 40318 8TH BATTALION NORTHUMBERLAND FUSILIERS
DIED FEBRUARY 24TH 1917 AGED 22

William was the third youngest of six children of Robert and Ann Cleminson, born at Ellerton before they moved along the dale to Grinton. The Cleminson's had been lead miners in Swaledale but by 1901 Robert was the cowman at Cogden Hall, and the family was living at nearby Grinton. Robert had been born at Low Row and Ann was from Riddings, near Reeth.

William travelled to Richmond to enlist and joined the 8th Battalion Northumberland Fusiliers, embarking for the front in September 1916. One of his other brothers was also on the Western Front, whilst another was in training.

In early March, his father Robert received news that Willie had died as the result of a bomb throwing accident. He was severely wounded internally and there was no hope of recovery. He died at the South African Hospital, Abbeville and was buried in grave 11.C.16. It is interesting to learn that his brother "Tott" was wounded when he went with a British force to Northern Russia in 1919, its aim being to help the White Russians against the Bolsheviks.

GUNNER JOSEPH METCALFE
NO. 148903 49TH DIVISION ROYAL FIELD ARTILLERY
DIED FEBRUARY 27TH 1917 AGED 27

Joseph was the son of Joseph and Elizabeth Metcalfe of Lofthouse, near Pateley Bridge, and had been born in Nidderdale. However, he had connections with both Linton and Burnsall through working on farms in these areas and his name is commemorated on the Burnsall memorial. When he enlisted at Keighley he joined the Royal Field Artillery as a gunner, but in the severe winter of 1916/1917 he was taken ill with pneumonia. He was taken to No. 12 Stationary Hospital, on the race course near the town of St. Pol, 30 kilometres SW of Bethune, where, on February 27th, Joseph Metcalfe died. He was buried in grave E.2. St. Pol Communal Cemetry Extension.

Joseph Metcalfe, formerly of Linton, Wharfedale
Courtesy of The Craven Herald

PRIVATE JOHN MARTIN
NO. 22010 16TH BATTALION WEST YORKSHIRE REGIMENT
DIED FEBRUARY 27TH 1917 AGED 19

John was born at Richmond, the son of George Martin, a mason's labourer from Oxfordshire and Alice Martin, a girl from the village of Crakehill, south of Thirsk. We have already seen that John's brother, George, had been killed in September 1914, whilst serving with the BEF. John enlisted at Richmond and eventually was posted to the 16th Battalion West Yorkshire Regiment.

He was killed in action at the beginning of the period when the Germans withdrew to their newly prepared defensive positions, known as the Hindenburg Line, and the Allies pursued them across an area devastated by the "scorched earth" policy of the retreating Germans.

On February 23rd the Battalion was in the vicinity of the village of Hebuterne, to the north of Albert, when nearby Gommecourt Wood was shelled by the Allies and the enemy's retaliation was directed on the trenches occupied by the 16th Battalion. On February 27th they took part in an operation against the enemy who were known to be evacuating their position.

At 6-30a.m. the Battalion made an attack on Rossignol Wood, with two companies attacking and two in support. The Battalion suffered heavy casualties chiefly from machine gun fire, High Explosive shells and shrapnel. It was during this attack that John Martin was killed. He is buried in Row A Owl Trench Cemetery, Hebuterne, 15 kilometres north of Albert.

SERGEANT SAMUEL ATKINSON
NO. 2395 5TH BATTALION YORKSHIRE REGIMENT
DIED MARCH 1ST 1917 AGED 28

Samuel's parents, Samuel and Mary Atkinson, worked on the Londesborough Park Estate, near Market Weighton, between York and Beverley. In 1901 their 13 year old son, Samuel, was working as a farm errand boy on a large farm on the estate, but some years later he became employed in working for the Hutton family on their estate at Marske, in Swaledale.

Samuel was in the Territorial Army and joined the 5th Battalion Yorkshire Regiment. The Battalion had taken part in the later stages of the Battle of the Somme in mid September 1916, receiving heavy casualties (in three days of fighting September 15th – 18th there were 252 casualties). In late October 1916 they were employed on road making, but still suffered 60 casualties. The whole of January 1917 was spent near Mametz Wood, in the Somme area, whilst in February, moves were made to Fresnes Wood and Triangle Wood.

However, it was in February that Samuel was taken ill and eventually was transported to the large military hospital complex at Le Treport on the French coast, 25 kilometres NE of Dieppe. It was there that he died of pneumonia and was buried in grave IV.C.8. Mont Huon Military Cemetery, Le Treport.

PRIVATE JAMES RUSSELL
NO. 71839 62ND COMPANY MACHINE GUN CORPS
DIED APRIL 2ND 1917 AGED 36

James's father, James Russell senior, was a farmer and carrier, living at Downholme, near Richmond, and his mother was Elizabeth Hird, a girl from Grinton, near Reeth. James, junior, had four sisters and one brother but sadly three of his sisters and his brother died relatively young. As a carrier, James's father collected coal from Tan Hill on his horse and cart. On Saturdays he carried the produce of Downholme villagers to Richmond market and brought back a box of kippers to sell to them. He also collected sand for local builders from the river bed of the Swale, near Marske Bridge, a dangerous task on a few occasions because of the notorious Swale torrent that could be unleashed in times of sudden downpours.

James Russell, junior, became a journeyman butcher and moved around the country. In 1901 he was working at Darlington, but in 1904 he married Ellen Hall, a

Collecting sand from the River Swale, near Richmond
Clive Torrens Collection

Fremington girl, at Grinton Church, and they started married life at Barton on Humber. By 1906 they were living at Burnley, where their son was born, but when James joined the army the family was living at Norton, in the suburbs of Stockton on Tees.

James joined a battalion of the Northumberland Fusiliers but he later became a member of a machine gun company and it was in the pursuit of the Germans, as they withdrew to the Hindenburg Line, that he was killed by shellfire. He left a widow and his young son, James. His name is commemorated on Bay 10 of the Arras Memorial.

SIGNALLER ELLIS RICHMOND NO. 180416
31ST BATTALION CANADIAN INFANTRY (ALBERTA REGIMENT)
DIED APRIL 10TH 1917 AGED 24

The parents of Ellis were John Richmond, born at Pateley Bridge, and Martha, born at Skipton. In the late 1880's they lived first at Pateley Bridge and then Skipton, but by 1893 the family was at Keighley, where John was a fence waller. Ellis, who was born at Keighley in 1899, was the youngest of three sons and he also had six sisters. The family moved to Grassington, where they lived at Edge Side Farm and Ellis became a clerk. By the time of the Great War, however, his parents were living at Linton Falls.

Ellis Richmond was no longer living with them, however, for two years before the start of the war he had emigrated to Canada. He returned on the outbreak of war and trained as a signaller with the West Riding Regiment, before transferring to the Canadian Infantry and the Alberta Regiment in November 1915. Ellis was to die at the Battle of Arras.

On April 9th 1917 the Canadians gathered themselves to attack Vimy Ridge, to cover the flank of the British Third Army as it attacked out of the subterranean tunnels and caves of Arras, towards Cambrai. The Canadian Infantry surged across the wreckage of the German first line before the few survivors could get out of their dug-outs and by 6-05a.m. were in possession of the trench system. The second line was reached, but machine gunners caused mounting casualties as the Canadians fought for the ruins of a large cellar, containing two German Battalion Headquarters.

Ellis Richmond from Linton Falls, near Grassington
Courtesy of The Craven Herald

Machine guns on Hill 145 took a further toll on the advance up the slope of the Ridge and the Canadian 4th Division ground to a halt. Resistance southwards was lighter and by 1p.m. three woods fell into Canadian hands. The northern part of the Ridge line was only gained after the tenacious German machine gunners on Hill 145 had been dealt with. The forward slopes were stormed before nightfall and the crest fell in the early hours of April 10th. By April 12th the Canadians were in full control of Vimy Ridge. Its capture was a remarkable feat of arms and gave signal proof of the Canadians' courage, skill and ability.

However, as they stormed the crest of the Ridge on April 10th, Ellis Spink was killed. His body was never discovered and he is commemorated on the imposing Vimy Memorial.

PRIVATE WILLIAM GORDON CAMPBELL
NO. 2304 46TH BATTALION AUSTRALIAN INFANTRY FORCE
DIED APRIL 11TH 1917 AGED 30

In 1901 William was 14 years old and working in the family woollen warehouse in Bradford. He had been born at Bradford, the second youngest of the five children of Thomas and Edith Campbell, and he attended Carlton Street Commercial School. Thomas was a "stuff (woollen) merchant and they lived at Merton Road, Bradford. At some stage before the war, William worked at Linton, possibly at the textile mill at Linton Falls, near Grassington, but in 1911 he emigrated to Australia with his younger brother, Arthur, to begin a fresh life as a farmer.

They settled in Finley, New South Wales, in the Riverina district, an area of extensive sheep grazing and wheat growing, well to the west of The Australian Alps and The Great Dividing Range. They named their new home "Wharfedale".

As with many Australians, William answered the call of the Motherland and arrived in France with the Australian Infantry Force. Just as with Ellis Richmond, he too would be killed in action at the Battle of Arras in April 1917.

As part of the 4th Australian Division they were launched in an assault against the Hindenburg Line in the vicinity of Bullecourt but had neither been able to make the preparations nor to bring up the artillery necessary for a normal trench attack, far less an assault on the defences of the Hindenburg Line. Tanks were used instead as a mobile barrage and wire destroyer, but only eleven could be obtained and it was not enough.

The tanks appeared to have an initial impact, causing a panic which sent part of the German garrison fleeing across the countryside, and the Australians broke into the Hindenburg Line. However, they then became the target of counter-attack from all sides. William Gordon Campbell was killed during these counter-attacks and his name is commemorated on the Villers-Bretonneux Memorial, 16 kilometres east of Amiens.

LANCE CORPORAL STANLEY HARDING MOORE
NO. 2418829 2ND/5TH BATTALION LINCOLNSHIRE REGIMENT
DIED APRIL 11TH 1917 AGED 19

Stanley was the youngest of the six children of James William and Amy Moore. James William Moore was a Reeth man but, for 16 years, he settled in the village of Holt in Wiltshire, to the east of Bath, where he had taken up the position of schoolmaster at Holt British School. He met and married Amy Harding of Holt and four of their children were born whilst in Wiltshire. In 1895 he returned to Reeth as head teacher of Reeth Friends School and sons Edwin and Stanley were born at their home, Langhorne Cottage. James William, a staunch Methodist and choir master at Reeth, remained as headmaster of the village school for the next 27 years.

Stanley Moore from Reeth

During the war, from 1916, J.W. Moore was Chairman of the Military Tribunal. His eldest son, William, was a Territorial and joined up at the beginning of the war, serving at the Dardanelles and in Mesopotamia, but he was affected badly in a gas attack and was discharged. Reginald also served in the army and after the war he became the school truancy officer for the Reeth district.

Stanley Moore

Stanley Moore had been employed in the offices of the woollen milling firm of Messrs. Pease and Partners at Darlington before enlisting in that town. He joined the Lincolnshire Regiment and as a 19 year old was promoted to Lance Corporal. The Battalion embarked for France in February 1917 and they were involved in the pursuit of the Germans to the Hindenburg Line.

Reeth Friends School c1910. Headteacher J. W. Moore stands on the left.
His wife Amy is seated on right of front row

Reeth Friends School Gardening Class 1909
Back row: 4th from left William Moore, 6th from left Edwin Moore. Headteacher J. W. Moore

However, it was in the early stages of the Arras Offensive that Stanley was killed.

At 3-30a.m. on April 11th they attacked towards Malakoff Farm, Cologne Farm and the Quarry, near Hesbecourt, a village to the east of Peronne. "A" Company carried the Quarry, which was very large, capturing machine guns , bombing dug outs and taking 40 prisoners. In the Quarry they were met by heavy machine gun and rifle fire and lost their CO. At 4-40a.m., "C" Company moved against the enemy trench and commenced bombing towards Malakoff Farm. They were strongly counter-attacked from Cologne Farm by 250 Germans and appear to have been surrounded and mostly captured, because very few men returned (254 men became casualties).

During the counter-attack Stanley Moore was killed and his body was never recovered. His name is commemorated on Pier and Face I.C. Thiepval Memorial

Memorial plaque in the Methodist Chapel, Reeth

PRIVATE RICHARD O'HERN
NO. 2018 1ST BATTALION ROYAL WARWICKSHIRE REGIMENT
DIED APRIL 11TH 1917 AGED 26

Richard was one of the eleven children of Richard and Annie O'Hern, a Roman Catholic family, born and bred in Richmond, with their father working as a foreman at the local paper mill. By the time Richard was killed in the war he was married to Winifred Sutton and they were living at 15 Hurgill Road with their daughter Joan.

Richard enlisted at Richmond and eventually joined the 1st Battalion Warwickshire Regiment. During February and March 1917 they had been involved in the advance to the Hindenburg Line. The Battle of Arras had already opened with the capture of Vimy Ridge on April 9th and on that same day the 1st Battalion had been in support at the storming and capture of Athies and Fampoux.

Two days later, the Battalion attacked towards Plouvain, resulting in many casualties from shell fire before starting, and the attack was almost at once checked by the enemy's machine guns. A few men managed to get to within 100 yards of the railway station, but were forced back.

Since the fire from the Chemical Works and Railway Embankment made further progress impossible, a line was ordered to be consolidated. This failure was due to the fact that they were in the view of the enemy as they came up to assembly and to the strength of the barrage they were then able to put down. When Richard O' Hern was killed in the attack on April 11th he was buried in grave II.H.9. Browns Copse Cemetery, Roeux, 8 kilometres east of Arras.

We shall find that his brother John died from pneumonia in early 1919 and is buried in Richmond Cemetery.

CORPORAL FRANK HIGHAM
NO. 242388 5TH BATTALION WEST RIDING REGIMENT
DIED APRIL 23RD 1917 AGED 19

Frank was born at Wetherby, but by 1901 he was living in the Hunslet area of Leeds with his parents, John and Annie Higham. John, a Bolton man, was working as a gardener. In the years immediately prior to the Great War, Frank arrived to work in the Rylstone area, between Grassington and Skipton, and it was in Skipton that he went to enlist and joined the 5th Battalion West Riding Regiment.

The Battalion was involved in the later stages of the Battle of Arras and Frank was severely wounded in an attack on the enemy lines on April 23rd 1917. He was taken to the Field Ambulance Station but he succumbed to his wounds and was buried in grave I.D.6. Vieille-Chapelle New Military Cemetery, Lacouture, 10 kilometres NE of Bethune.

On that same day, April 23rd, the market town of Richmond suffered a grievous loss when news was received of the death of four men from the town who were in the same Battalion of the Yorkshire Regiment and were killed in the same battle as Frank Higham.

CORPORAL THOMAS LAWRENCE BAINBRIDGE
NO. 200861 4TH BATTALION YORKSHIRE REGIMENT
DIED APRIL 23RD 1917 AGED 25

Thomas's parents were Richmond born and bred. Samuel James Bainbridge was a draper and tailor in the town and he and his wife Margaretta Annie Bainbridge, with their children, Clarence, Thomas, Margaret Doris and Joseph, lived at 5 Castle Terrace, Richmond. When he enlisted at Northallerton, Thomas joined the 4th Battalion Yorkshire Regiment, and by the time of his death he had won the Military Medal for gallantry.

AND

PRIVATE REGINALD BRAND
NO. 200090 4TH BATTALION YORKSHIRE REGIMENT
DIED APRIL 23RD 1917 AGED 25

Reginald was the youngest son and fifth out of the seven children of Charles and Esther Brand, living at 1 Gallowgate, Richmond. Their father, born at Gilling, had married Esther, a girl from Stanstead in Suffolk, and supported his family by working as a house painter.

AND
PRIVATE JOHN GEORGE BROWN
NO. 203799 4TH BATTALION YORKSHIRE REGIMENT
DIED APRIL 23RD 1917 AGED 26

John was born in Richmond, the eldest son of Potts and Margaret Brown, of Cornforth Hill. Potts was a Richmond cab driver and groom and we have already seen that another soldier son, Herbert, had died in September 1915.

AND
PRIVATE FREDERICK WILLIAM HORTON
NO. 200167 4TH BATTALION YORKSHIRE REGIMENT
DIED APRIL 23RD 1917 AGED 20

In 1901, four year old Frederick was living with his widowed mother, 38 year old Mary Horton, and sister Ellen, at the home of his grandmother, Mary Tate, at 33 Bargate, Richmond. Living at the same house was his uncle, Henry Tate, a bootmaker. Frederick enlisted at Richmond and joined his Richmond colleagues in the 4th Battalion.

The 4th Battalion Yorkshire Regiment billeted outside Arras in early April and reached the town on April 12th, being accommodated in the subterranean caves of Arras. On the night of the 22nd/23rd April they moved out and into position for an attack at 4-45a.m. on the 23rd. "W" Company met with much opposition from machine gun and rifle fire, whilst enemy artillery took its toll.

They moved into the German support trenches, filled with German dead, and captured three guns of a howitzer battery and then dug in. However, the machine gun fire remained deadly. The 4th Battalion was now down to 150 men and by 7-30a.m. the enemy was seen massing for a counter-attack, with infiltration occurring. A retirement by successive phases was now initiated, under heavy machine gun fire all the time. 360 men from the Battalion were either killed, wounded or missing.

All four men from Richmond were killed. The body of Thomas Bainbridge was never recovered and his name is commemorated on Bay 5, Arras Memorial. Reginald Brand is buried in grave IV.G.13. Feuchy Chapel British Cemetery, Wancourt. John George Brown is buried in grave V.B.8. Faubourg D'Amiens Cemetery, Arras, whilst Frederick William Horton lies at rest next to him in grave V.B.7.

LANCE CORPORAL THOMAS REYNARD
NO. 12767 9TH BATTALION WEST RIDING REGIMENT
DIED APRIL 25TH 1917 AGED 27

In 1901, eleven year old Thomas was living at Mock Beggars Hall (formerly Monks Hall), Appletreewick, the village in which he was born. With him were his father,

William Reynard, a widower and general labourer, and his 17 year old sister, Sarah, acting as housekeeper. An older brother who was working and living elsewhere, emigrated to Canada before the war. By the start of the war, however, Thomas's family was residing at Moor End Farm, Langbar, a small village between Bolton Abbey and Ilkley. It was from Langbar, in September 1914 that Thomas travelled to Ilkley to enlist, joining the 9th Battalion West Riding Regiment, and embarking for France in July 1916. In that same month he received wounds at the Battle of the Somme, from which he recovered. By November, his only brother was also out in France, serving with the Canadian Engineers.

Thomas Reynard of Langbar and the Bolton Abbey Estate

Having taken part in the Battle of Arras, Thomas and the 9th Battalion were ordered from the support line on April 24th to occupy trenches in Monchy Wood, to the east of Arras, ready for the attack on April 25th. At 3-37a.m. the enemy barrage began, shells falling over and just short of the first line trench, and a terrific machine gun and rifle fire barrage opened on the advancing troops. The advance continued upto 100 yards from the enemy trench, when whistles were blown and German machine gun fire grew even worse and the men were forced back to their trench, where they reorganised and were sent over again but met the same reception and again retired. For the third time they went over but had to retire, with the resulting casualties being serious.

Thomas Reynard was killed as he attacked the German line, but as his body was never recovered, his name is honoured on Bay 6, Arras Memorial, and on the Burnsall War Memorial.

PRIVATE JOHN WILLIAM TROTT
NO. 32868 2ND BATTALION DURHAM LIGHT INFANTRY
DIED APRIL 26TH 1917 AGED 25

Nine year old John William was living at Downholme, the place of his birth, in 1901. He resided, not with his parents, but with his grandfather, John Trott, a roadman and farm labourer, born at Newton le Willows, between Leyburn and Bedale, and his grandmother, Mary, who originated from Harmby, near Leyburn. When war was declared in 1914, John William Trott was living and working at Shotley Bridge, near Consett in County Durham, and he went to enlist in that town, joining the 2nd Battalion Durham Light Infantry.

The Battalion was stationed between Lens and Bethune, at Mazingarbe, in April 1917. They played no part in the Battle of Arras, but were in and out of the front line in the bleak coalfield region at Mazingarbe, including a period of front line trench duty between April 23rd and 27th. A good deal of shelling always took place and during the whole month of April, 22 men were killed, with 131 wounded or missing. One of those killed in routine trench warfare was John William Trott. He was buried in grave II.A.15. Mazingarbe Communal Cemetery Extension.

PIONEER SYLVESTER MOORHOUSE HARTLEY NO. 195384 THIRD ARMY HQ. SIGNAL COMPANY ROYAL ENGINEERS DIED APRIL 28TH 1917 AGED 30

Harper Hartley, Sylvester's father, was born at Linton and married Sarah Shiers Moorhouse of Summerscales, near Hazlewood, on the Bolton Abbey Estate. Their children were brought up on the Estate, at High Bank House, Storiths. Sylvester, or Ves, as he was known, was their third son and sang in the Priory Choir. He married a local girl, Emily Eliza Phillips, from Stank House, in the village of Bolton Abbey, and took a small farm on the Estate, called Lilac House, where they brought up their son, Basil. Ves travelled to Harrogate to enlist and trained as a signaller in the Royal Engineers, before embarking for France at the end of November 1916.

Sylvester Moorhouse Hartley from Storiths and Bolton Abbey

It was a dangerous occupation, and in the attacks on the Hindenburg Line near the end of April Sylvester Hartley was wounded. He was taken to a Field Ambulance Station on the outskirts of Arras, but died from his wounds on April 28th. He was buried in grave I.H.10. St. Nicolas British Cemetery, Arras. On a pew in the choir inside Bolton Priory is written, "Sylvester Moorhouse Hartley, a devoted singer in this choir from 1896 to 1914, who gave his life for his country in the Great War, April 1917."

PRIVATE THOMAS INGLEBY NO. 17670 8TH BATTALION WEST RIDING REGIMENT DIED APRIL 30TH 1917 AGED 19

In 1901, Adam Ingilby, his wife, Mary Jane, and young family were living at the small hamlet of Halton Gill, in Littondale, where Adam was a farmer. He was born at Thrushcross, near Blubberhouses, between Bolton Abbey and Harrogate, and had married Mary Jane, a Kettlewell girl. They farmed at Thrushcross, where four of their children were born, including Thomas, before moving to Halton Gill in 1900.

By 1914 Thomas Ingleby was working on a farm at Hawkswick, in Littondale, and was in the Territorial Army. However, it was not until January 1915 that he enlisted at Keighley, after attending a recruitment meeting at Arncliffe Schoolroom, addressed by Colonel Dawson. He joined the 8th Battalion West Riding Regiment and trained as a signaller in the Battalion. His brothers, Jimmy, Robert and William also served in the army during the Great War and thankfully survived.

The Battle of Arras (April 9th to 15th) was a British tactical victory but there was no breakthrough. However, the French offensive under General Nivelle (April 16th to

The Ingleby family of Littondale
Adam Ingleby with twins Maggie and Thomas, Billy Ingleby and Mary Jane Ingleby with Jimmy

Tom Ingleby of Halton Gill, Littondale

Tom Ingleby, Maggie Ingleby, Jimmy Ingleby

20th) was a disaster and so for the next few weeks General Haig continued with further attempts at attacking the German lines, to help the French. We have already seen that a considerable number of Dales servicemen died in these later battles and Thomas Ingleby became another casualty.

The 8th Battalion was in the front line at Reincourt, between Bapaume and Arras from April 24th to the 27th, sustaining 21 casualties. On the 28th and 29th April strong patrols were pushed out and the line advanced by 200 yards, but it resulted in 4 men being killed, 8 wounded and 5 taken prisoner on April 29th. One of those severely wounded was Thomas, with shell wounds to the right arm, buttock and back, received whilst carrying out his duties as a signaller. He was taken to No. 3 Australian Clearing Station, but died from his wounds on April 30th 1917. His body was buried in grave II.B.16. Grevillers British Cemetery, 3 kilometres west of Bapaume.

PRIVATE THOMAS CLARKSON
NO. 325648 9TH BATTALION DURHAM LIGHT INFANTRY
DIED APRIL 30TH 1917 AGED 27

Thomas was one of the children of John and Ann Clarkson, both of whom were born in Muker in Swaledale. In the early days of his marriage, John was a farm worker, lead miner, coal miner at Tan Hill and horse driver. Most of their children were born at the farmstead in Hartlakes, in the gorge below Kisdon Falls. They then came in the early 1900's to farm at the top of Kisdon, at Kisdon Lodge, with Tom helping on the farm.

Although Tom was not a conscientious objector, he always stated that he did not want to kill anyone. However, he still went off to war when he was called up at Richmond, joining first of all the Yorkshire Regiment, before being transferred to the 9th Battalion Durham Light Infantry. When he arrived in France and went into the front line for the first time, at the start of the Battle of Arras, he was severely wounded in the head within six hours of his first action (part of his head was shot away).

He was soon transferred to a hospital in London and was visited by his brother Jack, but he died on April 30th 1917. His body was returned to Swaledale and he was buried in St. Mary's Churchyard, Muker.

Thomas Clarkson from Swaledale, who died from wounds and is buried in Melbecks churchyard

LANCE CORPORAL ARTHUR CHRISTOPHER FRANKLIN NO. 30723 12TH BATTALION YORKSHIRE REGIMENT DIED MAY 1ST 1917 AGED 31

Arthur was born in Richmond, Surrey, not in Richmond, North Yorkshire. He was the son of Charles Franklin, a worker in a Richmond ironmongers, and Emily Franklin. However, by the start of the Great War, Arthur was living in the Richmond area of North Yorkshire and joined the 12th Battalion Yorkshire Regiment, a Pioneer Battalion, drawing its men mainly from skilled craftsmen such as fitters, carpenters, blacksmiths and masons..

Between June 1st 1916, when they first landed in France, and February 1917, the Battalion moved around a great deal to wherever they were required for construction work. When the Germans withdrew to the Hindenburg Line between February and April 5th 1917 they had laid waste to the countryside vacated. In late April, early May, the 12th Battalion was employed in the task of repairing roads in an area to the east of Peronne and the men were subjected to intermittent shelling, resulting in the death of Arthur Franklin on May 1st 1917. Arthur is buried in grave VII.H.7/8. Fins New British Cemetery, Sorel-Le-Grand, between Peronne and Cambrai.

We have already seen that the French offensive of April 16th-20th had been a disaster and as a result of this, mutiny broke out in the French Army. Renewed British attacks were made in early May to distract the Germans and in one of these Divisional attacks on the Hindenburg Line on May 3rd, four Wharfedale men were killed, two of them serving in the same Battalion.

LANCE CORPORAL TIMOTHY HOLMES SIMPSON NO. 20007 2ND/6TH BATTALION WEST RIDING REGIMENT DIED MAY 3RD 1917 AGED 20

Timothy Holmes Simpson from Hebden, before the Great War

In 1901 four year old Timothy Holmes Simpson was living at the Buckden home of his grandfather, Timothy Simpson, a widower and farmer. With him were his father William, born at Aysgarth, his mother, Laura, a girl from Burneston, Yorkshire and his older sister, Mary.

A few years later, William and Laura moved to Hebden, near Grassington, to take over the Clarendon Hotel. Five other children completed the family.

By the start of the Great War Timothy was living at

Timothy Holmes Simpson from Hebden

Croft House, Hebden, and was working as a farm labourer on a farm belonging to the Hebden firm of T. and A. Stockdale, grocers and provision merchants. A happy go lucky country lad, he enlisted at Skipton in April 1916 and was wounded on October of that year, returning to England to recuperate. He rejoined his regiment, 2nd/6th Battalion West Riding Regiment, but did not get sent out in a draft of men until April 1917, and found himself in the same Battalion as James Robert Atkins, from Deerstones on the Bolton Abbey Estate. Both lads would fall in battle on the same day.

AND
PRIVATE JAMES ROBERT ATKINS
NO. 267101 2ND/6TH BATTALION WEST RIDING REGIMENT
DIED MAY 3RD 1917 AGED 21

James's father, Henry Atkins, was the son of George and Margaret Atkins and was brought up at Deerstones, on the Bolton Abbey Estate. Henry married twice, firstly to Annie Swales at Bolton Abbey in 1880, with whom he had four children, but Annie died in 1888. In 1895, Henry married again, this time to Jane Ann Kitson, who had been born in Suffolk but was working for Henry as a housekeeper. Four more children were born, including James Robert in July 1895. Henry died in 1908, leaving Ann to raise a large family by herself. The farm extended to only 15 acres and would not bring in a large income, but James helped his mother run the farm. However, in 1916 he was called up and enlisted at Skipton, joining the 2nd/6th Battalion. His half brothers, Herbert and Charles, also served in the war and would survive the conflict.

As the French Mutiny was being quelled, renewed British attacks to distract the Germans' attention had already drawn German reserves to the northern front and this is where Timothy and James were killed. On May 2nd 1917 the Battalion proceeded to the Railway Embankment in order to take part in an attack by 62nd Division, to be launched at 3-40a.m. on May 3rd on Bullecourt and trenches of the Hindenburg Line west of Bullecourt. The Battalion suffered severe losses during this attack, sustaining 257 casualties, many caused by shelling and shrapnel, and the Battalion was relieved in the evening. However, two of the men killed by shell fire were Timothy Simpson and James Atkins, colleagues from the dales. Their bodies were not recovered and their names look down from Bay 6 of the Arras Memorial.

On that same fateful day, two more men from Wharfedale were killed, one from Grassington and the other from Burnsall.

PRIVATE SYDNEY WHITAKER
NO. 201989 2ND/5TH BATTALION WEST YORKSHIRE REGIMENT
DIED MAY 3RD 1917 AGED 20

We have already seen in the previous chapter that Sydney's brother, Edgar Whitaker, was killed on October 4th 1916. Sydney had travelled from Grassington to enlist at Skipton and joined the 2nd/5th Battalion West Yorkshire Regiment. By April it was fighting at Arras and on May 3rd took part in the attack on Bullecourt.

A hostile barrage caused casualties as the Battalion moved into position, but the men soon occupied German trenches to the south of the village, even though shells were crashing all around them. They were in the centre of the village by 5a.m.,

despite the severe machine gun and trench mortar fire. There was heavy machine gun fire from the SE corner of the village, from an abandoned tank and from unlocated positions.

By 6-30a.m. German bombing parties in the centre of Bullecourt drove back the Battalion and retirement was made to the Railway Embankment. By the end of the day's engagement, 267 casualties had been sustained and one of those killed, whose body was not recovered, was Sydney Whitaker. His name was inscribed on Bay 4 of the Arras Memorial. In the space of seven months William and Alice Whitaker had lost their two sons. After their deaths, Alice suffered dreadfully, her mind being affected by her sad loss.

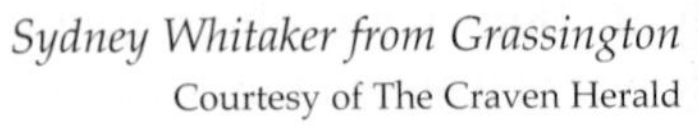

Sydney Whitaker from Grassington
Courtesy of The Craven Herald

CORPORAL JOSEPH GRIFFITH
NO. 300027 2ND/4TH BATTALION WEST RIDING REGIMENT
DIED MAY 3RD 1917 AGED 32

Joseph was the son of Mr. and Mrs. Thomas Griffith of Chester. He became a police constable before the war, serving at both Skipton and Burnsall. Although he was residing at Higher Broughton when war began he enlisted at Skipton and joined the 2nd/4th Battalion West Riding Regiment (when he was killed his name was inscribed on the Burnsall Memorial).

Joseph Griffith, formerly of Burnsall
Courtesy of The Craven Herald

The Battalion was stationed at Mory in late April 1917, just north of Bapaume, as the Allies prepared for a divisional attack just to the north of nearby Ecoust. At 3-45a.m. the attack began, but the first wave was not successful and a party of four officers and 90 men who had been forced to retire to the Railway Embankment were led forward by Captain Waller in a second attempt. At 6-15a.m. this party were again forced back, having had very heavy casualties. During the operation 241 men were killed, wounded or posted missing. The Battalion held the embankment with 2 officers and 150 men until the night of May 4th/5th, when the remainder of the Battalion returned to Mory.

Joseph Griffith's name joined those of Timothy Simpson and James Atkins on Bay 6 of the Arras Memorial.

PRIVATE JOHN HUTCHINSON
NO. 200321 4TH BATTALION YORKSHIRE REGIMENT
DIED MAY 4TH 1917 AGED 21

In 1901, five year old John Hutchinson was living with his 27 year old mother, Mary Ann Nelson, a single woman, at the Richmond home of his grandparents, William and Ellen Nelson. William was a general labourer and 13 inhabitants occupied the house, including another four of Mary Ann's children, who all took the name of their father. By the time of John's death in 1917, Mary Ann was living in Waterloo Street, Richmond.

John enlisted in the town and joined the 4th Battalion Yorkshire Regiment. As with so many other servicemen from the dales who perished in the Spring of 1917, he was involved in the Battle of Arras and in the battles of late April, planned to relieve the pressure on the French. John was wounded due to action in the Second Battle of the Scarpe, where the British troops attacked on a front of nine miles. The Battalion went into the attack on April 23rd and sustained 370 casualties from artillery and machine gun fire between April 21st and 23rd. John Hutchinson was taken to a casualty clearing station between Arras and Doullens, where he died on May 4th 1917. He was buried in grave X.F.10. Warlincourt Halte British Cemetery, Saulty, betwee Arras and Doullens.

SECOND LIEUTENANT CHARLES JOHN HOLDSWORTH
8TH BATTALION DEVONSHIRE REGIMENT
DIED MAY 8TH 1917 AGED 32

Charles was the son of Captain and Mrs. J.W. Holdsworth, of Richmond, although by the time of his death they had left the market town. The Battalion Charles joined as a Second Lieutenant had been formed in Exeter in 1914 and landed in France in July 1915.

His fate was to be the same as the other dales servicemen killed in actions around Arras between April 21st and early May. Charles John Holdsworth was killed in action on May 8th and buried in grave IV.H.15. H.A.C. Cemetery, Ecoust-St-Mein, between Arras, Bapaume and Cambrai.

CAPTAIN RANDAL WILLIAM SHUCKBURGH CROFT
"C" COMPANY 7TH BATTALION YORKSHIRE REGIMENT
DIED MAY 12TH 1917 AGED 27

Randal Croft was born at Richmond and in 1901, at the age of 11, he was boarding at the Friary School in Richmond (part of Richmond Grammar School). He was connected to the Richmond family of glaziers and gas fitters, who lived at Great Channel, near Ryders Wynd. Randal joined the local regiment and by early 1917 he was a captain and Commanding Officer of "C" Company, 7th Battalion Yorkshire Regiment.

After participating in the Battle of Arras, the Battalion spent time behind the lines reorganising and refitting. On May 1st and 2nd the men moved by buses back to Arras. An ammunition dump exploded and the Battalion lost most of its equipment. The 12th May saw "B" and "C" Companies moving forward under a shrapnel barrage. Dust and smoke from the barrage made observation impossible once the attack was launched. At 7-30a.m. a message was received reporting that Captain Randal Croft of "C" Company had been killed, but that all the objectives had been gained, with the exception of three trenches. Randal Croft's body was never recovered and he is commemorated on Bay 5, Arras Memorial.

General Haig, after the abortive renewal of fighting around Arras to relieve German pressure on the French, had determined to break through between the North Sea and the River Lys. The Ypres Salient was selected, but success could only be gained after first taking the dominating Messines Ridge. On June 7th 1917, the Battle of Messines began, after a 17 day general bombardment. British mines, packed with one million pounds of high explosive, tore a wide gap in the German lines on the Ridge. Under cover of this surprise, in a carefully planned and organised attack, General Plumer's Second Army successfully gained the position. The success of the battle would come, however, at the cost of more lives from the dales. Elbowroom had been gained for the main offensive, and the clear-cut victory bolstered British morale.

PRIVATE JOHN THOMAS ALDERSON
NO. 32528 8TH BATTALION YORK AND LANCASTER REGIMENT
DIED JUNE 7TH 1917 AGED 33

John was born at West Hartlepool, the son of James and Elizabeth Alderson. His parents were both born at Reeth, but had gone to the east coast town because of James's work as a bookkeeper. All their children were born there, but by 1901 John, his three siblings and parents were living at Oakworth, between Haworth and Keighley, where James was still bookkeeping, his daughter was a worsted weaver, two of his sons were carpenters and his youngest child, John Thomas, was an 18 year old butcher. However, by 1914, James and Elizabeth, together with John, were back at Reeth, living at Oakworth House and Elizabeth running a general provisions shop.

John Thomas Alderson enlisted at Reeth and eventually joined the 8th Battalion York and Lancaster Regiment. By May 12th 1917 the Battalion was in the Hooge sector of the Ypres Salient, preparing for the Messines Ridge offensive, the object of which was to free the Ypres Salient from the enemy observation under which it had long suffered.

On June 7th they suffered heavy casualties from artillery fire prior to and during their movement to their forward assembly position in the "Blue Line". "A" Company suffered particularly badly, losing many of its officers and NCO's. Just beyond the line carried by the 8th Battalion lay a hillock, known as the Knoll, on which a party of the enemy was established. It was essential that they be driven off and Second Lieutenant Fraser, with a small party of men, charged the position, putting to flight the Germans who had rallied there.

In the intensive shelling that took place on June 7th, John Thomas Alderson was killed, and, as his body was never found, he is commemorated on Panels 36 and 55 Menin Gate Memorial.

A second man from the dales to die that day at Messines came from Richmond.

PRIVATE FREDERICK AMBROSE MANSFIELD
NO. 26333 9TH BATTALION YORKSHIRE REGIMENT
DIED JUNE 7TH 1917 AGED 27

Frederick Mansfield was born in Richmond and in 1901 he was a ten year old child living at the Richmond Union Workhouse. Ten years earlier, in 1891, he had been a two month old baby living with his parents, 50 year old Robert and 57 year old Elizabeth and three older siblings, on Tower Street, Richmond. Robert, a native of nearby Hipswell, was a rural postman for the Richmond area and had married Elizabeth, who originated from Sunderland. Sadly, by 1901, Robert and Elizabeth had died and this resulted in Frederick being placed in the Workhouse.

Later, he worked in the market town and enlisted from there on November 10th 1915, joining first of all the 3rd Battalion and then the 9th Yorkshire Regiment.

On June 7th 1917 the 9th Battalion attacked at 6-50a.m., but after the first 200 yards the undergrowth became increasingly thick and snipers and machine gun fire caused many casualties, whilst a great deal of flanking fire held them up. The Battalion was forced to dig in on the southern edge of Battle Wood, owing to the heavy machine gun fire from emplacements making further advance impossible. 266 men from the Battalion became casualties on June 7th and one of those killed by shell fire was Frederick Ambrose Mansfield. His name joined that of John Thomas Alderson on the Menin Gate, on Panel 33.

His older brother, Robert, aged 32, had died from wounds and disease at Gallipoli on September 11th 1915. Before the war he had worked as a farm labourer for John Pickersgill of Village Farm, Hudswell (now Grange Close Farm). He was buried at Mudros Bay, on the island of Lemnos, but sadly his name is not commemorated on either the Richmond or Hudswell Memorial. He was, however, remembered by his employer, John Pickersgill, for the details of his death in the Dardanelles are inscribed on John's tombstone, in Hudswell churchyard.

A third man, this time from Starbotton, near Kettlewell, was killed in action on the second day of the Battle of Messines.

DRIVER RICHARD DENT TENNANT NO. 165461
2ND DIVISION AMMUNITION COLUMN ROYAL FIELD ARTILLERY
DIED JUNE 8TH 1917 AGED 23

Richard was the youngest son and sixth of nine children of Christopher and Edith Tennant of Bushey Lodge Farm, Starbotton. Christopher was born at Thoralby and married Edith, a girl from Walden, near West Burton, and they started farming at Newbiggin before moving to Cray, near Buckden. Four of their children were born there but in 1894 the family moved to Bushey Lodge and Richard was born that year. He worked on his father's farm when he left school, but when he was called up he enlisted at Skipton, and, being used to handling horses, he became a driver for the Royal Field Artillery, harnessing the horses to the guns and driving them into position.

The Battle of Messines was an artillery man's battle, with a preliminary bombardment lasting 18 days. The artillery was used effectively during the 7th and 8th June and needed to advance and keep up with the infantry. Bringing up the ammunition was a vital and dangerous job and the batteries and ammunition supply columns were important targets for the opposing German gunners.

Richard Tennant was severely wounded in action by the explosion of a large shell on June 8th and died shortly afterwards at the dressing station he was taken to. All he was heard to say was that he wished his mother was there. Richard was buried by the artillery chaplain just below the lines at 3p.m. on June 10th in grave I.A.17. Vlamertinghe New Military Cemetery, 5 kilometres west of Ypres.

A memorial service was held at Kettlewell Church, which was filled with a congregation from all parts of Upper Wharfedale. The Dead March was played by the organist, the National Anthem sung and the flag was flown at half mast.

The next soldier to die was not involved in the battles unfolding in the Ypres Salient, but was taking part in routine front line duties.

Richard Dent Tennant from Starbotton, near Kettlewell
Courtesy of The Craven Herald

PRIVATE JOHN FAWCETT
NO. 40330 18TH BATTALION WEST YORKSHIRE REGIMENT
DIED JUNE 16TH 1917 AGED 37

John was born at Castle Bolton, Wensleydale, in 1880, into a farming family keeping dairy cattle. By 1901 he was living with his mother Ann, a single woman of 58 years, and working on the family farm. However, by 1914, his mother had died and he was living with his cousin, Annie Wade, at Japonica House, and later Moorview Cottage, Halton East, on the Duke of Devonshire's Bolton Abbey Estate.

Enlisting at Halifax, he joined the 18th Battalion West Yorkshire Regiment and by June 10th 1917 they were providing working parties on the front line near Arras. 100 men, under the supervision of the Royal Engineers, carried trench boards to the support line and helped widen the trenches.

They relieved another Battalion in the front line on the Arras-Gavrelle Road on the 14th June but on leaving the trenches on the night of the 15th a High Velocity shell exploded at 9p.m., causing 13 casualties, one of them being John Fawcett. He was taken to the casualty clearing station but died the next day, June 16th, and was buried in grave III.H.36. in Aubigny Communal Cemetery Extension, 15 kilometres NW of Arras, on the road to St. Pol. John Fawcett is commemorated on both the Castle Bolton Memorial and the memorial at Bolton Abbey.

A soldier from Richmond died close by on that same day, whilst taking part in an attack.

PRIVATE FRED JOHNSON
NO. 32098 12TH BATTALION NORTHUMBERLAND FUSILIERS
DIED JUNE 16TH 1917 AGED 25

The Johnson family was living in Waterloo Street, Richmond, in 1901. George Johnson, a general labourer, had married Eliza, a Richmond girl, and Fred was the eldest of their four children. By 1917 George and Eliza were living at 20 Bargate, but Fred had already enlisted at Richmond and joined the 12th Battalion, Northumberland Fusiliers.

Early June 1917 found the Battalion in France, just to the SE of Arras, at Croisilles, close up to the new German front line. On the evening of June 15th they marched towards their assembly positions, passing through heavy shelling in the village of Croisilles and in the Sensee Valley, where a few casualties were sustained.

At 3-10a.m. on June 16th, under cover of a barrage, the attack began on a trench 300 yards away, but it was met by a heavy barrage and machine gun and rifle fire. Nearer to the objective they were met with showers of stick grenades. Despite this, an entry was made into Tunnel Trench by a small party from "D" and "C" Companies, where, after a desperate hand to hand fight, they were overwhelmed by superior numbers and all became casualties. "B" Company were mainly occupying shell holes in front of the enemy's trench. On the evening of June 16th the remains of the Battalion were forced to withdraw. Of the 401 men who attacked, 214 became casualties and Fred Johnson was one of those whose body was never recovered. His name can be found on Bays 2 and 3 of the Arras Memorial.

DRIVER/FITTER ROBERT GRAHAM WETHERELL
NO. 99991 "D" BATTERY 161ST BRIGADE ROYAL FIELD ARTILLERY
DIED JUNE 20TH 1917 AGED 37

I have been unable to find with certainty details about R. Wetherell from off the Richmond Memorial but he could possibly be Robert Graham Wetherell of the Royal Field Artillery. Born at South Shields and enlisting at South Shields he died of wounds in France, on June 20th after spending time at the hospital complex at Rouen. He was buried in grave P.II.P.4B. St. Sever Cemetery Extension, Rouen.

A British heavy howitzer battery in action on the Somme

PRIVATE EDWARD BOYLE
NO. 81865 97TH COMPANY MACHINE GUN CORPS
DIED JUNE 28TH 1917

Born at Newcastle-on-Tyne, Edward Boyle was working in the Richmond area at the start of the Great War and enlisted there, joining first of all the Royal Army Service Corps. By 1917, however, he had joined the Machine Gun Corps, formed in October 1915, using mainly Vickers machine guns. By the Battle of Messines, machine gunners were also employing creeping barrages, with fire falling ahead of the artillery barrage, to catch troops moving to the rear. They would concentrate on specific targets, or sweep the enemy ground behind his front. For these tasks, the guns were placed 1000 yards behind the advancing infantry and were moved up as soon as the enemy positions were captured. Machine gun tactics had in fact become more like those of the artillery than of the infantry.

Edward Boyle was killed in action on the NW fringes of the Ypres Salient on June 28th. His body was not recovered and his name is found on Newport Military Cemetery, Memorial 4, Ramscappelle Road Military Cemetery, near the Belgian coastal town of Nieuwpoort.

GUNNER JOSEPH BARRELL
NO. 64155 57TH SIEGE BATTERY ROYAL GARRISON ARTILLERY
DIED JULY 24TH 1917 AGED 28

Joseph was born at Polsted, a small village 8 miles north of Colchester, Essex, and when he was killed his mother Esther was still in that region, living at Frating, 4 miles east of Colchester. However, James was working in the Richmond area of North Yorkshire when he enlisted at the market town and was soon training as a gunner in a siege battery of the Royal Garrison Artillery.

The capture of Messines Ridge was almost the only true siege warfare attack made throughout a siege war and secured the high ground that had given the enemy complete observation of the British trenches and forward gun battery positions. Joseph had been involved in the success of the Battle of Messines, in which the artillery bombardment had lasted 18 days, and he had survived to fight another day. He was a gunner in a siege battery, which consisted of six guns, each of 9.2 inch calibre, and was involved in bombardment and counter-bombardment roles.

Six weeks after the conclusion of the Battle of Messines the offensive to capture Passchendaele Ridge began. The bombardment proper opened on July 22nd and continued for ten days. It was in the exchange of artillery fire between the British and German batteries that Joseph Barrell was killed by shell fire. His body was buried in grave I.G.7. Canada Farm Cemetery, 8 kilometres NW of Ypres.

On July 26th, five days before the infantry went "over the top" at the Battle of Passchendaele, a servicman from the Keld and Muker area was killed in the Ypres Salient on a raid to test the strength of the German positions before the main offensive started.

PRIVATE RICHARD ALDERSON
NO. 28136 "C" COMPANY 2ND BATTALION YORKSHIRE REGIMENT
DIED JULY 26TH 1917 AGED 21

Richard was the third of six children of William and Margaret Alderson, and was born at their farmhouse at Skeugh Head, near Angram, between Keld and Thwaite in Swaledale. Their other children were Sarah, Mary Alice, Jane, Margaret and John. When he left Keld School, Richard helped his father run the sheep farm, although by that time they were living at nearby Angram. In his spare time he was a member of Keld Band.

Richard Alderson, from Angram, between Keld and Muker

Richard enlisted at a recruitment meeting at Satron, near Gunnerside, and became a member of "C" Company 2nd Battalion Yorkshire Regiment. In the latter stages of the Battle of the Somme, Richard was wounded and returned to a convalescent hospital in England. On December 30th 1916 his eldest sister Sarah died, aged 26, after an illness that resulted in her having a leg amputated. He was able to come home to Keld to attend her funeral, the last time the family would see him, for in early 1917 he returned to his regiment on the Western Front. Before he left Keld he mentioned a number of times that he believed he would not return.

Richard Alderson, standing on the far left, whilst convalescing, after being wounded

The 2nd Battalion was in the Ypres Salient from May 1917. In late July they moved up to Dickebusche Huts in readiness for a daylight raid into the enemy lines, arranged for July 26th, five days before the "Big Push". "C" Company, with Richard Alderson, penetrated to Jeffrey Reserve Trench, following the barrage steadily, but as the barrage went on, the raiding party had to come back without any artillery protection, and the enemy was able to fire heavily upon it as it fell back from Jackdaw Beck. One German officer and ten of his men were brought back as prisoners, but 47 men became casualties. Richard's premonition became a reality when he was struck down in No Man's Land as they returned to their own lines.

A letter arrived at the Alderson farmhouse from Lieutenant Law stating, "There is no doubt about the fact that he was killed in the raid as I told you. He will be buried with the other men, but

Sarah Alderson, sister of Richard. He came home on leave to attend her funeral in December 1916.

Keld School 1911 (Waller Hutchinson died in the Great War)
Back row: Ralph Scott, George Scott, Ernest Harker, John Thornborrow, Waller Hutchinson, John George Reynoldson, Ernest Whitehead, Percy Metcalfe, Bob Thornborrow, Dick Scott
Next row: Mary Scott, Maggie Alderson, Lizzie Metcalfe, Janey Alderson, Jane Metcalfe, Jennie Hutchinson, Madge Metcalfe, Lizzie Matcalfe, Mary Ann Rukin, Jessie Parrington, Agnes Reynoldson
Next row: John Metcalfe, Frances Alderson, Gladys Alderson, Annas Alderson, Maggie Scott, Nanny Metcalfe, Chrissie Waggett, Mary Kilburn, Janey Metcalfe, Dick Scott, Bobbie Hutchinson
Front row: John Reynoldson, George Metcalfe, Sam Clarkson, John Herbert Clarkson, George Clarkson, John Metcalfe, John Willie Alderson, Ernest Reynoldson
Teachers Mr. Brooksbank and Margaret Elizabeth Metcalfe

Keld School 1917
Back row: Brian Fawcett, John Henry Kilburn, Edward Clarkson, George Clarkson, John Reynoldson, Dick Scott, Bobbie Hutchinson, Sam Clarkson
2nd row: Phylis Clarkson, Mary Scott, Sally Scott, Nanie Metcalfe, Francis Alderson, Olive Parrington, Mary Kilburn, Lizzie Clarkson, Edna Parrington, Maggie Alderson, Esther Parrington, Mary Metcalfe, Jean ?
Front row: George Alderson, Bob Scott, Will Alderson, Geoffrey Fawcett, Jack Alderson, George Alderson, James Robert Fawcett, Jack Scott, ? Calvert. Teacher Mr. Brooksbank

unidentified because on a raid no one wears their identity disc for fear of capture. A burial party went out as soon as it was dark and fairly safe and buried all the regimental casualties together. There are many nameless dead and many who are never buried except by shells. God bless and comfort you."

Another letter from friends at Thwaite reads, "Very sorry to hear of the death of your dear son. I have felt very uneasy since I received his last letter to say he had no faith of coming back to see us all. He has been able to see further than we could. For your dear son and our dear brother Tom (they were family of Tom Clarkson, who had been fatally wounded and brought home to be buried at Muker) it should never have had to be if this awful war had never begun. It feels very hard when it has come so near to us all, it is so hard to bear."

We have seen that his only grave was an unmarked, makeshift one on the battlefield and instead, Richard's name is commemorated on Panel 33, Menin Gate, at Ypres.

At 3-30a.m. on July 31st 1917 the Third Battle of Ypres (Passchendaele) began, with the infantry of twelve divisions advancing on an eleven mile front, to the accompaniment of torrential rain. On the opening day of the battle a man from the Langstrothdale area lost his life, the first of 23 dalesmen to die during the horrendous fighting of the next three and a half months.

Keld School 1919
Back row: Chris Alderson, Bobby Hutchinson, Edmund Clarkson, Nick Scott, Sam Clarkson, Henry Kilburn, Jack Alderson
Next row: Maggie Waggett (teacher), Mary Kilburn, Lizzie Clarkson, Chrissie Waggett, Frances Alderson, Nanny Metcalfe, Lilly Kirkbride, George Alderson, Esther Parrington, Teacher Miss Parkin
Next row: Brian Fawcett, Lena Kirkbride, Jack Scott, Mary Metcalfe, Bob Scott, Phyllis Clarkson, James Robert Fawcett, Amelia Alderson
Next row: Jack Alderson, Geoffrey Fawcett, Sarah Lizzie Alderson, Nellie Alderson, Will Alderson, Jack Alderson (Pat)
Front row: Nellie Alderson (Harkers), Annie Clarkson, Ella Harker, Lizzie Metcalfe, Alice Metcalfe

GUARDSMAN MATTHEW HOLMES
NO. 26923 1ST BATTALION GRENADIER GUARDS
DIED JULY 31ST 1917 AGED 27

In 1901 the Holmes family, consisting of parents Jeffrey and Isabella and children Margaret, 11 year old Matthew, Christopher and Albert were living at the isolated hamlet of Far Greenfield, at the head of Langstrothdale. Jeffrey, born at Hawes, as was his wife, was a gamekeeper working for Mr. Garnet-Orme of Low Greenfield Hall, and owner of the Greenfield Estate. After leaving Oughtershaw School, Matthew trained as a gamekeeper on the same estate and by the start of the war he was the head gamekeeper and shepherd. He lived at Throstle Nest Farm with his wife Edith and daughters Kathleen (b.1909) and Dorothy Margery (b. 1914). Matthew was called up in October 1916 and joined the Grenadier Guards, whilst Edith took the children to live in Kettlewell.

On July 31st 1917 the 1st Battalion Grenadier Guards were to attack towards Boesinghe. Whilst taking up their assembly positions on the 30th they suffered losses to enemy shelling, but at 4-28a.m. on the 31st they advanced behind the creeping barrage, some companies getting dangerously close. Fifty enemy prisoners were taken from German dugouts and the first objective, the Blue Line, was taken fairly easily. Further waves, meeting stronger resistance, took the second and third objectives and at 9-50a.m. the Battalion was ordered to withdraw. During the attack they had captured four machine guns and two Minenwerfers, but had sustained 119 casualties. One of those hit by an exploding shell was Matthew Holmes and he is commemorated on Panel 9 and 11 Menin Gate.

On the following day another Langstrothdale man died in the same battle, succumbing to his wounds.

Mathhew Holmes
from High Greenfield, Langstrothdale, near Buckden
Courtesy of The Craven Herald

PRIVATE MATTHIAS DIXON
NO. 18774 2ND BATTALION COLDSTREAM GUARDS
DIED AUGUST 1ST 1917 AGED 23

Matthias Dixon from Buckden
Courtesy of The Craven Herald

In the years before the Great War, the Dixon family lived at The Grange, a farmhouse between Buckden and Hubberholme. Edmund Dixon was born at Starbotton but raised at Kidstones Farm, Bishopdale. Aged 21, he married Jane, a girl from Thoralby, near West Burton. For 11 years they farmed at Walden, near West Burton, before moving to The Grange in 1896. Matthias was born at Walden and was the second eldest of four children, his siblings being Mary Jane, Jeffrey and Frances. Sheep provided the main income at the Grange, but Frances, the youngest child, remembered when the cows would be walked the 20 miles to Skipton market. As the eldest son, Matthias worked at The Grange as his father's right hand man. The whole family were church goers and in his spare time, Matthias was a chorister and bell ringer at Hubberholme Church.

However, on August 15th 1916 he travelled to Skipton to enlist and joined the Coldstream Guards, before embarking for France on January 31st 1917. Six months later they were in the Ypres Salient and about to take part in the new offensive. At dawn on July 31st the Battalion crossed the Yser Canal, passed through the 2nd and 3rd Guards Brigades which had attacked their objectives, and advanced to secure the crossing of the Steenbeek (a large stream). There was hostile shell fire and the casualties mounted.

As they reached their final objective, they began to dig in but the ground was very wet and the ranks were getting thin and so they had no great volume of rifle fire. All the night it rained in torrents and continued for the whole of August 1st. The trenches were ditches of water, with everyone standing in water up to their thighs and terribly cold. The Battalion HQ was in a concrete German blockhouse which was continuously shelled with all calibre of weapons..

Matthias Dixon was wounded on August 1st and taken to a casualty clearing station, where he died from his wounds. He is buried in grave II.D.4. Dozinghem Military Cemetery. The following week a memorial service was held for Matthias at Hubberholme Church by the Reverend Anderton.

PRIVATE BASIL GILL NEWALL
NO. 24770 "Y" COMPANY 8TH BATTALION WEST RIDING REGIMENT
DIED AUGUST 8TH 1917 AGED 19

Basil was a three year old child in 1901, living with his parents, Samuel and Mary Elizabeth Newall and older brother Alan and younger siblings Rex and Ellen, at the

Basil Gill Newall from Beamsley, near Bolton Abbey

Right: Rex and Alan Gill, brothers of Basil.

farmhouse home of his maternal grandparents, Thomas and Charlotte Gill. They lived at Deerstones, a tiny hamlet on the Bolton Abbey Estate, and later, a fifth child, Roy, would be born.

Samuel's mother, Isabella Newall, had gone to Stornaway on the Hebrides to help her brother run a farm and produce tweed, and it was there that Samuel was born. They returned to the Bolton Abbey area a few years later and eventually Samuel married local girl, Mary Elizabeth Gill. Prior to the Great War, their son Basil helped with the farm work but both he and his brother Alan were enlisted in the army at Keighley, with Basil joining in September 1916 and being posted to the 8th Battalion, before embarking for France in January 1917. Periods of training were often interspersed with opportunities for sporting competition and Basil showed an aptitude for long distance running, becoming the champion for his Battalion.

During 1917 Alan was travelling with his battalion by train across France. As the train came to a halt beside one of many orchards, the soldiers descended from the wagons to pick the fruit, and by tremendous coincidence, he discovered his brother Basil "scrumping" apples from the same tree. It was to be the last time that Alan saw his brother.

On Sunday 6th August, Basil's Battalion was in billets at Poperinghe, but the following day they arrived at the Canal Bank, Ypres, and took over the front line trench by the 7th. Between August 8th and 11th the Battalion was simply holding the line, sustaining casualties from shelling and gas.

During this period an attack by "Y" and "Z" Companies on a strongpoint opposite Langemarck took place and the position held till 4p.m. but they were forced to withdraw owing to heavy machine gun fire and the large, superior force of enemy. Basil was badly wounded in both legs and taken to No. 4 Casualty Clearing Station, where he passed away at 5-35p.m., a few hours after admittance. He was buried in grave II.F.5. Dozinghem Military Cemetery, to the NW of Poperinghe.

Thankfully, his older brother, Alan, would survive the war, whilst his younger brother, Roy, would serve in the Second World War and survive that conflict.

PRIVATE GILL MORRELL
NO. 267210 5TH BATTALION WEST RIDING REGIMENT
DIED AUGUST 16TH 1917 AGED 33

Gill's father, John Gill Morrell was born at Stainburn, a small village 8 miles to the SW of Harrogate and married Rachel, a girl from Ripon. They lived at Stainburn, where John was a farm labourer, and they raised six children, Gill being the second eldest. In 1901, his older brother, William, was a fish trader, whilst 17 year old Gill was a groom. However, by 1914, Gill was living on the Bolton Abbey Estate and working as a gardener at Bolton Hall.

He enlisted at Keighley and joined the 5th Battalion West Riding Regiment, finding himself in the front line trenches in the Ypres Salient during the early stages of the Battle of Passchendaele. Gill was badly wounded in early August, treated for his wounds and then brought back ten miles behind the lines to the village of Coxyde (Koksijde), where he died. He is buried in grave II.J.6. Coxyde Military Cemetery, Belgium.

GUNNER (CORPORAL) JOHN ALDERSON SCOTT
NO. 157720 287TH SIEGE BATTERY ROYAL GARRISON ARTILLERY
DIED AUGUST 16TH 1917 AGED 29

In 1891, John Scott, or Jack as he was known, was a two year old, living with his family at the hamlet of Whaw, in Arkengarthdale. His father, James, was a miner in the nearby Arkengarthdale lead mines and had married a local girl, Hannah Caygill. By 1901 the family was living close to the CB Yard, near Langthwaite, and, as a boy, Jack also worked in the lead mine, but the industry was coming to a close and so the family left the dale shortly after this and went to Ferryhill, 8 miles south of Durham, where the menfolk of the family worked at the Mainsforth Colliery.

John Alderson Scott from Arkengarthdale

Jack met Mather Daglish, a girl from Dipton, near Consett, and they married at Durham. By the time of Jack's death they had five children, the youngest being six months old. Despite such a large family, Jack volunteered and was in the army by 1915, joining a siege battery of the Royal Garrison Artillery, whilst Mather and their children went to stay at Langthwaite, in Arkengarthdale.

In July 1917, Jack's heavy siege battery was in the Ypres Salient and taking part in the 10 day bombardment prior to the Battle of Passchendaele. The British artillery strength totalled 3091 guns, of which 999 were heavy. The infantry attack on July 31st was relatively successful on the left but was held up on the right. The second blow across the narrow Steenbeek valley towards Langemarck, on August 16th, was a diminished replica of the first in its results. It was in this attack that Jack (John) Scott was killed.

In a letter from Major Withers, his CO, he says that Jack volunteered to assist the signallers, who were short handed, in forward observation duties during the attack on Thursday August 16th. He had appealed to his CO again and again for permission to go forward and see an attack and this time he reluctantly gave way. The party were caught by a machine gun and Jack was killed instantly. In the middle of such a large scale battle, with shells exploding all around, it is not surprising that his body was never recovered and John Alderson Scott's name is commemorated on Panel 6 to 7 and 162 Tyne Cot Memorial.

Jack's death left a widow and five young children. Mather Scott remained in Arkengarthdale, living at Calva View, Arkletown, until her death in the 1930's.

PRIVATE ARTHUR JAMSON
NO. 12759 10TH BATTALION DURHAM LIGHT INFANTRY
DIED AUGUST 22ND 1917 AGED 32

In 1901 Arthur Jamson was a 15 year old grocer's assistant, born in Richmond. He was living at Bargate in the town, with his father, Thomas, a hairdresser, mother Susannah, and five other siblings. We have already seen that Arthur's brother was killed whilst serving with the BEF in 1914. Arthur travelled to Darlington to enlist and joined the 10th Battalion, Durham Light Infantry.

The Battalion arrived at the Zillebeke Bund, SE of Ypres, on August 20th and the line was reconnoitred west of Inverness Copse. At 2a.m. on August 22nd the Battalion came forward through a bombardment of gas shells to occupy support positions for the attack.

By the time a hostile barrage in Sanctuary Wood was passed, casualties amounted to 60. Two hours later they joined in the attack in the vicinity of Dry Lakes, capturing a machine gun, reaching Herenthage Chateau and accepting the surrender of the garrison of 50 men.

Few of these POW's or guards survived the journey back to the British lines because of the intensity of the enemy shelling. Meanwhile, two platoons went forward and dug a post north of Inverness Copse, lying in a chain of shell holes in front of a trench they had taken.

Arthur Jamson, however, had been killed by enemy shellfire and his name is commemorated on Panel 128 to 131 and 162 and 162A Tyne Cot Memorial.

PRIVATE BERNARD TENNANT
NO. 43602 8TH BATTALION MANCHESTER REGIMENT
DIED SEPTEMBER 9TH 1917 AGED 23

Bernard was the youngest of two sons of John Drake Tennant, a Manchester butcher, and Margaret Tennant. Bernard, his brother James and sister Rosamund were born in Manchester and lived at Alexandra Road, with the family business located first at Cheetham Hill and then Mosside. The Manor House at Buckden, Wharfedale, with its associated farm and land, was also owned by John Drake Tennant and each weekend he would arrive by train at Threshfield Station and travel to Buckden by horse and trap, to work on the farm. During the week it was run by employees (we have already seen that one of these, Wilfred Ewart Holmes, had died of wounds in late 1916).

Bernard enlisted at Manchester in November 1914, eventually joining the 8th Battalion Manchester Regiment and going to France in July 1916, where he was wounded and returned home in March 1917. Meanwhile, his brother James had joined the Army Service Corps (Remount Section) and served at Gallipoli and in Salonika (it is interesting to note that their great uncle, Sergeant John Tennant, had fought in the Grenadier Guards at the Crimean War).

Bernard returned to the Western Front in June 1917 and went into the Ypres Salient. On September 7th the Battalion marched via the Menin Gate and Millcot to the front line, with headquarters at Low Farm. As preparations were made for a third strike into the enemy positions, planned for September 20th, Bernard Tennant was killed by shell fire whilst in the trenches on September 9th. At irregular intervals

Above: Bernard Tennant from Buckden and Manchester (in civilian life before the War)

Right: Bernard Tennant from Buckden and Manchester
Courtesy of The Craven Herald

during the day, British artillery put a five minute barrage on enemy strongpoints. Most of these barrages were replied to by hostile batteries, especially on Square Farm and the support companies. Orders for the relief came but casualties for September 9th were 6 men killed, 21 men wounded and 13 men gassed. A high explosive shell killed Bernard. The damage caused by such weapons meant that there was no possibility of a burial, and his name is commemorated on the Tyne Cot Memorial.

The next fatality occurred away from the action at Passchendaele, when a man from the Grassington and Colne areas was killed in France.

PRIVATE THOMAS (TOM) WATERS
NO. 29053 7TH BATTALION EAST LANCASHIRE REGIMENT
DIED SEPTEMBER 24TH 1917 AGED 22

Tom was the second eldest of the children of Albert and Elizabeth Waters, and in 1901 the family was living at the Raikes, Hartlington, near Burnsall, before taking up residence in Grassington. Albert had been born at Pateley Bridge and married Elizabeth, a girl from Eastby, near Skipton, supporting his young family by working as a stone mason. When Tom grew up he did what many people from the dales were forced to do and sought work in the Lancashire mill town of Colne.

It was from there that Tom enlisted and joined the 7th Battalion East Lancashire Regiment in August 1916, travelling to France in January 1917. Whilst in the front line trenches near Bailleul, close to the border with Belgium, he was wounded by shell fire and died on September 24th, after being admitted to hospital. The Battalion chaplain wrote to his mother, telling her that he was fond of Tom and had prepared him for his confirmation in July. He came to receive the Holy Communion regularly and took the last opportunity he had of receiving it before he went into the line for the last time.

Tom Waters was buried in grave I.B.8. Outtersteene Communal Cemetery Extension, Bailleul, France.

Between September 26th and 27th three men from Swaledale (Downholme, Reeth and Richmond) died at the Battle of Passchendaele whilst serving in the same Battalion.

Tom Waters of Grassington
Courtesy of The Craven Herald

LANCE CORPORAL GEORGE JEFFERSON
NO. 14492 6TH BATTALION YORKSHIRE REGIMENT
DIED SEPTEMBER 26TH 1917 AGED 22

Willie Jefferson of Downholme, brother of George

George's father, James Jefferson, was born at Downholme and married Jane, a Leyburn girl. He was a smallholder, but his main income came from the quarry he owned at nearby Stainton, where green slate for roofs was produced. George was the third eldest son out of a family of ten children, and when he grew up he helped his father and worked for the local council. He collected slate from the quarry on his horse and cart for Richmond Station and brought back coal for the villagers. George would also break up the stone from the quarry and use it to repair the roads for the council. When George enlisted he went to Leyburn and joined the 6th Battalion Yorkshire Regiment. In the same Battalion he was joined by Henry Haw from Reeth and John Robinson from Richmond, and all three would be killed within the space of two days.

AND
PRIVATE HENRY HAW
NO. 20312 6TH BATTALION YORKSHIRE REGIMENT
DIED SEPTEMBER 27TH 1917 AGED 22

In 1901 the Haw family was living at Ellerton Lodge, near Downholme, where Henry's father was a farmer and postman. He had been born at Marske, nearby, and had married Ada, who had been born in Jersey. Henry, aged 5, was the youngest of their three children in 1901 and all had been born at Marske. However, we have already seen that the Webster family arrived at Ellerton Lodge some years before the war, for the Haw family had moved to a farm at Marrick, near Reeth. Henry volunteered and enlisted at Richmond on February 6th 1915, training with the 3rd Battalion before being posted to the 6th Battalion Yorkshire Regiment, where he joined his near neighbour, George Jefferson.

AND
PRIVATE JOHN ROBINSON
NO. 26562 6TH BATTALION YORKSHIRE REGIMENT
DIED SEPTEMBER 27TH 1917 AGED 27

We have already seen that William Robinson, a Richmond man and the brother of John, was killed on November 19th 1914 with the BEF in Belgium (see Chapter Two for the family background). Unlike his brother, John was not a Territorial, and it was not until February 1916 that he was called up and joined the 6th Battalion.

After taking part in the main operations in the Battle of Passchendaele during August and incurring many casualties, the 6th Battalion spent the first three weeks of September in the vicinity of Poperinghe. On September 24th they moved by rail to Reigersberg and marched from there to dug-outs in the Yser Canal Bank, remaining here during the night and then taking over the front line trenches, or rather shell holes, where, during the three days of the tour, the Battalion came under very heavy shelling and sustained 93 casualties.

George Jefferson was killed by shell fire on September 26th and was buried in grave XI.A.14. Bedford House Cemetery, one mile south of Ypres. One day later, both Henry Haw and John Robinson were killed by shell fire, with Henry's name being commemorated on the Tyne Cot Memorial and John being buried in grave IV.C.17. Cement House Cemetery, near Langemark.

PRIVATE BENJAMIN BEAUMONT
NO. 41274 2ND BATTALION SUFFOLK REGIMENT
DIED SEPTEMBER 27TH 1917 AGED 23

Benjamin's father, Benjamin Beaumont senior, was born at Birkenhead and married Margaret, a Yorkshire girl. By the late 1870's they were living at Hebden, where their first child, Eveline was born in 1879. By 1901 they were living on Chapel Lane and seven year old Benjamin was the youngest of five children, with their father employed as a grocer's assistant. Benjamin's older brother Fred had a withered hand, but still managed to pump the church organ and became the caretaker at Hebden School. We can see from the photograph of the Grassington Volunteers, in Chapter Two, that Benjamin went into the army at a very early stage of the war and during the next three years he served with first the West Riding Regiment, then with the Sherwood Foresters and when he died he was with the 2nd Battalion Suffolk Regiment.

Ben Beaumont from Hebden
Courtesy of
The Craven Herald

They found themselves involved at Passchendaele,

Hebden School concert 1908
Left to right: Jack Moore, Tom Worsley, Ben Beaumont, John Kitching, Bayne Knowles, David Bell

especially in a series of limited attacks on narrow fronts beginning from September 20th, as the British inched forward against determined counter-attacks. Mustard gas was used here for the first time by the Germans, while German planes flew low to strafe British infantry. One of these attacks began on the 26th and the following day, as the Battalion attempted to push forward through the mud and desolation of the battlefield, against intensive shelling directed from the heights of the Ridge, Benjamin Beaumont was struck down. His name was yet one more to add to the mounting roll on the Tyne Cot Memorial.

LIEUTENANT MILES BENNISON
9TH BATTALION YORKSHIRE REGIMENT
DIED OCTOBER 1ST 1917 AGED 27

Miles Bennison had strong connections with Richmond. James Bennison, the father of Miles, was born at North Cowton, a village five miles to the east of Scotch Corner, and married Elizabeth, who came from Gunnerside. In 1901 they and their three children, including Miles, were still living at North Cowton, where James was a road labourer.

Early in the war, Miles , who was married by this time, was serving in the army and by July 1917 he and the 9th Battalion Yorkshire Regiment were in the Ypres Salient. On the night of September 30th they took over the front line south of Polygon Wood. At 5a.m. on October 1st the enemy opened a very intense artillery barrage, resulting in the severance of all communication. Four enemy planes flew low over the Battalion lines and worked in concert with the German infantry, causing many deaths through use of their machine guns.

One company came under infantry attack and their Lewis gun was knocked out. In great danger of being encircled, they were withdrawn. The men were reorganised under Lieutenant Miles Bennison, the Company commander, and were led forward by him in a counter-attack. During this advance Miles Bennison was struck down and the men were forced to retire as the Germans attacked once again. Miles Bennison's body was left on the battlefield and never recovered. His name has been added to the Tyne Cot Memorial. He left a widow, Marion.

GUNNER ROBERT GEORGE ALLINSON
NO. 20583 79TH BRIGADE ROYAL FIELD ARTILLERY
DIED OCTOBER 2ND 1917 AGED 30

Robert's brother, Thompson Allinson, had already been killed in September 1916 (see Chapter Four). The Allinson family from Grinton, near Reeth, sent four brothers to the war and two died whilst serving their country. Robert joined the Royal Field Artillery as a Gunner and in late September 1917 was wounded in France. He was taken to hospital but as a result of his wounds and the onset of pneumonia, he died on October 2nd and was buried in grave V.B.45. Duisans British Cemetery, Etrun.

Robert George Allinson of Grinton and Richmond

His brother Matthew had served in Gallipoli and Egypt and had been wounded, whilst his brother, James, serving in the Yorkshire Regiment, won the Military Medal for his bravery. On February 23rd 1918, James was the guest of honour at a gathering held in the Congregational Schoolroom at Reeth, when schoolmaster J.W. Moore presented him with five war saving certificates and a watch on behalf of the Reeth district inhabitants. Private Allinson had been recommended for the MM by his captain who was mortally wounded in a surprise attack. James had crossed open ground under severe shell and machine gun fire in order to fetch reinforcements to save the day.

PRIVATE OBADIAH WILLIAM PEACOCK
NO. 30520 8TH BATTALION EAST LANCASHIRE REGIMENT
DIED OCTOBER 6TH 1917 AGED 30

Obadiah's parents, Abel and Catherine Peacock, and their children, Mary Jane, Arthur, Lawrence, Margaret, Obadiah and Ellen, were all born in Arkengarthdale. Abel had been involved in lead mining, but as the industry declined, the whole family moved away to seek employment and in 1901 they were to be found at 20 Prince Street, Haworth, near Keighley, with Abel employed as a wool comber. Their second youngest child, 14 year old Obadiah, was working as a Worsted setter in one of the mills.

Obadiah William Peacock of Arkengarthdale and Haworth

Obadiah Peacock volunteered to join the colours in October 1914 and joined the Army Service Corps. Prior to this he had been employed by Messrs. Prince Smith and Son, Keighley, machine makers for the local mills, with their factory close to Keighley Railway Station. By this stage he was married to his wife Catherine and they lived at 3 Main Street, Haworth.

He spent nearly three years with the ASC, firstly in Ireland, and then in December 1915 he embarked for France. In 1917 he transferred to the infantry and joined the 8th Battalion East Lancs. Late September of that year saw them in the Ypres Salient and preparing for another "push" on October 8th in the Battle of Passchendaele. There was rain on each day from October 3rd and the conditions underfoot became atrocious, with glutinous mud and standing water.

However, two days before the launch of the attack, Obadiah was killed by shell fire whilst near the front line trenches. His name appears on the Tyne Cot Memorial, near Ypres, on the Haworth War Memorial, but not on the Arkengarthdale War Memorial at Langthwaite. Instead, his sister had a plaque put up in Langthwaite Church, in honour of Obadiah.

During the 24 hours of October 9th three more dalesmen fell, with another fatality on the following day.

PRIVATE THOMAS G. SIDDALL
NO. 260083 6TH BATTALION WEST YORKSHIRE REGIMENT
DIED OCTOBER 9TH 1917 AGED 33

In 1901, seventeen year old Thomas Siddall was working as an apprentice draper in Stockton-on-Tees and was lodging at the home of Sarah Taylor, on Palmerstone Street. He had been born in Richmond, the son of John and Anne Siddall, of Frenchgate, Richmond. John originated from Eppleby, west of Darlington, whilst Ann was a native of Well, near Masham. In Richmond they ran a family business, with John being a tailor and his wife a draper. Thomas, junior, returned to Richmond to enlist and joined the Northumberland Fusiliers, before being transferred to the 6th Battalion West Yorkshire Regiment.

The Battalion was in the Ypres Salient in early October and was to take part in the battle for the village of Poelcapelle (9th October) during Passchendaele. After the respite in September, rain fell almost unceasingly throughout October, and, with the continuing barrage, destroyed the few remaining signs of roads and tracks. By this time the whole area had reverted to a porridge of mud. Mules and horses (even men) were known to have sunk beneath it with their loads; guns could find no solid ground to fire from; and it took 16 bearers instead of 2 to carry each stretcher case the 4000 yards to the field dressing stations.

On October 8th, the day before the "push" for Poelcapelle, there was torrential rain. In terrible conditions, Thomas Siddall's Battalion began its advance and was met by intensive shelling and machine gun fire. Thomas was killed on this day and his body was submerged in the quagmire. There is no gravestone for the Richmond draper but instead his name is inscribed on the Tyne Cot Memorial.

PRIVATE (SAPPER) JOHN WILLIAM WHITFIELD
NO. 15182 10TH BATTALION WEST RIDING REGIMENT
DIED OCTOBER 9TH 1917 AGED 25

John was the only son and second youngest child of Thomas and Sarah Ann Whitfield. Thomas and Sarah Ann were born at Scrapton, but by the 1880's they arrived at Skirethorns, near Grassington, where Thomas worked in the quarry. All four children were born at Skirethorns but by 1901 they were living at Rock Cottage, Linton, and Thomas was working as a navvy.

John William Whitfield from Linton
Courtesy of The Craven Herald

John was employed on the Yorkshire Dales Railway as a platelayer on the Rylstone section. However, in January 1915, he travelled to Keighley to volunteer and joined the West Riding Regiment, being drafted to France in August 1915. After awhile, John was transferred to the Royal Engineers as a platelayer, where he remained until taken back to his old regiment in September 1917.

On October 4th the Battalion, which had been working on the French side of the border, moved by route march to Caestre, where they entrained for Ypres. Between October 5th and 10th, most of the Battalion were attached to the 2nd Battalion Canadian Railway troops for work in the construction of a light railway, which would allow supplies, ammunition and artillery guns to be moved more easily over the terrible ground conditions. Although they were just behind the immediate front line, they were constantly targetted by enemy artillery and John William Whitfield was posted missing. It was not until September 1918 that his family received official confirmation of his death. John's name is commemorated on the Tyne Cot Memorial.

SIGNALLER CLIFTON PREECE EMMOTT
NO. 24119 8TH BATTALION WEST RIDING REGIMENT
DIED OCTOBER 9TH 1917 AGED 20

In 1901 the Emmott family, consisting of Thomas and Lizzie and their only son, 4 year old Clifton (known as Cliff), were living at Thrush Street, Keighley, where Thomas was employed as a platelayer on the railway. He was a native of Rochdale, his wife originated from Rotherham, whilst Cliff was born at Keighley. The family then moved to "Glenview", Grassington, where Thomas continued his work as a platelayer, only now on the Yorkshire Dales Railway.

Cliff was an active member of Grassington Primitive Methodist Church and of the Sunday School Christian Endeavour and Choir. He enlisted at Skipton and joined the 8th Battalion West Riding Regiment, where he trained to become a

Company signaller and linesman. On the battlefield, he and his army pal, Vic Simpson, would try to mend the broken telephone wires, destroyed by shelling. They often carried a field telephone into battle, but it proved useless if the wires were broken and often they would use a carrier pigeon to send a message, instead.

On October 3rd 1917 they left the front line trenches in the Ypres Salient for billets at Houtkerque, where they bathed and cleaned up. On October 7th they moved back into the front line and at 5-20a.m. on the 9th, the Battalion took part in the attack on the village of Poelcapelle. 21 men were killed, 44 were wounded and 4 were missing. Cliff was killed an hour after they "went over the top". A friend told the family that he was reading his bible and singing hymns before they went up. They often noticed him reading his bible and he told them his father had asked him to read a little every day. Clifton Preece Emmott is commemorated on the Tyne Cot Memorial.

Clifton Emmott
from Grassington
Courtesy of The Craven Herald

On the following day, two men from Richmond in Swaledale, serving in the same Battalion, were killed in an attack on the ridge at Poelcapelle.

QUARTER MASTER SERGEANT THOMAS MORRIS
NO. 9565 6TH BATTALION YORKSHIRE REGIMENT
DIED OCTOBER 10TH 1917 AGED 25

Thomas was born at Clapham, London, in 1894, the son of Thomas and Jane Morris. By 1901 the family was living in Fulham, where Thomas, senior, was a cab proprietor, but before the start of the war they were living in Leeds and Thomas began work as a labourer after leaving school. He joined the local Militia (the 3rd West Yorkshire Volunteers) and in August 1910, at the age of 18, he enlisted in the regular army at Leeds, eventually joining the 6th Battalion, Yorkshire Regiment.

By 1917, he was married, with a young son, Harold, the family living at 2 Castle Terrace, Richmond. By this stage Thomas had risen to the rank of Sergeant in the 6th Battalion.

AND
PRIVATE ARTHUR THORNHILL
NO. 38264 6TH BATTALION YORKSHIRE REGIMENT
DIED OCTOBER 10TH 1917 AGED 33

Seventeen year old Arthur Thornhill, an assistant rag engineer at Richmond paper mill, was living with his widowed mother, Jane, a Richmond woman, and older brother, Thomas, at Chapel Wynd in 1901. Thomas also worked at the mill as a rag engineer, whilst Arthur's twin brother, Richard, was a private in the Yorkshire

Regiment and stationed in Sheffield (we have seen that Richard died in Egypt in 1915). Older brother Thomas had been born at Ferryhill, Co. Durham, but the family had moved back to Richmond, where the twins were born.

(*** Richmond Paper Mill was to be found on Mill Lane, off Reeth Road (nowadays the site of the caravan park). Paper making had required that the River Swale should be dammed, and above the dam was a deep stretch of river. By the 1930's the mill was no longer functioning and during the summer months many people in the town would flock for picnics and bathing. On the river bank was a tea hut, two changing cubicles and a diving board, with a series of wooden steps making access to the river easier. In winter, the mill ponds had been favourite skating places, with music sometimes being provided from a wind-up gramophone.)

Arthur enlisted at Richmond and served with the 6th Battalion Yorkshire Regiment, joining Swaledale colleagues, Thomas Morris, George Jefferson, Henry Haw and John Robinson. We have already seen that the last three men met their death by shell fire between September 26th and 27th. Just 13 days later, Thomas and Arthur would also die.

In early October 1917, the Battalion was to be employed in an attack against the main line of the ridge east of Zonnebeke, attacking the Poelcapelle line. The attack on October 9th against the "Brewery" met with heavy machine gun fire and consolidation of the line was required, during which many casualties were caused by machine gun and rifle fire at close range from both flanks.

The night of 9th/10th October was taken up with reorganisation and evacuating the many wounded, but early on the morning of October 10th the enemy guns again became active, putting down a very heavy barrage. It was during this artillery action that Thomas Morris and Arthur Thornhill were killed and the Tyne Cot Memorial received two more names to be added to the long list. Sadly, we shall discover that during the Second World War, Thomas' son, Harold, would be killed whilst serving in the Italian Campaign and his name join that of his father on the Richmond Memorial.

CAPTAIN MICHAEL DAY WADE MAUDE
9TH BATTALION YORKSHIRE REGIMENT
DIED OCTOBER 14TH 1917 AGED 27

The Maude family had lived at "The Fleets", Rylstone, for a number of generations and were large landowners in the district. Michael Maude's grandparents, Abraham and Anne, had worshipped at Rylstone Church for 31 and 42 years respectively from 1845 and enabled the rebuilding of the church, building of the school and schoolhouse and of the rectory. Michael was the youngest of the two sons of Lieutenant Colonel M.W. Maude, his elder brother Gerald Maude also serving in the army and, as we will see, succumbed to wounds received in India in 1919.

Michael, who was living at Ellinthorpe Hall, Boroughbridge, went into the army just before the war and went out to France in 1914 with the Seventh Division and was involved in the First Battle of Ypres. He was mentioned in despatches after the Battle of the Somme, when he was attached to the West Yorkshire Regiment. By September 1917 Michael was attached to the 9th Battalion Yorkshire Regiment as commanding officer of one of its companies, and they were in the Ypres Salient.

On September 20th the Battalion was in the vicinity of Sanctuary Wood and the men advanced towards Inverness Copse, through heavy shelling and machine gun fire. Numerous small parties of Germans had remained in the wood in dug-outs and shell holes and many of these put up strong resistance, attacking the 9th Battalion with bombs, machine gun fire and a hostile artillery barrage. Before reaching the Red Line, 8 out of 16 officers had been hit, including two of the company commanders. Captain Michael Maude received shrapnel wounds to the thigh and was brought back to England, where he entered a military hospital at Dover. It was there that he died and it was planned that his remains would be interred at Aldborough, Boroughbridge. However his body was brought to Rylstone and buried in St. Peter's churchyard.

Michael Day Wade Maude from Rylstone
Courtesy of The Craven Herald

The next serviceman to die was from Grassington and passed away before ever reaching the battlefield.

'Fleets', Cracoe. This was the home of Colonel and Mrs. Maude. One son was killed during the Great War and their surviving son died in India in 1919 whilst serving in the army
Clive Torrens Collection

PRIVATE HERBERT (BERTIE) BLAKEY
NO. TR5/104548 TRAINING RESERVE BATTALION
DIED OCTOBER 18TH 1917 AGED 18

In 1901, Bertie was two years old and staying with his grandparents, William and Margaret Blakey, at Rose Cottage, Grassington. William was a road contractor and his son Fred, Bertie's father, was a Grassington farmer and contractor. Bertie served in the Territorial Reserve and at the age of 18 enlisted in the army, joining the Training Reserve Battalion stationed on Cannock Chase, Staffordshire.

Shortly afterwards, he was admitted to Cannock Chase Hospital, Rugeley, and died from septic poisoning on October 18th 1917. Bertie's body was brought to Grassington and buried with military honours in Linton Churchyard on October 22nd. The coffin was draped in a Union Jack and covered in wreaths and was carried to the grave by his former schoolmates. Three volleys of shots were fired over the grave and the Last Post sounded.

Henry (Harry) Blakey from Grassington
Courtesy of The Craven Herald

SECOND LIEUTENANT CHRISTOPHER WILLIS WHARTON
3RD BATTALION LONDON REGIMENT (ROYAL FUSILIERS)
DIED OCTOBER 26TH 1917 AGED 32

Christopher, or Willis as he was known, was born at Gunnerside in 1885, the youngest of three sons of John and Ann Wharton. John was a lead miner, born and living at Satron, near Gunnerside, who married Ann, a local girl from Upper Swaledale. By 1891 the family had left the dale, as the lead mining industry declined, and was living in the village of Melsonby, between Richmond and Darlington, where John was employed as a limestone quarryman.

However, we find that by 1901, sixteen year old Willis had left his parents and three older brothers and was living with his cousin, John Alton, also born at Gunnerside, at the Lambeth, London, home of their widowed aunty, Elizabeth Harker, another native of Gunnerside. The cousins were trying to forge a better life for themselves in the metropolis, with John working as a shipping clerk and Willis as a draper's apprentice.

Willis Wharton volunteered for the army and joined a London Regiment (Royal Fusiliers) and by September 1917 had risen to the rank of Second Lieutenant in his Battalion. On October 26th, across atrocious ground conditions, they took part in the second attempt to take the ruined village of Passchendaele and the ridge it was on. The attack failed (it would not be until November 6th that the village would fall to the Canadians), and in the opening day's fighting, Christopher Willis Wharton was killed by shell fire. His body was not retrieved from the oozing, treacherous morass of mud that was the battlefield they fought over and his name is recorded on the Tyne Cot Memorial.

PRIVATE EDWARD BARKER NO. 17/769
17TH BATTALION (PIONEERS) NORTHUMBERLAND FUSILIERS
DIED NOVEMBER 2ND 1917 AGED 38

Edward's father, Robert Barker, was a Richmond man who had married Mary, a girl from Askrigg, and had set up home in Frenchgate, Richmond. Edward was the second eldest of five children and their father ran a plumbing business in the town. By 1901, Edward's older brother was a groom, his sister Edith was a teacher but he had left the family home and, aged 22, was living with his wife, Florence, a Gilling girl, and one month old daughter Mary, at Maison Dieu, Richmond. He was employed as a plumber by his father in the family business.

Edward enlisted at York in October 1914, together with a friend, John William Copeland, a plumber who had been born in Richmond but was living at York, and they both joined the same Battalion, the 17th Northumberland Fusiliers, which was a pioneer battalion engaged in construction work, digging and making foundations. The two men would die within the space of a fortnight of each other and were laid to rest in the same cemetery.

The Battalion was based near St. Jean, north of Ypres, in the latter stages of the Passchendaele Battle and was involved in road construction and repair in the swamplike conditions in the Steenbeek - St. Julien - Langemarck sector. Though the battle was drawing to a conclusion the dangers from shelling were ever present, even behind the immediate front line. On November 2nd Edward Barker was killed by shrapnel from a shell and was buried in grave V.B.38. Bard Cottage Cemetery, north of Ypres.

PRIVATE HERBERT HOLMES
NO. 53362 2ND/9TH BATTALION KING'S LIVERPOOL REGIMENT
DIED NOVEMBER 4TH 1917 AGED 36

Herbert's father, Harry Holmes, was a farmer and woodman, living at Moor View Farm, at Hazlewood with Storiths, on the Bolton Abbey Estate. He had married Hannah Moorhouse, a Pateley Bridge girl, and they raised three sons, George Arthur, Herbert and Tom. Herbert was not keen to be a farmer and by 1901, aged 19, he was to be found as a boarder at Russell Street, Skipton, and employed as a draper's assistant by Mr. Boothman (we shall find that Mr. Boothman, who was born on the Bolton Abbey Estate, would lose his son Clarence in 1918).

Herbert Holmes of Hazlewood, Bolton Abbey, and Doncaster
Courtesy of The Craven Herald

To further his career, Herbert travelled to Doncaster in 1905 and was employed by Messrs. Dennis Roberts and Sons, drapers of St. Sepulchre Gate, latterly as a buyer in their print department. Whilst still at Doncaster, he married Eleanor (Nellie) Cutler at Bolton Abbey in September 1908 and he and his wife lived at 47 Albany Road, Balby, Doncaster. In 1909 a son, Charles, was born and in 1911, a daughter, Norah. A popular figure in his business circles, Herbert was a well-known bowls player, being a member of the Hexthorpe Flatts Club.

Herbert joined the Colours on February 5th 1917

and went to France on September 15th with the East Surrey Regiment, before being transferred to the 2nd/9th Battalion King's Liverpool Regiment and sent to the Ypres Salient. They went into the front line on November 2nd for their first taste of action. For the previous seven days they had whale oil rubbed onto their feet to ward off the effects of "trench foot".

At 3-45p.m. on November 3rd three patrols were sent out on reconnaissance, returning after being fired on and one patrol being affected by gas shells. A heavy enemy barrage continued till after midnight, with 11 men killed and 3 wounded. On the afternoon of the 4th there was great enemy aerial activity, with no English machines sighted. The relief was to start at 5p.m. but from 4p.m. a heavy barrage between Langemarck Corner and Bongite continued until midnight and the Battalion suffered considerable casualties. One of those who was killed was Herbert Holmes and his name is honoured on the Tyne Cot Memorial.

The Holmes family in Doncaster, early 1912
Herbert Holmes, Charles Holmes, Eleanor Holmes with 6 month old Norah

LANCE CORPORAL HENRY (HARRY) KIRKLEY
NO. M2/182865 402ND MECHANISED TRANSPORT COMPANY
ARMY SERVICE CORPS
DIED NOVEMBER 8TH 1917 AGED 29

Harry's father, Thomas Kirkley, came from Northside Head Farm, Middlesmoor, at the head of Nidderdale. His wife, Margaret Jane (nee Moore), also came from a Nidderdale family and they began their married life at Burley-in-Wharfedale, where Thomas was employed as a weaver at the woollen mill. All six children were born at Burley-in-Wharfedale, including Harry in 1888, but by 1901 the family was living in Keighley, with Thomas and 12 year old Harry working in the textile mills.

Harry later became a bus driver in Grassington for Christopher Chapman, coach proprietor, subsequently returning to Keighley and driving a Corporation bus between Oakworth and Keighley. Everyone knew when the bus was approaching

Above: Harry Kirkley from Grassington (seated)

Right: Allan Kirkley (age 3), Jennie Kirkley and Winnie Kirkley (age 1)

Harry Kirkley with colleagues in France. He stands at the back (middle figure) with his hand on the shoulder of soldier in front

Harry Kirkley driving one of the Chapman's buses in Grassington c1910

Harry Kirkley driving a Keighley Corporation bus at Oakworth c1913

down Oakworth hill, as the solid tyres came into contact with the cobbled road. Harry met Jennie Briddon, who had arrived from Chesterfield in Derbyshire to work as a maid at the Golden Fleece, Oakworth, and they married at Slack Lane Baptist Chapel in 1912. A son, Allan, was born in 1913 and shortly after this the family moved to Grassington, where Harry obtained a job as chauffeur for Clement

Holdsworth JP, at Netherside Hall.

A daughter, Winnie, was born in 1915, but early in 1916 Harry enlisted at Skipton and joined the West Riding Regiment. After initial training, it was decided to put Harry's driving and mechanical skills to good use and he was sent straight to France, this time in the Army Service Corps. He served in the Battles of the Somme, Arras, Messines and finally at Passchendaele, rising to the rank of Lance Corporal.

On November 4th, an attack on the village of Passchendaele finally saw it captured on the 6th November. Harry, who was daily expecting to be sent home on leave, was driving through the quagmire that existed around Passchendaele, serving in a munitions supply column, when he was struck by a stray piece of shrapnel. He was taken to a field ambulance station but died of his wounds on November 8th. He was buried in grave I.M.9. Oxford Road Cemetery, NE of Ypres.

His wife, Jennie, was devastated, but remained in Grassington, where, 12 months

Harry Kirkley driving his bus at Oakworth c1913

Netherside Hall, near Threshfield, Grassington, the former home of Mr. C. Holdsworth, J.P. Today, it is a school

later, her health shattered by grief, she died on November 27th 1918, at the age of 28, and was buried in an unmarked grave in Linton churchyard. The two little children were brought back to Keighley to be brought up by relatives, but that was not the end of the tragedy, as Winnie died in a diphtheria outbreak in 1921, aged six years. Eight year old Allan had therefore lost his father, mother and sister within the space of four years.

The final fatality of a dalesman in the Battle of Passchendaele was the friend of Edward Barker, the plumber from Richmond, who had died on November 2nd, whilst serving in the same Battalion.

PRIVATE JOHN WILLIAM COPELAND
NO. 17/203 "C" COMPANY 17TH BATTALION (PIONEERS)
NORTHUMBERLAND FUSILIERS
DIED NOVEMBER 16TH 1917 AGED 37

The Copeland family was long established in Richmond. John's father, John Copeland senior, was born in the town but by 1901 he was a police constable stationed in York, and, with his wife Sarah, was raising a family of seven children. John junior, at 21 years, was the second eldest child, having been born in Richmond, before moving to York in 1883 when his father was stationed there. He was a plumber and gas-fitter on the North Eastern Railway, who had trained with and worked for Robert Barker, the Richmond plumber, and was friendly with his son, Edward. By the start of the Great War, John William Copeland was married to Laura and they were living at 22 Railway Terrace, Holgate Road, York.

Edward Barker arrived from Richmond and both men enlisted there, joining the 17th Battalion Northumberland Fusiliers. On November 2nd 1917 he had witnessed his friend, Edward Barker, being killed near Langemarck, whilst in the process of constructing roads, but on the 15th November the Battalion transferred from the 32nd Division to Railway Construction troops and began to reorganise for the change. They were still in danger from shell fire, however, and on the next day, the 16th, John Copeland was killed by shrapnel. He was buried in grave VI.B.41. Bard Cottage Cemetery, north of Ypres, a few yards away from his friend.

And so we come to an end of the account of the Battle of Passchendaele and its affect on the families in the dales. Within the space of fifteen weeks a total of 24 men had died and 24 families were left to cope with the grim news. The year still had eight more weeks to run its course, however, and during this period, thirteen more names would be added to the list.

GUNNER JAMES WILLIAM KEARTON
NO. 195035 ROYAL FIELD ARTILLERY
DIED NOVEMBER 20TH 1917 AGED 29

James was the son of Richard and Mary Kearton of 8 Sleegill, Richmond, and we will find that in April 1918 his brother John would be killed. Their father, Richard, had been born at Muker and worked as a lead miner. He married his wife, Mary, a girl from Marrick, and their eldest son, John, was born in that village. James and his sister Margaret were born at Grinton, but by 1901 the family had moved to

Middlemoor, in Nidderdale, where Richard was still employed in lead mining, although their eldest child, John, had remained in Marrick, where he was a domestic servant. By the outbreak of the war, however, the family had settled in Richmond.

James enlisted at Richmond and joined the Army Service Corps but later transferred to the Artillery, as a gunner. On November 20th 1917 General Haig launched an offensive against the Hindenburg Line, in the direction of Cambrai, that caught the Germans by surprise because there was no preliminary artillery bombardment during the previous days. Over 300 tanks headed the attack and results appeared promising on that first day of battle.

James Kearton's gun battery was positioned between Peronne and Cambrai, and although there was no preliminary bombardment, the artillery backed up the operation during the day. There was, as usual, retaliation from the opposition batteries and James was wounded. He was taken to a casualty clearing station but died from his wounds that same day. James William Kearton is buried in grave II.B.14. Fins New British Cemetery, Sorel-le-Grand, between Peronne and Cambrai.

A soldier serving in the regular army before the Great War, whose family lived in Richmond, was also killed during the Battle of Cambrai.

LANCE CORPORAL GEORGE ELLIS
NO. 5635 13TH BATTALION YORKSHIRE REGIMENT
DIED NOVEMBER 24TH 1917

Above: Dog tags, tobacco tin etc., belonging to George Ellis

Left: George Ellis from Richmond

George Ellis was born at Old Malton, just to the south of Pickering, and became a soldier in the regular army prior to the war. Whilst he was based at Richmond with the Yorkshire Regiment (Green Howards) he met Annie Emstock, a Richmond girl, and they were married. They raised their family of three sons and a daughter in accommodation at the Green Howards Barracks (now the Garden Village Estate, Richmond).

George had previously served in South Africa and when the Great War began, he went with the BEF to France. He fought throughout many of the campaigns on the

Western Front and survived but was killed in action on November 24th, four days into the Battle of Cambrai.

On November 20th the Battalion moved to Le Transloy, receiving warning to be ready to move off at a moments notice, for the Battle of Cambrai was about to begin. The 13th Battalion was brought up to the front line of operations by November 22nd. The attack was to be made at 10a.m. on November 23rd, the objective being Bourlon Wood and village. They went forward behind the tanks, meeting with some resistance at first from machine gunners on the flanks. By midday, the outskirts of Bourlon were cleared and then the village itself was cleared by hand to hand fighting. Bombardments and counter-attacks were made after 3p.m. The Battalion was then relieved by a unit of the Cavalry, but by then George Ellis was dead.

His body was never recovered and he is commemorated on Panel 5 Cambrai Memorial. When news of his death arrived back in Richmond, Annie and the four children had to leave the Barracks and they moved into a house in the Castle grounds. Life was difficult for Annie and to make ends meet she began taking in the washing of servicemen.

Another Richmond man was killed a few days later in a sector of the front line, adjacent to where the Battle of Cambrai was taking place.

PRIVATE SEPTIMUS FREDERICK HERBERT ALLAN
NO. 48457 9TH BATTALION NORTHUMBERLAND FUSILIERS
DIED NOVEMBER 25TH 1917

Born at Richmond and enlisting at Richmond, Septimus Allan first of all joined the Army Service Corps, before becoming a member of the 9th Battalion Northumberland Fusiliers. November 13th to the 23rd 1917 were spent in billets near Arras, but at 8a.m. on November 24th the Battalion paraded in fighting order and marched by companies via Mercatel and Henin, to the SW of Arras, towards the Hindenburg Line and relieved the 10th Battalion Lincolnshire Regiment by 2p.m. During the night six patrols were sent out and thoroughly cleared No Man's Land of the enemy, shots and bombs being exchanged with them.

At 9a.m. on November 25th the enemy retaliated to the Battalion's trench mortar shooting by putting some "pineapples" on to the front line, where two men were killed. Whilst off-loading rations at the Battalion Dump, a working party came under enemy machine gun fire, with one man being killed. That night, large enemy patrols were sighted but were dispersed by Lewis gun and rifle fire and the Battalion now had complete control of No Man's Land. However, one of the two men killed by the German shelling at 9a.m. was Septimus Allan. His name is commemorated on Bay 2 and 3, Arras Memorial.

PRIVATE JAMES METCALFE NO. 25/410
3RD BATTALION OTAGO REGIMENT
NEW ZEALAND EXPEDITIONARY FORCE
DIED NOVEMBER 28TH 1917 AGED 34

In 1901 the Metcalfe family was living in the parish of Kettlewell with Starbotton. 17 year old James (Jim) was the second youngest of four children of John and Alice

Metcalfe. John, who originated from Hawes, was a farm worker at Kettlewell, and the family had spent time at a number of farms, including ones at Deepdale and Cray (where Jim was born), before settling in the Kettlewell area, where Jim's elder brother, Ninion, was a shepherd.

At some stage before the war, Jim Metcalfe emigrated to New Zealand, becoming a farm worker in the beautiful province of Otago, on South Island. A year after the war broke out he joined the New Zealand Rifle Brigade and early in the Spring of 1916 arrived in France. While with the Brigade he was wounded in the Battle of the Somme on September 15th and was on sick leave in England (and so able to visit Wharfedale) until June 1st, when he returned to the Western Front.

James Metcalfe of Kettlewell
Courtesy of The Craven Herald

Throughout October and early November 1917 the Otago Battalion was involved in many attacks on the Passchendaele front and remained in the front line after Passchendaele had fallen. It was in late November 1917 that Private Jim Metcalfe, a stretcher bearer with his Battalion, was fatally wounded and died at No. 10 Casualty Clearing Station on November 28th. He was buried in grave XXVI.AA.1. Lijssenthoek Military Cemetery, 12 kilometres west of Ypres.

LANCE CORPORAL ROBERT LAYFIELD
NO. 30569 6TH BATTALION YORKSHIRE REGIMENT
DIED NOVEMBER 30TH 1917 AGED 27

Robert was born at Richmond, the son of Jane Layfield of 3 Chapel Wynd. In 1901 he was ten years of age and he and his mother, a single woman employed as a sheeter at Richmond Paper Mill, were living with his grandmother, Ann Layfield. When Robert enlisted at Richmond, he was by this time married to Mary and he joined the 6th Battalion Yorkshire Regiment.

On October 9th 1917 they had taken part in the attack on Poelcapelle, during the Battle of Passchendaele, and had received heavy losses. They were then stationed in France, in the region between Loos and Lens during November and December, where they were employed on working parties, building fire steps in the Reserve Line and deepening and improving the communication trenches. However, towards the end of November they experienced losses from the enemy artillery (13 men killed and 20 wounded) and one of those wounded was Robert Layfield. He died in a Casualty Clearing Station and was buried in grave IV.A.10. Noeux-Les-Mines Communal Cemetery Extension, south of Bethune.

PRIVATE FRANCIS WILSON LOVETT
NO. 26152 4TH BATTALION GRENADIER GUARDS
DIED DECEMBER 1ST 1917 AGED 19

In 1901, two year old Francis was the son of Harry and Mary Lovett, living at Incline Cottage in Kepwick Entire, a village on the fringes of the North York Moors and in the Hambleton Hills, and with them was their one year old daughter, Maud. Mary was from Ardenside, Yorkshire, where the two children were born, but Harry was a native of Honingham, Norwich, and was employed as a gamekeeper. A few years later, the family had moved to Downholme parish and Harry was working on one of the local estates.

Francis was a tall lad and when he enlisted he joined the 4th Battalion Grenadier Guards. On November 20th the Battalion took part in the Battle of Cambrai. Tanks would be used to break through the German wire, with the infantry following under the cover of smoke barrages. Initial advances were remarkable, but when a halt was called for on the 22nd November, it allowed the Germans to reinforce. The fighting was intense and by November 29th it was clear that the Germans were ready for a major counter-attack.

On December 1st the Battalion was involved in the difficult task of taking Gonnelieu and Quentin Ridge, advancing at 6-30a.m. over open sloping ground and being met at once by heavy machine gun fire. It was so intense that progress was arrested until a tank saved the situation. Number 2 Company suffered heavy losses, with one platoon practically wiped out.

Machine guns bristled from every building of the village, yet so determined and persistent was the onslaught of the 4th Battalion that isolated parties managed to penetrate into the village. However, a most gallant attempt by No. 3 Company to capture the village, resulted in horrendous losses. After extremely heavy fighting, the 4th Battalion was finally relieved on December 2nd, but Francis Lovett did not return. His body was never recovered and his name is commemorated on Panel 2 Cambrai Memorial.

PRIVATE THOMAS BENSON RENTON
NO. 82902 227TH COMPANY MACHINE GUN CORPS
DIED DECEMBER 1ST 1917 AGED 31

Thomas Benson Renton of Hetton
Courtesy of The Craven Herald

In 1901 the Renton family was living at West Marton, a village between Barnoldswick and Skipton, where Joseph, the father, was a foreman joiner and carpenter. He originated from near Pateley Bridge and his wife, Grace, came from Gargrave. Their daughter Mary was born at Gargrave but her younger brother, Thomas, was born at West Marton. However, before the Great War, the family came to live at The Nook (now called Bensons), Hetton, near Rylstone, where Joseph and Thomas practised as the local joiners and undertakers. They used a horse and cart to transport the timber, but it was also sympathetically draped in black material and used at funerals.

Thomas travelled to Keighley in November 1916 to enlist and first joined the York and Lancaster Regiment before transferring to the Machine Gun Corps. It was whilst he was taking part in the Battle of Cambrai that he was severely wounded and died at the 21st Casualty

Clearing Station. Thomas was buried in grave VI.A.5. Rocquigny-Equancourt Road British Cemetery, Manancourt, 13 kilometres north of Peronne.

PRIVATE THOMAS WHITEHEAD NO. 267162 2ND/6TH BATTALION WEST RIDING REGIMENT DIED DECEMBER 2ND 1917 AGED 25

Thomas, who was born at Pateley Bridge, lived at Moor View, Hebden, with his parents, Thomas and Mary (nee Shepherd) and brothers, Eddy and George. For a number of years before the Great War he worked for the Chapmans, driving the Royal Mail from Skipton to Buckden and back, and just prior to the war worked as a platelayer on the Rylstone section of the Yorkshire Dales Railway.

Thomas Whitehead from Hebden
Courtesy of The Craven Herald

Thomas enlisted at Skipton in March 1915, joining the 2nd / 6th Battalion, West Riding Transport Section, and went to France in February 1917. They were involved in the Battle of Cambrai, especially in the vicinity of Bourlon Wood and village. The Battalion helped to hold the village till 5p.m. on November 27th, when it was relieved and took up positions on a crest in Bourlon Wood. During the day the enemy shelled Bourlon Wood with very heavy guns, thereby causing many casualties and the Battalion was relieved.

On December 1st they moved back and dug a line of posts, which were occupied by night only and during the day the Battalion stayed in the old British line, but over the next two days were badly shelled and sustained some casualties on December 2nd, including Thomas Whitehead. He is buried in grave I.F.22. Lebucquiere Communal Cemetery Extension (8 kilometres east of Bapaume).

SERGEANT MICHAEL J. MURPHY NO. 33392 15TH SERVICE BATTALION (1ST GLASGOW) HIGHLAND LIGHT INFANTRY DIED DECEMBER 3RD 1917 AGED 35

I know very little about the background of Michael Murphy, except to say that he was born at Bury and had connections with Richmond, from where he enlisted, although he was living at Manchester with his wife, Sophia.

Eventually he was promoted to Sergeant in the 15th Battalion Highland Light Infantry (originally formed in 1914, with many members being Glasgow tramway employees) and by late November 1917 they were stationed in the recently extended Ypres Salient. Although the Passchendaele Ridge had been captured, the German artillery was as active as before, and on December 3rd Michael Murphy was killed by shell fire. His name is inscribed on the Tyne Cot Memorial.

PRIVATE JOHN DENT
NO. 202882 11TH BATTALION BORDER REGIMENT
DIED DECEMBER 4TH 1917 AGED 23

John Dent was born at Asby, a village six miles inland from Whitehaven, on the fringes of the Lake District, where his father was a farmer. By 1901, 7 year old John, the youngest of three sons of Robert and Mary Dent, was living with his parents at Scober Farm in the village of Warcop, six miles south of Appleby. His parents originated from Romaldkirk, near Barnard Castle, where their eldest son had been born.

John Dent of Rylstone
Courtesy of The Craven Herald

John worked on his father's farm at Warcop, but on January 20th 1917 he enlisted at nearby Appleby and joined the 11th Battalion Border Regiment, receiving four months training before going to the Western Front. It was at this time that Robert and Mary left Scober Farm and arrived at Rylstone, to begin farming at Burton House.

At 1-55a.m. on December 2nd 1917, the Battalion made a night attack on the German positions south of Westroosebeeke (near the recently captured village of Passchendaele) in conjunction with other units. The Battalion took its objectives and these were held all day until the enemy launched a counter-attack at 4-30p.m. and the Battalion fell back into the old line. Casualties had been heavy, with six officers killed, seven wounded and many men killed or wounded.

John Dent received shell wounds to the leg and left thigh and was taken to the 46th Casualty Clearing Station, where he died on December 4th. He was buried in grave VI.AA.58. Mendinghem Military Cemetery, 17 kilometres NW of Ypres. His older brother Edgar had been serving his country for the past three years in the Royal Army Medical Corps, whilst the eldest brother, Willie, helped on the farm. John Dent's name was later added to the Rylstone and district memorial.

PRIVATE CHRISTOPHER CHAPMAN
NO. 57377 2ND/7TH BATTALION WEST YORKSHIRE REGIMENT
DIED DECEMBER 5TH 1917 AGED 36

Christopher's father, Christopher senior, was a Grassington coach and mail proprietor. In 1901, he and his wife Elizabeth (nee Metcalfe) were living at Town End with three of their children, Nancy, 19 year old Christopher and Thomas, together with their grandson, John (the same Jack Chapman who had died in Egypt in 1915). The family lived at the Temperance Hotel, now known as Church House, and it was from there that the Chapman's Royal Mail and coaching business was run. Christopher senior, known as Kit, was born at Buckden and it was in that village that he began his business career as a local carrier. For 50 years he the family operated the Royal Mail service in this dales area and transferred their headquarters to Grassington. Eventually, 50 horses were stabled next to the Temperance Hotel.

Christopher junior, also known as Kit, had been born at Buckden in 1881 and was employed in driving the mail coach for his father. By 1907, however, the firm became mechanised with the purchase of a number of motor buses to add to their horse drawn transport.

In 1906, Christopher married Sarah Alice Easterby, a farmer's daughter from Halton Gill, Littondale, at Arncliffe Church. By the time of the Great War, he and his wife lived with their two children at 5 Hebden Road, Grassington. Christopher enlisted at York soon after the outbreak of war, but was discharged because of defective eye-sight. He was again called up in June 1917 and joined the 2nd/7th Battalion West Yorkshire Regiment (by this time his father had died, on the very day war was declared).

Christopher Chapman from Grassington
Courtesy of The Craven Herald

Christopher and the Battalion took part in the Battle of Cambrai (November 20th to December 3rd 1917). On November 26th they moved into Bourlon Wood and dug in. On the 27th they took part in an attack on the enemy's position, with 14 tanks leading the advance. Platoons of "D" Company were held up in the sunken road by heavy machine gun fire. Further advance was impossible

The Chapman family of Grassington
Back row: Robert (Bob), Mary, Jim, Sarah, Christopher (Kit) junior, Alice
Seated: Lizzie, Christopher (Kit) senior, Elizabeth, Maggie
Kneeling: Nancy, Tom
Christopher, junior, was killed in the Great War, whilst Alice's son, Robert Bownas, was also killed

and consolidation of the line took place.

Five or six small enemy counter-attacks were stopped and at 7p.m. the Battalion was relieved. 82 casualties were sustained and one of the wounded was Christopher Chapman, who had received a gunshot wound to the chest. At first his condition was thought not to be serious, but he rapidly grew worse and his wife was informed that he had died in No. 3 British Casualty Clearing Station at 5a.m. on December 5th. He was buried in grave VIII.D.18. Grevillers British Cemetery, 3 kilometres west of Bapaume.

GUNNER THOMAS DAVEY NICHOLLS
NO. 90375 ROYAL FIELD ARTILLERY
DIED DECEMBER 5TH 1917 AGED 23

In 1901, seven year old Thomas was to be found at Colne, the Lancashire cotton mill town in which he had been born. He was living with his widowed grandmother, Martha, a woman who had been born in Grassington, and when he died he was buried in nearby Linton Churchyard. His parents were Richard and Annie Nicholls, natives of Grassington and for some years before the war had lived in the village. His grandfather, Thomas Nicholls, had been a Grassington carrier.

Tom Nicholls, formerly of Grassington
Courtesy of The Craven Herald

Thomas junior was one of the first to join the army at the outbreak of war, joining the Royal Field Artillery as a driver of the horses (due to the family's experience with horses), but soon became a gunner in his battery. After training at Guildford and Aldershot, he went to France in February 1915, coming home on leave for Christmas 1916. He was wounded twice and also gassed and the latter event affected his chest and his breathing. After his discharge from the army in September 1917 he developed tuberculosis and died in Middleton Hospital, Ilkley, on December 5th 1917 and was buried in Linton Churchyard on December 8th.

PRIVATE JOHN GEORGE WALKER
NO. 51665 17TH BATTALION ROYAL FUSILIERS
DIED DECEMBER 7TH 1917 AGED 22

Hannah Walker was a single woman, who, in 1901 was living at Bargate, Richmond, with her five children, three daughters and two sons, and earning a living as a laundress. She had been born at Wensley and John, aged six, was the eldest of her two sons.

When John enlisted at Richmond, he first of all joined the Army Service Corps, before transferring to the 17th Battalion Royal Fusiliers. The Battalion was involved in action near the Cambrai front and John was wounded. He was taken to the Casualty Clearing Station near Bapaume but died from his wounds on December 7th 1917. John George Walker was buried in grave IX.E.6. Grevillers British Cemetery, 3 kilometres west of Bapaume.

PRIVATE CHARLES EDWARD HYMAS NO. 378783
257TH AREA EMPLOYMENT COMPANY
NORTHUMBERLAND FUSILIERS (LABOUR CORPS)
DIED DECEMBER 13TH 1917 AGED 27

Tom Hymas, father of Charles, originated from Burton Leonard, five miles south of Ripon, and married Margaret, a girl from Otley. Their first child, Linda, was born at Otley, but then they moved for a while to Thornton, a village near Pocklington, east of York, where Charles was born. The family then lived at Bingley for a number of years, where three more children were born, before settling down at Idle, in the northern suburbs of Bradford. Here, Tom Hymas was employed as a worker in a woollen mill.

Charles E. Hymas from Rylstone
Courtesy of The Craven Herald

Some years before the Great War, Charles Hymas left Bradford to work as a platelayer (ganger) on the Yorkshire Dales Railway at Rylstone and also became a porter. It was at Rylstone that he met Millie, who was working at the Bull's Head Inn and they married. Charles was known to the locals as "Chuck" and he and Millie settled down to married life in one of the two cottages at the far end of Green Lane, Rylstone. An

Bulls Head Inn at Cracoe c1905, where Millie worked. (The inn no longer exists.)

addition to the family came with the birth of their daughter Dorothy.

"Chuck" Hymas enlisted in the army at Keighley and it is no surprise that he became a member of a Labour Corps (257th Company Northumberland Fusiliers) because of his experience as a platelayer. He served in France, but during the cold and wet December of 1917, he was admitted to one of the largest military hospital centres in Northern France, at St. Omer. It was there that Charles Edward Hymas died from septic pleurisy on December 13th.

Charles was buried in grave IV.F.25. Longuenesse (St. Omer) Souvenir Cemetery. He left a widow and young child and after the war Millie Hymas married Jess Ibbertson and they had four other children.

As the last serviceman from these dales to die in 1917, Charles Hymas's death brought the total of local servicemen who had been killed in action or died during the year to 79. Their loved ones suffered almost unbearable pain and heartache but there would be no noticeable "let up" in 1918.

Opening of the Yorkshire Dales Railway 1902.
A considerable number of servicemen who had worked on this railway were killed or wounded during the Great War

CHAPTER SIX

1918 – WILL IT NEVER END?

On the first day of the new year the death occurred of a dalesman who was languishing in a German Prisoner of War Camp. Sadly, he would be the first of 72 dales servicemen to die during this final year.

PRIVATE GILBERT TENNANT
NO. 28016 10TH BATTALION LANCASHIRE FUSILIERS
DIED JANUARY 1ST 1918 AGED 43

Gilbert was born in 1873 at Buckden, the youngest of the children of John and Mary Tennant, who lived near to the Buck Inn. John was a carpenter, born at Buckden, who had married Mary, a girl from Stokesley, on the northern fringes of the North York Moors. By 1881 his eldest son, George, was helping him in the family business, but ten years later, John had died and his widow, Mary, was living at Buckden with her daughter Elizabeth, a dressmaker, and 17 year old Gilbert, a general servant.

Ten years later, in 1901, Gilbert was to be found in Kent, in the Chatham dockyards, where he was employed as a stoker, but by the outbreak of war he was in the Leeds area. He enlisted at Leeds and joined the Kings Own Yorkshire Light Infantry, before eventually finding himself serving on the Western Front with the 10th Battalion, Lancashire Fusiliers. Gilbert was taken prisoner by the Germans in 1917 and found himself in a POW Camp inside Germany. In the winter of 1917/1918 he was taken ill and died on New Years Day 1918. Gilbert was buried in the POW Camp burial ground, but after the war his body was exhumed and buried in grave III.C.9. Hamburg Cemetery.

GUNNER JOHN WILLIAM PEACOCK
NO. 129244 "A" BATTERY 223RF BRIGADE ROYAL FIELD ARTILLERY
DIED JANUARY 18TH 1918 AGED 22

John William, known to all as William, was the son of Joseph and Elizabeth Ann Peacock of Booze, a tiny hamlet in Arkengarthdale. Joseph was a chert quarryman, working in the quarry on Fremington Edge, at Reeth, but their son William had left Arkengarthdale before the outbreak of war and was working in Scotland. He enlisted at Perth and trained as a Gunner in the Royal Field Artillery.

John William Peacock was wounded in mid January 1918, whilst serving near Manancourt, 13 kilometres north of Peronne, as his battery was involved in the routine duty of day to day bombardment and counter bombardment against the enemy front line and support trenches, as well as shelling the rear areas. He was taken to No. 21 Casualty Clearing Station, where he died from his wounds on January 18th 1918 and was buried in grave IX.D.22. Rocquigny-Equancourt Road British Cemetery, Manancourt.

John William Peacock from Arkengarthdale

GUNNER WILLIAM MEE TOPLEY
NO. 155538 ROYAL GARRISON ARTILLERY
DIED JANUARY 18TH 1918 AGED 31

William Topley was born in 1887 at Cockerham, a small village a few miles from the Lancashire coast, between Garstang and Lancaster. His father Samuel, a Nottinghamshire man, was a butler in the Cockerham area and had married Annie, who came from Addingham.

William Mee Topley
of Bolton Abbey and Lancaster
Courtesy of The Craven Herald

William met and married Edith Whitaker, the daughter of Fred Whitaker of Bolton Abbey. Before the Great War, William and Edith settled in Lancaster, where William was employed as the manager for Messrs. Satterthwaite, grocers. He enlisted at Lancaster in April 1917 and went to France as a Gunner in the Royal Garrison Artillery on July 13th 1917.

William was severely wounded in the left ankle and above the knee by shell shrapnel on December 8th and went into the hospital at Rouen, in France, where his leg was amputated. The War Graves Commission indicates that William died at Rouen and was buried there but the report in the "Craven Herald" states that he was removed to a hospital in Dover and died from diphtheria on January 18th. William is commemorated on the Bolton Abbey War Memorial.

LIEUTENANT GEORGE WILLIAM ANNAKIN WATSON
1ST AIRCRAFT SUPPLY DEPOT ROYAL FLYING CORPS
DIED MARCH 7TH 1918 AGED 20

The Watsons were a Conistone and Kilnsey farming family of long standing. George's father, James Watson, had married a Thirsk girl, Emily Mary, and George was their eldest child. In around 1915 James died and Emily took her family to Headingly, Leeds, where George attended Leeds University on an engineering degree. He had a genius for invention, a new fuse and engine having been made to his design.

In his eagerness to serve, however, he left his engineering studies and enlisted at Leeds in the Royal Naval Division, before being sent to an important position in a Leeds shell factory. This did not content him and he joined the Royal Flying Corps, passing out of his novitiate period at the top of his class. George left for France to join the 1st Aircraft Supply Depot, only three weeks before he was killed.

George William Annakin Watson from Conistone, Wharfedale
Courtesy of The Craven Herald

The unit was based at the airfield at Marquise, between Boulogne and Calais and the issue section was at nearby Rety. Its job was to ferry new fighter and bomber aircraft arriving from England to the front line squadrons operating on French soil. George Watson was killed, together with his pilot, 2nd Lieutenant Lay, when their plane went down on March 7th 1918. He is buried in grave IV.G.1. Wimereux Communal Cemetery, 5 kilometres north of Boulogne. Emily Watson had lost her husband and two sons in the space of two years, the younger son dying in September 1917, after an operation (I have included George Watson, despite the fact he is not on the Kettlewell or Conistone memorials, because of his strong connections with Wharfedale).

Meanwhile on April 6th 1917 America had declared war against Germany, but with her small army of 210,000 men, it would take some while before her manpower resources could become a decisive factor. During the winter of 1917/1918 General Ludendorff realised that Germany's only hope of winning the war lay in a decisive victory in the West in 1918 before the weight of American man power began to tell. The Bolshevik Revolution of 1917 in Russia had resulted in that country being knocked out of the war.

Ludendorff therefore shifted most German forces from the East and prepared for an all out offensive to be launched as early as possible in the Spring, using "shock troops" as spearheads for the assault. He planned to smash the Allied Armies in a series of hammer blows, driving a wedge between the British and French forces, and then destroy the British in subsequent assaults. Preparations were made for this massive attack in the Somme area to begin on March 21st between St. Quentin and Arras, towards the goal of capturing Amiens.

16 servicemen from the dales would die during the "Kaiser's Battle", when overwhelming German forces would roll forward and swallow them up in the desperate weeks of late March and early April. The British were well aware of German intentions and made preparations for the inevitable attack. One of the most ironic re-deployments was to abandon the Passchendaele Ridge and form a tight defensive line around Ypres. All the sacrifices of the previous Autumn seemed as nought.

Liddell Hart, the military historian, wrote: "At 0430 hours on March 21st the sudden crash of some 6000 German guns heralded the breaking of a storm which, in grandeur of scale, of awe and destruction, surpassed any other in the World War. By nightfall a German flood had inundated 40 miles of the British front; a week later it had reached a depth of nearly 40 miles and was almost lapping the outskirts of Amiens, and in the ensuing weeks the Allied cause itself was almost submerged. Germany came desperately near to regaining that lost chance of victory which she had forfeited in early September 1914."

On the second day of this titanic battle, a soldier from Rylstone would be the first man from these dales to be "swallowed up" in the German tidal wave.

PRIVATE TOM SWALES
NO. 13653 9TH BATTALION WEST RIDING REGIMENT
DIED MARCH 22ND 1918 AGED 21

Tom was the son of Thomas and Grace Swales, and three months after Tom's death, his cousin, James Swales, would also die whilst serving his country. Their fathers, Thomas and Frederick, were brothers. Thomas and Frederick had been born into a farming family at Starbotton, but their parents then moved to run Dale Head Farm at Newhouse in Bowland, with Thomas working for his father. Another move was made to a farm at Flasby, near Rylstone, around 1884, and it was whilst there that he married Grace Bownass. It is interesting to note that his brother Frederick married Grace's sister Eleanor. Thomas and Grace Swale's son, Tom, was born and they moved the short distance to Rylstone, where they ran Yew Tree Farm, below the village pond. Siblings William (Billy), Doris, Martha (Mattie) and Grace completed the family. Before he enlisted Tom became a postman, based at Cracoe post office and delivered mail in the Rylstone, Cracoe and Hetton area.

Tom Swales of Rylstone
Courtesy of The Craven Herald

Tom went to enlist at Grassington and joined the 9th Battalion West Riding Regiment. By March 21st 1918 the Battalion was in the front line trenches near Havrincourt. On that day there was a great enemy bombardment using HE and gas shells. Gas masks were worn by all ranks for five hours. The companies moved into defensive positions under this bombardment and repulsed the enemy attacks by use of rifle and Lewis gun fire.

Orders were received on March 22nd to move back to defend the trenches around Havrincourt, leaving two companies to act as an outpost line. At 10a.m. the enemy made repeated attacks on the Battalion bombing saps but were repeatedly driven back, leaving many dead in the trench, with hand to hand fighting taking place. By 4p.m. the Battalion was forced to withdraw, although a concentrated rifle and Lewis gun fire caused the enemy attacks to be broken up without reaching the newly established line.

However, Tom Swales was killed on this day and his body was left behind, never to be recovered. His name is to be found on Bay 6 Arras Memorial.

PRIVATE THOMAS NOEL JOBEY
NO. 19801 9TH COMPANY MACHINE GUN CORPS
DIED MARCH 23RD 1918 AGED 25

Thomas's mother Elizabeth was born in Northumberland and married Thomas Jobey, from Newcastle on Tyne. Thomas, senior, became a butler and two children were born, one at Newcastle and another in Sunderland, before the family arrived in Frenchgate, Richmond, in 1888, where Thomas was again employed as a butler. Four more children were born, including Thomas, the second youngest, but by 1896 their father had died and their mother, Elizabeth, was left to raise six young children. They moved to live at 36 Bargate, with Elizabeth supporting her family by working as a laundress.

Thomas was living in Richmond at the outbreak of war, but it was at Chester that he enlisted and joined the Kings Royal Rifle Corps. In October 1915 the Machine Gun Corps had been created and at some stage in the war Thomas was transferred to the 9th Company of the Corps. Being the targets for every enemy weapon, they well earned the nickname of the "Suicide Club".

As the German onslaught continued and overwhelmed the leading elements of the British army on March 22nd and 23rd, Thomas Jobey was killed in action on the 23rd. His body was never recovered and Thomas is commemorated on Panel 90 to 93 Pozieres Memorial 6 kilometres NE of Albert (over 500 men of the Machine Gun Corps are honoured on the memorial for this period).

PRIVATE FRED ILEY
NO. 41646 4TH BATTALION GORDON HIGHLANDERS
DIED MARCH 25TH 1918 AGED 26

Fred was the son of James Iley, who lived at 10 Hurgill Road, Richmond, and the wife of May Iley.

Having joined the 4th Battalion Gordon Highlanders, they found themselves at the forefront of the action as the German juggernaut bore down on them. The pace of the German advance in those few early days, combined with the effects of intense artillery shelling, meant that many bodies left on the battlefield did not receive a burial. The testament to the sacrifice of Fred Iley is to be found on Bay 8 and 9 Arras Memorial.

SECOND LIEUTENANT JOHN BATTYE
5TH BATTALION YORKSHIRE REGIMENT
DIED MARCH 25TH 1918 AGED 21

John was born in 1896 at 62 Birks Street, Middlesbrough, the second son of Harry and Jane Ann Battye. His father, Harry, a Middlesbrough man, was a Colour Sergeant in the Yorkshire Regiment and had married a Richmond girl, Jane Ann

Salvin. In 1897 the family moved to live in Richmond, at Castle Yard. By 1914, however, John had left Richmond to work in Lloyds Bank at Stafford.

During the Great War, John and his older brother, Harry junior, enlisted, Harry joining the Royal Warwickshire Regiment, whilst John served with the 5th Battalion Yorkshire Regiment. Sadly, both lads would be killed towards the end of the Great War, within the space of 7 days of each other.

John Battye returned to Richmond to enlist in the 5th Battalion in July 1915. He served as a private, but was put forward for officer training and was commissioned as a Second Lieutenant in May 1917.

When the great German offensive began on March 21st the 5th Battalion was completing 10 days of training at Demuin, just to the east of Amiens. On that same day the Battalion entrained at Guillancourt, arriving at Brie, a bridging point on the River Somme south of Peronne, at 5a.m. on March 22nd. Marching to Hancourt, they began digging in but at 11p.m. withdrew and took up positions along the main Veaignes-Brie road at 8a.m. on the 23rd.

The withdrawal was not easy, as the Battalion was engaged with the enemy in a rearguard action as they crossed the Somme at Brie about 3p.m. They rested in a quarry near Villers-Carbonnel. By 2p.m. on the 24th, they filled a gap on the high ground NE of Licourt. John Battye, together with two Companies, were pushed forward to fend off any possible attack, which came in with heavy shell and machine gun fire at 9a.m. on March 25th. They held on until the end, resulting in heavy casualties and many men captured.

One of those killed was John Battye and his parents received the news at their home in Frenchgate, Richmond. His name is commemorated on the Pozieres Memorial, near Albert.

PRIVATE HENRY SWINBURNE
NO. 16757 4TH BATTALION YORKSHIRE REGIMENT
DIED MARCH 26TH 1918 AGED 26

Henry was born at Richmond in 1891, the son of George Swinburne, a stone mason from Pickering, and his wife Emily, a girl from Scarborough. In 1901 they were living at York Square, Richmond, together with Henry's three sisters. When Henry enlisted at Scarborough and joined the 4th Battalion Yorkshire Regiment, he was living and working at Malton, south of Pickering.

As the German offensive began on March 21st, the 4th Battalion were engaged in training at Ignacourt and received orders to be ready to move. They entrained for Brie, arriving at midnight, and after a six hour march, took up their positions at Hancourt. On the 22nd their CO was killed while rallying his men and on the 23rd they retired to a prepared position on the River Somme. Retirement continued, with the 4th Battalion fighting a rearguard action all the way back to Le Mesnil-Bruntel. One Company was ordered to hold the high ground east of Brie until all the British troops had passed through. This Company afterwards covered and held the enemy in check until all the bridges except one had been destroyed, and this was demolished immediately they had crossed the river by it. However, Henry was killed during these actions on March 26th and his name is commemorated on Panel 31 and 32 Pozieres Memorial, joining that of another Richmond man, Thomas Jobey.

DRIVER JOHN TATE
NO. 33772 "B" BATTERY 70TH BRIGADE ROYAL FIELD ARTILLERY
DIED MARCH 28TH 1918 AGED 24

John Tate was born at Richmond, the son of Mary Elizabeth Tate, living at 21 Bargate, Richmond. I believe he could have worked on a farm prior to the war, for when he enlisted at Richmond, he became a driver in a gun battery, riding the horses that pulled the howitzers into their new firing positions.

Between March 21st 1918 and his death on the 28th, John would certainly have been busy, harnessing and unharnessing the horses as the battery fired from its position, retired to fresh positions and withdrew yet again. On March 28th John Tate was severely wounded and succumbed to his wounds, being buried in grave VII.C.2. Faubourg D'Amiens Cemetery, Arras.

LANCE CORPORAL PETER FRED BERESFORD
NO. 12960 21ST BATTALION KINGS ROYAL RIFLE CORPS
DIED MARCH 30TH 1918 AGED 21

The Beresfords farmed at Cowside, a farm on the hillside above Newhouse, Deepdale in Langstrothdale (the farmstead is now derelict). George Beresford originated from Countersett in Wensleydale and married Jane Metcalfe from Starbotton, setting up home at Cowside. Peter was the third eldest child of six and the eldest son (Alice, Hannah, Peter, Frank, Norah, Eva).

Peter Fred Beresford
of Kettlewell and Langstrothdale

Their father, George, was about to take over a fresh farm at nearby Greenfield, when he died in 1905, aged 48. His widow and six children moved into a cottage in Starbotton and a few years later Peter began work as an under gamekeeper for the Holdsworth family on their Scargill House Estate. However, his mother, Jane, remarried just before the outbreak of war and the whole family went with their step father to live at Old Ing Farm, Horton-in-Ribblesdale.

It was to Keighley that Peter travelled to enlist and he joined the 21st Battalion KRRC. He fought in France with his Battalion but in November 1917 they were sent to Italy as reinforcements to help the Italians, who had fallen back in disarray at the Battle of Caporetto. For the next three months the Battalion was stationed in Italy, spending lengthy spells in the front line trenches.

On March 2nd they entrained at Bojand Station in Italy and arrived at Sombrin in France on March 8th. A few days later the life of the Battalion, as a unit, came to an end and the men were distributed amongst various Battalions of the Regiment. It was whilst taking part in actions against the onslaught by the Germans that Peter was wounded and was taken 40 kilometres west of Arras to the 6th Stationary Hospital at Frevent. His condition worsened and he caught influenza, resulting in his death on March 30th 1918. Peter Fred Beresford was buried in grave A.2. St. Hilaire Cemetery Extension, Frevent. He was highly regarded in the dale and even though his family now lived in Ribblesdale, a memorial service was held at Hubberholme Church, where he had been baptised.

*** (**The Beresford Band** It is interesting to note that other branches of the Beresford family living in Langstrothdale were musically gifted, playing instruments at dances and entertainments throughout the dale and further afield. In the late 19th century and during the earlier years of the 20th century, Peter Beresford of Oughtershaw, playing the fiddle, continued the tradition by playing in a small band, whilst during the late 1930's and into the 1940's and 50's, the band consisted of his son Jackie (accordian), George Beresford (accordian), Harry Cockerill (accordian) and later, Mickey Walker on the drums. During these times they played at the small village halls in Langstrothdale, Wharfedale, Coverdale and Hawes. On the occasion of the 1937 Coronation the Beresford Band was to be found playing at Stalling Busk, in Wensleydale).

SECOND LIEUTENANT HARRY BATTYE
8TH BATTALION ROYAL WARWICKSHIRE REGIMENT
DIED MARCH 31ST 1918 AGED 22

Seven days previously, Harry's brother, Second Lieutenant John Battye, had been killed to the south of Peronne and now a second dreaded telegram arrived at 65 Frenchgate, Richmond, the family home of their parents and younger brother, Richard, telling them of Harry's death.

Harry, junior, had left Richmond to work elsewhere, as his brother had done, but in 1915 he joined the 2nd/8th Battalion Royal Warwickshire Regiment. He received his commission on October 31st 1917 and eventually joined his Battalion in France on January 16th 1918. During the German push in March 1918 his Battalion was involved in repeated withdrawals and counter-attacks as the British forces were in danger of being overwhelmed.

Seven days after the death of his brother, Harry Battye was killed in action on March 31st 1918 and, together with his brother John, his name is commemorated on the Pozieres Memorial.

The next fatality from these dales occurred on the penultimate day of the German offensive to try and take Amiens. The day following this death, the offensive ground to a halt, having failed to take its final objective.

PRIVATE THOMAS HARKER
NO. 14471 3RD DRAGOON GUARDS (PRINCE OF WALES'S OWN)
DIED APRIL 4TH 1918 AGED 23

The Harker family lived at Hillside, near Scar House, above Langthwaite, in Arkengarthdale. In 1901 Joseph Harker was a farmer, who, with his wife Margaret, raised nine children at Hillside. Thomas, at six years of age, was the second youngest. His eldest brother, Robert, was a lead miner in the rapidly declining Arkengarthdale mines, whilst other older brothers were working on the farm.

When Thomas left school he joined his brother Joseph working on the farm and at the Fremington Edge chert quarry, near Reeth. They both enlisted in the army in Arkengarthdale, and partly because of their work with horses they became members of a cavalry regiment, the Dragoon Guards. They even found themselves in the same Battalion.

Thomas Harker from Arkengarthdale

The enemy was driving towards Villers-Bretonneux, 10 kilometres east of Amiens and between April 3rd and 6th, the 3rd Dragoon Guards, with the Royals and a Machine gun Squadron, were ordered to plug a gap at Bois de Vaire, east of Amiens, until the infantry could arrive. On April 4th, the Dragoon Guards was the advance regiment, leaving the wood in line of Troop Column under heavy shell fire.

As the 3rd Dragoon Guards galloped up towards the wood they came under heavy shell fire. They dismounted and took up positions with the Australian Infantry on their right and some mixed up British infantry on their left. The cavalry had been on hand to ride in quickly and support the infantry, otherwise the enemy would have got through. The enemy were attacking in large numbers under cover of heavy artillery fire, but they were halted by noon, although it was a "close call". Villers-Bretonneux was the key to Amiens and the 3rd Dragoon Guards had helped stop the Germans reaching it.

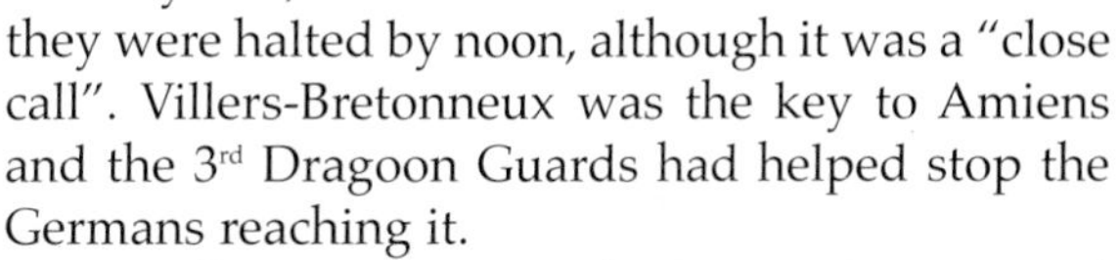

Joseph Harker and brother Thomas Harker

At Villers-Bretonneux the Regiment sustained 94 casualties and Thomas Harker was one of the men killed. Thomas and his brother Joseph were side by side on April 4th when Thomas was shot through the heart. His body was recovered and it was buried in grave II.A.3. Adelaide Cemetery, Villers-Bretonneux.

The Germans, finding that their advance was being brought to a standstill in the direction of Amiens, turned their attention further north and determined to threaten the Channel ports. On April 9th they began a concentrated attack along the River Lys, on the British and Portuguese front between Armentieres and La Bassee, and the fighting spread to Messines in Belgium. Further dalesmen would lose their lives as they fought to check the German advance in the north.

PRIVATE ROBERT BOWNAS
NO. 41255 4TH BATTALION EAST YORKSHIRE REGIMENT
DIED APRIL 10TH 1918 AGED 19

Robert was born at Arncliffe in Littondale in 1899, the eldest son of George and Alice Bownas. George had been born in Linton and married Alice Chapman (born at Buckden), the daughter of Christoper Chapman, senior, the Grassington coach and mail proprietor. George was employed as a coachman at Linton and young Robert began his school life at Arncliffe. However, a few years later, the family went to live at Moor Road Grassington and Robert became apprenticed to one of the Grassington tradesmen.

Robert Bownas of Grassington

In early 1916, a Recruitment Meeting was held in Grassington Town Hall in which seven more men came forward to enlist (William Cummings, Wallace Maxfield, Christopher Chapman, John Foster, Thomas Maxfield, Wilfred Gilbert Steel and Henry Oswald Harrison). At that same meeting, 17 year old Robert Bownas came forward, and on being rejected as not old enough, burst into tears. The officer, however, gave him a letter of merit as consolation, to show to his friends.

On May 14th 1917 Robert travelled from Grassington to Harrogate to enlist in the army, joining the 4th Battalion East Yorkshire Regiment. It was only on April 3rd 1918 that Robert arrived in France as part of a fresh draft and they were rushed to the front as a new German assault became apparent. Seven days later he would be dead.

The 4th Battalion had suffered dreadful casualties in late March as it helped to bring the German advance towards Amiens to a halt. Now it moved north into the area of the LysValley to reorganise and receive reinforcements, including Robert. On the night of the 8th/9th they arrived in defensive positions near Estaires, between Armentieres and Hazebrouck. The Battle of Estaires was about to begin.

At 9a.m. shell fire was very severe and they were ordered to advance to hold the Lys River, east of Estaires, as the Germans had broken through and were about to cross the river. The enemy machine gunners fired from houses overlooking a bridge spanning the river. Here, desperate fighting took place. "B" Company drove them back repeatedly and their fire power was remarkable considering the men were new to battle conditions. The bridge was blown up by the engineers.

On April 10th, "A" and "B" Companies were relieved, since they had suffered severe casualties, but one platoon of "A" Company went astray and was "lost". Heavy shell fire and machine gun fire had scattered "A" Company, whilst "B" Company dug in to act as a counter-attack force. Everywhere there was confusion, as the Germans had crossed the Lys elsewhere. The two forward companies were in a desperate position as they were virtually surrounded, but with splendid bravery, two Lewis gun teams went into position to allow the remnants of "C" and "D" Companies to escape

By the end of April 11th the Battalion strength was down to three officers and 120 men and Robert Bownas was one of the men killed on the 10th. His body was never recovered and his name can be found on Panel 4 Ploegsteert Memorial, Belgium.

Robert was reported as being "missing" and it was not until 13 months later that his parents were officially told that he was dead. It is sad to report that Robert's mother, Alice, had lost a brother, Christopher Chapman, in December 1917, a nephew, Jack Chapman in 1915 and now she had lost her son.

On the Messines Ridge in Belgium, a few miles away across the border from where Robert Bownas fell, a serviceman from Hetton was killed one day later.

PRIVATE FRED SLINGER NELSON
NO. 42761 4TH BATTALION SOUTH STAFFORDSHIRE REGIMENT
DIED APRIL 11TH 1918 AGED 19

Fred was the youngest of the family of five children of Joseph and Annie Nelson. Joseph had farmed in the Settle area and it was there that Fred was born. At some stage before the war the family was to be found at Rock Farm, Hetton, and Joseph became a church warden at Rylstone Church. Fred left school and became a draper in the employ of Messrs. Taylor and Hannam, in their shop on Sheep Street, Skipton.

Fred Slinger Nelson of Hetton
Courtesy of The Craven Herald

Fred enlisted in the army at Keighley in April 1917 and joined the 4th Battalion South Staffordshire Regiment. Sadly, two months earlier, in February 1917 his father, Joseph, had died and another brother had been called up in the same week as the funeral.

After fighting on the Somme in late March 1918, the Battalion was conveyed by train and bus to the Ypres Salient and moved into the line at Ploegsteert Wood. On April 10th the enemy attack opened at 3-30a.m. with heavy shelling of the back areas by gas shells. At 5-30a.m. the Germans opened a barrage on the front and support lines and then lengthened to hit the Reserve. "C" Company in the front line was wiped out. No. 6 platoon, "B" Company withdrew, owing to the heavy shelling, and when ordered to move forward at all costs, it was unable to re-occupy the position.

Similar heavy fighting took place on the following day and it was then that Fred Nelson was killed. His name was another one to be included on the Ploegsteert Memorial, on Panel 6.

PRIVATE JOHN CHAPMAN KEARTON
NO. 33236 4TH BATTALION YORKSHIRE REGIMENT
DIED APRIL 12TH 1918 AGED 34

John was the son of Mary Kearton of No. 8 Sleegill, Richmond, and the brother of James Kearton who had been killed in France on November 20th 1917. John had been born at Marrick in 1884 and in 1901 was still living there, employed as a servant. By the outbreak of war he was living with his wife, Eleonor, at Sleegill, Richmond, and it was from the town that he enlisted and joined the 4th Battalion Yorkshire Regiment.

The Battalion had sustained heavy casualties during the German offensive towards Amiens in late March 1918 and by March 29th its strength was only 300 men. It moved into billets at Bethune on April 2nd, where it received reinforcements of 22 officers and 800 men from England.

On April 8th the men were ordered to leave Bethune to play their part in the Battle of the Lys, relieving the decimated Portuguese battalions at Sailly-sur-Lys. The Germans attacked heavily on April 11th, forcing the men to retire. The whole of April 12th was passed in falling back from one position after another, incurring many casualties, but causing great loss to the enemy and by night-fall La Motte-au-Bois was reached, where some huts were occupied and rest was gratefully taken. However, John Chapman Kearton had not survived the day, and, with his body lost on the field of battle, his name is honoured on Panel 4 Ploegsteert Memorial.

SERGEANT JOHN HENRY ALDERSON
NO. 12329 18TH BATTALION DURHAM LIGHT INFANTRY
DIED APRIL 12TH 1918 AGED 28

The Alderson family of Barningham
Left to right: John Henry Alderson (killed in the Great War), Mary A. Alderson, David Alderson, David Alderson, Thomas Frederick Alderson

The Aldersons were long standing residents of the village of Barningham, near Richmond, and farmed at Hill Top Farm. David and Mary Alderson had three sons, David, Fred and John Henry. While the two older brothers worked on the family farm, John Henry Alderson worked in a shop at nearby Barnard Castle. At the out-break of war, it was the youngest son, John, a single man, who enlisted at

Sunderland and joined the 18th Battalion Durham Light Infantry, rising to the rank of Sergeant.

As with its sister Battalion, the 8th, they found themselves defending the bridge-heads across the River Lys against overwhelming odds on April 10th, 11th and 12th. The fighting was very stubborn, the Germans only succeeding in advancing five miles, despite the Battalion being so worn out by the March retreat towards Amiens that throughout these days of fighting some fell asleep even in the act of firing. During the intense fighting on April 12th John Henry Alderson was killed by shell fire and his body was eventually buried in grave II.F.7. Le Grand Beaumart British Cemetery, Steenwerck, between Armentieres and Bailleul. He is commemorated on the Richmond Memorial.

PRIVATE GEORGE BINNS
NO. 13788 4TH BATTALION WEST RIDING REGIMENT
DIED APRIL 14TH 1918 AGED 20

In 1901 George's father, George senior, was a sawyer at a woodyard at Burnsall. He was born at Burnsall and married Mary, a girl from the nearby village of Appletreewick. At Burnsall, in 1901, they were raising their family of Charles (6), George (3) and Mary (1), all born in the village. By 1914, however, the family was living at Park Cottage, Barden, on the Bolton Abbey Estate. As a boy, George junior was a member of the Barden Chapel choir and later, he was employed by farmer George Atkinson of Low House, Barden.

George Binns of Barden, near Bolton Abbey and also Burnsall
Courtesy of The Craven Herald

George enlisted at Ilkley on September 20th 1914 (he was underage) and went to France on August 23rd 1915 with the 4th Battalion West Riding Regiment. He was wounded on the first day of the Somme, July 1st 1916, and came back to England before returning to the front when he was fit.

During the second German "push" in early April 1918 the Battalion was involved in defending the positions in front of Bailleul, west of Armentieres. On April 12th the Battalion took up positions west of the town, along the railway, under severe enemy shelling. One shell caused 15 casualties among the HQ Detail. The morning of the 14th was quiet but soon after 12a.m. the enemy opened a very heavy bombardment of the town and its outposts. Early in the afternoon, enemy troops dribbled forward in the direction of Steam Mill, occupying it and threatening the whole line. "C" Company and two companies of the 7th Battalion West Ridings immediately counter-attacked. The situation was completely restored except that Steam Mill remained in enemy hands.

During the day's actions George Binns was killed by shell fire and his name appears on the Tyne Cot Memorial. He was the first Barden lad to be killed and his name appears on both the Bolton Abbey memorial and the Burnsall Memorial.

PRIVATE THOMAS WILLIAM JOHNSON
NO. 50674 2ND BATTALION LANCASHIRE FUSILIERS
DIED APRIL 22ND 1918 AGED 42

Thomas was born in 1876 at Hornby, a small village between Lancaster and Kirkby Lonsdale, the son of Thomas and Maria Johnson. However, Thomas junior was living in Richmond when he enlisted and he first of all joined the Army Service Corps, before transferring to the 2nd Battalion Lancashire Fusiliers.

Thomas Johnson was killed by shell fire on April 22nd 1918, during a heavy enemy bombardment on the southern fringes of the German advance into the Lys Valley. His name is recorded on the Loos Memorial.

SERGEANT MAJOR TOM WARD NO. 50876
ARMY GYMNASTIC STAFF NORTHAMPTONSHIRE REGIMENT
DIED APRIL 27TH 1918 AGED 26

At Reeth, in 1901, the village post office was in a house called Edgmont, next to the Wesleyan Manse. Living at that address was John Thomas Ward, the sub postmaster and Registrar of Births and Deaths, his wife Louisa Alice and children Alice (13), Elizabeth (11), Tom (9) and Annie (8), all born at Reeth. The members of the family were very strong Methodists.

Tom enlisted in the army at Darlington and rose to the rank of Sergeant Major in the Northamptonshire Regiment, with responsibility for drill and fitness. However, in April 1918, there was an explosion of munitions at their base in France and Tom was wounded in the blast. He was admitted to hospital near the French town of Cassel, 50 kilometres SE of Calais. It was there that he died on April 27th 1918 and was buried in grave I.E.6. Arneke British Cemetery, near Cassel.

PRIVATE JOSEPH JACKSON WILSON
NO. 46482 12TH/13TH BATTALION NORTHUMBERLAND FUSILIERS
DIED APRIL 27TH 1918 AGED 23

Joseph was the fourth youngest of the nine children of John and Margaret Wilson. John, who was born at Reeth, had married Margaret, a Bainbridge girl, and they were living on a farm near Marske Rectory. All nine children had been born at Marske but by 1914 John Wilson was farming within Downholme parish.

Joseph was possibly working well away from home at the outbreak of war because he enlisted at Sunderland and joined the Durham Light Infantry, before transferring to the Northumberland Fusiliers. The Battalion was on the Messines Ridge, at Wytschaete, on April 10th 1918, when the Germans launched their offensive. They came under heavy shelling as the enemy attacked but succeeded in repulsing the enemy on the evening of April 11th.

By April 15th they had moved into the line, Kemmel to Vierstraat, where they were attacked on the high ground and 11 officers and 320 men became casualties by the 16th. At 7p.m. on April 25th the Battalion was ordered to relieve the 1st Lincolnshire

Regiment. April 26th saw very heavy shell fire in the afternoon and through the evening and night, with 87 casualties being sustained and after only one day in the line, they were relieved. Joseph Jackson Wilson was one of those killed in the shelling and his name is to be found on the Tyne Cot Memorial and on the plaque in Downholme Church.

CORPORAL CHARLES HORNER
NO. 266239 6TH BATTALION WEST RIDING REGIMENT
DIED APRIL 29TH 1918 AGED 23

Six year old Charles Horner and his eight year old brother William were living with their grandmother, Rebecca Hughes, at Halton Gill, Littondale, in 1901. They were the sons of farmer Anthony Horner and his wife, Agnes, and had been born at Halton Gill.

Charles Horner of Burnsall
Courtesy of The Craven Herald

Charles enlisted soon after the outbreak of war and had been three times wounded. As the Lys offensive came to a halt, the 6th Battalion was just over the border in Belgium on April 20th 1918, with the enemy still attacking their line. Whilst in Reserve at Poperinghe on the 24th, many bombs were dropped by hostile planes and several men were badly affected by gas shells.

The Battalion was in the front line near Kemmel on April 26th. At about 7-30p.m. on the 28th, the front line was very heavily bombarded for two hours from La Clytte to Ypres. At 3a.m. on April 29th, the enemy opened a terrific bombardment on the front line and back areas. This continued on the front line till 7a.m. when the enemy attacked in great force along the front of the whole Division. Everywhere he was completely repulsed and he suffered great casualties. Bombardment of the back areas continued until 10a.m., with many gas shells being used. The casualties were relatively light, but one of those killed was Charles Horner and he was buried in grave VI.D.5. La Clytte Military Cemetery, 8 kilometres west of Ypres.

Writing to Charles's bereaved mother, Agnes, (Anthony had died by this stage and Agnes was living at Morecambe) Lieutenant Hopwood of Skipton wrote, "Your son was killed by a piece of shell last Monday and his death was instantaneous. I have known your son for a long time personally, seeing that I live in Skipton, and I took rather a greater interest in him than in most of the other fellows. He was a boy of great promise and if he had lived, his promotion with us would have been very rapid."

Agnes Horner had two other sons fighting on the Western Front, one with the Manchester Regiment, and the youngest with the Coldstream Guards.

PRIVATE HENRY LANCASTER
NO. 240211 4TH BATTALION WEST RIDING REGIMENT
DIED APRIL 30TH 1918 AGED 24

Henry was the son of Henry Lancaster, a general labourer from Escombe, a village near Bishop Auckland, and his wife Mary, a native of York. Two daughters were born in the Middlesborough area, Henry was born in 1894 at the village of Melsonby, between Richmond and Darlington, whilst in 1900 the family moved to No. 1 Chapel Wynd, Richmond, where three more children were born. Eventually, in later years, Henry, junior, moved away from Richmond when he married and lived at 3 Brunswick Yard, Albert Street, Lockwood, near the centre of Huddersfield. He was employed in the Lockwood factory of David Brown and Sons, the largest manufacturers in the British Empire of gears for the newly developing car industry (by 1935 the same firm began producing the world renowned David Brown tractors).

When he enlisted at Huddersfield, Henry joined the 4th Battalion West Riding Regiment and during his time on the Western Front was awarded the Military Medal for bravery. At the time of Henry's death his Battalion was in the front line east of Poperinghe, involved in serious fighting on April 27th and 29th. However, Henry Lancaster was not with his colleagues. He had been wounded in earlier fighting in the German offensive towards Amiens, and by the end of April was in a hospital near Cassel, SE of Calais. Henry died on April 30th 1918 and was buried in grave II.D.23. Arneke British Cemetery. He sadly left a widow and young child back in Huddersfield.

LIEUTENANT J. NORMAN PROCTER
6TH BATTALION WEST RIDING REGIMENT (MC)
DIED MAY 2ND 1918 AGED 23

Norman was the younger son of William Atkinson Procter and Rebecca Procter of the Manor House, Rylstone. They owned much land in the area as part of the Cracoe Estate and were local benefactors. Norman was educated at Gresham's School, Holt, in Norfolk, and joined the forces in November 1914, receiving a commission in the 6th Battalion West Riding Regiment.

J. Norman Procter from Rylstone
Courtesy of The Craven Herald

He went to France at the beginning of August 1915, a week after his 21st birthday, as Signalling Officer for his Battalion. He was mentioned in dispatches in April 1916 and received the Military Cross on January 1st 1918 (for gallantry and devotion to duty as Signalling Officer, especially in the trenches near Hulloch in June 1917, when, under mortar, shell and gun fire, he laid new lines when the former had been cut. He also did the same in August 1917 when serving near Nieuport). By January 1918 he was acting as Signalling Officer for his Brigade.

The Battalion had been heavily involved in stemming the German offensive on the River Lys in early April 1918, suffering many casualties, but by

April 25th they were in the vicinity of Poperinghe in Belgium and entering the front line, near Kemmel, on the Messines Ridge. Digging their line under continual shell fire, the Battalion was not attacked until the 29th when the Germans made desperate efforts to break the whole line. The shelling, mostly from big guns, lasted incessantly from 3a.m. to 4p.m. and was the heaviest ever experienced by the Battalion. In the attack that followed, the enemy had to be driven out of the trench by a bayonet charge.

Norman Procter had been wounded by shell fire in the left shoulder and chest and was admitted to the 3rd Australian Casualty Clearing Station. He died from his wounds on May 2nd 1918 and was buried in grave II.B.15. Esquelbecq Military Cemetery. His Commanding Officer wrote, "Your son was a model of an English officer and gentleman. As regards his work, I cannot speak too highly of him; he was most able and devoted to his duty; he was of the greatest assistance to me and my commanding officers and I shall be quite unable to replace him. Your son died doing his duty in a way that could not have been done better. We sadly mourn his loss."

By the end of April Ludendorff called off the offensive. No breakthrough had been effected and the Channel ports were safe. The cost had been great, another 100,000 British casualties – but again, German casualties were almost as great. Ludendorff's carefully trained and prepared shock troops were sadly depleted, the morale of the survivors badly shaken.

The next fatality from these dales occurred far away from the Western Front, at Salonika, to the north of Greece. Bulgaria had entered the war in August 1915 on the side of Austro-Hungary and her ally Germany, with its main aim of attacking Serbia and so regaining part of Macedonia which Serbia had seized from Bulgaria in 1913. The Greeks, and an Anglo-French force despatched from Gallipoli, were too late to help the Serbs, being pushed back by the Bulgars onto the port area of Salonika. Evacuation made good military sense but, after the Gallipoli disaster, it would have been unthinkable, politically. So an Allied force of Serb, Greek, British, French, Italian and Russian contingents held the Salonika area more or less passively until 1918. The inaction of the Allies resulted in the Germans referring to the enclave as their "largest internment camp", and with 500,000 Allied troops in the area, such a description was possibly justified.

CORPORAL JOHN BARKER
NO. 17370 9TH BATTALION SOUTH LANCASHIRE REGIMENT
DIED MAY 6TH 1918 AGED 26

John Barker's grandfather, also called John, was the Charlesworth family's Estate Agent and head gamekeeper on the Grinton Estate, living first with his family at Grinton Lodge and then at Langhorne House, in Reeth. His son, Adam George Barker, was John junior's father, and we find that he certainly had "itchy feet".

At the age of 16 Adam ran away from home and enlisted in the army, becoming a military musician (playing the clarinet) in the Grenadier Guards for 18 months, before leaving the army. Back in the dale, he became a gamekeeper and in 1886 married his wife, Dorothy Ann. With farming and lead mining in the dale in decline, Adam, Dorothy and their daughter emigrated to Canada, where Adam served as a musician in the Canadian Army 1887 – 1890. In 1890 he spent some months by himself in Australia, before returning to Canada to serve in the army once again.

John Barker was born in Canada in 1892 but shortly afterwards his family moved to America, living there until 1899, with Adam serving in the American Army. Dorothy and the children returned to England and Reeth in 1899, and then to Healaugh, but Adam remained in the American Army, helping to fight the Spanish in the Philippines for two years and managing to get himself shipwrecked off Nagasaki, Japan.

However, Adam's father, John senior, died and by 1902 Adam returned to his family at Healaugh and Reeth. He still could not resist travelling, first of all moving to Wharfedale as a gamekeeper and then in 1909 going by himself to New York State as a military bandsman until returning in 1911, when, at the end of the year, he died.

John had inherited some of his father's wanderlust. In December 1907 he had been sent by Adam to Aldershot, where he joined the West Riding Regiment, but on his father's death in 1911 he bought himself out for £18. At home for just three months, he

John Barker of Reeth, Swaledale, (Scottish Rifles), is seated

John Barker, South Lancashire Regiment with French and British colleagues in Salonika. He stands on the extreme right

then enlisted in the Scottish Rifles in 1912 and served in Malta. In 1914 he again bought himself out and joined his two sisters in Pittsburgh, Pennsylvania, working as a telephone operator in a Veteran's Hospital.

When war broke out, his brother George sent a postcard asking him when he was returning to do his duty. John arrived home and enlisted in 1915, joining the 9th Battalion South Lancashire Regiment and being posted to Salonika. His letters home make grim reading for he writes that he feels life is passing him by and that for 18 months he has never been away from the sound of guns.

However, in early May 1918 he was severely wounded when a trench mortar blew up during an instruction course and he died from his wounds. John Barker was buried in grave D.680. Sarigol Military Cemetery, Kriston, 40 kilometres north of Thessalonika. His brother George served in the Royal Marines Band before the war (playing his father's clarinet) and fought at the Battle of Jutland 1916, helping to lay the guns in the gun room.

LANCE CORPORAL JOHN WILLIAM RINGROSE
NO. 238222 2ND BATTALION WEST YORKSHIRE REGIMENT (MM)
DIED MAY 25TH 1918 AGED 20

In 1901 John was three years old and living in Richmond with his father, John Ringrose, mother Carol Annie and younger siblings Harold and Alice. His father originated from Lincolnshire and owned a glazing business in Richmond. For many years he was on the Town Council, was an Alderman, and the Mayor of Richmond 1912 - 1913. He also did much to help in founding the District Nursing Association.

John Ringrose, junior, enlisted at Richmond and joined the Yorkshire Regiment, winning the Military Medal during the Ludendorff offensive of March and April 1918. However, the Battalion sustained severe casualties and John found himself transferred to the 2nd Battalion West Yorkshire Regiment. On May 4th they travelled by train and bus across France to take up duties in a supposedly quiet section of the French front in the Champagne area, between Soissons and Rheims.

On May 20th they relieved the Devon Regiment in the front line trenches in front of La Mussette and during the next five days, patrols were sent out to reconnoitre at night. On the 23rd a night patrol encountered a strong enemy patrol and during the fight seven enemy were accounted for, with two men wounded and three missing. It was during this period of night patrols that John Ringrose lost his life. His body was never recovered and he is commemorated on the Soissons Memorial.

Just two days later, Ludendorff launched his next major offensive, this time in the Champagne countryside, the very area a number of British Battalions had been sent to in order to recuperate from the terrible mauling they had received during March and April. Two serviceman from these dales, both natives of Richmond, would die on the first day of the offensive.

PRIVATE WALTER GORNER BARKER
NO. 240643 5TH BATTALION YORKSHIRE REGIMENT
DIED MAY 27TH 1918 AGED 29

We have already seen in Chapter Five that on November 2nd 1917, Walter's brother,

Edward Barker, was killed. Their father was a plumber in Richmond, but Walter appears not to be employed in the family business, for when he enlisted at Scarborough, he was living in the village of Sledmere, ten miles SE of Malton.

He joined the 5th Battalion Yorkshire Regiment and on May 27th they were in the front line between Soissons and Rheims.

AND
PRIVATE EDGAR CYRIL FAWCETT
NO. 76479 22ND BATTALION DURHAM LIGHT INFANTRY
DIED MAY 27TH 1918 AGED 18

Edgar Cyril Fawcett had been born at Walburn, in Downholme parish in 1900, the youngest of five children of John and Elizabeth Fawcett, all born in the parish. John came from Castle Bolton, in Wensleydale, whilst his wife, Elizabeth was a native of Thornton Rust. In 1901 the family moved the short distance to Richmond and settled in Frenchgate. John's occupation was a Hide and Skin agent and collector. At a Hide and Skin works the carcasses of cattle would arrive to be cut up to obtain the offal and bones, whilst at a later stage the skins were cured. Salt petre and sand were placed in layers around the hides to dress and cure them. Sheep and pigs' intestines were cured and dressed to be made into sausage skins and the animal bones were collected and sent off to be ground down and made into glue.

In late 1917 Edgar enlisted at Richmond and joined the Durham Light Infantry. Until 1918 it was against the regulations to knowingly allow soldiers below the age of 19 to fight abroad, but in the desperate fight for survival in March and April 1918, resulting in severe losses of manpower, a law was passed to revoke the ruling, allowing those soldiers of 18 years of age to embark for the killing grounds. As with so many of these young, inexperienced soldiers, 18 year old Edgar Fawcett was rushed to France to make up the numbers in the decimated battalions.

May 27th saw the third great German offensive on the Rivers Marne and Aisne. By May 30th they had reached the Marne but at this point the newly arrived American forces were flung against the nose of the German offensive, held the bridges, then counter-attacked and drove the Germans back across the Marne. Throughout June and July further German assaults were repulsed and on July 18th the Allies went on the offensive themselves on the Aisne and Marne. The initiative had been wrested from the Germans and Ludendorff's gamble to conclude the war successfully, had failed. Allied morale soared as that of the Germans dropped.

However, on the first day of the German offensive, Walter Barker and Edgar Fawcett were killed. About 1a.m the enemy bombardment opened with every kind and calibre of shell, including gas, and heavy casualties were caused in the forward posts on the plateau, and nearly all the rearward communications were cut within a very short time. The ordeal was made more trying by crouching, semi-suffocated in gas masks. At 4a.m., the grey waves of German soldiers advanced out of the swirling mist and reached the crest of the ridge in the centre, uncovering the flank of the 50th Division and forcing many of the survivors to fall back down the slope. The plateau was enveloped on both flanks by 6-30a.m..

The hostile barrage was maintained to the last and many men were killed or captured before they could leave their deep dug-outs. Smoke and dust made observation impossible, whilst the HQ Company was fighting around the

Commanding Officer's command post and appeared to be surrounded. All attempts to organise any defence at this point had to be abandoned and the retreat was continued. Walter Barker and Edgar Fawcett were killed in those early hours of May 27th. As with so many British soldiers on that first day of battle, their bodies were never recovered and their names are inscribed on the Soissons Memorial.

Another Richmond man was the next to die, but on this occasion, as a POW, in the hands of the Germans.

PRIVATE WILLIAM HUTCHINSON SHIELDS NO. 35071
7TH BATTALION KINGS OWN YORKSHIRE LIGHT INFANTRY
DIED JUNE 21ST 1918 AGED 36

The Shields family was living in Richmond by 1901, with father William employed as a farm worker. He had been born at Barton, a village five miles south of Darlington, and spent some years with his wife Ann at Darlington, where a daughter, Ada, was born. By 1882, however, they arrived in Richmond, where William, junior, was born in that year and Rose and Frank would complete the family. By 1901, however, their mother, Ann, had died and 19 year old William was employed as a grocer's apprentice in the town.

William eventually enlisted at Richmond, serving in the army, and joined the Yorkshire Regiment, before transferring to the 7th Battalion KOYLI. In the Ludendorff offensives of March 21st and April 9th, many British soldiers were wounded or captured. One of those wounded and taken prisoner by the Germans in April was William Shields. He was treated behind the German lines but he died on June 21st and was buried by the Germans in grave I.A.7. Le Quesnoy Communal Cemetery, 15 kilometres SE of Valenciennes.

SAPPER RALPH RUTTER NO. 249342
50TH BROAD GAUGE (RAILWAYS) OPERATING COMPANY
CORPS OF ROYAL ENGINEERS
DIED JUNE 25TH 1918 AGED 30

In 1901 the Rutter family was living at Whin Hall, an isolated farm house in the wilds near Winterings, high up on the hillside above Gunnerside. Cyprian Rutter was a farmer and lead miner, living with his wife, Annie Elizabeth, born at Blades, and children John Thomas (16) born Heights, Ralph (13) born Dyke Heads, James Lockey (8), Ernest (5), Matthew (3) and Margaret (3 months). Ralph's older brother, John Thomas, was a lead miner like his father and became the last miner to work at the Old Gang Mine.

However, Ralph left Swaledale in the years before the Great War to work on the railways, mainly as a platelayer, and by 1914 he was living in Haworth. He enlisted at nearby Keighley and joined the West Riding Regiment, but his skills gained in civilian employment could be put to better use by the Royal Engineers and he became a member of the 50th Broad Gauge (Railway) Operating Company. Their task was to construct and maintain the track and rolling stock bringing supplies and munitions up to the front line, as well as providing track for the large artillery pieces to operate on. It was a dangerous job because they worked at times close to the front

The Rutter family of Gunnerside, Swaledale. (Ralph Rutter died in the Great War.)
Back row: Matthew Rutter, Ralph Rutter, Cyprian Rutter, John Thomas Rutter, James Lockey Rutter
Front row: Annie Elizabeth Rutter, Margaret Rutter, Cyprian Rutter, Ernest Rutter

line and were obvious targets for the German gunners.

In June 1918 Ralph was taken ill and was admitted to a Casualty Clearing Station and hospital, but he died on June 25th and was buried in grave IV.L.47. Aubigny Communal Cemetery, 15 kilometres NW of Arras. (Ralph's brother, James Lockey Rutter also enlisted in the army and served with General Allenby against the Turks in Palestine).

Earlier in the year, a Wharfedale man had lost his life in France, whilst serving in the RAF, and now another RAF man from the same dale was shot down and killed.

SECOND LIEUTENANT CLARENCE DUCKMAN BOOTHMAN 210 SQUADRON RAF DIED JUNE 26TH 1918 AGED 22

David Boothman, the father of Clarence, was a draper who owned a gents outfitters on Otley Street, Skipton, and in 1901 the family was living at Hothfield Terrace, Skipton. David and his wife Sarah had been born in small villages adjacent to each other, he at Langbar, she at Beamsley, on the Duke of Devonshire's Bolton Abbey Estate. In 1901, we find that their eldest son, 17 year old Herbert, who had been born

Sopwith Camel 210 Squadron

at Bedale, was now working in his father's store, whilst 7 year old Percy and 5 year old Clarence were born at Skipton.

By 1914, Clarence and his parents were living at Oakfield, Beamsley, and in October 1914 Clarence enlisted as a private in the West Riding Regiment, embarking for France in April 1915. While in France he was offered a commission. He came home, passed his examination for the infantry, but volunteered for the Flying Corps, where he passed all his tests and went out to France to join 210 Squadron.

210 Squadron was part of 11th Army Wing and was based at the airfield of Sainte Marie-Cappel, 12 kilometres east of St. Omer, Northern France. They had recently been equipped with the Sopwith Camel, a supreme dogfighter that had the honour of shooting down more enemy aircraft than any other type. A deadly weapon in the hands of a skilled pilot, it was the despair of the novice. Clarence Boothman arrived at St. Marie-Cappel in early June and three weeks later he was dead.

On June 26th he took off in Sopwith Camel D9614 on "Operation Armentieres - Lille" He was last seen over Armentieres between 7p.m. and 10p.m. and was shot down east of the German lines by Lieutenant Jacobs of Jasta (Jagdstaffel) 7 (a fighter squadron of 14 aircraft). Badly wounded in the crash, Clarence died on the same day and was buried by the Germans in grave IV.H.31. Pont-Du-Hem Military Cemetery, La Gorgue, between La Bassee and Estaires. His name is also commemorated in Bolton Priory.

ORDINARY SEAMAN JAMES THOMAS SWALES
NO. SS/8309 HMS "VICTORY" ROYAL NAVY
DIED JULY 3RD 1918 AGED 19

James Swales (known as Jim) was the cousin of Tom Swales from Yew Tree Farm, the Rylstone postman, who was killed on March 22nd 1918, on the second day of the Ludendorff offensive. Now, just three months later, Jim Swales died.

He was the only son of Fred and Eleanor Swales. Fred Swales was born at Dale Head Farm, Newhouse in Bowland, to the west of Settle, where he lived with his brother Thomas, the father of Tom Swales.

At the age of eight he went with his family to a farm at Flasby, between Gargrave and Hetton. With many brothers in the family, he had to seek work elsewhere and began farming at Far Hill, Bolton by Bowland, near Guisburn. However, in 1898 he married a Flasby farmer's daughter, 19 year old Eleanor Robinson Bownass, at Gargrave Parish church and they settled to married life at Bolton by Bowland, where a son, James Thomas Swales, was born on July 29th 1899.

A few years later they returned to continue farming at Flasby, where a daughter, Freda, was born. Eventually, the family moved the short distance to run a farm at Threaplands, on the outskirts of Cracoe, across the fields from Swinden Quarry.

James Swales from Cracoe
Courtesy of The Craven Herald

Jim attended Cracoe Council School before commencing at Ermysted's Grammar School in September 1912 at the age of thirteen. Although only at the school for three

The Swales family at Threaplands
Jim Swales, Eleanor Swales, Fred Swales, Freda Swales

years he was a bright student. He left school on 27th July 1915 and went to work on the family farm.

On reaching his 18th birthday, July 1917, he was called up and joined the West Riding Regiment. However, in April 1918, five weeks before his death, he joined the Royal Navy and began his training at HMS "Victory", a shore-based establishment at Portsmouth.

However, he caught a chill which developed into double pneumonia and he died on Wednesday July 3rd. Fortunately his parents were able to get to him on Monday night, just before he lost consciousness, which he never regained. There was a very large attendance at the funeral at Rylstone Church on Sunday July 7th.

James and Freda Swales

As the Germans began to withdraw on the Marne front, the French and Americans, with a British contingent, began an offensive on the Marne and Aisne, between July 18th and August 5th. A serviceman with Wharfedale connections would die from the wounds he received.

SERGEANT GEORGE EMSLEY WILKINSON NO. 240112 (MM)
5TH BATTALION WEST RIDING REGIMENT
DIED JULY 26TH/27TH 1918 AGED 23

George was the third son of R.A. and Jane Wilkinson who farmed Cote Farm, Kilnsey, near Kettlewell, before moving to Lane Head Farm, Kirkburton, a village just to the south of Huddersfield. George worked for the firm of Messrs. Taylor and Hobson, cabinet makers of Huddersfield. He was a Territorial soldier before the war and went to France in April 1915 with the 5th Battalion West Riding Regiment. Three other brothers also joined the army, and one of them, Felix, who had been born at Litton, in Littondale, had been missing since May 3rd 1917. Eventually, his mother would receive the news confirming his death.

George won the Military Medal on the night of August 13th 1917 when the trenches were heavily shelled and all the wires were broken. Corporal Wilkinson, with his linesmen, went out under heavy shell fire and repaired the lines, whilst men were being killed around them. He did the same on other nights during that period. Later, he was promoted to Sergeant.

On July 18th 1918 the Allied offensive began on the Marne, with the 5th Battalion ordered to capture the Bois du Petit Champ on July 22nd. At the centre of the wood they met with serious opposition from a strong point difficult to locate, and sustained heavy casualties. Meanwhile "C" Company were threatened with envelopment by a very strong counter-attack and were eventually surrounded. The enemy captured the most forward post, then charged the other two posts of the Company with fixed bayonets. A Lewis gun was put into action and compelled the enemy to retire temporarily. They came on again using stick bombs and the position became untenable.

During the desperate fighting on July 22nd George Wilkinson was severely wounded and taken to the Casualty Clearing Station, where he died on July 26th. He was buried in grave 79 Vertus Communal Cemetery, a village 30 kilometres west of Chalons-en-Champagne. His mother, Jane, by now a widow, received the news of his death at "Park View", Kirkburton, the second of her children to be killed in the war. George Wilkinson's name is not on the Kettlewell memorial, but I have included him because of the family's strong connection to Kilnsey and Littondale.

Sadly, the next man to lose his life had survived the dangers on the battlefield, only to die as a Prisoner of War.

PRIVATE JOHN THOMAS IDESON
NO. 37122 23RD (TYNESIDE SCOTTISH) BATTALION
NORTHUMBERLAND FUSILIERS
DIED JULY 28TH 1918 AGED 32

John Thomas Ideson of Barden, near Bolton Abbey
Left to right: Lilian Ideson, Dennis Ideson, Thomas Ideson, John Thomas Ideson

John was the only son of Charles and Sarah Ideson and was born in 1886 at Rose Cottage, Howgill, a small cottage next to Howgill Farm, on the Bolton Abbey Estate. Charles was a farmer, born at Barden, who met Sarah Phillips when she came from Burnley to work in service on the Estate. A daughter, Jessie, completed the family.

In his earlier years, John worked on the farm but later he became a woodman on the Estate. He was a good all-round cricketer and a member of Barden Cricket Club. In 1907 he married Lilian Platts from Grassington, who was housemaid at the house next to Howgill Farm, and they began their married life at High Gamsworth, Barden, a smallholding, on which they kept a few animals. Six children were born (Rennie 1907, Phyllis 1908, Mary Ethel 1910, Charles 1912, Tom 1914 and Dennis 4th September 1916). In 1915, John's mother, Sarah, died.

John enlisted at Keighley on January 25th 1917 and went to France on April 25th 1917, but was admitted to hospital in France with septic poisoning and returned to England on November 30th. After a period of recuperation he returned to France on February 20th 1918. When John came home on leave, Lilian would take the children to meet their father and a great fuss would be made of him on the way home. When it was time for him to return, Lilian walked from Barden with him all the way to Skipton Station and then returned alone. Sadly, February 20th 1918 would be the last time she waved goodbye to him on Skipton Station.

On March 21st 1918, John was captured by the Germans on the first day of the Ludendorff offensive. He eventually arrived at a prison camp in Germany, called Lazaret, and on June 27th Lilian received a postcard from John, dated May 30th, stating that he was a POW in Germany and was not wounded. Sadly, news arrived

John Thomas Ideson is second from the right, on the back row

in August that John had died in the camp on July 28th, due to lung problems. Internment took place on July 31st in the Allies POW Cemetery near Munster city. There was a funeral in which the coffin was followed by his comrades, who laid a beautiful floral tribute, the ribbons of which would be sent to the family (After the war, his body was reburied in grave XVIII.B.29. Cologne Southern Cemetery).

Tragically, four months after the death of John Thomas Ideson, his sister Jessie, aged 29, died in childbirth. Meanwhile, Lilian and her six children remained at High Gamsworth, with Charles, her widower father-in-law, moving into the house to help in raising the family.

LANCE CORPORAL ARTHUR NEWBOULD NO. 39021
2ND BATTALION THE LOYAL NORTH LANCASHIRE REGIMENT
DIED JULY 30TH 1918 AGED 23

Arthur was the eldest child of John and Alice Newbould. John, a native of Burnsall, was married to Alice, a Hebden girl, and he was employed as a gamekeeper. After six years of married life in Burnsall, the Newboulds moved to Hebden, although in later life Arthur maintained his Burnsall connections by singing in the Church Choir and remained a member of the Hartlington Band of Hope.

Arthur Newbould of Hebden and Grassington
Courtesy of The Craven Herald

Arthur enlisted at Bradford in November 1915 and after serving as a driver in the Army Service Corps he was transferred to The Loyal North Lancashire Regiment and went to Egypt in July 1917. Another brother, Harry, was also serving in the army, as a gunner in the Royal Garrison Artillery. In May 1918 Arthur was transferred to France and took part in the Allied offensive on the Marne (July 18th - August 5th). He was severely wounded on July 30th and died the same day at the 63rd Casualty Clearing Station. His body was buried in grave II.B.50. Senlis French National Cemetery.

PRIVATE WILLIAM JOHNSON
NO. 40785 2ND BATTALION SOUTH STAFFORDSHIRE REGIMENT
DIED JULY 31ST 1918 AGED 27

William was born at Skipton, the second youngest of five children of Spencer and Mary Johnson., all born at Skipton. Spencer was from Beamsley and Mary was from nearby Bolton Abbey, but they lived in Skipton until the mid 1890's, where Spencer was a cabinet maker. By 1901 the family, minus William, was back at Town End, Beamsley, where Spencer continued his trade and also farmed. 10 year old William, however, was living with his grandfather, Thomas Johnson, at Hazlewood and

Storriths, on the Bolton Abbey Estate.

When William enlisted at Skipton in March 1917, he was living at nearby Bradley, and he joined the 2nd Battalion South Staffordshire Regiment, embarking for France in July 1917. He was taken by the Germans as a POW on March 24th 1918, during the first Ludendorff offensive. His parents received a postcard from him on July 14th, from his POW camp at Parchim in Northern Germany, saying that he was quite well.

William Johnson of Beamsley, near Bolton Abbey
Courtesy of The Craven Herald

However, there is a mystery as to what happened after that, when, in November, they received information that he had died of pneumonia on July 31st. The mystery is that he had died at a POW hospital at Conde, which was some miles behind the German front line at Valenciennes. This POW camp was 500 miles from Parchim, and just behind the Western Front.

Whatever the reason, William Johnson was buried in grave A.80. Conde-Sur-L'Escaut Communal Cemetery, north of Valenciennes.

SERGEANT ROBERT RIGG
NO. 27582 "D" BATTERY 232ND BRIGADE ROYAL FIELD ARTILLERY
DIED AUGUST 7TH 1918 AGED 33

Robert Rigg, formerly of Grassington
Courtesy of The Craven Herald

Robert Rigg was born at Baldersby, a village between Thirsk and Ripon, and in 1901 he was a 16 year old cattleman on a farm in the nearby village of Kirklington. However, a few years later there was a change of direction in his life when he became a police constable and for three years was a popular officer at Grassington, before moving on. (it is for this reason that I have included Robert, for you will not find his name on the Linton Memorial, covering the Grassington area.).

He was serving in the Normanton area, between Wakefield and Castleford, when he enlisted there in August 1915 and first of all joined the West Riding Regiment, embarking for France in January 1916. Robert transferred to the Royal Field Artillery and was killed on August 7th 1918, as his Battery prepared for the great British offensive to be launched on the following day. His body was buried in grave A.5. Montigny Communal Cemetery on the Amiens to Contay road.

PRIVATE JOHN (JACK) WATKIN
NO. 306730 "A" COMPANY 8TH BATTALION TANK CORPS
DIED AUGUST 9TH 1918 AGED 20

John Watkin's father, Robert, was a painter and decorator in Richmond. He met his future wife Eliza when she came to Richmond from Kirkby Stephen, in the employment of the Wesleyan minister. They had three children, Jack, Jane and Thomas and the family lived at Newbiggin, Richmond.

Jack served his apprenticeship as a plumber for Lord Zetland, at Aske Hall, near Richmond, but then enlisted in the market town and first joined the Royal Engineers, before transferring to the Tank Corps.

Jack Watkin was killed on the second day of General Haig's Amiens Offensive (August 8th – September 4th 1918), which caught the Germans off guard by a well mounted assault, secretly prepared. Troops advanced without preliminary bombardment, preceded by tanks, and bit deep into the German positions. General Ludendorff stated that August 8th had been the "Black Day" of the German Army.

John Watkin from Richmond
Left to right: John (Jack) Watkin, Thomas Watkin

Between August 1st and the 7th the 8th Battalion Tank Corps brought their tanks by train to Amiens and then established a base east of the town, preparing the tanks for battle. At 8-20a.m. on August 8th an action took place, with 6 tanks being damaged or destroyed (8 men were killed and 14 wounded). They rallied in nearby Amy Wood. At 4a.m. on August 9th four tanks of "A" Company were in action at Vauvillers, 22 kilometres east of Amiens. Three of these were knocked out with the loss of five men killed and seven men wounded and at 5p.m. the three remaining tanks were brought back to Bayonvillers.

One of those who was killed was Jack Watson, but his body was not recovered and his name is found on Panel 11 Vis-En-Artois Memorial, 10 kilometres SE of Arras.

PRIVATE GEORGE RUSSELL NO. 41062
1ST INFANTRY LABOUR COMPANY LINCOLNSHIRE REGIMENT
DIED AUGUST 20TH 1918 AGED 26

Thomas and Jane Russell, the parents of George, were born in Richmond. Thomas was a general labourer and he and Jane raised five sons and two daughters. George enlisted at Richmond and joined the Lincolnshire Regiment in a Labour Battalion, mainly employed in digging trenches, preparing foundations and constructing roads.

It was still dangerous work, as they were often in the front line and even in the back areas they were targeted by German artillery. In August 1918 George was wounded by shell fire and taken for treatment, but died in a Casualty Clearing Station and was buried in grave II.F.28. Esquelbecq Military Cemetery, France, close to the Belgian border.

Throughout August and early September the Amiens offensive continued and by September 2nd the entire German situation deteriorated, necessitating retirement to the final position – the Hindenburg Line. General Haig's forces needed to re-organise, after all his reserves had been expended, and the storming of the Hindenburg Line did not begin until September 27th. However, between September 2nd and September 27th, probing of the German positions continued and in these operations, a number of dalesmen lost their lives, whilst others died in Italy and Salonika (it is an interesting but sad fact that in the last two months of the war, 34 dales servicemen died).

PRIVATE JOHN WILLIAM WELLOCK
NO. 235314 9TH BATTALION WEST RIDING REGIMENT
DIED SEPTEMBER 8TH 1918 AGED 22

John was the son of Jenkinson and Ellen Wellock and the sister of Mrs. M. Clark of Valley View, Burnsall. The Wellock family had farmed at High Garnshaw Farm, on the hillside above Hebden, for nearly 400 years and in 1881, 16 year old Jenkinson was to be found working on the farm with his father Robert and mother, Mary, a native of Bellbusk. Just before 1891, Jenkinson married Ellen, a girl from Hartlington, near Burnsall, and they lived at the farm. John was born in 1896, but in 1901 there is no sign of Jenkinson, Ellen or 4 year old John William on the 1901 census. I believe they could have emigrated to Canada or Australia for a few years, before returning to England. It is certainly the case that John William Wellock enlisted at Keighley, joining the 9th Battalion West Riding Regiment. On September 8th 1918 he was killed by a German sniper and his name is commemorated on the Vis-En-Artois Memorial, SE of Arras.

John William Wellock from Hebden and Burnsall
Courtesy of The Craven Herald

PRIVATE WALTER LIMMER
NO. 13659 10TH BATTALION WEST RIDING REGIMENT
DIED SEPTEMBER 12TH 1918 AGED 22

We have seen in Chapter Four that Walter's brother, John Thomas Limmer, had been killed on July 10th 1916. His parents, Robert and Mary Ann Limmer, had settled at

Chapel Fold in Grassington, after arriving from Normanby, Middlesborough, and Robert was employed as a brick layer. Walter, their youngest son, worked as a farm labourer on George Wade's farm at Kelbrook, between Skipton and Barnoldswick.

Walter Limmer from Grassington

Courtesy of The Craven Herald

Walter Limmer enlisted in September 1914, joining No. 4 Platoon 10th Battalion West Riding Regiment, before going out to France in August 1915 . He was transferred to Italy in November 1917, after the Italian defeat at Caporetto. He came home on leave to Chapel Fold on August 10th 1918, where by this stage his father had died. Whilst on leave, he married 23 year old farmer's daughter, Alice Wade from Kelbrook, at Skipton Register Office on August 19th but within a few days of his marriage Walter returned to the Italian front and three weeks later he was dead, leaving a young widow back home.

He had acted as an officer's batman and in a letter to his wife, his officer writes, "We had just finished tea when a shell came over that gave us no chance, and burst in the midst of us. Walter, I found, was badly wounded in his head. We immediately dressed his wounds and rushed him off to the doctor, but I don't think he ever regained consciousness until the following day, when he died at 4-30a.m." Walter Limmer was buried in grave I.D.9. Cavalletto British Cemetery, 12 kilometres south of Asiago, Italy. Another son of Mary Ann Limmer was lying wounded in hospital and a fourth was serving in France.

PRIVATE ROWLAND PARKER
NO. 58441 12TH BATTALION CHESHIRE REGIMENT
DIED SEPTEMBER 18TH 1918 AGED 23

Rowland Parker of Deepdale, Langstrothdale, and Rochdale

The Parker family had farmed for generations at Deepdale, in Langstrothdale. Rowland Parker, senior, had married Rebecca Thwaite, a Kettlewell girl, and their family consisted of sons, William (21), John (12), Richard (9), Rowland (6) and daughters, Elizabeth, Jane and Maggie. A flock of 500 sheep was kept on the two farms run by Rowland senior and his sons at Deepdale, and butter from a few cows was sold at local markets.

By 1914, however, Rowland, junior, the youngest son, was living at Ashworth, near Rochdale, and it was from there that he enlisted and joined the Lancashire Fusiliers. At some point he was transferred to the 12th Battalion Cheshire Regiment and by mid 1918 he was serving with the Salonika Force, north of Greece, and preparing for an offensive against the Bulgarians.

The Bulgarian forces were well dug in, in mountainous country. The Cheshires were involved in the second phase of attacks, launched on September 18th against a complicated network of emplacements and dug outs dominating the high ground around Lake Doiran, but the first day did not go well. The attack on the 18th was against Pillar Hill, and following the repulse of the initial attack by the Bulgars, the remnants of the Brigade fell back to the old line, where a defensive line was formed and a muster of the unwounded men was taken.

The Battalion had only one officer and sixty men still available. The process of collecting the wounded and dead from the slopes and their evacuation under fire proceeded throughout the day and the body of Rowland Parker was buried in grave VI.D.7. Doiran Military Cemetery, Greece.

PRIVATE JOSEPH MORGAN
NO. M2/052018 "K" SIEGE PARK, MECHANICAL TRANSPORT
DIED SEPTEMBER 18TH 1918 AGED 42

Joseph Morgan was born at West Hartlepool in 1876. He became employed as a domestic groom by a gentleman from the nearby village of Thornley, who was a shareholder and had interests in the lead mines around Hurst, in Swaledale. Joseph drove him to the isolated village on a regular basis and he became friendly with a Hurst resident, Elizabeth Frankland, the daughter of Henry Frankland, a lead miner. They were married and lived at West Hartlepool, before settling at Thornley, where seven children were eventually born. Joseph was still employed as a groom in the village. However, his employer bought a car in the early 1900's and Joseph became familiar with the workings of the internal combustion engine.

Joseph volunteered for service in the army and was placed in the Army Service Corps because of his driving and mechanical skills. After a while, in 1915, Elizabeth went with her children to stay in Swaledale and settled in Grinton.

It was while preparations were being made for the storming of the Hindenburg Line, deadlined for September 27th, that Joseph was killed on September 18th whilst transporting war supplies near the front line at Hancourt, east of Peronne. His body was buried in grave F.17. Hancourt British Cemetery.

Joseph Morgan from Grinton, near Reeth, and of South Shields

LIEUTENANT LEWIS MARSDEN BULL
1ST BATTALION AUSTRALIAN INFANTRY FORCE
DIED SEPTEMBER 18TH 1918 AGED 22

Lieutenant Bull was born at Burwood, New South Wales, Australia, the only child of Lewis Daniel and Mary Amelia Bull. Although not born in this country, he volunteered for duty and came to fight on the Western Front. At some stage in 1917 he was wounded and was seriously ill, necessitating a period of recovery in England. He was recuperating in the Skipton area and in 1917 and part of 1918 regularly attended the services at Rylstone Church, where he received a most friendly welcome. He returned to his Battalion and on September 18th 1918 was killed near Hesbecourt, east of Peronne. Lieutenant Lewis Bull was buried in grave II.H.6. Roisel Communal Cemetery Extension.

On Sunday October 31st 1920 at St. Peter's, Rylstone, a short Memorial Service was held, and an oaken tablet was dedicated by the Rector, to the memory of Lewis Bull. His parents had the tablet erected because they wished him to have a memorial in the church he had so often attended, and of which he had grown so fond.

LIEUTENANT JOHN KINGSLEY MILLER
24TH (DENBIGHSHIRE YEOMANRY) BATTALION
ROYAL WELSH FUSILIERS
DIED SEPTEMBER 19TH 1918

I am afraid that I have no background information about this serviceman or how his name comes to be on the Richmond Memorial. His actual service record is also something of a mystery.

The 24th Battalion served in Egypt, Sinai and Palestine, entering Jerusalem with Allenby in late 1917 and Jericho in February 1918. In April 1918 they were in France and by late June were taking part in an offensive near the French-Belgian border. For the remainder of the war they were stationed on the northern sector of the front, in Belgium. Yet, on September 19th, John Kingsley Miller was killed far away to the south, in France, north of St. Quentin. The Regimental records do not list him. Whatever the explanation, he was buried in grave III.B.30. Unicorn Cemetery, Vend'Huile, 19 kilometres north of St. Quentin, and his name is commemorated on the Richmond War Memorial.

In late September a mother, recently widowed and living on the Bolton Abbey Estate, received news that her two sons had been killed within one day of each other.

PRIVATE WILLIAM (WILLIE) YOUNG MITCHELL
NO. 11091 1ST BATTALION SCOTS GUARDS REGIMENT
DIED SEPTEMBER 20TH 1918 AGED 30
AND
LANCE SERGEANT JOHN MITCHELL
NO. 12888 9TH BATTALION WEST RIDING REGIMENT
DIED SEPTEMBER 21ST 1918 AGED 34

In 1901 the Mitchell family were living at Strid Cottage, near the Strid, on the Bolton Abbey Estate. John and Annie Mitchell came from Scotland and John was the Chief

Woodman on the Estate. Their two sons and two daughters were born at Bolton Abbey.

John Mitchell, junior, was an old Skipton Grammar School boy and, prior to enlistment, was under his father, the head forester for the Duke of Devonshire, whom he was going to succeed after the war as head forester. He was assistant forester at Hornby Castle, and also on the Marr Brodsworth Estate. When he was killed, he left a wife and one child. Willie Mitchell was educated at the Keighley Trades and Grammar School. A single man of 30, he served his time as a mechanical engineer and was with the firm of Messrs. Brown and Co., Clydesdale Works, Glasgow, up to his enlistment. Both their sisters were playing their part in the war effort, with one working in War Agricultural Work and the other involved in nursing.

Willie and John Mitchell from Bolton Abbey
Courtesy of The Craven Herald

John was one of the first men from Bolton Abbey to enlist, joining the West Ridings in September 1914. He went to France in July 1915, was wounded and returned to England in September 1915, before returning to France in February 1916 and transferring into the Military Police. Three weeks before his death he returned to his old Battalion. John was killed by a sniper at 2a.m. on September 21st. He was conducting two officers from the Machine Gun Corps to another part of the line, to which he knew the best way, and it was while he was returning with the officers that he was caught by a sniper's bullet, being instantly killed. Other officers went out, found his body and brought back his personal effects. John had been promoted to Lance Sergeant a week before his death, as he had done some magnificent work in an earlier attack that week. He was buried in grave IV.B.2. Gouzeaucourt New British Cemetery, 15 kilometres SW of Cambrai.

Willie Mitchell had also enlisted in September 1914, in Glasgow, joining the Scots Guards, and went to France in February 1915, before being wounded and returning to England in August 1915. He returned to France in March 1916, was again wounded and sent home in July 1917, returning to France in December 1917. On September 18th 1918 he was once more wounded and was taken to a Casualty Clearing Station, but this time he succumbed to his wounds and died on September 20th. Willie Mitchell was buried in grave II.D.18. Sunken Road Cemetery, Boisleux-St.Marc, 8 kilometres south of Arras.

Their father, John, had predeceased his sons in January 1917.

PRIVATE WOODWARD SUNTER
NO. 88295 17TH BATTALION MACHINE GUN CORPS
DIED SEPTEMBER 21ST 1918 AGED 31

Known to family and friends as Woody, his parents were Thomas and Elizabeth Sunter. They were born at Grinton, but Thomas and his parents lived at Bank Heads, along the Crackpot road, on the opposite side of the river from Gunnerside. They farmed on a small scale but mainly worked in the Gunnerside Gill lead mines. As a child, Thomas would walk with his mother to work on the dressing floor of the Sir Francis Level and Old Gang Lead Mines, for lead mining was a family affair. Gangs from the same family would work a section on piece work and the women and children helped in dressing the ore. Even the children who went to school would be given time off on occasions to help in cutting the peat, used as fuel in the smelt mills.

Jim Sunter from the Gunnerside area, brother of Woodward Sunter

As the prosperity of the lead mines declined, it was Thomas, who, as he grew up and married Elizabeth, became the first in the Sunter family to provide a living solely from farming at Bank Heads.

By 1901, Thomas and Elizabeth were farming at Spring End Farm, near Satron, Gunnerside, and raising their family of Thomas William, Sarah Ann, 13 year old Woodward, Elizabeth, Rose, Jim, Josua, Spensley and William. Woody married Ruth Cottingham from Lodge Green, Gunnerside, a school teacher at the village school and two sons, Will and Jack, were born. During the war, Woodward Sunter's brother Jim joined the Border Regiment and was wounded in the arm, whilst young Spensley joined the Tank Corps near the war's end but never served abroad. Woodward enlisted at Gunnerside and joined the Yorkshire Regiment, before transferring to the Machine Gun Corps. During the period prior to the planned offensive, he was wounded and died in a Casualty Clearing Station 3 kilometres SE of Bapaume. Woodward Sunter was buried in grave B.13. Thilloy Road Cemetery, Beaulencourt.

The next dalesman to be killed was a farmer from Keld, in Swaledae, and he fell on the third day of the great British offensive, attempting to break into the Hindenburg Line ("The Advance To Victory").

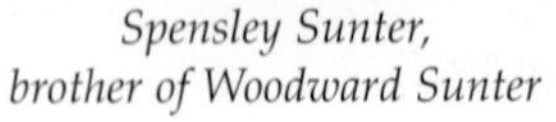

Spensley Sunter, brother of Woodward Sunter

PRIVATE ROBERT RUKIN
NO. 38180 2ND BATTALION YORKSHIRE REGIMENT
DIED SEPTEMBER 29TH 1918 AGED 35

Robert Rukin from Keld in Swaledale

In 1901, eighteen year old Robert was the eldest of the five children of James and Sarah Rukin, and was working in Swaledale for his father, on the family farm, Park Lodge, Keld. James had married Sarah Kearton and besides working the farm, he would supplement his income by working down the coal mine near Tan Hill. A younger son, John Rukin, eventually became the Keld postman and would travel between Keld and Tan Hill in all extremities of weather.

Robert travelled to Richmond to enlist in 1916 and joined the 6th Battalion Yorkshire Regiment. By October 1916 they were at West Hartlepool and witnessed its bombing by a Zeppelin. Robert was part of a draft of men who embarked at Folkestone in January 1917 as reinforcements for the 6th Battalion. They were involved in the Battle of Messines, 1917, and were in and out of the line during the Battle of Passchendaele, receiving heavy losses.

Throughout February to July 1918, he and other members were attached to the 1st. Corps, Royal Engineer Yard in France, involved in moving supplies such as coal and timber. He was then transferred to the 2nd Battalion Yorkshire Regiment and they prepared for the forthcoming offensive against the Hindenburg Line.

They moved up on September 26th 1918 to a position to take part in the Battle of the Canal du Nord, fixed for the 27th September. The Battalion commenced to attack Epinoy about 3p.m. The village was reached by 6p.m., progress having been slowed on the outskirts by the fire from three machine guns. "A" Company suffered heavily on entering the village. As further progress was made on the 28th and 29th the Battalion suffered much from heavy gas shelling and machine gun fire, with 126 men killed, gassed or wounded. Robert Rukin had been killed on September 29th and was buried in grave A.18. Sucrerie Cemetery, Epinoy, between Cambrai and Douai.

PRIVATE GEORGE MARTINSCROFT
NO. 839 20TH BATTALION DURHAM LIGHT INFANTRY
DIED OCTOBER 1ST 1918 AGED 37

In 1901 Frances (Fanny) Martinscroft lived in part of Hill House, Reeth (nowadays the Burgoyne Hotel) with her children, Samuel (23), an electrical lamp trimmer working for the Burton family's Electric Light Company, and Matthew (20), a rural postman. Fanny, born in Arkengarthdale, had left the dale in earlier times and settled in Bolton, where she married James Martinscroft, a native of Worsley, between Manchester and Bolton. During this period, Bolton was well known for its cotton mills and iron founderies and James worked at one of these iron founderies in a Bolton steel mill. It was at 72 Rishton Lane, Greater Bolton, that all their children were born. Their third son, George (20), was the twin brother of Matthew. After James died, Fanny returned with her family to her native Swaledale and Arkengarthdale, but George was not to be found at the family home in 1901, living and working elsewhere. By 1914, however, George was living in the dale and enlisted at Darlington, joining the 20th Battalion DLI.

In late September 1918 the Battalion was at Ypres, in the front line, left of the Canal Sector. On September 28th they attacked the enemy's lines and took Hill 60, Canada Tunnels and Klein Zillebeke and advanced on Zantvoorde. At 7p.m. on October 30th they advanced on the Gheluwe Switch, but were held up by heavy machine gun fire and barbed wire entanglements. October 1st saw the attack continued but it only advanced 200 yards, for they were again held up by a strong line of pill boxes, entanglements and heavy machine gun fire. It was on this day that George Martinscroft was struck down and killed, his body being buried in grave I.D.10. Zantvoorde British Cemetery, 8 kilometres SE of Ypres.

TROOPER FRANCIS (FRANK) KENDALL
NO. 36342 10TH HUSSARS
DIED OCTOBER 8TH/9TH 1918 AGED 27

The Kendall family lived on a farm in Buckden, called Firth Demense, across the main road from the Buck Hotel. In 1901, George and Cecily Kendall lived there with their seven children, Frank being the eldest child, aged nine years. George originated from Muker and Cecily from Aysgarth, but all the children were born at Buckden. Frank and his brothers worked on their father's farm, but during the war, both he and his brother, George, served in the army, with George joining the West Riding Regiment and their younger brother, Mark, remaining on the farm to help his father.

Frank Kendall of Buckden
Courtesy of The Craven Herald

It was not until late 1917 that Frank enlisted at Skipton, and being a farmer's son and used to horses, he joined the Cavalry, serving with the 10th Hussars. They arrived in France in April 1918 and when the offensive was launched against the Hindenburg Line in late September 1918, the Cavalry was made use of in the more fluid movement that took place during that first week.

On October 3rd the Brigade moved up to Bellenglise and the 10th Royal Hussars came under heavy machine gun fire from many aeroplanes, also some gas shelling, and were forced to find a fresh position of readiness. They were subjected to considerable bombing by enemy aircraft during the night. During the march, one enemy bomb fell into the middle of a column of German prisoners and 70 were killed.

At 5a.m. on October 9th they advanced, their role being to push through and occupy the high ground west and south west of Le Cateau, the main objective being the village of Honnechy. "C" Squadron, 10th Hussars, came under machine gun fire from the outskirts of La Sabliere Wood, but after stubborn resistance, Honnechy was captured. The 10th Hussars had suffered many casualties, in men and horses, from shelling, machine gun fire and by aircraft attack. The village of Honnechy was inhabited by civilians and many lost their lives in the bombardment that followed. Red Cross flags were flying from most of the houses and from the church. Seven men from the Hussars were killed, 63 were wounded and 100 horses became casualties. Frank was killed by a bomb and was buried in grave II,B.4. Honnechy British Cemetery, 8 kilometres SW of Le Cateau.

LANCE CORPORAL WILLIAM HENRY BEW
NO. 47693 7TH SQUADRON MACHINE GUN CORPS (CAVALRY)
DIED OCTOBER 10TH 1918 AGED 38

William, or Henry as he was known, was born at Nottingham in 1880, the son of William Bew, a law clerk, and Helen Bew. At Nottingham, in 1901, Henry was employed as a lithographic artist and at some later stage in his working life was living at Richmond. When war broke out he was living with his wife, Sarah, in Darlington, and enlisted at Gateshead. He eventually joined the section of the Machine Gun Corps which worked in conjunction with the Cavalry.

In early October 1918, his Squadron was supporting the action of the 10th Hussars at Honnechy, in which Frank Kendall was killed and on the following day, October 10th, William Henry Bew was also killed. He was buried in grave I.D.1. St. Souplet British Cemetery, 6 kilometres south of Le Cateau, and his name is commemorated on the Richmond Memorial.

PRIVATE WILLIAM HENRY TOWNSON
NO. 44627 4TH BATTALION NORTHUMBERLAND FUSILIERS
DIED OCTOBER 11TH 1918 AGED 42

William Henry Townson of Kettlewell
Courtesy of The Craven Herald

The Townson family lived on Chapel Street, Hebden, in 1901. William's father, Thomas, was born at Embsay and he now worked as a labourer at the Linton Falls cotton mill. He and his wife, Esther, a Hebden girl, lived with their children, Agnes, William and Thomas. By 1914, however, William Henry Townson was married and was landlord of the Blue Bell Inn at Kettlewell.

He enlisted at Skipton on June 16th 1916 and joined the 4th Battalion Northumberland Fusiliers. He had twice been wounded, the second time before Christmas 1917, but had returned to France at the New Year. When the Ludendorff Offensive began on March 21st 1918, the Battalion was rushed by train to try and help stem the advance. On March 23rd the Battalion crossed the Somme at St. Christ, taking up a position commanding the bridgehead. "C" Company held the river crossing against great odds until relieved at 1p.m by the 8th Division arriving. However, on the 23rd March, William Henry Townson was captured by the Germans.

In late October, William's wife, living at Dale House, Kettlewell, received news through the Geneva Red Cross that her husband had died in Germany on October 11th. However, for some unknown reason there is no grave in Germany and instead his name is honoured on the Pozieres Memorial, NE of Albert, and on the Kettlewell Memorial.

SECOND LIEUTENANT NORMAN CROWTHER
3RD BATTALION CHESHIRE REGIMENT
(ATTACHED TO THE 15TH SUFFOLK REGIMENT)
DIED OCTOBER 14TH 1918 AGED 27

Norman was the only son of Arthur and Mary Catherine Crowther of "Brooklyn", Grassington and 21 Hall Road, Shipley. He was educated at Pannal Ash College, Harrogate, leaving there to enter the banking profession, and when war broke out he had secured a good position in the chief office of the National and Provincial Bank at Leeds.

Norman Crowther
from Grassington and Leeds
Courtesy of The Craven Herald

He enlisted in 1915, joining the 5th Battalion The Buffs and gaining his commission in June 1917. He transferred to the 3rd Battalion Cheshire Regiment and sailed with them to Egypt, being one of the expedition to Palestine, but did not enter Jerusalem with General Allenby because he had to spend some time in hospital.

He was recalled to France in May 1918 and saw much severe fighting in the neighbourhood of Merville, being mentioned for gallantry in action. By this stage he was attached to the 15th Suffolk Yeomanry and his death came only two days after retuning from home leave. He and one of his men were sheltering in a shell hole when a shell buried them. They were both dead by the time help arrived and Norman was buried in a cemetery near Chateau-de-la-Valee, 12 miles from Lille. After the war he was re-buried in grave V.A.6. Aubers Ridge British Cemetery.

PRIVATE ROBERT VICKERS
NO. 40919 6TH BATTALION DORSETSHIRE REGIMENT
DIED OCTOBER 26TH 1918 AGED 21

Robert was born in 1897 in the area of Stanhope, in the remote Wear Valley of County Durham, the son of William and Jennie Vickers. At the time of his death his parents were living at St. Johns Chapel, near Stanhope, but Robert had sought employment in the Richmond area and it was from the market town that he enlisted.

He first joined the Royal Field Artillery but by September 1918 he was an infantryman with the 6th Battalion Dorsetshire Regiment. At some stage in early

October he was wounded and was admitted to hospital at Sangatte, Calais, the centre of a large hospital complex. Robert Vickers succumbed to his wounds on October 26th and was buried in grave VI.B.2. Les Baraques Military Cemetery, Sangatte, Calais, whilst his name is commemorated on the Richmond War Memorial.

CAPTAIN ROBERT CLEMENT PERKS
10TH BATTALION WEST RIDING REGIMENT (DSO)
DIED OCTOBER 27TH 1918 AGED 23

Robert was the second son of Thomas Probert Perks and Alice Lydia Perks of Halifax and The Green House, Hebden, near Grassington. His father was a Barrister-at- Law. In 1901, 6 year old Robert was a boarder at a private school at Lytham St Annes and later attended Heath Grammar School, Halifax, before going up to Merton College, Oxford.

Robert Clement Perks from Hebden and Halifax

He was in his second year at Oxford when he enlisted in January 1915, and, as an ex-Cadet of the Officer Training Corps, he was gazetted as Temporary Second Lieutenant that month. He was three times wounded, in July 1916 and in June and September 1917, and was awarded the DSO for leading a bombing party after being wounded.

By October 1918 the 10th Battalion was in Italy and preparing to take part in what would be the final offensive against the Austrians. On October 21st 1918, British forces took over the River Piave Front from Salletuol to Palazzon, serving as part of the Italian Tenth Army. On the night of October 23rd, the main channel of the river was crossed using small boats and the bridging of the Piave proceeded rapidly, although strong currents resulted in the two bridges frequently breaking and many men were drowned.

The Allied attack east of the Piave began early on October 27th. Despite stiff resistance and difficulties with bringing forward supporting troops across the river, the Austrians were forced back over the next few days until the Armistice came into effect on this front on November 4th.

Sadly, Captain Robert Clement Perks was killed on the first day of the attack whilst leading his Company against a machine gun emplacement. He was buried in grave 5.A.5. Tezze British Cemetery, Italy, north of Venice and his name is honoured on the Linton Memorial and on a plaque in St. Peter's Church, Hebden.

GUNNER MAJOR WALLACE
ROYAL GARRISON ARTILLERY
DIED OCTOBER 27TH 1918 AGED 32

In 1901 the Wallace family was living at The Kennels, on the Gledstone Hall Estate, near West Marton Hall (West Marton is a village between Skipton and Gisburn). Francis (Frank) Wallace, the head of the household, was Head Gamekeeper on the estate. He was born at Conistone, near Kettlewell, and had married Sarah Hathey, born in Bamburgh, Northumberland, having met her when she was head cook at Netherside Hall, near Grassington. At West Marton they were living with their five children, Evoline, William, Major, Francis and Violet, all born in the village.

Major Wallace
of Kettlewell and Leek
Courtesy of The Craven Herald

Both William and Frank would become gamekeepers, like their father, but Major worked for the coach and mail contractor, Christopher Chapman of Grassington, driving the six in hand between Grassington and Buckden. By the outbreak of war their parents were residing at Kettlewell, where they had taken over the running of the King's Head Inn. Sarah persuaded her three sons to enlist in the Artillery, believing it would be safer for them (sadly, both Major and William would die during the war).

With his skill in handling horses, Major joined the Royal Garrison Artillery, becoming a Driver and then a Gunner. However, in November 1917, he received serious wounds and burns to his body as a result of shelling from enemy counter-bombardments and was admitted to Netley Hospital in Southampton. Discharged from the army, Major seemed to make reasonable progress and married the Irish nurse who tended to his needs, starting married life at No. 9, Smith's Cottages, Wheetwood Lane, Headingley, Leeds, and even took up employment again as a cab driver. However, he suffered a relapse after his wounds re-opened and died from influenza, broncho-pneumonia and heart failure on October 27th 1918. He was buried at Killingbeck, Leeds, on October 30th. Two days later, his elder brother, William, died of influenza in a French hospital.

GUNNER WILLIAM WALLACE
NO. 77477 160TH SIEGE BATTERY ROYAL GARRISON ARTILLERY
DIED NOVEMBER 1ST 1918 AGED 32

William Wallace, or Bill to his friends, became a gamekeeper and before the outbreak of war was working in the Peak District of Derbyshire on the Chatsworth Estate of the Duke of Devonshire, at Highlow, near Hathersage. He had married Jeannie Ann, a Scottish girl from Kirkaldy in Fifeshire and was one of the first men from Hathersage to enlist. He joined the Royal Garrison Artillery and became a Gunner in a Siege Battery, surviving four years of bloody war, only to be taken ill and die ten days before the Armistice.

During the second half of 1918 and into 1919, the "Spanish Flu Pandemic" swept the world. It is now believed that the pandemic, a form of bird flu transmitted from person to person, originated in an army camp at Etaples, in France. Whatever the case, William Wallace was one of its victims. He was taken into a hospital at Rouen, in France, and died on November 1st 1918, being buried in grave S.II.BB.17. St. Sever Cemetery Extension, Rouen. (their brother Frank, also serving in the Artillery, was badly gassed and yet lived to a good age).

William Wallace of Kettlewell and Hathersage
Courtesy of The Craven Herald

GUNNER JAMES WITHAM THOMPSON
NO. 204305 "A" BATTERY 106 BRIGADE ROYAL FIELD ARTILLERY
DIED NOVEMBER 1ST 1918 AGED 27

James's parents, John and Catherine Thompson were living at St Martin's House, Richmond, when they received news that he had been killed by shell fire. However, when the war started James had been living on the southern fringes of the North York Moors, at Helmsley, from where he enlisted. He joined the Royal Field Artillery and was killed near the war's end, as the Allies pursued the retreating Germans. His body was buried in grave B.10. Crucifix Cemetery, Vendegies-Sur-Ecaillon, 12 kilometres south of Valenciennes, and his name is inscribed on the Richmond Memorial.

GUNNER ARTHUR SWAINSTON
NO. 66052 86TH ARMY BRIGADE AMMUNITION COLUMN ROYAL FIELD ARTILLERY
DIED NOVEMBER 2ND 1918 AGED 21

Arthur's parents, Henry and Mary Swainston, were both born at Richmond, as were their six children, with Arthur being the youngest. They lived on Castle Hill, Richmond, from where Henry ran his tailor's business. Richmond had a large Roman Catholic community and the Swainston family was part of it. After the war, Arthur's brother, Fred, carried on the tailoring business, whilst brother George ran the Talbot Hotel.

Arthur enlisted in Sunderland and became a Gunner in the Royal Field Artillery. It was always going to be a dangerous occupation, as bombardment of enemy positions was followed by an enemy counter-bombardment, but it proved even more dangerous in the last few weeks of the war as movement became more fluid and the gun batteries followed on the heels of the infantry. Arthur died in a Casualty Clearing Station on November 2nd and he was laid to rest in grave I.E.21. Premont British Cemetery, 20 kilometres SE of Cambrai.

PRIVATE FREDERICK STANLEY EARL NO. 39245 16TH BATTALION LANCASHIRE FUSILIERS DIED NOVEMBER 2ND 1918 AGED 25

Fred was the third youngest of the eight children of George and Jane Earl. The children were all born in Richmond and George earned a living as a general labourer. Fred enlisted in Richmond and for some time was a member of the Army Service Corps, before transferring to the 16th Battalion Lancashire Fusiliers. He became another victim of the inflenza pandemic, when he was admitted to a hospital in the medical complex at Etaples, south of Boulogne, and died on November 2nd 1918. Grave XLIX.A.12., Etaples Military Cemetery, received the body of Frederick Stanley Earl.

COMPANY SERGEANT MAJOR JOSEPH DAYKIN NO. 236161 9TH BATTALION WEST YORKSHIRE REGIMENT DIED NOVEMBER 4TH 1918 AGED 36

The Daykin family was a Swaledale family of long standing, in the Muker and Gunnerside area. Jonathan Daykin was a farmer who was born at Muker and farmed at Gunnerside. He was a widower by 1901 and he took his children, Isabella, Mary, Hannah, Joseph, Elizabeth and Ethel to farm at Hauxwell, a village near Leyburn. By 1909, however, the Daykin family was to be found at Manor Farm in Bellerby, near Leyburn. As the only son, Joseph worked on the farm, but early in the war, he travelled to enlist at York and joined the 9th Battalion West Yorkshire Regiment, in which unit he rose to the rank of Company Sergeant Major.

In Autumn 1918, Joseph arrived home on leave at Manor Farm in order to marry his fiancee, Miriam Mawer from Studda Farm. As he returned, little did she realise that she would never see her husband again, for a few weeks later he was dead.

Joseph Daykin
(Bellerby and Gunnerside)

By November 3rd 1918, with only days to go before the war would finally end, the Battalion was making steady progress in its advance eastwards into France, as they pushed hard against the retreating German forces. They were 10 kilometres east of Valenciennes and little opposition was met from enemy infantry but opposing gun batteries were very active. They were ordered to dig in on rising ground forward of the railway between Curgies and Jenlain.

They continued the advance at dawn, moving forward through thickly wooded country and the River Aunelle was crossed. Le Triez was cleared, with a number of prisoners being secured and many civilians in the village were released. The advance continued towards Roisin, but failure of the Division on the right to get into line put the right flank "in the air". A retirement was carried out to a sunken road on the outskirts of the village, during which many casualties occurred. Heavy shelling took place till dusk, causing further casualties.

During that one day's action, 18 men had been killed, 63 wounded and 41 were missing. Joseph Daykin was one of the men killed and he was buried in grave A.35. in Sebourg British Cemetery, France, 10 kilometres east of Valenciennes.

Three days later, three more men from the dales lost their lives.

PRIVATE GEORGE HENRY SIMPSON
NO. 46403 7TH BATTALION LEICESTERSHIRE REGIMENT
DIED NOVEMBER 7TH 1918 AGED 19

The Simpson family was living at Railway Cottages, Saint Martins, Richmond, in 1901. James Simpson, born at Brompton on Swale, was a railway porter employed by North Eastern Railways at Richmond. His wife, Isabelle, was a native of nearby Hudswell, and they had started married life at Darlington, where their first child, a daughter, had been born. Three more children, including George, were born at Richmond.

George Simpson enlisted in 1918 at Richmond and joined the 7th Battalion Leicestershire Regiment, which, in early November 1918 was pushing north eastwards through France, towards the Belgian border. On November 7th, four days before the Armistice, the Battalion was approaching Maubeuge when George Henry Simpson was struck down and killed. He was buried in grave D.30. Maubeuge Centre Cemetery, NE of Le Cateau.

PRIVATE RONALD ALLAN NO. 235470
9TH BATTALION KINGS OWN YORKSHIRE LIGHT INFANTRY
DIED NOVEMBER 7TH 1918 AGED 21

In 1901, four year old Ronald was living at the Allan homestead at Ashlands, Reeth, close to the present day garage. His father, Joseph, was a dry stone waller and farmer born at Melbecks, Swaledale, whilst his mother, Mary Elizabeth Longstaffe, was a Reeth girl. Children Leonard and Mary were born at Aske Moor, near Richmond, Rose was born at Richmond, but by 1892 the family was living at Reeth, where Peter and Ronald (November 13th 1896) were born.

Ronald Allan of Reeth

At the age of 19, in 1916, Ronald went before the Military Tribunal at Reeth, chaired by schoolmaster Mr. Moore, and was granted three months exemption on the grounds that he was working for his father as the cowman on the family farm. However, he finally enlisted at Reeth and first of all joined the Northumberland Fusiliers before transferring to the 9th Battalion KOYLI.

By November 5th 1918 the Battalion was advancing through the Forest de Mormal, 35 kilometres east of Cambrai, though progress was difficult since the railway bridges and road centres had been badly mined and blown up. At 8a.m. on November 7th they formed up at Limont Fontaine and began an attack. The advance was held up and the objective could not be reached because of intense artillery and machine gun fire.

Ronald Allan stands in the middle of the back row

In the afternoon another attack was arranged on the villages of Limont Fontaine and Eclaibes, where a strong stand was made by the enemy and fierce fighting took place in front of and in the streets of the villages, but by 9-30p.m. the villages were cleared of the enemy. But in the earlier fighting of that morning, Ronald Allan had been wounded and died later that day from his wounds. He was laid to rest in grave B.37. Ghissignies British Cemetery, SW of Le Quesnoy.

CADET ROBERT (ROBIN) EMMANUEL BARKER
NO. 183681 8TH CADET WING RAF
DIED NOVEMBER 7TH 1918 AGED 18

Robert Emmanuel ('Robin') Barker with his mother Marie and sister Lorna. He came from Reeth

Robert, or Robin as he was known to his family, was the son of John Barker, the Grinton Estate Agent and Head Gamekeeper. We have already seen that one of John's sons, Adam, had lived a life of adventure in Canada and America, and that his grandson, John, had died in May 1918 while serving in Salonika.

When John Barker, the Grinton Lodge Estate Agent, became a widower he married again in 1897. His second wife, Marie Angela, was a French lady in service with the Darby family. They often came for the shooting on the Charlesworth family's Grinton Estate and this is where they met. A daughter, Lorna, was born, and in 1900 Robin was born, 36 years younger than his half brother, Adam. Robin went to school at Barnard Castle until July 1917, when he began work at the Masham and Bedale branches of Barclay's Bank.

However, he soon left his place of work to enlist and joined the RAF as a Cadet in the 8th Cadet Wing. Within six weeks of his initial training he was taken ill with pneumonia and admitted to Sandgate Hospital in Kent. The toll of victims from the flu pandemic was mounting and "Robin" Barker's name was added to the grim list when he died on November 7th 1918. His body was brought back to Swaledale and he was buried in the north east part of St. Andrew's Churchyard, Grinton.

CORPORAL THOMAS HUTCHINSON
NO. 33009 4TH BATTALION YORKSHIRE REGIMENT
DIED NOVEMBER 9TH 1918

Inscribed on the Reeth War Memorial is the name Thomas Hutchinson. I am afraid I cannot be 100% sure that I have got the right man, nor have I found a definite connection with Reeth, but I believe Corporal Thomas Hutchinson may be the man we are dealing with.

Thomas was living and working at Urlay Nook, just West of Stockton on Tees, when he enlisted at Northallerton and joined the 4th Battalion Yorkshire Regiment. At some stage in 1918 Thomas was taken prisoner by the Germans and placed in a POW Camp near Poznan, in Poland. The flu pandemic claimed another victim when Thomas died on November 9th 1918 and he was buried in grave IV.B.6. Poznan Old Garrison Cemetery.

A Keld man was the next to die and he too succumbed to the outbreak of pneumonia and influenza.

PRIVATE WILLIAM WALLER HUTCHINSON
NO. 51425 1ST BATTALION LINCOLNSHIRE REGIMENT
DIED NOVEMBER 11TH 1918 AGED 20

Born in 1898 at Kirkby Stephen, William Waller Hutchinson, known to all as Waller, was the third child and eldest son of the six children of William Robinson Hutchinson and Harriett Garnet Tyson. When they married, William was working as a carrier, bringing people from the station to the Black Bull in Kirkby Stephen. William stayed at the Black Bull while Harriett came to the Cat Hole Inn at Keld in 1906, with her five children and another child on the way. The Hutchinson family stayed at the Inn until around 1950.

William Waller Hutchinson of Keld, Swaledale

Waller played in Keld Brass Band and became apprenticed to Thomas Parrington, the Keld cobbler. His father, William senior, never lost his interest in horses and went to Shildon, a coal mining area near Bishop Auckland, to look after the pit ponies, and it was from Shildon that Waller enlisted and joined the army, eventually joining the 1st Battalion Lincolnshire Regiment. Sadly he

Golden Wedding photo of William and Jane Rumney Hutchinson 1911 at Kirkby Stephen
Back row: Beatrice Levison, Matthew Levison, Harriet Hutchinson, William Robinson Hutchinson, Sarah Wayper, W. Wayper
Second row: Stanley Hutchinson, William Hutchinson, Jane Hutchinson, William Waller Hutchinson, Edith Hutchinson
Front row: Lucy Hutchinson, Robert Hutchinson, Jane Hutchinson

The Cat Hole Inn at Keld in 1904, when Amos Smith was landlord.
Shortly afterwards William Waller Hutchinson's family took over the tenancy

The Cat Hole Inn at Keld c1910. The sign over the door says 'William R. Hutchinson'. It was Waller Hutchinson's mother who ran the inn

Five soldiers from Keld and Muker.
Back row: Richard Alderson, Jack Metcalfe, Dick Scott (gamekeeper)
Front row: Tom Parrington (cobbler), Waller Hutchinson
Richard and Waller died whilst serving their country

became ill and entered hospital near Cambrai, in France, and died of pneumonia on Armistice Day, November 11th 1918. His grave, I.A.3., is to be found in Caudry British Cemetery, 10 kilometres east of Cambrai.

Inspired by the Communists and sparked by a mutiny of the German High Seas Fleet, disorder, revolts and mutinies flared inside Germany between October 29th and November 10th. A new Socialist government took power and proclaimed a republic on November 9th, whilst the Kaiser fled to Holland on the 10th. A German delegation negotiated an armistice at Compiegne, France, at 5a.m. on November 11th and hostilities ceased at 11a.m. After nearly four and a half years of fighting the war had come to an end.

Celebrations took place throughout the dales. At Beamsley, on the Bolton Abbey Estate, one of the sisters at the Almshouses rang the chapel bell till her arms ached; two of the other sisters took a turn, so spreading the message that peace had arrived.

At Skipton, a mill buzzer helped to acquaint people with good news. Flags began to appear on public buildings and private houses. By noon, the streets were crowded and children were running around waving little Union Jack flags. In some of the weaving sheds in the mills, the looms were decorated with small flags of the Allies. Several mills closed down at noon, the employees proceeding home singing patriotic songs. A merry peal was rung on the parish church bells and a public thanksgiving service was held at the church in the evening.

At Arncliffe, the church bells were rung and flags flew from windows. On Friday evening a dance was held in the schoolroom and over 100 young people gathered together, the music being supplied by Mr. Bolland. On Saturday there was a bonfire and fireworks were set off, the materials having been collected before the war.

Such scenes were repeated throughout many other villages in all the dales. However, even as these joyous celebrations were taking place, people were still suffering from the effects of the war. Private Maurice Bramley of Litton, wounded in France, was that same week in Sheffield Hospital, having had one of his legs amputated.

As the story of Swaledale and Wharfedale's involvement in the Great War comes to a conclusion, it is of great disappointment to me that there are seven servicemen who I have been unable to place with any certainty, both with regards to their background details and service records. All seven men had Richmond connections, for their names are listed on the market town's war memorial. They are **R.A. Bennison** (in 1901, 4 year old Reginald Augustus Bennison was living with his parents, Thomasin and Margaret, and five siblings at Catterick village. The whole family had been born there, with his father employed as a bricklayer's labourer and his mother being a grocer. One year later, in 1902, the family moved to Richmond, where Thomasin became a hide and skin merchant. However, I cannot find out with any certainty his war record. We shall find that in the Second World War, his younger brother, Harry, would be killed in action and his name was also inscribed on the memorial.), **H. Fawcett**, **J.A. Garvey**, **H. C. Matthews**, **H. Parker**, **H. Clarke** (could be Private Harry Clarke No. 202818 10th/11th Battalion Highland Light Infantry, killed south of Ypres on April 9th 1918 during the German "push". His name is on the Ploegsteert Memorial. He was born at Leicester, the same city as Job Clarke, who is also on the Richmond Memorial) and **J. Sillini** (his family was of Italian extraction and he attended services at the Roman Catholic Church at Newbiggin, Richmond). Although the information about their lives and deaths does not appear within these pages, their names are commemorated in the book with the same degree of pride as their colleagues. **(As the book goes to press I have discovered that J.A. Garvey emigrated to Canade before the Great War and returned to fight with the Canadian forces. The man on the Richmond Memorial is: John Andrew Garvey, Shoeing Smith 8th Brigade Canadian Field Artillery No. 115274, the eldest child of Edward and Jane Garvey of Sunderland, husband of Alice Garvey of Barrow-in-Furness, who died in the "Advance to Victory" on August 31th 1918 aged 34 and was buried in grave IV.G.59. Aubigny Communal Cemetery Extension, 15 kilometres NW of Arras). Edward and Jane were born in Sunderland, as were all their eight children. Edward was a blacksmith and horse shoer, and in 1901 the whole family was living in the Wensleydale village of**

FURTHER INFORMATION

By 1915 Bobby Murray had been attached to the Royal Munster Regiment, remaining with them until his death in July 1916. He was with the regiment when they landed at Gallipoli in 1915, where he was recommended for a gallantry award and suffered, as so many did, from dysentry. Having recovered, he went with the Fusiliers to France and took part in the Somme offensive. On July 7th 1916 he and two of his lieutenants dashed to where a shell had landed in the trench nearby, to assist with the wounded. Sadly, a second shell exploded on the parapet wall and killed all three men. The two lieutenants were buried on either side of Robert Murray in Philosophe British Cemetery.

Captain Robert Murray (Richmond)

See page 156

Whilst living at the Bainbridge Smithy John went to Yorebridge Grammar School. The Garvey family, Roman Catholic in their faith because of their origins in Ireland, returned to Sunderland in 1909, where his father Edward died that same year. Four of the Garvey brothers eventually emigrated to Canada, with John working as a blacksmith in Manitoba and Saskatchewan. He enlisted in the Canadian forces at the small town of Moosomin, Saskatchewan. By the time of his death he had married Alice, a girl from Sunderland.

Sergeant Shoeing Smith John Andrew Garvey (Richmond)

See page 288

STOKER 1ST CLASS HARRY PARKER SS/107255 HMS "QUEEN MARY" ROYAL NAVY DIED MAY 31ST 1916

See page 288

Since going to print, I have discovered information about H. Parker, commemorated on the Richmond Memorial. Harry was born in Aberdeen, but his family moved south to run a hotel at Croft, in County Durham. He entered the Royal Navy before the Great War and rose to become a Stoker 1st Class. He married Mary Garvey, from Sunderland, sister of John Andrew Garvey, the shoesmith in the Canadian forces, and at Sunderland a son. Harry, was bom. By August 1914 Harry senior was on board the 31,000 ton battle cruiser HMS "Queen Mary" in action against German naval vessels in the Battle of Heligoland Bight, raiding into German waters. On May

31st 1916, "Queen Mary" was part of Vice-Admiral Sir David Beatty's Battle Cruiser Fleet, known as the 'Ocean Greyhounds', the spearhead of scouting and offensive operations, as they raced to meet the German High Seas Fleet under Vice-Admiral Scheer. They would meet that day in the waters separating Denmark from Norway, at the Battle of Jutland.

Contact was made between the opposing scouting cruisers at 3-48pm but within forty minutes two of Beatty's great ships would be lost. With a thunderous roar the "Indefatigable" went up in flames at 4-05pm and at 4-30pm "Queen Mary" succumbed after she had come under the concentrated fire power of "Der Fflinger" and "Seydlitz". Only twenty crew-men out of 1,266 survived. Harry Parker is commemorated on the Portsmouth Naval Memorial and his name is found on the Richmond Memorial because his wife Mary and son Harry left Sunderland to live at Sleegill, Richmond, near the war's end and later St. Martin's.

Harry Parker (Richmond)

See page 288

James Russell Junior was the eighth of twelve children, six of whom died whilst very young. James and his wife Ellen had four children before James was killed in 1917. His father had died in 1916 and his mother passed away in 1919. See page 182

Carrier James Russell and family in front of North House, Downhoime cl892. Left to right: Jane Elizabeth Russell, James Russell, Elizabeth Russell, Mary Russell, James Russell, (killed 1917.)

Further acknowledgements: Richard Lawson, Norah Taylor, Mike Wood/ Dodd Barnard.

Bainbridge, where 16 year old John was helping his father in the smithy. The family eventually returned to Sunderland to run a livery business but John and another brother emigrated to Canada before the Great War. They both returned with the Canadian forces, John serving as a Shoeing Smith. Sadly he was to die on the battlefield of the Western Front.

However, between the Armistice and the end of 1920, fifteen more servicemen from the dales would die from wounds received during the war or from the effects of the flu pandemic, and their names would be added to the lists of men commemorated on the dales' war memorials. News of the deaths of loved ones as a result of the flu virus must have been very hard for their families to accept. They had survived against the odds on the battlefield, only to succumb to the killer virus. For this First World War generation there was no protection. For them, this epidemic was a cruel epilogue to the suffering they had endured in four years of fighting. It was, as one historian has written, the gleaner of the war's harvest.

PRIVATE JOHN WILLIAM HASKEY
NO. M2/200417 709TH MOTOR TRANSPORT COMPANY ASC
DIED NOVEMBER 16TH 1918 AGED 29

John William Haskey was born at Castleford in 1890, the eldest of the children of John and Hannah Haskey. John, a coalminer from Hunslet, had married Hannah, from Castleford, and all their children were born in her home town. However, John William came to work in the Richmond area, possibly employed in the driving of motor vehicles, and married Alice Jane.

He joined a Motor Transport Company of the Army Service Corps when he enlisted and served in the Salonika Force, fighting the Bulgarians. In late October he caught influenza and died in hospital on November 16th 1918, being buried in grave J.12. Skopje British Cemetery, Macedonia. The great majority of these burials are of men of the Army Service Corps (MT) who died of influenza after the armistice with Bulgaria.

PRIVATE JOHN IRVINE HARGRAVES
NO. 62726 7TH BATTALION WEST YORKSHIRE REGIMENT
DIED NOVEMBER 19TH 1918 AGED 19

Born in 1899 at Appletreewick, John Irvine Hargraves, known as Jack, was the second son of Irvine Hargraves of Appletreewick and his wife Jane (nee Abbot). He had an older brother, Harry, and younger brothers Wilfred and Cecil. Their father was a builder and contractor who built Burnsall, Appletreewick and Kilnsey Village Halls and did the work of altering and extending both Parceval Hall and Mock Beggars Hall, Appletreewick.

Jack attended Skyreholme School and then worked as a gardener/handyman for the rector of Burnsall. He enlisted for the army on November 9th 1917 and went to France on Whit Monday 1918, together with another Wharfedale man, Herbert Longthorne (it is likely that Herbert's youngest sister was Jack's girlfriend). Jack was with his friend, Herbert, sheltering in a barn on October 15th, when there was a gas attack and Jack was badly affected. He was eventually admitted to the 20th General Hospital at Etaples, on the coast south of Boulogne, where he died from the effects of gas and the onset of pneumonia on November 19th 1918. He was buried in grave L.C.32. Etaples Military Cemetery and his name is commemorated on Burnsall War Cemetery.

Jack's brother, Harry, also served in France, where a bullet took a small piece out of the bottom of his nose. Herbert Longthorne was badly wounded, soon after the October 15th gas attack, when his jaw was shattered, and he returned to England, where he was in a Birmingham hospital until March 1919.

John Irvine Hargraves of Appletreewick, near Burnsall

LANCE CORPORAL TOM DUCKETT
NO. 40362 8TH BATTALION NORTH STAFFORDSHIRE REGIMENT
DIED NOVEMBER 24TH 1918 AGED 19

In 1901, two year old Tom Duckett was living with his parents, Thomas, a native of Threshfield, and his mother, Annie Louise, from Millom in Cumberland. Thomas was a shepherd at New House Gill in Bishopdale, near Thoralby, but Tom had been born in Grassington. A sister, Violet, was born and eventually they moved back into the Grassington area. However, before Tom enlisted in the army during the war years, his father died and his mother went to live in Bradford, from where Tom enlisted in the 8th Battalion North Staffordshire Regiment.

Tom Duckett of Grassington
Courtesy of The Craven Herald

On November 5th 1918 they were south of Valenciennes, pursuing the German forces. During the afternoon the enemy put down a heavy barrage of all calibres, including machine guns. Owing to this enemy activity, the darkness and the heavy rain, it was not possible to capture the final objective. The attack continued the next morning, with heavy machine gun and artillery fire encountered, and the companies dug in, whilst sending patrols across the river. Machine gun fire and snipers along the railway and in the woods made this impossible. The shelling all day was very heavy, and never for one moment ceased.

It was during this day's actions that Tom Duckett was seriously wounded and eventually transferred to the hospital complex on the French coast, at Le Treport, NE of Dieppe. It was there that Tom died on November 24th 1918 and was buried in grave X.B.5A. Mont Huon Military Cemetery, Le Treport. His name was also honoured on the War Memorial in Linton Churchyard.

JAMES CARTER SPENSLEY, MA, AIC, FCS, RESEARCH CHEMIST AT THE GOVERNMENT MUNITIONS FACTORY, GRETNA, DIED DECEMBER 16TH 1918 AGED 32

James's grandfather, Carter Spensley, a farmer and blacksmith, was born at Grinton, near Reeth, and married Elizabeth White, a Marrick girl, in 1855. They lived at Feetham Holme, Whitaside, near Healaugh, and one of their children was John Joseph Spensley, the father of James.

John Joseph Spensley eventually became the head teacher at Gunnerside School 1882 – 1894 and married a local girl, Mary Ann Woodward in 1884. Their children, James Carter Spensley and Elizabeth Mary, were born at Gunnerside. However, the family emigrated to South Africa in the late 1890's, settling at Knysna, 350 miles east of Cape Town, on the southern coast of South Africa, where John Joseph taught and became a JP.

His son, James Carter, eventually became a Professor and lecturer in Chemistry at the University of Pretoria. However, when war broke out in 1914, his life was drastically changed. When the South African leaders, Botha and Smuts, planned a campaign against German South West Africa, it displeased many Africaners and a rebellion broke out. James Carter Spensley joined the South African forces and helped put down the rebellion by July 1915. However, he was invalided from the army due to wounds received, but when he recovered he looked for other means to serve the Allied cause.

By 1915 there was every chance of Britain losing the war through a lack of ammunition for her armed forces, until 30,000 women and men from all over the world came to work at a newly built munitions factory on the Solway Firth, near Gretna, in Scotland. Many scientists from universities across the Empire and from the mining companies in South Africa were brought to Britain to work at the factory. One of the research chemists who arrived from South Africa, in May 1917, was James Carter Spensley.

The Gretna Munitions Factory became the largest in Europe, with the townships of Gretna and Eastriggs being built to house the workers. The factory had 125 miles of rail track on site, together with 35 locomotives, its own power station, a bakery producing 14,000 meals and 13,000 loaves daily and a laundry that could clean 6000 items daily. The Solway factory produced more than all the other plants in Britain put together.

It was in the factory that a paste was made known as "The Devil's Porridge", a mixture of nitro-glycerine and nitro-cotton. The dried paste was made into cordite for shells and bullets. James Carter Spensley was one of the research chemists and he was housed in a hostel for professional people, called "The Ridge", at Eastriggs. He served on the staff of the Central Laboratory, working in connection with the Solvent Recovery Problem.

An urgent call came in the spring of 1918 for chemists to travel to another factory involved in work at one of the most deadly forms of "chemical warfare", one where the staff and workers ran great risks of injury, and James answered that call. Sadly, an accident at the factory resulted in him receiving a dosage of the chemicals he was dealing with, rendering him very ill, and for many weeks he was "at death's door". He made a partial recovery, though his heart was weakened, and he returned to Gretna, where he had a mild attack of influenza. His case was making satisfactory progress, but suddenly heart trouble intervened and he died at the Gretna Works Hospital on December 16th, at the age of 32, the last casualty from the dales to die in the final year of the war.

DRIVER THOMAS FREDERICK CURTIS
NO. T2/015960 CLEARING OFFICE ROYAL ARMY SERVICE CORPS
DIED JANUARY 21ST 1919 AGED 36

Thomas was born in Richmond in March 1882, the son of Walter and Mary Curtis. Walter originated from York and had arrived to work as a groom at the racing stables in Richmond. He married Mary Mattison, a Richmond girl, and they and their children lived in Waterloo Street, with Mary supplementing the family income by working as a laundress. By 1919, however, the Curtis family was living at 2 Cornforth Hill, Richmond. During the war years Thomas had joined the Army Service Corps and thankfully survived the horrors of war, but he was struck down in the flu pandemic and died on January 21st 1919, at the London Temperance Hospital. He was buried in grave C 54 Richmond Cemetery.

CORPORAL RICHARD J. EBDELL
NO. 54421 28TH FORTRESS COMPANY ROYAL ENGINEERS
DIED JANUARY 30TH 1919 AGED 31

In 1901 the Ebdell family was living at Doncaster, with father, Edmund, a native of Ripon, employed as a sanitary engineer. His wife, Anne, was from Newsholme, five miles to the north of Goole, and they began their married life in Ripon, where their daughter Isabelle was born. They next moved to Skipton where, in 1887, Richard and another son were born, before they moved on to Doncaster, where their sister worked as a school mistress.

Edmund and Anne eventually settled at "Grasmere" in Grassington and Richard began work in the Grassington area, but he returned to Doncaster to enlist in the army and joined the Royal Engineers. By the end of the war Richard was stationed with the 28th Fortress Company on the island of Malta, but he contracted influenza and died on January 30th 1919. He was laid to rest in grave B.X.X.X.5. Pieta Military Cemetery, Malta.

LANCE CORPORAL JOHN O'HERN
NO. 200238 4TH BATTALION YORKSHIRE REGIMENT
DIED FEBRUARY 1ST 1919 AGED 35

We have seen in Chapter Five that John's brother, Richard O'Hern, was killed on April 11th 1917. They were the sons of Richard and Annie O' Hern of Richmond and before the war John had married Violet, a girl from the village of Wolsingham, between Stanhope and Crook, in County Durham. He was taken ill in January 1919 and died of pneumonia on February 1st, being buried in grave A 69 Richmond Cemetery.

PRIVATE OSBORNE ROBINSON
NO. 3462A 1ST AUSTRALIAN PIONEERS
DIED FEBRUARY 8TH 1919 AGED 27

The Robinson family was living at West Hartlepool in 1901. 31 year old Edward Robinson, born in West Hartlepool, was a merchant of foreign produce, and was married to Edith, a Wakefield girl. Mary (10), Osborne (9) and Elsie (2), all born in the east coat port, completed the family. By the outbreak of war, however, their mother was living at Osborne Cottage, Reeth, whilst Mary was in Warminster, Wiltshire, and in 1913 Osborne had migrated to Australia where he was involved in farming.

He joined the 1st Australian Pioneers and arrived in Egypt in 1915, where they performed garrison duty. By 1916 the Battalion was in France and taking part in the Battle of the Somme, where, in September, he was wounded. He had been carrying a pick-axe, and three fingers of his left hand were badly damaged by the fire from a machine gun. He was in a Birmingham hospital during the latter part of 1916, recovering from the injury and from the effects of shell shock.

Osborne returned to France and survived the further actions he was involved in, but early in the New Year of 1919 he suffered from the outbreak of influenza. He was being nursed by his sister, Mary Robinson, at No. 6 Smallbrook Lane, Warminster, when he died of septic pneumonia and influenza, and was buried in St John's Churchyard, Warminster.

PRIVATE DAVID ABBOTT
NO. 41253 DEPOT OF YORK AND LANCASTER REGIMENT
DIED FEBRUARY 20TH 1919 AGED 25

David's father, George Abbott, was born in Richmond and became a journeyman tailor. By 1901, he was living at The Green, Richmond, with his wife, Mary, born in St Helens, Lancashire, and their children, Annie (13) and David (7), both born in Richmond.

Having joined the York and Lancaster Regiment during the war, David Abbott was at the main depot of the Regiment in England when he was struck down by influenza in late January 1919 and died on February 20th. He was buried in grave Z57 in Richmond Cemetery.

Raymond Chapman from Grassington
Courtesy of The Craven Herald

PRIVATE WILLIAM RAYMOND CHAPMAN
NO. 121066 53RD BATTALION SHERWOOD FORESTERS
DIED FEBRUARY 23RD 1919 AGED 18

In 1901, ten month old Raymond was living with his parents, John and Jane Chapman, on Main Street, Grassington. His father, a Grassington man, was a chemist (drug and patent medicine tender) whose shop was in the Market Square. Towards the end of the war, Raymond was called up and began service with the Sherwood Foresters. He was in training with his Battalion at Catterick Camp, near Richmond, in late January 1919, when he was admitted to the camp hospital and died of pneumonia, following influenza, on Sunday February 23rd. His body was brought for burial to Linton Churchyard.

RALPH BRADLEY
WIRELESS OPERATOR IN THE MERCHANT NAVY
DIED MARCH 7TH 1919 AGED 22

Ralph was born in 1897, the youngest of the three sons of Charles and Margaret Bradley, all three born in Goole. Charles and Margaret were both from Silsden, between Keighley and Skipton, but Charles's work as a clerk had taken them to Goole. Proximity to the sea and activity in the port possibly encouraged Ralph to join the Merchant Navy, where he trained as a wireless operator. His parents, meanwhile, went to live and work on the Bolton Abbey Estate, residing at The Bungalow, Bolton Abbey.

Ralph joined the Merchant Navy in late 1915 and had escaped a number of attempts to torpedo his ships, one of which damaged the vessel. He had just returned from Galveston, USA, the ship being berthed at Salford Docks, when he was taken ill with pneumonia and admitted to Pendleton Hospital, Manchester. It was there that he died on March 7th 1919.

PRIVATE CHARLIE WOOD
NO. 34381 5TH BATTALION WEST RIDING REGIMENT
DIED APRIL 2ND 1919 AGED 19

In 1901 the Wood family was living on Water Lane, Grassington. Hubert Wood, a Grassington man, was employed as a stone mason, and had married Jane, a native of Redmire, Wensleydale. Charlie was the youngest of their six children, all born at Grassington. Sadly, their son, Hubert, had been killed in France in November 1916 and now they were to lose another son.

Charlie Wood from Grassington
Courtesy of The Craven Herald

Charlie joined up in July 1917, being drafted out to France at Easter 1918. Having been involved in many attacks, he was wounded twice and gassed, included being wounded in the hand by shrapnel. When the Armistice was signed, he was drafted to Germany with the Army of Occupation and whilst there he was taken ill with influenza, followed by pneumonia. Charlie was sent to a hospital at Boulogne, where he succumbed to that disease, coupled with the effects of the gas, on April 2nd 1919. He was buried with full military honours in grave XV.B.45. Terlincthun British Cemetery, Wimereux, on the outskirts of Boulogne, his parents being present.

LANCE CORPORAL THOMAS H. LONGSTAFFE
NO. P/5214 CORPS OF MILITARY POLICE
DIED APRIL 15TH 1919 AGED 31

In 1891 the Longstaffe family was living at the small hamlet of Whaw, in Arkengarthdale. By 1901, although they were still in Arkengarthdale, they had moved to Raw Moor, between Langthwaite and Reeth. Thomas was the third eldest of the eight children of John and Mary Longstaffe. John, a farmer, road contractor and lime burner, was born in Reeth but his wife Mary and all eight children were born in Arkengarthdale.

When Thomas joined the army he became a Military Policeman and thankfully survived the war, only to succumb to the dreaded flu virus that was sweeping the world. He died on April 15th 1919 and was buried in Langthwaite Churchyard.

Thomas Longstaffe, Military Police, from Arkengarthdale

CAPTAIN GERALD WILLIAM EDWARD MAUDE
1ST BATTALION YORKSHIRE REGIMENT
DIED NOVEMBER 5TH 1919 AGED 30

Gerald William Edward Maude from Rylstone
Courtesy of The Craven Herald

In Chapter Five we saw how Gerald Maude's brother, Michael, died from his wounds in October 1917. They were the sons of Lieutenant Colonel M.W. Maude of The Fleets, Rylstone, landowner and benefactor in the parish.

Gerald had served eight years in India with his Regiment and in the Spring of 1919 he was badly wounded by a bullet penetrating one of his lungs during a skirmish near Fort Dokka, in Baluchistan (Afghanistan). After three months sick leave in Kashmir, he recovered sufficiently to resume duties. On being granted a year's leave, he was hoping to embark for England on November 7th 1919, but unfortunately he contracted a cold, which probably affected the injured lung. Pneumonia developed and Captain Maude died on November 5th at the Military Hospital, Peshawar. He left a widow and young son, Michael.

Gerald Maude was buried at Peshawar and his name

is commemorated on the Delhi Memorial (India Gate).

DRIVER JOHN INMAN
NO. 801103 (MM) ROYAL FIELD ARTILLERY
DIED SEPTEMBER 26TH 1920 AGED 25

John was born in 1895 at the Tennants Arms, Kilnsey, in Wharfedale, the son of the landlord, Henry Inman, and his wife, Mary Agnes. He was a local man, who also kept the Anglers Arms at Kilnsey, but Mary Agnes Atkinson originated from Leece, near Barrow in Furnace. John went to school and was christened in Conistone and later came to work for Dean Brothers, farmers and butchers, at Grassington, with the family living at Woodland View, Threshfield. John became a journeyman butcher and by 1914 was working in the Manningham area of Bradford.

He enlisted in the West Yorkshire Regiment in 1915 and served for a time in Ireland, where he was involved in putting down the Easter Rising of 1916. In July 1917 he married Elsie Hodgson from Girlington Road, Manningham, Bradford. Meanwhile, he had been transferred to France and joined the Royal Field Artillery, where his expertise in handling horses could be put to use. John was awarded the Military Medal for his bravery, but during his time on the Western Front he was gassed and his lungs were badly affected.

John returned to civilian life as a butcher in Bradford but his health was blighted by the gas attack and he died from Lobar Pneumonia at 167 Girlington Road, Manningham, on September 26th, after 13 days of suffering. He was buried in the family grave in St. Mary's Churchyard, Conistone, and his name was commemorated on the Linton War Memorial, due to the family's connection to Threshfield.

And so we come to an end of the account of the men of these dales who were killed or died during the Great War, or who died later from injuries or illness associated with that period. And yet, it is worth mentioning that within both the Swaledale and Wharfedale areas, the casualties inscribed on the war memorials do not provide the full picture. On the Skipton Memorial is the name John Easterby, who was born at Halton Gill, Littondale, and yet is not to be found on the Arncliffe Memorial. In the case of James Watton, his name is commemorated on his parent's grave in Downholme Churchyard, Swaledale, because of his mother's connections with Downholme and Richmond, but again, his name does not appear on either of their war memorials. This kind of situation was repeated throughout both of the dales, and indeed, throughout the country, and shows that the loss of loved ones affected many more people than would appear to be the case.

PRIVATE JAMES HUBERT WATTON
NO. 204161 5TH BATTALION WEST RIDING REGIMENT
DIED NOVEMBER 24TH 1917 AGED 31

James was born at Hunton, between Leyburn and Bedale, the youngest son of John and Frances Watton. John was born in Ireland and married Frances, a Richmond girl, with connections to Downholme. He was a gardener, and by 1901 the family was living at Spennithorne, near Leyburn, with John working in the gardens at the Hall. By 1914, their son James was living and working in the Potteries, but it was at Bradford where he enlisted and joined the West Riding Regiment.

Having survived the fighting in the latter stages of Passchendaele, James was killed in the Ypres Salient a fortnight later and was buried in grave III. D. 9, Dochy Farm New British Cemetery, NE of Ypres.

PRIVATE JOHN EASTERBY RIFLEMAN NO. 49718
6TH BATTALION THE KING'S (LIVERPOOL REGIMENT)
DIED APRIL 14TH 1918 AGED 35

John Easterby, better known as Jack to his family, was born at Halton Gill, Littondale, in 1882, the son of George Easterby, a farmer who originated from Bentham, and Dorothy Easterby (nee Chapman), from a farming family at Stone-Beck, in Upper Nidderdale. Children, William and Sarah Alice, completed the family (we have already seen that John's sister, Sarah Alice, married Christopher Chapman, from the Grassington coaching firm, who had died from his wounds in 1917).

John Easterby of Skipton and Halton Gill

After finishing his schooling at Halton Gill, he left the family farm to make his home at Skipton, obtaining employment at Stockdale and Helms in Skipton, where he was employed as a grocer. It was there that he met a colleague, Annie Hargreaves from Earby, a traveller for the same firm, and they married at Thornton in Craven in 1909. They lived above the store, at 4 Sheep Street, Skipton, and in 1911 their son, Harry, was born.

The Easterby family in 1914. John Easterby, Harry Easterby, Annie Easterby

Eventually, John enlisted and joined the West Riding Regiment (Service Number 30606), before being transferred to the 6th Battalion The King's (Liverpool Regiment). During the great German Spring Offensives of March and April 1918, John was severely wounded and was taken to the large hospital complex at Boulogne. It was there that he succumbed to his wounds and died on April 14th 1918. He was buried in grave VIII. I. 193 Boulogne Eastern Cemetery and his name is commemorated on a brass plaque in Skipton Parish Church. By the time of his death his parents had passed away and this may explain why John's name is not on the Littondale Memorial, in Arncliffe Church.

There has probably never been a more prolonged and appalling experience for ordinary soldiers in all the history of the British Army than the four years of trench warfare, 1914 – 1918. And now, after living through such nightmare conditions, the survivors could look forward to returning to the beautiful surroundings of the dales.

Though victory had been achieved, the cost was enormous in both manpower and material, with 900,000 Empire troops killed and a further two million wounded. Those who survived came back to a "land fit for heroes" and were promised that the Great War had been "the war to end all wars". The sentiments seemed appropriate at the time but history would make a mockery of them.

As a silence fell over the battlefields, the dales counted their loss of so many dalesmen, but those who arrived safely back gave thanks that they had survived the horror of war. Swaledale, Wharfedale and the associated dales were grateful for the war's end and wished to see the survivors take up their civilian lives again. However, within the space of 19 years, the dales folk would once again find themselves confronting the prospects of conflict against Germany and the possibility of world wide conflagration.

On a somewhat brighter note, a national holiday was held on July 19th 1919 when Peace Celebrations were held in towns and villages throughout the land. However, in Wharfedale the dales folk appear to have chosen their own time to celebrate.

Peace Celebrations were held at Burnsall on Friday 22nd August and Saturday 23rd. On Friday the returned soldiers and their wives were entertained to a meat tea, with a dance and supper in the evening. On Saturday the Sports, including open and local fell races, were followed by a public dance in the Village Hall (the local fell race was won by S. Longthorne, with T. Worsley second). The following Thursday there was a motor trip to Blackpool for the soldiers.

Rylstone Sports and Peace Celebrations were also held on Saturday 23rd August. The weather was dull but fine and the 600 people who were in attendance were entertained by the Carleton Brass Band. There were some good displays of wrestling, both in the open and local events, with the latter being won by W. Foster of High Fleets, whilst the fell race was won in 22 minutes. In the afternoon, 100 scholars took tea in the school room and afterwards the children were presented with a mug each by Mr. W.A. Procter as a Peace Souvenir. The day's proceedings were finished off by a dance in the marquee till 11-30p.m.

Appletreewick's celebrations took place on August 29th and 30th. Friday sports were held at 2-30p.m. in a field lent by Mr. Chapman of High Hall and continued on Saturday afternoon, with a free tea, supper and dance also provided. The dancing

Unveiling and dedication of the temporary was memorial in front of Grassington Town Hall, October 13th 1919 (later, a permanent war memorial was erected in Linton churchyard)

lasting till 2a.m. the following morning, with the music provided by piano and violin. 21 men from the district had joined the Colours, with one being killed. A solid silver medal with attachments for a watch was presented to each man.

The celebrations in Littondale took place at Arncliffe on a Thursday in mid September 1919. Tea was provided and enjoyed in a marquee, the interior of which was gaily decorated. The participants then retired to a field in front of Amerdale House, where sports were contested until dusk. Returning to the marquee, there was dancing until 11-30p.m., the music supplied by Mr. Bolland.

The temporary was memorial in front of Grassington Town Hall, October 13th 1919

The Peace Celebrations in Grassington were postponed from early September to Monday October 13th 1919. The celebrations on Monday were essentially for the children but were spoilt by wet weather. Prior to assembly in the Market Place the children were presented with badges by school-mistress Mrs. Chapman and Miss Spencer. Hymns and patriotic songs should have been sung but were

Cracoe War Memorial Institute and Club, opened by the benefactor, Colonel Maude of 'The Fleets', Saturday June 17th 1921

dispensed with owing to the heavy rain.

A procession was formed, and headed by the Grassington Boy Scouts and a detachment from Brougham Street School, Skipton, proceeded along Wood Lane, Long Lane, to the Town Hall. In front of the Town Hall, a specially erected temporary cenotaph had been placed, draped in white muslin and decorated with ivy, the lower part adorned with bows of flowers on a background of moss, together with four floral corner posts, each surmounted by the Union Jack.

Portraits of the fallen of Grassington, enclosed in a wood frame, was placed on the cenotaph. The Town Hall was also decorated with flags and bunting (at a later date a permanent war memorial was erected in Linton churchyard).

Beautiful wreaths were placed on the cenotaph by Mr. and Mrs. Whittaker (lost two sons), Mr. and Mrs. H. Wood (two sons), Mr. and Mrs. Robert Chapman (a nephew), Mrs. Ellis Lambert, Mr. and Mrs. Blakey, Mrs. Limmer (two sons), Mrs. Chris Chapman (husband), John Crowther (a son), Mrs. T. Duckett, Mrs. Holmes, Mr. and Mrs. G. Bownas and Mr. and Mrs T. Emmott.

The Scouts formed a guard of honour, and to the muffled roll of drums, the children marched past, placing their floral tributes at the foot of the cenotaph, at the same time saluting. The pastor of the Primitive Methodist Church, Rev. Waters, then addressed a few words to the crowd, the proceedings concluding with the singing of the National Anthem and the playing of the Last Post. A tea for the soldiers and the relatives of the fallen was held in the Town Hall.

During the evening the weather imroved, enabling sports to be held in bus proprietor Robert Chapman's field, on Wood Lane, in front of the Old Hall. At dusk, there was a brilliant display of fireworks and the ascent of balloons. At 6pm, John

Crowther, chairman of the Peace Celebrations Committee, lit a bonfire and three large flares on the old Beacon Hill in Bastow Wood. This was followed by a torch-light procession down the centre of the wood into Lea Green and then down the old Grassington Road, entering the town by Old Bank Cottage, and terminating in front of the Town Hall. Later that night, there was a dance in the Town Hall, with supper for the soldiers and sailors.

It was during the years just after the war that the dales' parishes raised money to provide some sort of memorial to honour the names of those who had died.

At Cracoe, on Saturday afternoon June 11th 1921, four year old Michael Maude opened the War Memorial Institute and Club. The young lad was the son of Captain Gerald Maude, who had died at Peshawar in 1919 and grandson of Lieutenant Colonel Maude of The Fleets, Rylstone, who had also lost his only other son, Michael, in the Great War. The Institute, decorated in National Colours, was the gift of Lieutenant Colonel Maude, in memory of the men of Cracoe, Rylstone and Hetton who lost their lives in the war and those who served and survived. An oak tablet, inscribed with the names of these men, was erected in the Memorial Institute and Club and the benefactor remarked that he hoped the Hall would last a few years (in fact, it performed its role in a sterling manner for 75 years, until replaced by a modern building). Each serviceman was presented with a copy of "Craven's Part in the Great War", provided free by Walter Morrison, MP.

The wooden building was one of two huts that had housed German prisoners of war in a POW Camp at Raikes Wood, Skipton. One of these was purchased for the inhabitants of Arncliffe, for use by a Gun Club, whilst the second now graced the site next to Cracoe School. A two bed flat also formed part of the building, to be used rent free by a caretaker and his family. The Lieutenant Colonel was staunchly anti-communist and made certain that a clause was inserted into the regulations pertaining to the running of the Institute, stating that Bolsheviks and Atheists should be barred from peddling their propoganda in the building.

Cracoe Cairn (war memorial) on the fellside above the village of Cracoe. Built in 1922, it honoured the men of Cracoe, Rylstone and Hetton who lost their lives in the Great War

The memory of those servicemen from the Rylstone, Cracoe and Hetton area who lost their lives was also to be honoured by the building of a Memorial Cairn on the fell side, on Watt Crag, 1661 feet above sea level. One attempt had already been made, using the dry stone wall method, but it had collapsed to the ground. Jack Moore of Cracoe, Richard Baines of Malham and Hetton, John Tomlinson and other local men then took over the project, completing it in six weeks, in the early summer of 1922, at a cost of £56.

Cracoe Cairn (war memorial) built in 1922

The obtuse obelisk was 23 feet six inches in height and 9 feet square at the base, tapering to 3 feet at the top. In the first section was placed a sealed bottle, a copy of the Craven Herald and some coins. Local sandstone was taken from the fells nearby, sand for the cement was crushed from the softer sandstone, whilst water was collected in a railway wagon sheet borrowed from Rylstone Station and stored in barrels. The stone was dressed by Jack Moore. When the work was being done, the men lived in a tent near the site during the week, cooking on a primus stove. Crates of bottled beer were sent up at the start of the work. All the materials and plant used were carted up to Joe Lawson's fellside barn, stored, and then "sledded" by local farmers to the site.

Throughout all the dales, memorials were being erected in the 1920's. Tragically, events around the world were conspiring to increase international tension between certain nations, especially in Europe, and the prospects for war were building up once again.

A view of the war memorial and High Row, Reeth, 1950's

Unveiling Reeth War Memorial
Colonel Charlesworth and Thomas Brown,
in the early 1920's

The war memorial near Keld, Swaledale, honouring those who lost their lives from the Keld, Thwaite and Muker area, during the Great War. It was built by the local Keld builders, Frank and Bob Metcalfe

Armistice Day, Richmond Market Place, 1920
Wenham Collection

Unveiling of Green Howards Memorial July 1921
Wenham Collection

Unveiling and dedication of Richmond Town Memorial
Wenham Collection

CHAPTER SEVEN

THE INTER-WAR YEARS IN PHOTOGRAPHS

Keld School 1929.
Back row: George Fawcett, Thomas Hall, Frank Kipling, John Alderson, Chris Calvert, Willie Whitehead, Dick Metcalfe, Willie Calvert
Next row: Maggie Alderson, Mary Cox, Lizzie Metcalfe, Jennie Scott, Isobel Alderson, Harriet Alderson, Mary Ellen Fawcett, Lizzie Appleton, Maggie Appleton, Lizzie Calvert
Next row: Hilda Cox, Hannah Scott, Jennie Rukin, Mary Clarkson, Elizabeth Phyllis Fawcett, Edna Scott, Ethel Sinclair, Jennie Hunter
Front row: Ernest Whitehead, Kitty Peacock, James Appleton, Raymond Harker, Stanley Harker, Simon Fawcett, Jimmy Alderson, George Calvert, James Peacock, George Peacock

Keld School

Laying of the foundation stone for Keld Public Hall. Money was raised by subscription and local labour was provided. It was built by Frank and Bob Metcalfe, builders of Keld, who also built Keld War Memorial. It was opened in 1926

A view of Swaledale from west of Keld during the late 1920's
Clive Torrens Collection

The Gunnerside Smithy belonging to the Calvert family, 1942
Clive Torrens Collection

Gunnerside in 1926, looking from the east

A view of Muker from the south, early 1930's
Clive Torrens Collection

The Farmers Arms Inn at Muker late 1930's
Clive Torrens Collection

A view of Muker from the west, 1930's
Clive Torrens Collection

The opening of Muker Public Hall in 1922. The speaker is believed to be Marmaduke Clarkson, a local vet who gave the land for it to be built on. It was built by John Dougill of Gunnerside, who died before the completion of the porch

The band leads the procession on the day that Muker Public Hall was opened, in 1922

Muker showground
Clive Torrens Collection

Judging the sheep at Muker Show, 1920's
Clive Torrens Collection

Tim Scratcherd's bus at Muker, in Swaledale.
He provided the first bus service between Keld and Richmond

Muker Chapel in the mid 1930's. It was opened in 1934 and the last service was held in 2001.
It is now a dwelling

Tommy Thompson, from Blades, near Low Row, driver of the first bus through Swaledale

The Punch Bowl Hotel, Low Row, in the 1930's
Clive Torrens Collection

View of the village of Healaugh, Swaledale, showing West Farm, 1939
Clive Torrens Collection

Arkengarthdale School c1924
Back row: Edwin Hilary, James Harker, George Scott, Jim Scott, Bertie Hutchinson, Arthur William Scott, Robert Hird, Albert Harker, X
Next row: Sarah Hannah Scott, Emma Longstaffe, Maggie Harker, Olive Longstaffe, Thora Carter, Phyllis Piercy, ? Scott, X, Fremmy Hutchinson
Next row: Gwen Scott, Eva Longstaffe, Kathleen Piercy, Josephine Lauder, Blanche Lauder, Mary Woodward, Manie Harker, Lizzie Hutchinson, Doris Siddall, Mary Coates, Nancy Scott
Front row: Newton Hutchinson, X, Mary Scrafton, Mary Hall, Nellie Scott, Annie Harker, James Enoch Atkinson, Jack Scott

The meeting of the hounds takes place at the Punch Bowl Hotel, Low Row, in 1939/1940

Susan Peacock, landlady of the Tan Hill Inn, Arkengarthdale, late 1920's.
The highest public house in England at 1732 feet above sea level
Clive Torrens Collection

John Rulin from Keld was the postman for the head of Swaledale.
His 'patch' included the remote Tan Hill Inn

Party of snow cutters at Tan Hill Inn, winter of 1933

Punch and Judy Show at Reeth Show c1922

High Row, Reeth, in 1928
Clive Torrens Collection

West side of the green, Reeth, 1929
Clive Torrens Collection

High Row, Reeth, showing Victoria House
Clive Torrens Collection

A charabanc is parked on Reeth green in the late 1920's. The Buck Hotel and Hill House (later The Burgoyne Hotel) are clearly seen at the top end of the green
Clive Torrens Collection

High Row, Reeth, 1933
Clive Torrens Collection

Reeth village green 1948. The showground has its show tents pitched
Clive Torrens Collection

Reeth Friends School group and their teacher, Mr. Shepherd, in the early 1930's.
(William Hammond, on the front row, was killed in the London Blitz.)
Back row: Jim Calvert, Norman Sunter, Wilfred Coates, Robert Bainbridge, Dick Peacock, Tom Milner, Maurice Porter, Percy Fawcett
Next row: Harry Calvert, Alice Sunter, Marjorie Cherry, Lizzie Stoddart, Evelyn Johnson, Isobel Burton, Martha (Matty) Hammond, Hugh Raw
Next row: Albert Wallace, Tarn Bainbridge, Mary Johnson, Annie Petty, Evelyn Robinson, Alice Metcalfe, Nancy Woodmass, Reggie Allinson, Fletcher Coates
Front row: Arthur Kendall, William Hammond, Maurice Barningham

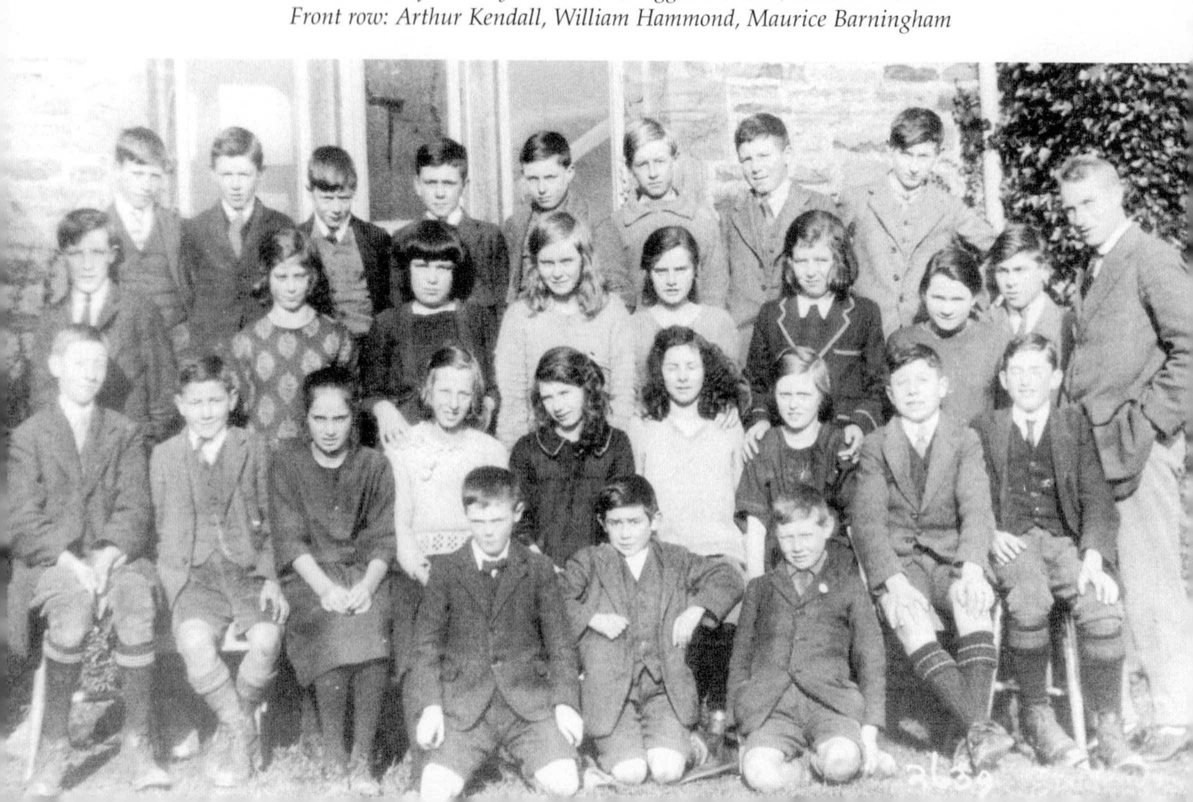

Widening of Grinton Bridge 1930's.

X, Joe Jackson, John Hutchinson, X, Ian Allen

Ike
Billy Tom X Jim Roland Cleminson Lockey Raw
Martin Close X Broadbury Allen X Jimmy
Hird

Billy Martin would be killed whilst serving in the Second World War

Downholme children on Jack Park's horse and cart from Holme Farm

Market Place, Richmond 1920's
Clive Torrens Collection

Market stalls, Richmond
Clive Torrens Collection

Richmond Market Place 1929

Richmond Market Place 1929

View of Buckden 1934. The road on the right leads to Hubberholme
Clive Torrens Collection

A view of Starbotton, Upper Wharfedale, late 1920's
Clive Torrens Collection

Conistone village green, Wharfedale, in 1926
Clive Torrens Collection

Conistone with Kilnsey School 1927/1928, with pupil Ellis Spink, who would be killed flying with the RAF during the Second World War
Back row: William Mallinson, Arnold Hall, Norman Daggett, Walter Ibbotson, Ellis Spink, Aubrey Spink, Phillip Hall
Middle row: Herbert Metcalfe, Richard ?, Doris Metcalfe, Margaret Ibbotson, Margaret Daggett, Mary Robinson, Annie Ibbotson, Elsie Joy, Miss Ormoroyd
Front row: John Joy, Alfred Metcalfe, Doreen Richmond, Kathleen Hill, Rene Campbell, Hazel Ibbotson, Doris Hill, Thomas Lister

The Kettlewell Football Team of 1937/1938, including Horace Mallinson, who would be killed during the Normandy campaign, 1944.
Back row: G. Hanson (manager), W. Hales, G.J. Horner, C. Hanson, John Henderson (J.P., president), J. Horner, T. Parrington (vice-captain), S. Parrington (trainer)
Front row: W. Busfield, S. Mallinson, H. Maxfield, Horace Mallinson, J. Easterby, J. Procter, R. Dickens

The hamlet of Halton Gill, at the head of Littondale

Grassington Square in the more tranquil 1930's
Clive Torrens Collection

The square in Grassington, late 1920's, showing Harker's Post Office. Even on this sunny day a parking place is readily available
Clive Torrens Collection

A coach from the Grassington firm of Chapmans waits outside the Red Lion, Burnsall c1930. Two members of the Chapman family died whilst in the army in the Great War

The Forester's Arms, Grassington, in the 1920's. For the few who could afford a car, the late 1920's and 1930's must surely have been the great age of motoring

Leaving Threshfield on the Skipton Road, 1940
Clive Torrens Collection

Threshfield School early 1930's. (Brothers Edward and Richard Gilbert are on the Linton Memorial.)
Back row: Mollie Johnson, Joan Pratt, Jack Ellis, Jack Taylor, John Pickles, Robert Firth, Richard Gilbert, Norman Stubbs, Edward Gilbert
Third row: Doreen Hammond, Jenny Chaney, Chrissie Taylor, Doreen Richmond, Isobel Bustfield, Mona Wiseman, Beatrice Pratt, Gwen Warhurst, Edward Brennand
Second row: Douglas Binns, Harriet Chaney, Connie Titterington, Kathleen Cowling, Marion Hogarth, Jean Firth, Doreen Lowcock, Mary Kerfoot, Hannah Woodrup, Norman Hodgson
Front row: Arthur Chaney, Robert Chaney, Frank Smith, John Pratt, Roy Dicken, Jack Middleton, Tommy Latham

The main street of Hebden, near Grassington, showing the Wesleyan Chapel.
The school can be seen on the right
Clive Torrens Collection

The Post Office at Hebden, late 1920's

Burnsall, in Wharfedale, showing the Red Lion Hotel, 1920's
Clive Torrens Collection

Skipton High Street during the late 1920's, taken from the church tower. One can see from the tall chimneys that it was still a mill town
Clive Torrens Collection

View of Skipton High Street taken in the late 1940's
Clive Torrens Collection

CHAPTER EIGHT

THE DALES AND THE SECOND WORLD WAR

As the 1930's drew to a close, the everyday lives of the dales folk were rudely over-shadowed by the increasing prospects of war in Europe, due to the repercussions from the growing tensions on the international diplomatic scene. The political climate in Europe was changing and "war clouds" loomed on the horizon. The strains imposed by economic collapse during the years of the "Depression" and the bitterness caused by the outcome of the Versailles Peace Treaty, settled in 1920, had found certain countries' democratic institutions wanting. Fascist and Nazi regimes had won favour (Mussolini in Italy and Adolf Hitler in Germany), determined to push their aggressive foreign policies in the belief that the remaining democracies were ill-prepared to defend their rights.

The threat of war was tangible during 1938 as General Franco's forces gained the ascendancy during the Spanish Civil War 1936 – 1939 and a German ultimatum led to the appointment of several Nazi German ministers in the Austrian cabinet. On March 11th 1938 German troops entered Austria and the Anschluss, or forbidden union of Austria with Germany, was established. As the year 1938 progressed, many people in the dales would possibly think back to the period of the Great War and wonder if the madness of those times could be returning to haunt them.

Tension increased in other areas of Europe, especially in Czechoslovakia, where Hitler demanded further considerable concessions by October 1st, in default of which, Germany would "march". The Czech army mobilised on September 23rd, France on the next day.

In Britain, Territorial Anti-Aircraft and coastal defence units, the Observer Corps and Auxiliary Air Force were called up on September 26th and the British Fleet was mobilised on the 28th. Gas masks were distributed to civilians throughout the country and provisional air raid shelters were dug in London parks.

Prime Minister Neville Chamberlain visited Hitler at Bad Godesberg and Berchtesgaden, without result, and on September 28th Hitler invited the British and French premiers to meet with Mussolini at Munich next day. At this meeting, to which no Czech representative was admitted, it was agreed that German occupation of the areas demanded should proceed in stages between October 1st and 10th. Chamberlain was able to return to London claiming "Peace in our time" and most of Britain breathed a collective sigh of relief. Appeasement had apparently "won the day".

Relief turned to concern, when, in March 1939, Hitler ignored certain conditions of the Munich Agreement and occupied Bohemia and Moravia, without British or

French government intervention. Sensing a weakness of resolve throughout the European democracies, Hitler turned his attention to Poland during the summer months. War clouds were looming once again over Europe, for at last, Chamberlain spelt out clearly in Parliament British condemnation of Hitler's latest aggression and made it clear that an attack on Poland would not be tolerated. On April 26th Britain reintroduced conscription.

The weakness displayed by Britain and France in Munich was Hitler's most powerful incentive to plan the attack on Poland, first for August, then for September 1st 1939. He believed that Poland could be defeated in isolation, as Czechoslovakia and Austria had been before, especially when, on August 23rd, Germany and Soviet Russia signed a Non-Aggression Pact. Hitler's way to Poland seemed open, but on August 25th the signing of the Anglo-Polish Alliance was announced in London and Hitler realised that his attempt to isolate Poland had failed.

At 11-15a.m. on Sunday September 3rd 1939, Neville Chamberlain announced to a hushed nation that Britain was at war with Germany. It was the beginning of the greatest conflict the world has yet seen.

THE EVACUEE SCHOOL CHILDREN

The British government had been shaken by the seriousness of the international situation in 1938, during the Munich Crisis, and realised the dangers facing the civilian population from possible indiscriminate enemy bombing if Germany and Britain ever went to war. The Government therefore began to plan for the evacuation of women and children from the industrial areas into the more rural districts. During early 1939, therefore, local authorities in such districts began to identify those households which would be willing to take evacuees and the area of the Yorkshire Dales became a prime area for such evacuation.

In March 1939, six months before war began, it is interesting to note that many of the residents of Cracoe, between Skipton and Grassington, were willing to play their part when a reporter from the "Leeds Mercury" visited the village in the last week of February.

Mrs. Thompson of West Garth told him she thought that relatives at Bradford might wish to come to them, but she was prepared to take one child, whilst Mr. and Mrs. Smith Tillotson of Brookside House, although getting on in years, would willingly take girls, for they believed that boys might prove too much for them.

Another resident of the village, Mrs. M.A. Daggett of Toppan Farm, although a widow, having all her rooms occupied, would take a couple of city children if necessary, even if it meant rearranging the furniture. Mr. R.G. Procter of Rudd House had already arranged for a relative to bring her two children from Bristol in the event of war but he had offered two sitting rooms to be made into dormitories.

At the Devonshire Arms, Cracoe, Mr. and Mrs. L. Bower believed they would have several spare bedrooms and had already put themselves down for eleven children to be billeted there, plus a teacher, if the worst came to the worst.

As the might of Germany's armed forces swept across the Polish frontier on Friday September 1st and Britain still remained at peace, the reality of the situation was brought home to the people of Swaledale and Wharfedale with the arrival of special trains at Richmond and Skipton, bringing evacuee school children from the industrial areas to be billeted in the dales. The evacuees had arrived, and with them the realisation that this time there was no "turning back".

Over 8000 children from Bradford were expected in the Craven district, arriving at Skipton Station on either the 1st or 2nd September. On the first day, unaccompanied children would arrive and on the second day, accompanied children. All schools were to be closed on the Friday to facilitate the arrangements and during the previous week, members of the Women's Voluntary Services had visited the houses where accommodation had been promised. It was planned for the town of Skipton to receive 900 pupils and for the outlying rural district to receive 3,354. Three trains would arrive at 9-30a.m., 12-30p.m. and 2-30p.m. The control officer at the station was William Daggett, assisted by T.C. Sharples, T.E. Berry and M. Gough, the Skipton headmasters. The children were to be taken from the trains to the Belle Vue Mills welfare room where people were ready to allocate them to the different districts. Two days worth of rations would be supplied to them and 20 buses would be on hand to take them to the different rural districts. Those who alighted from the first train were to be taken to Kettlewell, Buckden, Conistone, Kilnsey, Grassington, Cracoe, Burnsall, Appletreewick, Hebden, Embsay, Beamsley, Gargrave etc.

When the day came, the numbers were not quite as large as expected (3000 children and adults instead of the 8000 expected). On the second day the train arrived with mothers and young children, expectant mothers, nursery school children and priority cases amongst the adults (including 70 adult blind people and their helpers. The adult blind were temporarily billeted in the Hebden Guest House and Newfield Hall, another guest house). With less evacuees, Grassington, Kettlewell, Bolton Abbey and Barden schools did not receive any of these evacuees. A week later, the Skipton schools opened up and 200 St. Joseph's Roman Catholic School pupils began lessons.

Richmond Station was the scene of great activity when the first train arrived at 10a.m. with mainly Sunderland pupils, although there were only 400 instead of the 650 arranged for. Alderman A. Brand, the detraining officer, was assisted by C.R. Douglas, the station master. 300 children were destined for the Swaledale villages and Boy Scouts and Girl Guides from Richmond directed the groups to Richmond National School, where headteacher Mr. R. Hornby directed arrangements for their distribution by bus. The girls from Bede Grammar School, Sunderland, also arrived and were soon to begin lessons at Richmond Grammar School in the afternoons, whilst the Richmond boys received their education during the morning period.

A second train arrived at 1-30p.m. with 450 Gateshead pupils, most destined for the dale, whilst the third train arriving at 4-40p.m. contained 298 children instead of 500 expected for billeting in Richmond borough. They were welcomed by the Mayor, Councillor W. Robinson.

Three more trains would bring mothers and young children, the aged, expectant mothers, the blind and the disabled. Later, another 60 evacuees arrived from Sunderland and were taken by bus from Richmond Station to Reeth.

600 evacuees had been expected in Swaledale in the first two days and there were some discontented people when fewer people turned up, especially when meals and preparations for them had been made, whilst some evacuees left after a short period without giving any notice, saying they felt lonely and could not settle in the countryside.

In September 1939 the number of children on the Gunnerside school registers rose considerably. Miss E. Rutter taught the infants and Miss W.K. Packman, the newly appointed headmistress, divided the rest with the evacuee teacher. As the two classes were taught in one room with only a curtain to separate them, the process of education was difficult. The evacuees would join in with many of the Gunnerside children's activities, including the annual play put on in the Institute, and on the Friday before the Harvest Festival, the teachers took all of the children to Hag Wood, just across the River Swale, to collect fern brackens and red silver birch berries to decorate the Chapel. When the evacuee children left the village school to continue at the Richmond schools they ceased to wear clogs and suffered cold feet as a result. One who left and returned to the village for holidays remarked that she knew she was home when she lay in bed in the morning and heard the ring of clogs on stone.

Shepherded by a Boy Scout, Gateshead evacuees walk through Richmond on Friday September 1st 1939. Note their cardboard boxes containing gas masks

Courtesy of the Darlington and Stockton Times

The winter of 1939 - 1940 was often referred to as the "Phoney War", since no fighting took place between Germany and the Anglo-French forces in Europe and the anticipated bombing of British towns and cities did not materialise. Many parents of evacuee children therefore took their children back home. However, when the Germans successfully invaded the Low Countries and France in May and June of 1940, fresh batches of school children arrived in the dales on July 7th 1940.

Not everything went smoothly in the Reeth district when this second influx arrived. There were problems when some families refused, for certain reasons, to take the children billeted on them and the Reeth Rural District Council refused to push forward their prosecution. The Reeth Billeting Committee resigned and there were heated arguments in the letters section of the Northern Echo and the Darlington and Stockton Times.

Cicely Hoye was one of the evacuee children who arrived at Keld in Swaledale in July 1940 (in 1939 she had been evacuated to Northallerton for two weeks, before returning). She was just 8 years old and was a pupil at Askew Road Mixed Infant School, Gateshead. With their red blazers and labels attached to their button holes, they were taken by tram car to Central Station, Newcastle, and by train from there to Richmond. A bus from Percival's "Swaledale Bus Services" of Gunnerside arrived at Richmond and transported them deep into Swaledale, into a landscape that was so different from the one they were used to. Some children were dropped off at Gunnerside, others at Muker, but most travelled on to Keld, with their teacher, Miss M. Andas.

They were deposited in Keld Village Hall, in strange and frightening surroundings for an 8 year old girl from the industrial North East. Mr. Waggett, the Keld post master and shopkeeper, was one of the billeting officers and as she stood alone, he came across and without saying a word wrote his name on her label.

Cicely Hoye (evacuee) with the Waggett family of Keld. Cicely Hoye, Chrissie Waggett, Mary (Polly) Waggett, James Waggett

The Waggetts lived at Butt House, Keld, with the shop and post office in one room of the house. Cicely was fortunate, in certain ways, for it was a seven bed-roomed house, had electricity supplied from a generator, a bathroom and flush toilet and another flush toilet outside. Most of the other houses only had earth closets. Keld had a communal tap outdoors for use by the villagers, but James Waggett, his wife Mary (Polly) and daughter Christiana (Chrissie) had their own supply inside the house. It was still all very different to Cicely, for she was used to gas in her terraced house in Gateshead.

Young Cicely was terrified of the house at first, for after her two roomed terrace home, the house at Keld seemed huge, but she soon got used to it, for she was made to clean it as one of her many tasks. Other jobs included feeding the chickens and taking telegrams, although for this she was paid 4d.

Miss Emily Marshall, a strict disciplinarian, was the headmistress of Keld School. At the start of their stay the evacuees were placed in the nearby Village Hall, with an extra teacher employed to deal with them.

In December, 1940, Mrs. Jeannie Mee, the wife of the Rev. Arnold Mee, minister of Keld Congregational Church, gave a BBC radio broadcast after the one o'clock news, on the life of the evacuee children:

"In the first evacuation we received children from Sunderland, but they gradually drifted back. The present evacuees are old hands at leaving home, most of them having been evacuated last year to Northallerton, so when they came to Keld on a beautiful sunny afternoon in July we had few tears or wailings to go back home. My husband, who is chief billeting officer, and his staff, had a busy time getting the right children to the right places, but it was worth while. All the boys wanted to live on farms, and fortunately we were able to oblige most of them. It was funny to see their faces when they heard they were to be billeted at such high-sounding places as Starling Castle and Crackpot Hall – which are really only an

Keld School 1940's
(Keith and Gordon Wilson were evacuees sent privately by their parents to Keld, paying for their keep.)
Back row: Agnes Scott, Marion Calvert, John Coates, Jack Alderson, Albert Alderson, Tommy Haykin, George Hird, Mollie Alderson, Amelia Hunter
Second row: Annie Clarkson, Elsie Scott, Mabel Scott, Renne Scott, Margaret Alderson, Ellie Hird, Romie Hird, Joan Mee
Front row: Clarence Sinclair, Keith Wilson, John Alderson, Simon Calvert, Sidney Clarkson, Waller Metcalfe, Gordon Wilson, William Calvert

ordinary cottage and a farm.

"One of the things we found was that none of the children had footwear suitable for our roads, as most of them have a three or four mile walk to school. One of the foster-parents went to the village shoe-makers at Bridge End with a pair of their town shoes and asked him to put thicker soles and toe-caps on them. But now, they have clogs and strong boots.

"Of course, at the beginning they all missed the cinemas and fish-and-chip shops. But in spite of such a different life they have all settled admirably. The boys have learnt quite a lot about "tups and ewes" and pig-killing has been a time of great interest to them."

For Cicely, there was not a great deal of leisure time for she was employed in tasks around the house but she was allowed to take part in the activities of a Concert Party formed during these war years and which continued for a few years after the war.

The Concert Party, known as "The Blackout Belles" and based in Keld, was started by Mrs. Jeannie Mee, the Keld minister's wife, and Albert Edward Wright from Skeugh Head, near Angram. Albert was a former schoolmaster from Darlington who came into Swaledale, partly to escape the bombing and partly for health reasons. He had been a talented entertainer in the Teesside area and relished the chance to harness the latent entertainment talent of the local young women of the Keld and Muker area, such as Jennie Rukin of Keld, Elizabeth Calvert from Hoggarths Farm, Hilda Alderson from Skeugh Head, Mollie Alderson, Marion Calvert, Eleanor Hird, Betty Metcalfe, Chrissie Waggett with her monologues and young Cicely Hoye, the evacuee from Gateshead.

Sketches, monologues and singing were practised at the Keld Manse and concerts were held during the war years at public halls and institutes at Keld, Muker, Gunnerside, Low Row, Reeth and Arkengarthdale. They were often followed by a supper and a dance. The concert at Muker was for the provision of Red Cross Parcels for POW's and was held in October after the sheep sales had taken place, so that a large amount of money could be raised. When the war was over the concert party continued to entertain for a number of years, changing its name to "The Victory Belles" and performing as far afield as Mallerstang.

In succession to
KELD BLACKOUT BELLES

THE VICTORY BELLES

present an original and New-style Entertainment

ELIZABETH CALVERT — JENNIE RUKIN
HILDA ALDERSON — MOLLIE ALDERSON
MARION CALVERT — ELEANOR HIRD
BETTY METCALFE — CICELY HOYE

Directed by Albert E. Wright.

THE INSTITUTE LOW ROW
MONDAY APRIL 22nd 1946
COMMENCING AT 7 30 p.m.

PROGRAMME 2d.

During the Second World War the Keld area raised a concert party named 'Keld Blackout Belles' to keep people's spirits up in Upper Swaledale. After the war they were known as 'The Victory Belles'

Throughout the war years, the dales' villages contributed significant sums of money to fund raising, whether for comforts for the soldiers, Red Cross parcels, relief for the Russians or raising money for war weapons.

In early December, 1941, Low Row in Swaledale held a Gift Sale in aid of Mrs. Churchill's "Aid For Russia Fund". It began in a field lent by Leslie Sunter, when upwards of 30 sheep, together with poultry, were sold and resold several times. This was followed by a "Bring and Buy" sale in the Institute. Tea was served and a concert held afterwards, with proceedings closing with a supper and dance, the MC being T.H. Kendall. A total of £333 was raised.

In January 1942, Reeth, Healaugh, Grinton, Harkerside, Ellerton, Marske, Marrick, Hurst and Fremington set themselves a target of £500 for the same fund, but actually raised £730. Another Gift Sale, conducted by Tom Peacock, helped swell the takings, and in the evening a concert was presided over by Mrs. Radcliffe of Draycott Hall. Arkengarthdale were not to be outdone and in February 1942 raised £621. By the end of February, Swaledale and Arkengarthdale had contributed £2020.

For the forthcoming "Warship Week" the following slogan was suggested by Mr. A. Scarr of Barclay's Bank, Reeth: "You have given generously, lend liberally." The Reeth R.D.C. was linked with HMS Pimpernel during "Warship Week" of 1942. They adopted the corvette, which was used on convoy duty and was also stationed in the Atlantic on weather-ship duty to provide the RAF with information for their bombing missions. HMS Pimpernel was on escort duty on the last Atlantic convoy which arrived at Liverpool on June 5th 1945.

When Neville Chamberlain had announced to the nation that Britain was at war with Germany on September 3rd 1939, it was not long before the people from the dales, especially from Swaledale, learned that they would not be spared. Any false hopes were dashed when news came to the people of Richmond that one of their men had lost his life whilst serving in the RAF.

AIRCRAFTMAN FIRST CLASS BASIL NORMAN BLADES (WIRELESS OPERATOR) NO. 55071 233 SQUADRON RAF DIED OCTOBER 10TH 1939 AGED 19

Basil's father, Norman, had been born at 37 Market Place, Richmond, the son of Francis Blades, a Richmond hairdresser, and Rebecca Pearson, a West Hartlepool girl. Norman worked with his father in the shop and they would often travel to Aske Hall to cut the servants' hair.

Basil Blades of Richmond

As a Territorial Army man with the Yorkshire Regiment, Norman was called up straight away in 1914 and thankfully survived the war. In 1917 he had married Jane, a Sunderland girl living in Richmond. Their son, Basil, was born at Earl's Orchard, Richmond. Norman did not want to continue as a hairdresser and began training as a policeman in the North Riding force.

From a very early age Basil was fascinated by aircraft. Whilst living at Morton-in-Cleveland, consternation was caused when he could not be found one day and it was discovered that the six year old boy had cycled off to Thornaby-on-Tees Airfield to watch the aircraft. It was at Morton that Basil's sister Jean was born. Other moves were made, including to Lingdale, near Guisborough, and it was from there that Basil entered Cranwell RAF College as a boy entrant. The family then moved to Grangetown, east of Middlesborough, from where police sergeant Norman Blades was transferred to Wath Police Station near West Tanfield and Ripon, in July 1939, just a few months before Basil's death.

Sergeant Blade's "patch" covered a wide area and he could often be seen riding his bicycle to meet his constables stationed at Dishforth, Boroughbridge and Kirklington.

By 1939 Basil was serving with 233 Squadron, stationed at Thornaby-on-Tees, the airfield he had cycled to as a young lad, to watch the planes. Around June 1939 he helped deliver a number of Anson aircraft to Aden, in the Middle East, returning by boat through the Mediterranean Sea, and enjoying the experience. 233 Squadron then received Lockheed Hudsons at Thornaby, eventually transferring to RAF Leuchars in Scotland.

At the time of his death, Basil was serving as Aircraftman First Class and had just passed to become a wireless operator. He was aboard a Hudson Mk. 1 aircraft (Serial number N7226) of 233 Squadron No. 18 Group, Coastal Command, that took off from RAF Leuchars, situated between the golfing town of St. Andrews and the Firth of Tay, Scotland. It flew into high ground one and a half miles south of Freuchie, near Glenrothes, Fifeshire, 12 miles SE of Perth, whilst returning from a North Sea patrol, with the loss of all four crew members.

His parents and family were devastated by the news. He was buried in St. Mary's Churchyard, Wath, with full military honours, after evensong on the Sunday. The coffin, draped in the Union Jack, was borne on a trailer drawn by a RAF lorry. Preceding the vehicle, the RAF escort marched with reversed arms and a RAF unit acted as bearers. RAF units and police detachments from Grangetown and Wath were formed around the grave. Three volleys of shots were fired over the grave and two trumpeters sounded the "Last Post", immediately followed by the "Reveille".

On VE Day, Norman Blades was promoted to inspector and served first at Thornaby-on-Tees and then at Whitby, from where he retired to live in the village of Skeeby, near Richmond.

Just seven weeks later, another Richmond serviceman died in Scotland.

TROOPER ERIC BURN NO. 316711 9TH LANCERS AND 3RD CAVALRY TRAINING REGIMENT ROYAL ARMOURED CORPS DIED NOVEMBER 30TH 1939 AGED 28

Eric was the son of Mr. and Mrs. David Burn of 9 Sleegill, Richmond. By October 1939 he was training with the 3rd Horsed Cavalry Training Regiment, near Edinburgh, when he fell ill and was taken to the Military Hospital, Edinburgh, where he died of asthma and acute cardiac failure. Eric was buried in grave D.70. Edinburgh (Comely) Cemetery.

THE YEAR 1940

Throughout the dales, rationing was introduced in January 1940, although ration books had been stored for the previous 18 months. Butter, sugar, bacon and ham were first on the list, but things did not get really bad until 1942. At Reeth, Mr. Wagstaffe installed the Food Office in Moor Garth, and, to augment the coal rations, some Swaledale folk went onto the moors to cut peat. Gas masks had also been made ready since the 1938 crisis and these were ready for collecting from the Council storage above what is the hairdressers in Reeth at the time of writing. In the Grassington and Skipton area, the West Yorkshire buses were painted a drab grey to help them blend in with the landscape and so make them less easily seen by enemy aircraft. More standing room on these buses was created by removing and re-siting the seats around the sides of the buses.

Meanwhile, news of the deaths of Brian Blades and Eric Burn brought home to many dales' families that for the second time in living memory, their loved ones could be taken away from them.102 men from these dales would perish during the Second World War, compared to 236 lost during the Great War. It meant that 102 more families would receive the sad news of bereavement and the war would be brought closer home to the civilian population by the ever present threat of aerial bombardment during the "Blitz".

The villages and towns of Swaledale, Arkengarthdale, Wharfedale, Littondale and Langstrothdale were never involved in receiving the terrible effects of enemy bombing, although the flight paths of Luftwaffe bombers crossed the area as they flew from east to west to target the west coast ports and Belfast. There was, of course, the nightly reminders of throbbing engines overhead, whilst the need for maintaining the "Blackout" was constant.

Action from the air, however, did occasionally impinge on their lives a little more directly, for there were many crashes in the area of the Yorkshire Dales, especially ones concerning the Allied airforces.

On a Saturday night, May 30th 1942, a Wellington bomber crewed by Canadians crashed onto the moors near Owlands House, close to Hurst in Swaledale, "belly flopped" across the moor, crashed through 19 yards of wall on the top of Fremington Edge and rested there. Virtually all of the crew were killed in the accident but the sole survivor, an injured navigator, was guided down the steep slope in pitch darkness by the cackling of Carson Alderson's geese in Reeth. He ended up at Burton's electricity generating mill, near Arkle House.

A few weeks earlier, on January 31st 1942, another Wellington bomber, crewed by Polish airmen from an Operational Training Unit, crashed between Starbotton Fell and Buckden Pike. They had set out from Bramcotes in Northamptonshire, on a training exercise. Joe Fuzniak was the only survivor, making his way through the snow by following fox tracks, to eventually reach the White Lion Inn at Cray, where he was helped by the Parker family. In 1972 a memorial was erected to those who died, near Buckden Pike.

On December 14th 1942 a low-flying, crippled Hampden bomber from a Training Unit, skimmed Castle Keep, Richmond, and hit the hillside above Prior House, Quaker Lane. It burst into flames and the ammunition began exploding in spectacular fashion.

A two seater war plane crashed into Blackburn Edge, on the edge of the moor above Skeugh Head, near Angram and Keld, in Swaledale. The two Dutch airmen only managed to bale out at the last moment, with insufficient altitude to make a safe landing by parachute. A search party of local inhabitants, including Tom Wilson, the head gamekeeper from Keld Lodge (later, it became Keld Youth Hostel), found the men, one of whom was in a sitting position, but sadly, both men were dead. A gate was used as an improvised stretcher to carry the bodies down the slope to Skeugh Head, and from there William Alderson wheeled the bodies in a barrow as far as Angram, where an ambulance waited. For some years after the war, the parents of the two men would arrive at Angram on an annual pilgrimage and be taken to the site where the airmen landed.

The Air Raid Prevention units (ARP), with their wardens, had been in training before the war started and sprang up in even the remotest dales' village. One of those in charge at Reeth was Harry Blenkiron, with the sandbagged office of the local garage on Arkengarthdale Road being used as the headquarters. It was not until later in the war that Reeth received an air-raid siren and until then a hand-held football supporter's rattle was used for warning of an impending attack, and the blowing of a police whistle sounded the "all clear". In the field near the cemetery, on the Richmond road, an Observer Corps post was built to track enemy aircraft.

As with many villages, Reeth had its own wartime Auxiliary Fire Service, headed by Cuthbert Croft. Their small pump was trailed behind a car and was stored in a garage along Silver Street. It was well-known that the Germans used the west to east flowing River Swale as a route marker on clear, moonlit nights, following the silver thread westwards on their way towards Merseyside and other destinations.

On December 3rd 1941 the largest fire Reeth had seen erupted in Ernest Bagshaw's joinery shop behind Anvil Square. It was a clear, moonlit night, but thankfully, that night was the only one during the last fortnight of clear skies that the Germans never came. Stocked with all sorts of flammable material, including 5 gallon drums of petrol, the flames reared high into the night sky. To add to the drama, the car would not start and the firemen had to drag the pump down to the hydrant on the village green.

However, if we return to the Autumn of 1939 we find that the British Expeditionary Force had embarked for France, together with men from the Yorkshire Dales, but no hostile action was pursued as the opposing sides faced each other across the Siegfried and Maginot Lines during the bitter, freezing winter of 1939/1940, in the period known as the "Phoney War".

It was during that winter, on March 2nd 1940, that the first fatality from the dales for that year was recorded.

MATTHEW BRODERICK (ERIC) CHERRY
RADIO OFFICER (MERCHANT NAVY) SS "ALBANO"
DIED MARCH 2ND 1940 AGED 23

Matthew Broderick Cherry was known to family and friends as Eric. His grand_father, Matthew, was born at Grinton and married Ruth, a local girl. By 1901 they were living at Ivelet, a hamlet near Gunnerside in Swaledale, where Matthew was employed as a game-keeper on Captain Lyell's Gunner-side Estate (later owned by Lord Rochdale).

Shooting party, Gunnerside area.
Back: Simon Cherry (Eric's father), X, X
Front: Jack Cherry (Simon's brother)

Their two sons, Simon and Jack, both became gamekeepers on the same estate. Simon married and he and his wife Lizzie lived at Merlins, a cottage in Gunnerside, where their only child, Eric, was born in 1916. Eric was educated at Gunnerside Methodist School and then Rich-mond Grammar School, between 1929 and 1934 (where he received a distinction in Divinity in his School Certificate and won the Divinity Prize). He was closely identified with Gunnerside Methodist Church, where his mother had been at one time the organist. Eric decided to enter the Merchant Navy and in 1935/1936 he began training as a signaller and radio officer at the Signalling School at Conway, North Wales.

He received his appointment in early 1940, his first voyage being to South Africa. He returned home for a few days leave and was recalled to join the SS "Albano", belonging to the Wilson Steamship Line (based at Hull and mainly trading with the Scandinavian ports). Eric became part of the 16 man crew of the small steamship, SS "Albano" (1176 tonnes).

At the beginning of March 1940 the SS "Albano" was sailing from Hull to Bergen, in Norway, with a general cargo, when, on Saturday March 2nd, it struck a German laid mine and sank with the loss of nine lives, seven and a half miles off Coquet Island Light, off the port of Amble, in Northumbria. Eric was first reported to be one of seven crew to be picked up by a naval vessel but this was proved to be incorrect.

Eric Cherry's body was never recovered and his name is commemorated on Panel 4 Tower Hill Memorial, London (32,000 Merchant Navy personnel died during the Second World War).

PILOT OFFICER (PILOT) HARRY PETER JOSEPH RADCLIFFE NO. 90293 607 SQUADRON RAF (AUXILIARY AIR FORCE) DIED MARCH 24TH 1940 AGED 25

Harry was the third son of Sir Everard Joseph Radcliffe 5th Bt. KCSG JP and Lady Radcliffe, of St. Trinians Hall, in Easby Parish, Richmond. During the war, Lady Radcliffe was the Roman Catholic District Representative for the Northern Command, organising the mending of garments for 7000 troops, and helped run the Catholic Women's League for the welfare of soldiers' wives. Her eldest son, Captain J.B.E. Radcliffe, was captured by the Germans at Calais in June 1940 and her fourth son, Major Michael Radcliffe of the Yorkshire Hussars, was taken prisoner in Italy in 1944. Major Hugh Radcliffe was in command of an Anti-Aircraft unit and Lieutenant D. Radcliffe was in the Irish Guards.

Harry Radcliffe was a member of the firm of Stockbrokers, Messrs. Wise, Speke and Co. of 53 Grey Street, Newcastle, of which his father used to be a partner, but, as a member of the Auxiliary Air Force, he was already with the RAF at the start of the war. He served with 607 Fighter Squadron , which in December 1938 converted to Gladiators, a biplane fighter that was already "out of date", and these were taken over to France in November 1939 to join the Air Component of the BEF. 607 Squadron was based at Vitry-en-Artois, a few miles NE of Arras, and in late March began receiving the first batch of Hurricanes to replace the Gladiator. Harry never had the chance to fly in the superb new aircraft, for, on March 24th 1940 his Gladiator collided with another Gladiator near Vitry-en-Artois and Harry Radcliffe was killed. His body was buried in grave L.11. Douai Communal Cemetery, 25 kilometres NE of Arras.

A few weeks later, on May 10th , the "Phoney War" came to a shattering close as the German Armed Forces invaded the Low Countries in their plan to defeat France and eliminate the British Expeditionary Force. As the remorseless might of the Wehrmacht and Luftwaffe drove the British back on their long retreat to the Channel coast and Dunkirk, 7 men from the dales were killed or died from wounds they received. On the 21st May, two men from Richmond were the first to die.

TROOPER HENRY ROY WOOD McGILLIVRAY
NO. 882174 7TH ROYAL TANK REGIMENT RAC
DIED MAY 21ST 1940 AGED 29

Henry was the husband of Muriel McGillivray and at the start of the war was in the Tank Regiment. He was in the 7th Regiment whilst another Richmond man, Alexander Millar, was in its sister Regiment, the 4th, and would be killed seven days after Henry.

The 7th Tank Regiment only landed in France on May 6th, four days before the German Blitzkrieg began, taking over from Alexander's 4th Regiment at Doullens. By the 14th May they had moved by rail to Waterloo, near Brussels, but were ordered to withdraw. Stuka dive bombers had demolished the local station and so the tanks from now on went by road and were continually breaking down. The long withdrawal was hampered by hordes of refugees and civilian traffic on the roads.

News came through that they were to be deployed in the Arras area, where they found the 4th Regiment already in position on the ridge. On May 21st the Battle of Arras commenced as a British counter-attack attempted to link up with the French at Cambrai. The 4th Regiment, who had no Matilda tanks, were reinforced by six vehicles from the 7th. The CO and other officers were killed as they ran into anti-tank positions, leading to confusion and loss of control. Anti-tank guns on the Doullens-Amiens road were destroyed by the Matildas but the speed of the advance had slowed down by 16-50 hours. Achicourt and Beaumetz were captured by "A" and "B" Squadrons but at 18-00 hours the 7th Regiment was ordered to withdraw and casualties had been heavy. 16 Mark 1's and 10 Matilda's were out of action, some due to mechanical breakdown and casualties were 4 officers and 25 men killed, 4 officers and 10 men wounded and 19 men missing. One of those killed was Henry McGillivray and he lies buried in grave 8.B.7 Longuenesse (St. Omer) Souvenir Cemetery.

PRIVATE HARRY WELLS BENNISON
NO. 4384167 4TH BATTALION GREEN HOWARDS
DIED AROUND MAY 21ST 1940 AGED 33

In 1902, the Bennison family came to Richmond from Catterick village, where their father, Thomasin and mother, Margaret Ann, had at one time run the Angel Hotel, although in 1901 Thomasin was a bricklayer's labourer and Margaret was a grocer. Harry was the youngest of 16 children, although a number died of consumption. At Richmond, Thomasin had a tanning business, with the family living at 2 Bridge End.

In November 1932, Harry married Elizabeth Bringloe from Skelton, who was working as a maid in Richmond and raised their children, Patricia and William, at 3, The Green, Richmond. During the 1930's he worked as a general labourer on farms and building sites, including the building of the Methodist Chapel in 1938. Harry was also a member of the Territorials (Green Howards), on many weeks receiving "The Stick" for being smartly turned out. Mobilised at Middlesbrough, as soon as war was declared, he went with the 4th Battalion to France in January 1940. He had not been home since joining up, because leave kept being cancelled, and his family would never see him again. Together with him in the Battalion were two other Territorials from Richmond, Eric Vale and George Algar Salvin, and all three would die as a result of their experiences in France and Belgium.

Harry Wells Bennison of Richmond, Swaledale

Some weeks were spent near Amiens, then on to Lille, where they stayed until May 16th, when they moved forward to counter the German threat. Confusion was in the air, as order and counter-order, marches and counter marches saw even their Commanding Officer at one time separated from them by 70 miles. They were constantly on the move, often without rations, with companies and platoons fighting for long periods on their own. Attacked on land and from the air by greater numbers they made their way back to Dunkirk and were evacuated on June 2nd. Harry Wells Bennison was not with them, however, for round about May 21st he was killed in action. In the confusion of battle he was reported missing and Harry's death was not confirmed to Elizabeth until 1942. He is buried in grave 2.A.14. Athies Communal Cemetery Extension, France, 5 kilometres east of Arras.

PRIVATE GERARD FRAIN
NO. 4387410 5TH BATTALION GREEN HOWARDS
DIED MAY 26TH 1940 AGED 26

Gerard was the husband of Lilian Frain of Richmond and May 10th 1940 found him with his Battalion opposing the German breakthrough in Belgium and France. On May 21st, they too were involved in the Battle of Arras, attacked by both armoured vehicles and aircraft over the next three days. They withdrew towards Douai, Bailleul and Lille on May 24th, often involved in heavy fighting, but in the early hours of May 26th they were ordered to retire to the south of Armentieres and then make their way to Ypres, which they reached at midnight. The going had been very slow because of congestion on the roads and attacks from the air, and it was on this day that Gerard Frain was killed. Since his body was never identified, his name is inscribed on Column 49 Dunkirk Memorial.

DRIVER WILLIAM NASH
NO. T/60588 ROYAL ARMY SERVICE CORPS
DIED BETWEEN MAY 26TH AND JUNE 2ND 1940

William was from Richmond and served as a driver with the RASC in France and Belgium. By the 26th May the BEF was withdrawing to the beaches and harbour of Dunkirk. The German Panzer Groups were more powerful and in greater numbers than the British armour and the Luftwaffe controlled the skies, with the Stuka dive bombers wreaking havoc, destruction and terror on the roads, already congested by the fleeing civilian population. Vehicles on these roads provided a sitting target and sometime between May 26th and June 2nd William Nash was killed by enemy action. Like his Richmond colleague Gerard Frain, his body was never recovered and William's name is also found on the Dunkirk Memorial, on Column 138.

LANCE CORPORAL ALEXANDER MILLAR
NO. 7877427 4TH ROYAL TANK REGIMENT RAC
DIED MAY 28TH 1940 AGED 35

Alexander, who had strong Richmond connections, was the son of John and Christine Millar and the husband of Dorothy Millar of Dunfermline, Fife. We have seen from the account of Henry McGillivray that the 4th Royal Tank Regiment fought alongside the 7th Regiment at the Battle of Arras on May 21st, where Henry was killed.

At Arras the German armour had wheeled northwards in three prongs, from the sea coast to Arras. A task force, including the 4th Regiment, was sent to bolster the right flank and counter-attack the German armour at Arras, but this effort was repulsed by General Erwin Rommel's 7th Panzer Division on May 21st. The severely depleted 4th Regiment withdrew on the 22nd to Vimy Ridge, but by May 25th the remaining tanks of 4th Regiment had to join with the 7th Regiment to form a composite Regiment. Its final action was at Neuve Chapelle, in which they assisted in the extrication of two infantry battalions who had been cut off, but in doing this they lost 8 of their remaining tanks.

They withdrew under shellfire to Dunkirk to embark for England and on May 27th all transport was abandoned in a field after it had been put out of action. They proceeded to the harbour on foot on the 28th and were subjected to incessant bombing, shelling and machine gun fire as the Germans strove to prevent embarkation. Sadly, Alexander Millar was killed during this period of intense fire and eventually he was buried in grave 2.A.31. De Panne Communal Cemetery, on the coast, a few kilometres north of Dunkirk.

SERGEANT ERIC VALE
NO. 4794786 4TH BATTALION GREEN HOWARDS
DIED MAY 29TH 1940 AGED 37

A Territorial soldier (Reservist) before the war, he and the 4th Battalion Green Howards were mobilised at Middlesbrough at the start of the war. Eric was the son of Albert and Mary Jane Vale and the husband of Mildred Alice Vale. They lived at 11 Maison Dieu, where they raised their family of two girls and a little boy. Before his marriage, Eric had spent some time working in Canada.

Eric went off to war with his Richmond Territorial colleagues, Harry Bennison and George Algar Salvin. As we have seen, Harry was killed around the 21st May. By May 27th the Battalion was in Belgium, south of Ypres, where they were subjected to a great deal of sniping and mortaring. The enemy had penetrated a sector of the defences and despite good work with the mortar, part of the post was practically surrounded.

At 6p.m. on May 28th they were ordered to withdraw to the woods north of Poperinghe, after first destroying all their kit and stores (Belgium had just surrendered). On arrival at the wood in the early hours of May 29th they took up defensive positions. At 4p.m. two German armoured cars came up against the forward posts and captured a platoon of "A" Company. At 9p.m. the enemy subjected Battalion Headquarters to rifle fire and shelling. During these fierce exchanges of action, Eric Vale was killed and his grave, 16.B.1., is found at Nine Elms British Cemetery, west of Poperinghe, Belgium.

In April 1940, just over a month before Eric's death, his wife, Mildred, had died after a brief illness, resulting in their three young children becoming orphans.

SERGEANT GEORGE ALGAR SALVIN
NO. 4385623 4TH BATTALION GREEN HOWARDS
DIED JUNE 1ST 1940 AGED 30

George Algar Salvin of Richmond
Courtesy of the Darlington and Stockton Times

Known to everyone as Algar, his parents, James and Hannah Salvin, lived at Carter's Yard, Newbiggin, Richmond. Employed for 12 years as a gardener for the Reverend N.G. Lawson of Temple Lodge, he married his wife, Lillian Jessie, and they too lived at Carter's Yard.

With Harry Bennison, Eric Vale and his brother, Joseph Salvin, he was in the Territorials (for 13 years) and they were all in France with the 4th Battalion by late January 1940 (he had been home on leave at Christmas). Algar was fighting for his life in May, round about the time that Harry Bennison was killed, and was severely wounded, being tended by his officer, Captain Metcalfe, who had also been wounded. Two colleagues carried Algar for two days until they brought him to safety near Dunkirk.

He was transferred to England but died from his wounds in a Liverpool hospital on June 1st, leaving a widow and four year old daughter. Thankfully, his brother Joseph returned safely from Dunkirk. Algar Salvin was laid to rest in grave 13.B.52. Richmond Cemetery.

The dire military situation of the Allies and the British Army was brought home to the people of the dales in early June 1940 when soldiers who had been evacuated from the beaches of Dunkirk arrived by train at various stations.

A number of Dunkirk soldiers arrived, dirty and exhausted, on the village green at Reeth. The Royal Army Service Corps unit and No. 45 Motor Ambulance Company RASC came to recuperate and reform. They had arrived at Darlington Railway Station and marched all the way to Reeth. Remnants of the 501 Ammunition Company RASC had landed at Dover, entrained for Darlington, and slept in the swimming baths there, before travelling on by train to Richmond and marching up the dale to Reeth. Billets were found for them in buildings such as the Methodist Sunday School (now the Museum), whilst for a short spell Hill House (now the Burgoyne Hotel) became a convalescent house for servicemen, who could be distinguished by their blue suits and red ties. The Dunkirk evacuees' one and only vehicle was used for collecting rations and transporting the men to Catterick Camp for their weekly baths.

THE HOME GUARD

During these dark days of 1940 dales folk rallied to the cause, when, on May 14th, Anthony Eden broadcast to the nation that volunteers were required for a new force called the Local Defence Volunteers (nicknamed "Look, Duck and Vanish"), later to be re-named the Home Guard.

The Home Guard for the Rylstone area, No. 6 Platoon "A" Company 32nd West Riding Battalion, had its headquarters in buildings provided by Dennis Standeven of Scale House. The Standevens were mill owners from Halifax, for whom Scale House was their country retreat. One of their main look out posts was to be found at the ruins of Norton Tower, high up on the skyline of the fell.

At nearby Grassington, the platoon's headquarters were in Hardy Grange, whilst

Hebden Home Guard c1940 near Bridge House.
Left to right: Major Bill Dennis, Fred Longthorne, George Whyte, Harry Lunham, Alec Bowdin, Jack Allen, Fred Bowdin, Thomas Bowdin, William (Bill) Simpson, Tom Horner, George Richards, Jim Green

Grassington and district Home Guard unit 1941/1942
outside the guard house on Hardy Grange, Grassington.
Back row: Tommy Odgers, Walter Blakey, John Masters, Bill Dennis, Tommy Tompson, Walter Eccles, George Cousins, X.
Front row: Horace Maxfield (Mossy), Jesse Billsborrow, Billy Scott, Ken Odgers, Percy Waring, Jack Capstick, Wallace Maxfield

Hebden made its own vital contribution to the homeland defence. Major Dennis was in charge at Hebden and Grassington. The story is told, always with a knowing wink, that on one occasion the Grassington contingent marched out of their headquarters, but the officer forgot to give the order "Left march!" and they marched straight ahead into the Devonshire pub, instead.

Each village platoon relied heavily upon the wartime knowledge of the old Great War soldiers, but also received instruction from regular army personnel and trained on occasions with regular army soldiers. Swaledale villages were fortunate that on their doorstep was the large army camp at Catterick, whose officers could provide expertise. Richmond was a barracks town, the headquarters of the Green Howards, and the town's Home Guard had its HQ in Richmond Barracks, along Gallowgate. On one occasion, when they went on manoeuvres with the regulars, it resulted in a big fuss and a sound "ticking off" for one of its members. A contingent of the Home Guard lay in ambush behind a high hedge bordering the road leading out of Richmond towards Brompton-on-Swale, awaiting two army bren-gun carriers to

Richmond Home Guard, Second World War

pass by. Armed with flour bags representing grenades, they prepared to lob their "deadly weapons". One individual, however, had placed a rock inside his bag, which struck the driver, resulting in the vehicle crashing into a wall.

Reeth Home Guard Platoon (including Healaugh and Low Row) met in their headquarters in the Memorial Hall (formerly Conservative Club), with other platoons located at Arkengarthdale, Muker and Keld. In charge at Reeth was Major Tom Porter, the post master. In the first few weeks, only two members possessed a rifle, and at an inspection by the King and Queen at Richmond, some men wore civilian clothes with a Khaki arm band and carried scythes, sickles and pitch forks. This situation was soon rectified and the Platoon took on the shape of an army unit. They now possessed Canadian Ross 300 calibre rifles, heavy but accurate, but soon discovered they had the wrong ammunition. Eventually their weapons included sten guns, Lewis guns, a PIAT mortar and even a mobile 2 pounder anti-tank gun.

During the dark, anxious days of 1940, with the German forces poised across the Channel, Reeth Home Guard, together with all other units country wide, spent night after night on guard duty, on the look-out for possible enemy paratroopers. Their guard posts consisted of a wooden shed on the moorland road between Reeth and Leyburn, and an old bus positioned above Watson House, on Reeth Low Moor, near Rawcroft. It has to be said that instead of dealing with paratroopers, they occasionally shot grouse instead. Their shooting prowess was obviously to be envied, for the Platoon once won the Buchanon Cup for shooting at Catterick, in competition with other units. At a sports meeting against other units, held at Catterick Stadium, the Swaledale/Arkengarthdale Company won the tug-of-war, with Bobby Guy of the Muker Platoon acting as the anchor man. Training and manoeuvres, however, were taken seriously and could be dangerous, for on one occasion, near Grinton Smelt Mill, one of the regular army soldiers was blown up with a hand grenade.

We have seen that Swaledale villages took pride in their brass bands, but these were disbanded as the war progressed, due to their members enlisting in the forces.

Reeth Home Guard at the back of the Memorial Hall, Reeth.
Winners of the shooting cup competition against other units.
Back row: X, Arthur Thompson, Jack Waiton, Lawrence Barker, Ben White, Alan Blenkiron, Albert Hammond, Robert Bainbridge
Next Row: X, Corsan Alderson, John Peacock, Joe Jackson, X, Tony Swainston, Alan Scarr, Stanley Bainbridge, Freddy Dodds, Cecil Duffin
Front row: Ralph Porter, George Graham, Norman Sunter, Robert Morgan, Harry Chapman, Jim Kendall, Simon Cherry, Jimmy Allinson, Jimmy Atfield, Tarn Bainbridge, Oliver Kendall

Reeth Home Guard Band
Back row: Nickles, Lawrence Barker, Bertie Hutchinson, Tom Longstaffe, Jake Stubbs, Sid Hird
Next row: Bob Carter, Jimmy Hatfield, Stan Gay, Hind Hutchinson, Willie Stubbs, X, X, X, James Allinson, Ralf Porter
Front row: Owen Hall, Vince Coates, Jim Kendall, John Stubbs, Kenneth Longstaffe

Reeth Home Guard unit outside the Kings Arms.
Back row: Dick Peacock (butcher), Arthur Johnson (electrician), Henry Wallace (painter), Kenneth Barningham (joiner), Sergeant Jim Kendall (local butcher)
Front row: Raymond Thompson (joiner), Sergeant James Allinson (roadman), John Attwood (butcher), Simon Coates senior (cattle waggon business)

Reeth Home Guard Officers.
Back row:
Simon Cherry (farmer and milk round), X,
James Kendall (butcher),
Harry Chapman (ganger and lengthsman)
Front row:
Jack Wagstaffe (Chert Quarry in Arkengarthdale),
Tom Porter, William Hutchinson (gamekeeper)

Reeth Home Guard, with their sheep mascot

The Green Howards' 1st Battalion Military Band also disbanded and therefore the Reeth Home Guard Band came into existence in late 1943. Many of its members came from the Arkengarthdale Band, for these men were often exempt from joining the services because they were quarry workers, whilst three other members were from the Military Band. One important occasion was when the band played at a march past in Leyburn for the whole of the Wensleydale Home Guard, at which Lord Bolton took the salute. Reeth butcher, Jim Kendall, was the bandmaster, but the Green Howards Band sergeant helped fine tune the band.

Even the remote villages further up the dale had their Home Guard detatchments, including Keld, whose members, including George Metcalfe, gamekeeper at Thorns, Laurie Rukin, Dick Metcalfe from Crackpot Hall, John and William Whitehead and gamekeeper Dick Scott, were led by Tom Wilson, Lord Rochdale's head gamekeeper at Keld Lodge. The latter two members had served in the Great War. The platoon would meet at their guard post at Kisdon Lodge, high up on the fell side and it was fortunate that the gamekeepers could provide their own weapons, for in the early days the rifles provided by the authorities came surplus of ammunition.

Hudswell Home Guard, near Richmond, met in their HQ, a sectional wooden building in the MOD waterworks complex. Major Hart was in charge, with other officers being Company Sergeant Major Green (a Great War soldier), Sergeant Charlie Hunter (manager of the waterworks) and Corporal Gerald Sowerby (joiner and foreman of builders on Catterick Camp). Other members were Harry Hodgson, Maurice Race, Arklie Pickersgill, Ronnie Brown, John Baggley, Bert and Jim Hutchinson, whilst Edwin Coates and Arthur Chandler were dispatch riders, since they had their own motorbikes.

In the early days of the war they did guard duty on a shift basis in a wooden hut on the moor, towards Downholme. Parades were held at Catterick, with a 3 ton truck arriving to take them there, whilst weapons training was held at the Green Howards practise range at Hazelbeck, near Richmond. On other occasions they went with other units to Marske Hall for lectures on stripping Lewis guns down.

Gamekeepers at Keld. Both Dick Scott and Tom Wilson were members of the Keld Home Guard, with Tom Wilson in charge of the platoon.
Left to right: Simon Fawcett, Tom Wilson, Dick Scott

Members of the Downholme Platoon, Home Guard, (Swaledale) in November 1940.
In front of the Bolton Arms Inn, forming up for Armistice Day Church Parade, 1940.
Back row: Joe Dixon, Jack Whitehead, Ernest Whitehead, Douglas Webster, X, Harold Weller, Richard Allison, X, Ian Raine.
Front row: Michael Webster, Ronald Calvert, Thomas Brown, Eric Lochart, Jack Dixon, X, Kenneth Calvert, Matthew Lambert (officer in charge)

Downholme Home Guard Platoon 1940

Removing the road signs in North Yorkshire, late May 1940

An official dump for signposts, taken down in the North Riding of Yorkshire on June 10th 1940. It caused more confusion to the native English than to any possible German Parachutist

THE ARMY IN THE DALES

With Catterick Army Camp being close at hand and the rugged countryside of the dales being "on the doorstep", it is not surprising that the intrusion of the regular army into the dales was very marked during the war years.

Many soldiers came to train in the Cracoe area, between Skipton and Grassington. During the war, as many as 3000 soldiers passed through a six weeks course at an officers' training camp, situated at Raikes Cross, Cracoe, in the fields off Thorpe Lane. In other fields to the left of Fell Lane, Cracoe, was a searchlight battery of three searchlights, together with their generators and air raid detection equipment, whilst eight army huts were constructed to house the men. The unit was part of a network set up to protect Bradford and was linked up with a similar battery at Gargrave. Whist drives and dances were held in the Memorial Hall, Cracoe, and many soldiers attended these popular events.

The army arrives in Grassington.
The 71st Regiment from Sheffield marches over the Bridge, Grassington

Officers and men of the 71st Regiment stationed at Grassington

At Grassington, the 71st Royal Artillery Regiment from the Sheffield area arrived for training, with their HQ and officers housed in the Town Hall. Many soldiers were billeted with local families and the Southwood Lane houses were requisitioned. A semi-detached house was made into one and became a medical centre. The Regiment's shooting ranges were high on Grassington Moor. The Army also transported a large number of tanks by railway to Threshfield Station, from where they made their way onto the moors for firing practise. When they became "clapped out" they became targets for the artillery. Eventually the 71st Regiment went to fight in both the North African and Italian Campaigns.

The Reeth and Arkengarthdale areas were popular training grounds for the army units from nearby Catterick Camp. It became a common sight to see tanks and bren gun carriers grinding their way up the Arkengarthdale road to the firing ranges on The Stang, on the road leading across to Barnard Castle. Their aim was not always accurate and farmers expressed the view that "every other sheep found dead on the moors was killed by the army".

Bren gun carriers practised river crossings in the River Swale at Grinton. Travelling past Blackburn Hall, they swung right, down into the waters of the Swale and then under the bridge itself. Here, there was a large hole and on occasions they sank out of sight, with belongings floating to the surface. One bren gun carrier's track lay buried for years in the gravel, but when retrieved, it was created into a dragon by local sculptor, Mike Kusz.

In 1942/1943 the Reconnaissance Corps (The Recces) arrived in Reeth, attending courses at the newly created Battle School. The Corps was an infantry unit organised to carry out protective reconnaissance, the armoured element consisting of carriers and scout cars. Always to be found in the forward positions, it assisted in gathering information of possible enemy movements. Personnel needed to be taught survival in different battlefield situations and to become independently minded during their six week courses at the School. Battle Schools had operated at

Staff of the Reeth Battle Training School, Reconnaissance Corps, 1943/1945, in front of Hill House, later the Burgoyne Hotel

Members of the Reconnaissance Corps in front of Hill House (Burgoyne Hotel), Reeth, whilst taking part in training at the Battle School between 1943/1945

Scarborough and at Lochmaben in Scotland, but in August 1943 the two centres were combined at Catterick under Major Parry, with the Battle School at Reeth being the largest of several in the area.

Officers were billeted at Cambridge House, Reeth, with HQ (Administration) and accommodation at the requisitioned Hill House (now the Burgoyne Hotel). Billets for the men were in the Methodist Sunday School (now the Swaledale Museum), where they slept on straw palliasses, in the Congregational Sunday School and at the Reeth wood yard. A canteen for the soldiers was set up by the local ladies in a building set back between the Black Bull and the King's Arms (nowadays called The Mews).

An assault course was constructed, known by the locals as the "Burma Road", along the Arkle Beck and in the woods below Fremington Edge, past Woodyard Farm and as far as Castle Farm. An aerial rope way was constructed, rope bridges crossed the beck and were given names such as Bridge of Sighs, whilst "Smoky Joe's Cabin" had to be reached by climbing a rope up a steep slope. At all times during training exercises, live ammunition was used.

Reeth youngsters could watch soldiers practising leaping in and out of moving lorries and using bayonets on sandbag gibbets along Arkengarthdale road. Most of the gunnery training and work with bren gun carriers was, however, completed on other courses on Leyburn and Bellerby Moors and at Staithes.

The arrival of the army affected some local people in other ways. For seven farming families in the Marske area it proved to be a time of terrible upheaval and distress. During the 1920's, both the Hutton family of Marske Hall and Lord Bolton sold land to the army, south of the River Swale, towards Downholme. But in May 1940, the army bought more land from off the Huttons, including seven farms in the Feldom and Cordillera area. Willie Thwaites (High Feldom), William James Hodgson (Low Feldom), the Lawsons (East Feldom) and Miles Alderson (West Feldom), Edward Hodgson (Wham Farm), the Tweddles family (Cordilleras Farm) and the Thwaites family (Waitgate Farm) received just six weeks notice to move.

As they left on May 14th, none of the families had anywhere to go. Most of the families had a sale advertised and the army said they could farm the land but not live on it. To farm the land would mean agreeing only to go on the land when the army allowed. Despite these restrictions, William James Hodgson and the Lawsons decided to farm the land whilst residing elsewhere (the Hodgsons moved some distance away to Owlands House, near Hurst). Some of the other families, such as the Aldersons, sought a new farming life over in Teesdale. For the next seven years the Hodgsons had to travel between the two areas of land, starting before 9a.m. and ending early so that it could be used as a firing range. For years afterwards, live mortar rounds would be found on the land.

The use of the moor land by the army in nearby Arkengarthdale and the discarding of live ammunition would bring tragedy to three families in that dale in 1943. Already, on November 21st 1941, a ten year old Reeth boy, Ivor Alderson, was killed and his companion injured when they were run over by a military lorry on the Reeth to Richmond road. The son of a Reeth stone mason, working on the Catterick Camp, Ivor was leaving Fremington School, and on running from the lane leading to the school, on to the main road, ran into the lorry.

On May 17th 1943 , three children were tragically killed in the explosion of live army ammunition, near Langthwaite. Alan Keith Carter was the seven year old son of Aircraftman Willy Carter and wife Hannah Carter who lived at the back of CB Yard, behind the CB Inn. Frances May Ramm was eight years old. Her grandparents ran the CB Inn and during the war her father served in the RAF. She and her mother came from Thirsk to live at the CB Inn. Jeremy Nicholls, the eldest child, aged 10, was an evacuee from Stockton, who came to live with his grandfather, Mr. Hobbs, at Plantation House, Newhouses, just before the turning for The Stang and Barnard Castle. Between 1940 and 1943 he was a choir boy at Langthwaite Church.

Whilst playing and exploring on the moors on the Monday evening, May 15th, Jeremy came across what later proved to be an unexploded piece of army ordnance. After bringing it to Mr. Hobbs house at Newhouses, his housekeeper, Edna Jane Parker, told Jeremy to place the rusty article in a sack of salvage that was kept in the scullery. There it remained for two days until May 17th, when at some point, Jeremy retrieved the object, and together with Keith and Frances, took it to a nearby shed, where, after placing it in a vice and striking it, the ordnance exploded, resulting in the death of all three children. The sadness felt was even greater because of the unnecessary ending of such young lives. Alan Keith Carter and Francis May Ramm were buried next to each other in Langthwaite Churchyard, whilst Jeremy Nicholls was cremated.

We have seen that on June 1st 1940 George Algar Salvin had died in England from wounds received whilst fighting in France. It would be just two more months before word arrived confirming the death of another serviceman from the dales, this time a man from the Grassington area.

The sad death of three young children from Arkengarthdale, killed by the explosion of munitions found on the moor. Left to right: Jeremy Nicholls, Frances May Ramm and Keith Carter

PRIVATE JAMES WILLIAM PICKLES
NO. 13034629 PIONEER CORPS
DIED JULY 29TH 1940 AGED 27

Jimmy, as he was known, was the eldest of the two sons of Newton and Lucinda Pickles of Lambert Close, Netherside, near Grassington. His father, Newton, originated from Hebden Bridge, where he was employed as a surveyor on the roads. He arrived in Grassington where he performed the same work and where he met his wife Lucinda, an Irish girl.

James William Pickles of Threshfield, Grassington

Jimmy's siblings were Eddy and Annie, with his younger brother working at Skirethorns Quarry. Jimmy was employed as a waiter at the Fell House Hotel at Burnsall. He joined the army in May 1940, just seven weeks before he died, and served in the Army Military Pioneer Corps, stationed at Topcliffe, five miles south of Thirsk. His brother also joined up at this time, serving with the Royal Leicestershire Regiment.

On Sunday July 28th Jimmy was admitted to the Military Hospital, Catterick Camp, where an abdominal operation was carried out to remove an intestinal obstruction, but sadly he died the following day, July 29th, aged 27. He was the first of Grassington's servicemen to die during the War and his funeral took place at Linton Church on Friday August 2nd 1940. The bearers of the coffin were members of the newly formed Grassington Home Guard.

By June 4th 1940, the evacuation of Dunkirk was completed and 338,000 men had been lifted from the beaches. On June 5th Hitler had decided on the invasion of Britain and Operation "Sea Lion" was begun. Having no adequate surface force to oppose British naval strength, the Luftwaffe's task was first to defeat the RAF and then to neutralise the Royal Navy.

In the first phase of the Battle of Britain, August 8th - 18th, the Germans planned to coax the British into combat by attacking sea ports and fighter bases. Aided by radar, Fighter Command still dominated the air over Britain. Phase two, August 24th - September 5th saw the German attack shift to concentrate against the main inland RAF bases and by sheer weight of numbers came close to cracking Fighter Command. The British were partly saved by a change of plan by the Germans. London now became the target for incessant aerial bombardment and Fighter Command was able to concentrate its dwindling force. During this third phase, a Spitfire fighter pilot from Richmond was killed in action in the South-East of England.

FLYING OFFICER (PILOT) ARTHUR PETER PEASE
NO. 72447 603 SQUADRON RAFVR
DIED SEPTEMBER 15TH 1940 AGED 22

Known to all as Peter, he was the eldest son of Sir Richard Arthur Pease J.P. D.L. M.A. 2nd Bart and Lady Pease (nee Kissel) of Richmond. Although connected to Middleton Tyas, the family home was Prior House, on Quaker Lane, Richmond. With an immensely tall, gangly figure, Peter had a deep love of music, history, writing and sports. The Pease family had strong connections to Darlington, especially with regards to the early railway era, with one member having been involved with the company opening the Stockton and Darlington Railway. The family's fortune and influence came from the woollen mills they owned in Darlington. Peter was educated at Eton and later, Cambridge, where he joined the University Air Squadron.

Peter Pease of Richmond
Courtesy of
the Darlington and Stockton Times

As a fighter pilot, flying Spitfires with 603 (City of Edinburgh) Squadron, he had not been involved in the earlier stages of the Battle. Instead, the pilots had been undergoing a two week crash course with Montrose Flying Training Command in Scotland and it was only on August 27th that the Squadron took off from Turnhouse and flew south to their new airfield at Hornchurch, Essex. They would be pitched into the action straight away. Nineteen days later, Peter would be dead.

The bombing of London reached its crescendo on Sunday September 15th, when more than 1000 bombers and some 700 fighters swept all day over the city and SE England, in wave after wave. On that day, 56 German planes were shot down at the expense of 26 British planes. One of those who lost his life on this vital day in the Battle of Britain was Peter Pease.

Flying Spitfire X4324 he was shot down on patrol in combat with ME 109's over Kingswood, just SE of Maidstone, Kent, at 1505 hours. He was chasing an enemy machine when a Messerschmitt latched onto his tail 150 yards away. Peter Pease was buried with full military honours in St Michael's Churchyard, Middleton Tyas, near Scotch Corner. An RAF contingent and band preceded the cortege from the village to the church, the coffin draped in the Union Jack on the back of a military vehicle.

By mid October the Battle of Britain had been won and Hitler cancelled Operation "Sea Lion" on October 12th. However, sporadic German hit-and-run bombing raids continued on London. One of these raids was on October 19th and a ground crew member of the RAF from Reeth in Swaledale was killed whilst on duty in the capital.

LEADING AIRCRAFTMAN WILLIAM WOODWARD HAMMOND NO. 1110571 RAFVR 907 BALLOON SQUADRON DIED OCTOBER 19TH 1940 AGED 29

William was the eldest son of Edward (Ned) and Mary Margaret (Polly) Hammond, their other children being Robert and Elizabeth (three other siblings died in infancy). Ned was a Swaledale man who had worked for many years at the Chert Quarry on Fremington Edge and also for awhile at the Punchard Colliery in Arkengarthdale. He had married Polly Woodward in 1905 and they brought up their family of three children, Elizabeth, William and Robert at Arkle House, Reeth, which Polly ran as a guest house.

William Woodward Hammond of Reeth, Swaledale

Ned had a carrier business and also kept a few animals on a small holding. He delivered items for people up and down the two dales, whilst also collecting the dust bins. He cut and sold ling (heather) from the moor for use as kindling on domestic fires. One day, Ned's horse dropped dead as he was cutting ling. The people of Reeth clubbed together to buy him another horse, but Polly got hold of the money and bought a piano for Arkle House and the guests. Polly was the driving force behind Arkle House Guest House. She was a good business woman and was determined her children should "amount to something".

When William left school, he was first a shop assistant for Hillary's grocers and corn merchants at High Row, Reeth, before becoming an insurance agent for the Prudential, at Catterick. At Reeth, he was honorary secretary of the Badminton Club, a playing member of the Cricket Section of Reeth Athletic Club and a member of the Worker's Educational Association. He attended Reeth Methodist Chapel and was a member of the Wesleyan Guild.

William was not physically strong, for he suffered from chest problems, asthma and bronchitis and his parents believed he would be exempt from serving in the forces. They were surprised when he was accepted into the Pioneer Corps, as part of the ground staff in the RAF at the beginning of the war. Spending some time in hospital, it was again a surprise and worry to them when the RAF sent William to recuperate in London, for the bombing of London was continuing.

He was attached to 907 Balloon Squadron (maintaining 45 balloons), with its headquarters at RAF Stanmore, North London, and he found himself with 11 others, based in a wooden hut at Highbury Fields, a park in North London, close to Arsenal Football Ground. Large anti-aircraft guns were stationed in the park and William's unit helped to man the search lights and barrage balloon.

On the evening of October 19th 1940 he had spent a few hours leave at his cousin Martha's house, before returning to duty at Highbury Fields, with all 12 servicemen crowded into the hut, when, at 9-53p.m. a German bomb scored a direct hit on the park. William and another man took the full force of the blast and were killed, whilst the others were wounded. A newspaper he had brought from Martha's home, found in his pocket, had his cousin's address on it, enabling the authorities to notify Martha. Sadly, William had been expecting a 48 hour pass to visit his home in Reeth, but this was not to be.

His RAF unit paid their last tributes to William when his coffin left London for the north. Members, led by the Commanding Officer, followed the coffin, draped in the Union Jack, through the streets to Kings Cross Station. As the train left, officers and men saluted. William's funeral service was held at Reeth Methodist Chapel and he was buried in grave N.1. in the new cemetery at Grinton.

Three weeks later, another member of the RAF was killed, above the waters of the Mediterranean Sea.

FLYING OFFICER ERIC GEORGE BIDGOOD
NO. 42098 261 SQUADRON RAF
DIED NOVEMBER 16TH 1940 AGED 22

Eric George Bidgood, RAF, son of the vicar of Langthwaite Church, Arkengathdale

Eric's parents were the Reverend George Bidgood and Muriel Bidgood. The Reverend Bidgood only arrived from Hartlepool as vicar of Langthwaite Church, Arkengarthdale, in 1944, and it is almost certain that Eric had never been to the dale in his life. His father had served as Army Chaplain 1916 - 1918 and again 1939 - 1944.

For the last three weeks of June 1940, the important Mediterranean island of Malta could only put up three Sea Gladiator biplanes to fend off more than 200 Italian planes. "Faith", "Hope" and "Charity" as they were known, performed heroically but in July they were supplemented by four Hurricanes.

Morale on Malta received a boost on November 11th when Swordfish torpedo bombers of the Fleet Air Arm from the new carrier "Illustrious" put three of Italy's six battleships out of action in an epic night attack on the harbour of Taranto. Four days later, on November 15th, Force H, including the aircraft carrier "Argus", carrying twelve Hurricanes of 261 Squadron (Malta Fighter Flight), including Eric

Bidgood, sailed from Gibraltar on Operation "White", its objective being to reinforce the air squadrons at Malta. The aircraft would be serviced by ground crew who had travelled to the island by submarine.

On November 16th it was decided to fly off the Hurricanes, plus two Skua guide aircraft, for Malta. Tragically, out of fourteen aircraft, only one Skua and four Hurricanes succeeded in landing at Malta, with their fuel almost exhausted, the rest having crashed into the waters of the Mediterranean. Although some enemy activity may have contributed, the main reasons for such a loss was an unexpected easterly wind of considerable force and the reduction of visibility in the vicinity of Malta. Eric Bidgood was one of the pilots who was killed, and, as his body was never recovered from the Mediterranean Sea, he is commemorated on Panel 5 Runnymede Memorial.

Reverend Bidgood, vicar of Langthwaite 1944 - 1948 and father of Eric George Bidgood

LEADING AIRCRAFTMAN JOHN EDWIN CRAIG NO. 867751 RAF 938 BALLOON SQUADRON DIED NOVEMBER 28TH 1940 AGED 32

Edwin Craig was the son of Thomas and Elizabeth Craig. The family was not from the dales, but from the NE of England. Edwin married Vera Winifred Murray from the Gosforth area and when war began, his mother Elizabeth came to live at Healaugh, near Reeth.

Edwin joined the RAF, becoming a Leading Aircraftman, and was posted to 938 Balloon Squadron, based at Newcastle as part of No. 15 Balloon Centre. The Blackout was introduced at the beginning of the war and accidents to motorists and pedestrians increased dramatically. It was on November 28th 1940 that Edwin Craig died in Stockton and Thornaby Hospital due to a fractured skull, caused by the side-car in which he was a passenger colliding with the rear of a stationary lorry in the Stockton area. He was buried in the cemetery at Reeth.

GUNNER JOHN ROBERT DUNN NO. 1682612 "Z" BATTERY 146 AA REGIMENT ROYAL ARTILLERY DIED DECEMBER 7TH 1940 AGED 29

John was the son of John William and Agnes Dunn of 38 Frenchgate, Richmond. He was married and he and his wife, Eva, lived at 21 The Green, Richmond. John was a civilian worker in the Royal Army Ordnance Corps at Catterick when he joined up in late July 1940, having previously been employed by the Richmond firm of Messrs. Singleton and Sons. Joining the army he became a gunner in an Anti-Aircraft Battery of the Royal Artillery, defending the cities and towns from possible German air attack. John died in St. Luke's Hospital, Bradford, from tuberculous meningitis on December 7th 1940 and was buried in grave 53 Richmond Cemetery, with representatives from his battery present. He was the last serviceman from these dales to die in 1940.

1941

British and Empire troops of the Western Desert Force had advanced 500 miles in North Africa by February 1941. However, the arrival of General Erwin Rommel and his Afrika Korps in March 1941 saw the British forces driven back by May 30th. Throughout April and May, the world witnessed the evacuation of British forces from Greece and then Crete. In both these spheres of operations dales' soldiers would be killed in action.

The main sphere of German operations for 1941, however, became Russia, when Operation "Barbarossa" was launched on June 22nd, whilst America was drawn into the war when the Japanese launched their surprise attack on Pearl Harbour on December 7th. 1941 would see the loss of 5 men from these dales. Three of them died on home soil due to accident or natural causes, but they were in uniform and serving their country at the time of their deaths.

SAPPER WILLIAM JOSEPH BROOKBANKS HUNTER
NO. 1860161 ROYAL ENGINEERS
DIED JANUARY 25TH 1941 AGED 40

William was the son of Thomas and Margaret Hunter. He was born in May 1900 at Tynemouth, Northumberland. His father, a boiler maker in the shipyard, had married Margaret Reid and they lived in the Chirton area of Tynemouth. The family lived at Kirkby Fleetham before moving to Hudswell, near Richmond, where Thomas became licensee of the George and Dragon. By the time of his son's death, Thomas and Margaret were living just outside Richmond, in the village of Skeeby.

William was a Reservist in the Royal Engineers and had served in France from September 1939 until Dunkirk. Earlier in his life he had worked in Canada and before being called up he was in the Royal Army Ordnance Corps in a civilian capacity. Formerly, he had been a steward of the R.E. Services Club at Catterick Camp.

By 1941 he was stationed at Barton Stacey Camp, five miles east of Andover, Hampshire. He became another victim of the "Blackout" when he sustained a fractured skull by misadventure, being knocked down by an unknown vehicle on the night of January 25th. William's body was returned to Richmond and he was buried, with full military honours, in grave M94 Richmond Cemetery, after a funeral at the Methodist Chapel.

CORPORAL BERTRAM HENRY PEART
NO. S/94244 ROYAL ARMY SERVICE CORPS
DIED JUNE 11TH 1941 AGED 23

Bertram came from Richmond and was the son of John and Mary Peart. He volunteered on the day war broke out and served in the Royal Army Service Corps. Bertram was with the BEF in France in May and June, 1940, and was evacuated at Dunkirk, before being sent out to North Africa. By April 1941 he found himself involved in the campaigns in Greece and Crete.

In anticipation of German intervention in the Balkans, Wavell was ordered to send his best Middle East Command troops to Greece. 57,000 men arrived during

March 1941. As Yugoslavia was being overrun, the Germans also invaded Greece and the British were forced to withdraw southwards, an evacuation of the mainland being completed on April 27th, as 43,000 troops were rescued, leaving all their heavy equipment, including RASC vehicles, behind.

16,000 of these troops landed on Crete and were joined by 12,000 more from Egypt, ready to defend the island, but equipment was inadequate and RAF planes were forced to withdraw. On May 20th, German Airborne and Mountain troops landed from the air and forced the British and Greeks back. Some defenders were evacuated by the Royal Navy but the rest were forced to surrender on May 31st. It was during the defence of Crete that Bertram Peart died. He was wounded and taken prisoner, but died in captivity some days later, being buried near Canae, Crete. His name is commemorated on Face 8 of the Athens Memorial.

SAPPER CLARENCE VIVIAN HALL
NO. 2134089 280 FIELD COMPANY ROYAL ENGINEERS
DIED JUNE 13TH 1941 AGED 25

Before the war, Clarence was employed as a foreman joiner for George Wade, the Richmond builder, and was living at Beacon House. Serving with the Royal Engineers in East Suffolk, in the Lowestoft area, Clarence Hall died due to enemy action during war operations on June 13th 1941. His body was returned from Lowestoft and was buried in grave W.110 Richmond Cemetery, the RASC providing a gun carriage and firing party.

LANCE BOMBADIER RICHARD MARTIN PROCTER
ROYAL ARTILLERY
DIED OCTOBER 7TH 1941 AGED 26

Richard had lived with his parents, Robert George and Violet Procter, at Rudd House, Cracoe. They were landed gentry owning large estates in the area. Robert, Richard's father, was the brother of Lieutenant Norman Procter who had been killed in the Great War. Their father, William Atkinson Procter, had lived at the Manor House, Rylstone, and was a generous benefactor to the district. Lance Bombadier Richard Martin Procter died in England on October 7th 1941, whilst serving with his Regiment, when he was involved in an accident whilst riding his motor bike. He is buried in Rylstone Churchyard.

The last serviceman from these dales to die in 1941 was from Richmond.

FUSILIER THOMAS WILLIAM DOHERTY
NO. 4278525 1ST BATTALION NORTHUMBERLAND FUSILIERS
DIED DECEMBER 9TH 1941 AGED 21

21 year old Thomas lived with his parents, John and Elizabeth Doherty, in the St. Martins area of Richmond. He joined the 1st Battalion Northumberland Fusiliers, who had been in Egypt since 1939. Between September 1940 and December 1941 they were in the desert without a break, and constantly in close touch with the enemy.

Throughout April and May 1941, Rommel's Afrika Korps drove back the British forces and on April 6th most of the British 2nd Armoured Division was surrounded and captured. The Fusiliers were further back from this action and in the general withdrawal, acted as a rearguard unit. They found themselves gradually drawn into the defences of the fortress of Tobruk, a port on the coast of North Africa. With the reverse, the British Commander, Wavell, was determined to hold Tobruk at all costs – to deprive Rommel of a base port and to threaten the German and Italian flank.

For the next seven months the Fusiliers were to play a vital role in Tobruk's defence. Everyone lived in sweltering hot dugouts, camouflaged from the frequent attacks of Stuka dive bombers. Through May and June the Tobruk defences held out against repeated attacks. In November, plans were made for a British offensive from Egypt, to be accompanied by offensive operations by the Tobruk garrison, so containing enemy forces. One of the fiercest engagements took place on November 29th, with "Z" Company especially to the fore as they helped storm and then defend the enemy position at El Duda. Serious casualties occurred as the Company came under constant fire from 210-mm. guns, mortars and tank rounds. They lost nearly two platoons in this engagement, but by December 3rd Tobruk had been relieved.

As the pursuit of Rommel's forces continued over the next few days, with the Afrika Korps fighting a vigorous rearguard action, Thomas Doherty was killed in action. His body was not retrieved and he is commemorated on Column 86 Alamein Memorial.

1942

In just over two years of warfare 21 servicemen from these dales had lost their lives, but during 1942, as the spheres of conflict widened, 21 more servicemen would die in this year alone. Only 1944 would see a greater number of deaths occurring in one twelve month period.

The Japanese advance through Malaya and their capture of Singapore claimed a victim, Bomber Command losses would claim a number of other lives, whilst the North African campaign continued to claim even more victims.

SERGEANT ALFRED WATERWORTH (AIR GUNNER) NO. 936068 51 SQUADRON RAFVR DIED JANUARY 26TH 1942

Alfred, known as "Smiler" to his friends, had lived with his parents, before his marriage, and worked as a bus conductor for the West Yorkshire Road Car Company in the Grassington area (Chapmans had sold out to them in 1930, with Bob Chapman acting as manager for them in the district). Alfred married Nellie Boothman from the King's Head Inn at Kettlewell and they came to live at "Fell View", Skirethorns Lane, Threshfield.

Alfred had joined up by September 1939 and trained as an air gunner in the RAF. His Squadron, Number 51, was based at Dishforth, North Yorkshire, and the 5 man crew flew twin engined Whitley bombers. Just one week before his death he had been home on leave at "Fell View".

January 26th 1942 saw Whitley bomber Z9315 take off at 1703 hours for a leaflet raid (nicknamed a Nickel raid) over the Emden area, but it failed to return. Only Sergeant Mancini, a Canadian crew member, survived, with the rest being buried with full military honours at Meppen, NW of Osnabruck and close to the Dutch border. After the war they were reburied in collective grave 14.D.1-4 Reichswald Forest War Cemetery. Out of 31 aircraft sent out over Emden that night, 2 Whitley bombers were lost. It is even more poignant to realise that they lost their lives whilst dropping pieces of paper over Germany.

Alfred (Smiler) Waterworth of Skirethorns Lane, Threshfield, near Grassington

SERGEANT (W.OP./AIR GUNNER) JOHN HAMMOND HARKER NO. 1360531 RAFVR DIED FEBRUARY 10TH 1942 AGED 27

John's father, Watson Harker, had been the sub-postmaster in Grassington and John eventually took over that position. His mother Elizabeth and siblings Robert and Ella completed the family.

In April 1938 John married Muriel Whitehead of Hebden and he enlisted in August 1940. Completing his training by August 1941 (and now the father of a baby daughter, Janet) he was posted to Thornaby-on-Tees and also Silloth before arriving to join a Ferry Training Unit at Honeybourne, in Worcestershire, 8 miles SSW of Stratford Upon Avon, in October 1941. He too had been home on leave the week prior to his death

Sergeant John Hammond Harker of Grassington

On a training exercise on February 10th the aircraft on which John was wireless operator crashed near Brayspool in Cardiganshire, Wales, with possibly the bad weather contributing to the causes of the crash. The entire crew was killed.

Internment took place at Hebden Church on Saturday February 14th at 3-30p.m. The coffin was draped with the Union Jack and a guard of honour from the Home Guard was in attendance, whilst two RAF sergeants represented his comrades.

SERGEANT ARTHUR L. ROBSON (W.OP./AIR GUNNER) NO. 996823 RAFVR DIED FEBRUARY 11TH 1942 AGED 23

Arthur was the son of Arthur and Catherine Robson of The Green, Richmond. He was a member of the crew of Whitley bomber N1439 of No. 10 Operational Training Unit, No. 6 Group, Bomber Command, which took off from RAF Abingdon, 6 miles south of Oxford, on a "Circuits and Landings" training flight at 21-29 hours on February 11th. Piloted by a Canadian and a Canadian trainee pilot, the aircraft struck trees one minute after take off and crashed, coming down in Upwood Park, Frilford Heath, on the NW side of the airfield. The cause of the crash was obscure. Only the air-gunner, Sergeant Hughes, survived out of the crew of four. Arthur Robson was buried with full military honours in grave U157 Richmond Cemetery.

SUB LIEUTENANT MICHAEL HOLDSWORTH 830 SQUADRON FLEET AIR ARM RNVR HMS "ST. ANGELO" DIED FEBRUARY 24TH 1942 AGED 20

Michael's parents were George Bertram and Mabel Holdsworth. George was brought up at Netherside Hall, near Grassington, and the Holdsworth family were in business as spinners and upholstery manufacturers at their Shaw Lodge Mills, Halifax (making upholstery for the seats on public transport, train seats and c harabancs). The family also owned Catteral Hall, Giggleswick, and the shooting lodge, Scargill House, near Kettlewell.

When he married, George and his wife lived at Catteral Hall, where their children, John, Michael and Bill were brought up. Their father was Master of the Catteral Beagles and entertained grouse shooting parties on his Conistone Moor estates. When Mabel died in 1934, the family moved to Scargill House.

Sub-Lieutenant Michael Holdsworth of Kettlewell

Michael had been educated at Harrow and had just gone up to Cambridge University when war was declared. He left and went into the Fleet Air Arm (his elder brother John went into the army and was killed in 1945, whilst younger brother Bill joined the RAF, becoming a Spitfire pilot and serving with the fighter ace, Johnny Johnson).

Michael eventually learned to land on aircraft carriers and on winning his commission, was posted to 830 Squadron, based at St. Angelo on Malta. The Squadron was equipped with Swordfish torpedo aircraft that searched for ships and submarines in the Mediterranean Sea. On February 24th 1942 his aircraft was part of the night time sweeps for enemy shipping off Tripoli, North Africa. His Swordfish aircraft (P4085) was shot down in flames whilst attempting a torpedo attack on two ships which were accompanied by destroyers.

Michael has no known grave and is commemorated on Bay 4 Panel 1 of the Lee-on-Solent Memorial (Fleet Air Arm).

PRIVATE JOHN HATHAWAY
NO. 4858299 1ST BATTALION LEICESTERSHIRE REGIMENT
DIED APRIL 11TH 1942 AGED 23

John, known to everyone as Jacky, was the second of four children of Walter and Jane Elizabeth Hathaway (Thomas, John, Peggy, Lawrence). Walter was an Otley man who came to work in a racing stables at Middleham. He met his wife, a Richmond girl, and eventually they moved to Carlton in Coverdale. With little work to be found in the dale, John moved to live with his grandmother at Waterloo, Richmond, and worked as a bricklayer for George Wade, the builder.

John Hathaway from Richmond

In 1936 he was persuaded by his mates to join the army, joining the Leicesters and going out to Palestine. They were stationed in India when war broke out. The Battalion returned home and in 1941 it was involved in the fighting on Crete, with John fortunate to be safely evacuated.

The 1st Battalion was then posted to Singapore, from where they were ordered to the Malayan Peninsula, to meet the Japanese amphibious landings to the north, on December 8th 1941. The Japanese, veterans of combat in China, swept aside the relatively light British covering force, including the 1st Battalion. By December 18th the Battalion had suffered so severely, they were amalgamated with the East Surreys, to become known as the "British Battalion". Putting up a stiff resistance at the Battle of Kampar and losing many men, the survivors, including John Hathaway, were taken off by the Navy on January 28th and landed on Singapore Island.

Lawrence Hathaway, visiting his brother John's grave on Singapore Island.
'Sleep on dear son, in a far-off land, in a grave I will never see.'

The Japanese assault began on February 8th 1942, following a protracted air bombardment. The crossing in armoured barges was covered by intense artillery fire and British counter-attacks were broken up by dive bombers. Despite foot-by-foot resistance, the city's reservoirs were captured. The 70,000-man garrison thereupon surrendered unconditionally on February 15th. John (Jacky) Hathaway had survived the ordeal, but in the terrible conditions found in the Japanese POW camps on the island, where dysentery and malaria were rife, he died on April 11th 1942, although his family did not get to hear of his death until 1944. He was buried in grave 7.A.11. Kranji War Cemetery and after the war his mother asked for these words to be inscribed: "Sleep on, dear son, in a far off land, in a grave I will never see. Loving mother." She regretted that no one from the family would ever see it but much later, his younger brother Lawrence was able to visit the site.

SERGEANT ARTHUR WILLIAM NEWHOUSE
NO. 645144 (W.OP./AIR GUNNER)
53 SQUADRON RAF COASTAL COMMAND
DIED MAY 4TH 1942 AGED 23

Arthur was the son of William and Florence Newhouse and was born at Troutbeck Farm, Linton, near Grassington. He attended Threshfield School, but when his parents took over the tenancy of the Slaters Arms Inn at Bradley, near Skipton, and the farm connected to it, he attended Bradley School. He then attended Earby School until leaving to become a farm labourer in Kelbrook, between Skipton and Colne, on the farm of Mr. Tempest.

Sergeant Arthur Newhouse, formerly of Linton

After joining the RAF he became an air gunner and joined 53 Squadron, Coastal Command, based at North Cotes in Lincolnshire, 4 miles south of Grimsby, flying Lockheed Hudsons. Arthur's plane, AM530, took off from North Cotes on May 4th 1942 for a mission over the North Sea, in an area off the Dutch coast, but failed to return. Their bodies were recovered by the Germans and the crew are buried in plot 85.C.11. New Eastern Cemetery, Amsterdam.

The next two dales men to be killed, one from Buckden and the other from Richmond, died fighting Rommel's forces in North Africa.

PRIVATE THOMAS DINSDALE
NO. 4347960 4TH BATTALION EAST YORKSHIRE REGIMENT
DIED BETWEEN MAY 31ST AND JUNE 4TH 1942 AGED 29

Thomas was the only child of James (Jim) and Jane Dinsdale. Jane Alderson was from Gunnerside and was in service with Miss Stansfield of Buckden House and owner of the Buckden Estate. Jim was the gardener for Miss Stansfield and when Jane and Jim married they lived at the cottage next to the Buckden blacksmith., where Thomas was born in 1913. After leaving school, Thomas joined his father in working in the gardens. He was a shy lad, but popular, and enjoyed cycling in the dales in his spare time. When Thomas enlisted he joined the 4th Battalion East Yorks and went with them to North Africa, where they became caught up in the disastrous Battle of Gazala.

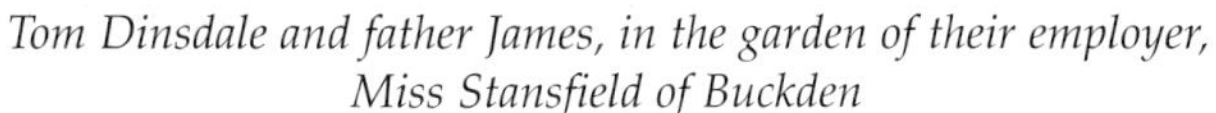

Tom Dinsdale and father James, in the garden of their employer, Miss Stansfield of Buckden

Tom Dinsdale from Buckden, in Wharfedale

On May 28th Rommel attacked the British forces, hoping to envelop their desert flank and roll up the position. The 4th Battalion was part of the infantry support within the main British defensive position, "Kingsbridge Box". Here, a tremendous tank battle raged from May 30th to June 1st between Rommel's Panzer column and British armour. Ammunition for the British inside the "Box" was running very low and on May 31st Rommel threw all that he had against them – artillery fire, tanks, infiltrating infantry covered by machine gun fire – from every side.

Short of ammunition and water, pounded day and night, with tanks no match for the German heavies, the Brigade fought grimly on in an ever contracting ring. Company positions were overrun one after another. By 2p.m. on June 1st the action was over, overwhelmed by vastly superior forces. The 4th Battalion had suffered severely in dead and wounded. "B" Company had refused to surrender, fought on and were virtually wiped out. The 4th Battalion ceased to exist. Thomas was posted missing and his death was not confirmed for a long time, causing great distress for his mother, Jane. Thomas Dinsdale's name is commemorated on Column 70 Alamein Memorial.

The disastrous British defeat at Gazala in May - June 1942, in which Thomas was killed, was a battle even Rommel thought he was going to lose. Yet somehow, the Eighth Army Commander, the hapless General Ritchie, managed to snatch defeat from the jaws of victory.

PRIVATE JOHN HETHERINGTON
NO. 4390167 4TH BATTALION GREEN HOWARDS
DIED JUNE 1ST 1942 AGED 29

John was the son of Robert and Mary Guy Hetherington and the husband of Lily Hetherington of Richmond. Serving with the 4th Battalion Green Howards, John, too, found himself in the same North African defensive box called "Knightsbridge", as Thomas Dinsdale had been in.

At first light on June 1st, Rommel's forces attacked on all fronts. There was much heavy shelling and the enemy advanced with tanks, close support guns and 3-ton carriers packed with troops at the point where a gap had been made in the minefield in front of No. 12 Platoon on the previous day. The Platoon fought until their ammunition ran out and then were forced to surrender. By 9a.m. "B" and "C" Companies had also been overrun. They fought gallantly but were desperately short of ammunition. Most were killed or taken into captivity, with only a few escaping. John Hetherington's body was never recovered and like Thomas Dinsdale, his name is found on the Alamein Memorial, on Column 60.

SERGEANT (AIR GUNNER) JOHN ROBERT THOMPSON NO. 989028 76 SQUADRON RAFVR DIED JUNE 2ND 1942 AGED 22

John lived at Richmond with his parents, John and Mary Kirsop Thompson. Joining the RAF, John trained as an air gunner and was posted to 76 Squadron based at Middleton St. George, between Darlington and Stockton, in County Durham.

The first 1000 bomber raid on Cologne had just taken place on the night of May 30th/31st and on the night of June 1st/2nd, 956 bombers headed for Essen, in the Ruhr. Failure was the outcome. Despite copious use of flares, bombing was scattered and very little material damage was caused to Essen, although surrounding areas suffered. 33 planes were lost that night.

The 6 man crew of Halifax bomber W1064 took off from Middleton St. George at 2306 hours. While homeward bound the starboard inner engine began to vibrate and within a short time seized. The Halifax was then attacked by a night fighter, piloted by Heinrich Prinz zu Sayn-Wittgenstein, and crashed at 0145 hours just south of Leuven, in Belgium. Two men, including John Thompson, were killed, two were taken prisoner and two evaded capture. John is buried in grave 2.E.1. Heverlee War Cemetery, between Brussels and Leuven.

LEADING AIRCRAFTMAN CLIFFORD DOBSON NO. 754202 235 WING, BASED IN NORTH AFRICA, DIED JUNE 8TH 1942 AGED 23

Clifford was the son of George Henry and Edith Elizabeth Dobson, who, by the end of the war were living at Billingham, County Durham. However, Clifford and his family had strong connections with Richmond. He joined the RAF as a member of the ground crew and became a Leading Aircraftman, maintaining the aircraft.

In May and June 1942 Clifford was involved in maintaining the planes that attacked viciously against Rommel's armour as the Panzers poured into the "Knightsbridge Box". Rommel erected a "fortress" in an area called "The Cauldron" inside the British lines. His armour debouched from "The Cauldron", threatening the rear of the entire Eighth Army and General Ritchie ordered withdrawal on June 13th. It was partly the Desert Air Force, under Air Vice-Marshal Coningham, of which Clifford Dobson was a member of the ground staff, that saved the Eighth Army from total destruction in the aftermath of Gazala. However, on June 6th, Clifford Dodson was killed as the German armour penetrated the British rear positions. He is buried in grave 8.G.6. Halfaya Sollum War Cemetery.

FLIGHT SERGEANT (NAVIGATOR) FRANK EBRAY LAWSON NO. 1109242 7 SQUADRON RAFVR DIED JULY 29TH 1942 AGED 32

Frank was the son of John and Mary Lawson of 6 Pottergate, Richmond (later 41 Darlington Road), and attended Richmond Grammar School. His father was a painter and decorator, with a shop in Pottergate. Frank had a fine baritone voice, being a member of the Church Choir, Richmondshire Musical Society and the Operatic Society. A keen cyclist, he was a member of Richmond Cycling Club and of the Cyclist Touring Club and played rugby for the Old Boys of the Grammar School. In 1939 he married his wife, Adelaide Nunn of Darlington, who was also a fine singer.

Frank Ebray Lawson of Richmond
Courtesy of the Darlington and Stockton Times

Frank joined the RAF in 1940 and trained as an Observer in Bomber Command, before joining 7 Squadron, flying Stirling bombers out of RAF Oakington, four miles north of Cambridge. Adelaide had gone to live near the aerodrome where he was stationed and was with him on the day he was called to go on the operation.

On the night of 28th/29th July 1942, Stirling bomber W7533 took off at 2228 hours, its destination the port of Hamburg. It was part of a large raid and 33 planes were lost, including two from 7 Squadron. Frank Lawson's plane crashed at Klein Horsten, 16 kilometres SW of Wilhelmshaven. One crew member became a POW, another was critically injured but died a few hours later and the others died in the crash. Frank Lawson is buried in grave 3.A.9. Sage War Cemetery, 24 kilometres south of Oldenburg, Germany.

SERGEANT/INSTRUCTOR RALPH LAWRENCE SEEGER NO. 2066820 6TH BATTALION WEST YORKSHIRE REGIMENT (LATER ROYAL ARMY ORDNANCE CORPS) DIED AUGUST 19TH 1942 AGED 33

Ralph Lawrence Seeger of Appletreewick and Shipley

A single man, Ralph lived with his parents, Lawrence and Annie Seeger, at Nab Lane, Shipley. Lawrence, his father, was in partnership with his other son, Ralph's twin brother Norman, in the family textile weaving business in the Shipley area. Ralph had become a textile designer and worked in the Bradford area. Before the war his parents rented a couple of rooms at Reynoldson's farm in Skyreholmes, near Appletreewick and later bought a semi-detached house on the main road running through Appletreewick. This explains why Ralph's name appears on the nearby Burnsall War Memorial.

During the late 1920's and early 1930's, Ralph,

Norman and a friend, Douglas Illingworth, went on walking trips, including ones in Europe. In 1928 they walked through Switzerland, with their luggage being sent ahead (in their luggage they had to include a dining suit)

Ralph was a member of the Territorial Army and was called up before war began. As a member of the Royal Army Ordnance Corps he later became involved in the operation of Radar, acting as an instructor at Nottingham in this vital, secret weapon of World War Two. Sadly, he was taken ill and entered one of the Nottingham hospitals, where he died on August 19th 1942. Ralph Seeger is buried in grave C.C.51. Bingley Cemetery.

PILOT OFFICER ROBERT (BOBBY) MACKINNON WATSON NO. 121415 39 SQUADRON RAFVR DIED SEPTEMBER 6TH 1942 AGED 22

Bobby was the son of Edward and Elizabeth Gray Watson, of Spion Kop, Seal Houses, near Langthwaite, in Arkengarthdale. His brother Edward completed the family. Bobby's parents were Scottish and in 1926 they came from the Teesdale area, with Edward taking the position of gamekeeper on the Arkengarthdale Estate belonging to Colonel Wilson.

Robert (Bobby) Watson, son of gamekeeper, Langthwaite, Arkengarthdale

Their father, known affectionately to dales folk as Uncle Ned, also broke in horses. Later, he became the gamekeeper for Sir Tommy Sopwith, when the world famous airman, yachtsman and inventor bought the Estate in 1942.

Bobby Watson went from Arkengarthdale School to Richmond Grammar School (1933 to 1937). He joined the RAF as war began and eventually was posted to 39 Squadron as a pilot. By January 1941 the Squadron was based at Shandur, Egypt, and was carrying out armed photo-reconnaissance sorties over the Western Desert, Greece and Crete, using Martin Maryland aircraft.

In August 1941 the Squadron was equipped with the Beaufort torpedo fighter bomber, crewed by four men and carrying one torpedo. They conducted maritime reconnaissance and torpedo strikes. On January 23rd 1942 members of the Squadron torpedoed the Italian liner (troopship) "Vitoria" and on March 9th sank a destroyer, crippled a cruiser and merchant ship and shot down two enemy aircraft.

During 1942 the Squadron became fragmented, with detached flights operating from Malta and various airfields in Egypt. Taking off from Malta on September 6th 1942, Bobby Watson was killed when his Bristol Beaufort (AW305) went missing from an attack on a convoy off Taranto, Italy. His name is commemorated on Panel 3 Column 1 Malta Memorial.

WARRANT OFFICER CLAUDE SIMPSON MAXFIELD
NO. 936753 104 SQUADRON RAFVR
DIED SEPTEMBER 8TH 1942 AGED 22

Claude was born in 1920, and he and his younger brother Colin were the sons of Wallace and Helen Maxfield, of Wood Lane, Grassington. Wallace was the shop foreman for a local building firm and also did undertaking work. Educated at Threshfield School and Ermysted's Grammar School, Skipton, Claude worked as a green keeper at Threshfield Golf Club whilst waiting to join the RAF. He had always been keen on sport and played rugby for the Upper Wharfedale team. A strong believer, he had been a server at Linton Church, together with Reginald Douthwaite, another Grassington man who would be killed later in the war, and both were friends of the Rector, Frederick Arnold Mosby.

Claude Maxfield of Grassington, stationed in England

Claude joined 115 Squadron at Marham in Norfolk and, after operations over France and Germany, the crews flew Wellington bombers out to join 104 Squadron in the Middle East, mainly operating against troop concentrations in the Mersa Matruh and El Alamein fronts. After attacking harbour installations on the coast on July 8th 1942 the plane developed engine failure and they crash landed in the desert, behind enemy lines, 30 miles from Sidi Barrani. After setting off walking on a desperate attempt to regain the British line, they were sighted by a Baltimore twin-engine plane, which landed and took off, heavily laden with relieved passengers.

Claude Maxfield of Grassington, relaxing whilst off duty in North Africa

After this incident, there were operations over Crete, Greece and Palestine but very little flying was done by Claude and his crew. He had completed 30 operations and was rested but because the Squadron was "pushed" for men, he was brought back. On September 8th 1942 Claude Maxfield was sadly killed whilst on a mission, attacking the port of Tobruk, which was now in German hands. His body was never recovered (although later a grave was exhumed to reveal the body of the plane's tail gunner, Sergeant Wood) and his name is commemorated on Column 249 Alamein Memorial. A stained glass window in Linton Church is dedicated to Rector Mosby, Claude Maxfield and Reginald Douthwaite.

CHIEF PETTY OFFICER (BLACKSMITH 1ST CLASS) SYDNEY GARGET NO. C/MX45530 HMS "CURACOA" ROYAL NAVY DIED OCTOBER 2ND 1942 AGED 37

Sydney was the son of William and Elizabeth Mary Garget and husband of Margaret Gertrude (Gertie) Garget. His grandfather was a Richmond blacksmith, living and working at Craven Gate in the town. His father, William, also became a blacksmith at the Craven Gate smithy, and when Sydney left school, he was apprenticed to his father, although he learned the skills of a white smith (making railings and a variety of iron work). However, with high unemployment and less demand for such work during the Depression years of the early 1930's, Sydney decided to join the Royal Navy.

Sydney Garget of Richmond

It was whilst he was stationed at Chatham that he met his future wife, Gertie, who came from Maidstone, and it was there that they set up home. However, for the next five years he was away from his wife as he served with the Royal Navy on the North China Station, from the naval base at Wei-Hai-Wei.

Sydney was serving on board HMS "Curacoa", a light cruiser, in 1942.

When America entered the war on December 7th 1941, it would be some time before large numbers of American troops would arrive in Britain. However, by the later stages of 1942 troops were arriving and a large contingent of 11,000 men set sail from New York on the "Queen Mary" on September 27th, bound for Liverpool. With

Left: Sydney Garget at Wei-Hai-Wei, China, during the 1930's

Below: Peter Starvis at the grave of his uncle, Sydney Garget, on the Isle of Skye

a top speed of over 30 knots, it was decided that she would sail unescorted, for she could outpace German U-boats.

The greatest danger facing the "Queen Mary" would be when she neared this coast and had to reduce speed. Therefore a rendezvous was arranged to the west of Northern Ireland, where she would reduce speed and be met by HMS "Curacoa" and a destroyer escort, which would lead her into Liverpool, in a full blaze of publicity.

Disaster struck on October 2nd, when, due to mistakes being made on both ships during countermeasure manoeuvres against U-boats, the "Queen Mary" struck HMS "Curacoa" amidships. She was cut in half and sank immediately. At the top level it was decided that the normal rules of the sea would not be adhered to, and instead of stopping to pick up survivors, so providing a target for U-boats and losing the lives of American soldiers (it would not look good if heralded across the newspapers by the press reporters waiting in Liverpool) the liner and escorting destroyers would carry on to Liverpool. When the liner arrived in great publicity, a news blackout was placed on the fate of the "Curacoa". 338 casualties out of a crew of 430 resulted from the loss of the naval vessel, including Sydney Garget. Eventually, the bodies of six sailors, including Sydney Garget, were washed up on the shores of the Isle of Skye (nine more would later be washed up). Sydney is buried in grave M.1. Ashaig Cemetery, Isle of Skye, a few miles from the Skye Bridge, Invernessshire.

The Cunard Shipping Company made an interim payment of £40 to the dependants of all those lost and at an enquiry after the war, a further payment of £300 each was made.

PRIVATE ERNEST FRANCIS BERESFORD NO. 2824324 2ND BATTALION SEAFORTH HIGHLANDERS DIED NOVEMBER 2ND 1942

Ernest Beresford of Newhouse, Langstrothdale

Ernest was born at Newhouse in Langstrothdale. His father, Robert, born at nearby Cowside, was the brother of Peter Fred Beresford who had been killed in the Great War. Robert married Mary Campbell, a local girl, and they farmed at Newhouse. The origins of the Beresford family were in Derbyshire, where they had been lead miners.

Three of their children died in infancy but Robert, Ernest, Arthur, Ada and Barbara went to Oughtershaw School. During the 1930's, their mother Mary supplemented the income by providing teas and refreshments for hikers passing through the dale. By the start of the war, however, Mary, her son Arthur and daughter-in-law had moved to Chapel le Dale, between Ingleton and Ribble Head, where they took over the Hill Inn and associated farm.

Ernest joined the army and became a member of the 2nd Battalion Seaforth Highlanders. In October

Newhouse Farm in Deepdale, Langstrothdale.
The Beresford family worked the farm before the Great War and into the late 1930's

Oughtershaw School group, Langstrothdale, 1930's.
Ernest Beresford 2nd left on back row. Arthur Beresford 3rd from right on back row.
Ada Beresford 2nd from right on back row. Barbara Beresford 3rd from left in the middle

1942 they prepared to take part in the Battle of Alamein, the turning point of the war in the Western Desert. Minefields were opened up by the infantry, including Ernest's Battalion, through which the 10th Armoured Corps advanced, whilst a diversionary attack was made to the south. On October 26th, General Montgomery threw his weight against the coastal area. For a week, a ferocious tank battle raged in the minefield south of the coastal road. The Axis armour, under constant aerial bombardment, "shrank" rapidly.

Rommel committed his last reserves, extricated his infantry from encirclement and dug in again on November 1st. Montgomery renewed his attempted break-through on November 2nd. Behind a rolling barrage, the infantry cleared a corridor through the minefields for British tanks. A desperate Panzer counter-attack momentarily snubbed the breakthrough, but by the day's end only 35 German tanks remained in action. The enemy minefields and shelling had taken its toll on the infantry, however. On November 2nd 1942 Ernest was killed in action. He was yet another dalesman whose name is found on the Alamein Memorial, on Column 70.

PRIVATE ROBERT FAWCETT DIXON
NO. 14298206 GENERAL SERVICE CORPS
(ATTACHED TO ARMY PHYSICAL TRAINING CORPS)
DIED NOVEMBER 3RD 1942 AGED 21

Robert (Bob) Fawcett Dixon of Halfpenny House, between Bellerby and Downholme, Swaledale

Robert, or Bob as he was known, was the son of John Anthony and Mary Elizabeth Dixon. John was born in Ravenstonedale and married Elizabeth Fawcett from Marske. They lived at Castle Farm, Scargill, near Barnard Castle, for awhile. They came to live at Halfpenny House, a farm and former toll bar house, between Bellerby and Downholme.

Bob was born there, the youngest of children Joe, Jack, Annie and Nellie. He left Downholme School at 14 years of age and helped on the family farm, where he took a keen interest in the care of the sheep. Their father, John, was killed in 1937 when he was knocked down by a car in front of Halfpenny House, and Joe and Jack took over the farm, with Bob continuing working there.

Bob joined Downholme Home Guard in June 1940 and gave much of his time to night duty and training. He was a keen rifle shot and in 1942 he joined the Army and was posted to Brancepeth Castle, SW of Durham, but it was only shortly afterwards that he fell ill. It is possible that a misdiagnosis resulted in his treatment for appendicitis and peritonitis being too late and he died on November 3rd 1942. If he had been at home he would almost certainly have received speedier medical attention. Robert Dixon was buried in grave 14, St. Michael's Churchyard, Downholme, on December 4th. The local detachment of the Home Guard formed a guard of honour, the coffin was draped with the Union Jack and was borne by Home Guard members.

Downholme School 1930/1931.
Back row: Walter Brown, Douglas Webster, George Clemminson, Ernest Whitehead, George Brown, Harold Weller.
Next row: Robert Dixon, Harry Taylor, Jack Dixon, R. Thorpe, John Clemminson, Freda Metcalfe, ? Thorpe, Mary Whitehead, Nellie Dixon, E. Taylor, Betty Wade.
Kneeling: Jimmy Smith, Annie Dixon, Peggy Close, Myra Bessie Webster, Mary Robinson, Peggy Wade, Kenneth Webster.
Robert Dixon and Harold Weller died whilst serving their country during the Second World War

GUNNER WILLIAM HUNTER MARTIN
NO. 1738047 95 BATTERY 48 LIGHT ANTI-AIRCRAFT REGIMENT ROYAL ARTILLERY
DIED NOVEMBER 6TH 1942 AGED 37

William Hunter Martin of Grinton and Reeth

Known to everyone as Billy, he was born at Alston in Cumbria, the son of William Martin, a regular army man, who eventually worked in the quarries. His mother Emily was a Hunter, connected to the Swan-Hunter family. With nine children in the family, they moved to live at Station House, Frosterley, near Stanhope, where William worked in the quarry.

At 18 years of age, Billy moved to Swaledale, where he was employed as a farm worker by Bert Horn at Sorrell Sykes Farm, Fremington, near Reeth. It was here that he met his future wife, Marjorie Elizabeth Peacock, from Grinton. Three boys, Peter, John and Ken were born at Grinton. Billy left Sorrell Sykes to farm for Thomas Brown at Scar House, Harkerside, Grinton, but he never really enjoyed life on the farm and finally began working for the local council, repairing the roads.

When he was called up in December 1940 Thomas Brown said he could go back on the farm to receive exemption, but Billy said, "I've worked for him once and that's enough." He enlisted and joined the Royal Artillery, serving in an Anti-Aircraft Regiment. They embarked for the Far East in late 1941/early 1942, their destination Java in the Dutch East Indies (Indonesia).

We have already seen that the Japanese had been victorious in Malaya and were about to attack Singapore. Thousands of British and Empire servicemen entered Java in February 1942, shortly before the Japanese invasion of the island. Two fighter squadrons plus anti-aircraft batteries continued to defend the island of Java until February 27th. On March 1st the Japanese landed and soon defeated the defending force.

The prisoners were housed in intolerable conditions in a POW camp, with harsh treatment meted out by their guards. Disease was rife and Billy became sick with dysentery in the rudimentary hospital. He was moved to a hospital camp a mile away, where he died on November 6th 1942. His pals carried him to his resting place. Billy's family was not officially informed about his death until 1946. His grave, 4.L.8. is now in the Jakarta War Cemetery, Indonesia.

DRIVER CURTIS WALKER
NO. T/113820 ROYAL ARMY SERVICE CORPS
DIED NOVEMBER 14TH 1942 AGED 24

Born in 1918, Curtis was the youngest of the three sons (William, Norman and Curtis) of Curtis and Annie Walker of Hetton, near Rylstone. Their father was a painter and decorator and they lived at the cottage next to the Angel Inn, Hetton. After leaving Cracoe School, Curtis junior went into the family business. He was mechanically minded, drove the business vehicle and possessed a motor bike.

Curtis Walker
from Hetton, near Grassington

He enlisted in October 1939, and it was not surprising that he became a driver in the RASC and went with the BEF to France with the 50th Division Petrol Company, before being evacuated from Dunkirk.

At Easter 1941 he married Mabel Newhouse from Linton and a few weeks later he embarked for Egypt in North Africa. He was never to see his daughter, Barbara, who was born in late 1941.

Curtis's unit was part of the garrison of Tobruk that capitulated to Rommel's Afrika Korps on June 21st 1942. As a prisoner of the Italians he found himself in a camp at Benghazi, and later, Tripoli.

On November 13th 1942 an Italian ship, SS "Scillin", grossly overloaded with 814 people on board, mainly British POW's, sailed from Tripoli to Trapani in Sicily. Half the men had dysentery and during the day only five men at a time were allowed up on deck to draw water. She sailed without lights and no flag.

Two British submarines were on patrol and the "Sahib" spotted the "Scillin". It fired twelve shots from her 3-inch guns on November 14th. The "Scillin" stopped and transmitted an SOS. The Italian guards placed solid heavy timbers over the hatches, so that the POW's could not escape. At 1950 hours, even though the submarine commander knew there were POW's on board, one torpedo was fired into the "Scillin" engine room and she sank in less than two minutes. Only 36 Italians and 27 POW's were rescued and taken to Malta.

The submarine commander had orders only to fire torpedoes at Africa bound ships, but his actions on November 14th were approved by his superiors. The MOD erroneously gave out information that the ship carried 200 Italian soldiers and had ignored warning shots across her bows. It was not until January 15th 1944 that Mabel discovered more about how he had died and sadly she continued to get letters from the War Office saying he was likely to be alive. Curtis Walker's name is commemorated on Column 79 Alamein Memorial.

Reg Rymer and his young helper, Curtis Walker, beside the Rymer's greengrocery van. The van travelled the dales in the 1930's

Cracoe Village School 1930/1931.
Back row: Dorothy Hymas, Marjorie Carr, Hilda Moore, Helen Foster, Margery Dowbiggin.
Next row: Eva Seely, Mary Tennant, Evelyn Foster, Dorothy Dpwbiggin, Eleanor Tennant.
Next row: Peggy Robinson, Winnie Rathall, Ronald Bolton, William Verity, Norman Carr, Curtis Walker.
Next row: Edward Taylor, Norman Reeday, David Ibbotson.
Front row: Joan Metcalfe, Florence Hunter, Joe Lawson, ? Bolton, Frank Shuttleworth, ? Bolton, Amy Verity, Peter Carr, Agnes Mason, ? Bolton

LANCE CORPORAL MOSES EDWARD KINCHIN NO. 7691214
115 PROVOST COMPANY CORPS OF MILITARY POLICE
DIED NOVEMBER 14TH 1942 AGED 27

Eddy, as he was known, was one of the two sons of Moses and Sarah Thomason Kinchin of Richmond. His father was a barber in the Market Square, close to the Market Hall, and the family lived above the shop.

When Eddy Kinchin enlisted he joined the Corps of Military Police and in November 1942 he was set to take part in the Battle of El Alamein, on the border of Egypt and Libya.

The Military Police had a vital and dangerous role in any battle zone. They were often to the fore front, dealing with route signing, marking out the roads, and guiding traffic in the battle area. Their role was to keep the lines of command clear and help reinforcements to be guided through more quickly. As they had to be conspicuous, they wore white helmets and white gloves, and so could provide an easy target for any sniper.

El Alamein was a success for the Eighth Army and they continued the pursuit of Rommel's forces. In this pursuit, Eddy Kinchin was killed on November 14th 1942. Again, in the confusion of battle and with the use of artillery, tank rounds and mortar fire, Eddy's body was not recovered and his name is to be found on Column 84 Alamein Memorial.

BOMBADIER JOHN MOODY SKINNER
NO. 6215403 4 MARITIME BATTERY ROYAL ARTILLERY
DIED NOVEMBER 22TH 1942 AGED 31

John had been born in West Hartlepool, the son of Henry and Mary Helen Skinner. He married Mary Hall, daughter of Charles Hall of Richmond, with the married couple living at 9 The Avenue, Richmond. In the late 1930's he was employed as a clerk in the Richmond branch of Barclay's Bank.

When he enlisted, John was eventually posted to a Maritime Battery of the Royal Artillery. The Maritime RA was engaged in ship defence, with its trained gunners being sent to serve on board merchant ships, to man the guns with which they had been equipped for defence against air and sea attacks.

However, John Skinner was taken ill with tuberculosis and by the time he was admitted to the Municipal Hospital, Middlesbrough, he had been discharged from the army. John died at the hospital from pulmonary tuberculosis on November 22nd 1942 and was buried in grave Y.7-92. Richmond Cemetery. He left a widow and twin children, born just a few weeks before his death.

The last fatality amongst the servicemen from these dales during 1942 was an air gunner in Bomber Command.

FLIGHT LIEUTENANT (AIR GUNNER)
CHARLES GUTHRIE SHIELDS BAIN NO. 118058 9 SQUADRON RAF
DIED DECEMBER 17TH 1942

The son of Finlay and Janet Bain of The Grove, Richmond, Charles attended Richmond Grammar School, as did his brothers, John and Finlay Bain. Their

Scottish father, Finlay, senior, had won the Military Cross during the Great War, whilst serving as an officer in the Cameron Highlanders. After the war he continued a career in the regular army, serving with the Royal Engineers at Catterick Camp for 20 years. When he retired to Richmond, he had a large part of The Grove converted to flats that could be rented out. After leaving Richmond Grammar School, Charles began work in the Naafi, on Catterick Camp.

Charles Bain of Richmond as a grammar school boy

During the war Charles enlisted in the RAF and became an air gunner with 9 Squadron, flying in Lancasters from Waddington in Lincolnshire. His skills were recognised and he became the Squadron's gunnery leader. There was miserable weather from September 1942 to the end of the year, but small raids were still launched, with losses disproportionate to the results achieved. One such raid occurred on 17th/18th December when aircraft from Nos. 3 and 5 Groups attempted to bomb a variety of small

The show goes on despite the war. The Swaledale Ram Show was held on Thursday 28th October 1943 at Kirkby Stephen, where the champion ram was sold for £175. Mr. Metcalfe of West Stonedale, the owner and breeder is shown holding the prize ram.
Standing, left to right: J. Whitehead, J. Alderson, R. Thornborrow, Mr. Kipling, R. Bousfield, T. Sisson, J. Dixon

industrial towns spread across Germany.

The 5 Group Lancaster Force (of which 9 Squadron belonged) lost nine of its twenty seven bombers, with 9 Squadron losing two of these.

Lancaster W4155 took off from Waddington at 1712 hours, its target Diepholz, between Osnabruck and Bremen. It crashed at 1932 hours, 20 miles to the north west. Five men were killed and two were taken prisoner. Charles Bain and four others were buried in the Evangelical Friedhof, but after the war he was reburied in grave 17.B.22. Rheinberg War Cemetery, south of Wesel, Germany. We shall find that Charles' brother, Major John Brain, would be killed in Burma, whilst Captain Finlay Bain of the Gurkha Rifles, though wounded, would survive the war. Meanwhile, their father was serving with Western Command in a civilian capacity.

1943

For British soldiers in 1943, the main theatre of operations was North Africa (especially Tunisia), Italy and the Mediterranean, where six dales men would lose their lives. In Northern Europe, the sole means of striking at the enemy had to come from the air and five airmen paid the price with their lives. Meanwhile, four servicemen with dales' connections came to be buried on home territory during 1943, bringing the total of servicemen who died during that year to fifteen.

SERGEANT (NAVIGATOR) GEORGE ERIC JOHNSON
NO. 1124496 214 SQUADRON RAFVR
DIED FEBRUARY 3RD 1943 AGED 21

George Eric Johnson of Richmond
Courtesy of the Darlington and Stockton Times

Known as Eric to his family, and "Porky" to his friends at Richmond Grammar School, he was the only son of Lawrence George and Hilda Mary Johnson, who, since 1941, lived at 19 Langholme Crescent, Darlington, but before then lived at "Beaumont"on Gilling Road, Richmond. Lawrence Johnson was a pork butcher whose shop was at the bottom end of the Market Square and had been a member of Richmond Town Council for eleven years.

Eric attended Richmond Grammar School (1930 to 1938) before entering the offices of the Borough Treasurer, Richmond. He had offered his services in the RAFVR and was eventually accepted by the RAF, becoming a navigator, after training in Canada and the USA. By early 1943 he was serving with 214 Squadron, operating Stirling bombers from RAF Chedburgh, Suffolk, five miles SW of Bury St Edmond. Just a fortnight before his death Eric had been home on leave.

The seven men crew of Stirling bomber R9282 took off from Chedburgh aerodrome at 1827 hours on February 3rd, its target the German port of Hamburg. It was shot down by a night fighter piloted by Christian Koltringer and crashed at Benschop, 17 kilometres SSW of Utrecht, in Holland. Four of the crew were taken prisoner but three men, including George Eric Johnson, had been killed and were buried in a collective grave in Benschop General Cemetery.

PRIVATE ERNEST PARKIN
NO. 4389730 4TH BATTALION GREEN HOWARDS
DIED FEBRUARY 22ND 1943 AGED 34

Ernest's parents were Frederick and Catharine Parkin. The family originated from Alnwick, Northumberland, and moved to Stockton on Tees, where Frederick was a pharmacist. The children in the family were Jack and the twins, Ernest and Fred.

Their father split up from his wife and in 1917 Catharine and the boys arrived at the village of Hudswell, near Richmond, where she became the postmistress and shopkeeper for awhile.

The twins' employment proved to be varied, for both travelled to Canada and became lumberjacks. On returning home, Ernest worked on the farm of Mr. Whitby, at Vicar's Green, Hudswell, whilst Fred was a farm worker at Ravensworth. They were also engaged in employment at the Boiler Room at Catterick Camp.

Ernest Parkin of Hudswell, near Richmond

Ernest had met Kathleen Morley, a Northallerton girl who came as a supply teacher to Hudswell School and lodged at Mr. Whitby's farm, and they married. A son, Derek, was born. Both Ernest and Fred were in the Territorial Army and so were called up straight away and both went with the 4th Battalion Green Howards to France and were evacuated from Dunkirk. In 1942 the twins were in Egypt and taking part in the actions there, but Ernest contracted diphtheria and died in the hospital centre at Tel-El-Kebir on February 22nd 1943. He was buried in grave 4.N.1. Tel-El-Kebir War Memorial Cemetery, 110 kilometres NNE of Cairo.

The next serviceman to die, with connections to the dales, is not on any memorial but was buried with military honours in Rylstone churchyard because of family association with that parish.

AIRCRAFTMAN 2nd CLASS STANLEY EARL SPENSLEY FIELDEN
NO. 1624171 RAFVR
DIED MARCH 8th 1943 AGED 18

Stanley's father, Earl Bateman Fielden, was born in Skipton, the son of John Fielden, a tailor and outfitter in that market town. Each week John made extensive arduous journeys on carriers' carts and often on foot into the dale's villages of Rylstone, Grassington, Burnsall, Appletreewick and Barden. Soon after the end of the Great War, Earl, who was not interested in tailoring, joined the RAF and became a fine pilot during the following few years.

In the late 1920's he left the RAF. He had married Sabina Joy Spensley from a farming family at High Gate Farm, Gargrave, with strong connections to Rylstone, where the Spensley family members were buried in St. Peter's churchyard.

Stanley Earl Spensley Fielden of Bentham (Lancashire), with connections to the Rylstone area at the age of 15

The Fieldens settled at Bentham, between Settle and Kirkby Lonsdale, where sons John, George, Stanley and Derrick, and daughter Mary were born. It was during the late 1920's and 1930's that Earl Fielden became one of the chief pilots for Alan Cobham's Flying Circus that toured British towns and cities, giving flying displays and taking members of the public for flights at the cost of ten shillings. (Alan Cobham, a fine aviator, was renowned for his long distance flights to Europe, North Africa, Rangoon, Cape Town and Australia). Earl Fielden later worked for Imperial Airways until 1939.

Captain Earl Fielden, father of Stanley Fielden, who served with Alan Cobham's touring 'Flying Circus' and Imperial Airways during the 1920's and 1930's

John, Stanley and Derrick went to Lancaster Grammar School, whilst at the age of fifteen George began farming with the Spensleys at High Gate Farm. During the Second World War, John, Stanley and Derrick left the Grammar School to join the RAF, following in the footsteps of their father.

Stanley enlisted in 1942 and as an aircraftman began his training for flying operations. Meanwhile, his father, although in his late forties was employed as a pilot for secret work with a government organisation.

As an 18 year old, Stanley was stationed near the South Coast in early 1943. On March 8th he was on night time manoeuvres with colleagues on the cliff line when he accidentally fell to his death. His body was brought to North Yorkshire and buried with military honours in St. Peter's churchyard, Rylstone, the traditional burial ground for the Spensley family.

WARRANT OFFICER ROBERT SIMEON SANDELIN
NO. P82680 (W.OP./AIR GUNNER)
59 SQUADRON ROYAL CANADIAN AIR FORCE
DIED MARCH 26TH 1943 AGED 24

Robert, or "Sandy" as he was known, is not named on any war memorial in these dales but he has strong connections with Gunnerside, Swaledale, and his service headstone is found in the graveyard there.

Robert Sandelin was a Canadian, from the town of Cornwall in Ontario, on the northern bank of the St. Lawrence Seaway. The youngest son in the family, he joined the RCAF on leaving school and became an air-gunner. Arriving in England, he met Winifred Weir, an English girl who was serving in the WAAF. Winifred was a niece of Mr. and Mrs. Hudston Ward of Hillway, Gunnerside. Mr. Ward was masseur to Lord Rochdale of Gunnerside Lodge, the owner of the Estate. Lord Rochdale was an invalid and Mr. Ward attended to his needs. He was transported onto the moors for shooting parties in a special carriage. During the war years, Winifred stayed with the Wards when not on duty and "Sandy" would visit when on leave. In September 1942, Winifred and Sandy were married at Gunnerside.

Sandy was a member of 59 Squadron of Coastal Command, based in early March at Thorney Island in Hampshire and was involved in anti-shipping and anti-submarine patrols, very often patrolling off the Dutch coast. The Squadron flew both Liberators and Fortresses. On March 26th 1943 "Sandy" was on board the heavy bomber, Fortress No. FA698 that flew into a hill at Luscott Barton, near RAF Chivenor, in Devon, on returning from a patrol. His body was brought back to Gunnerside and buried in the churchyard, far away from his Canadian homeland. The pall bearers were four Canadian pilots.

LIEUTENANT COLONEL JOHN HIGHT BLUNDELL DSO, NO. 17207 ROYAL ENGINEERS, ATTACHED TO KING GEORGE V'S OWN BENGAL SAPPERS AND MINERS DIED APRIL 6TH 1943 AGED 41

Born in 1901, John was the eldest son of Major Alfred Hubert Blundell and Amelia Blundell of Mock Beggars Hall (Monk's Hall), Appletreewick. His father, Alfred, was head of a London firm of solicitors and the family had associations with the dale going back many generations. Alfred was an old boy and governor of Giggleswick School and also a Trustee and governor of Burnsall School. John was educated at Wellington College and chose the Royal Engineers as his career. He went out to India in 1931, where he served with the Bengal Sappers and Miners, mainly at their training establishment at Roorkee.

He served through the Waziristan Campaign of 1930-1940, receiving the Order of the British Empire and being mentioned in dispatches. He was put in charge of the 2nd Training Battalion at Roorkee but left there to join an Indian Division in North Africa as Royal Artillery Divisional Commander and had been decorated on the field with the DSO on March 23rd 1943.

We have seen that Montgomery's Eighth Army had defeated Rommel in early November 1942 at El Alamein and pursued the Afrika Korps westwards across Libya and into Tunisia. On November 8th 1942 Operation "Torch" saw a combined American/British/French force land in Algeria and push eastwards towards Tunisia. The plan was to squeeze the Afrika Korps between the two Armies in Tunisia and force its surrender.

It was to be in Tunisia that John Blundell was killed on April 6th 1943. Prior to that, on the night of March 22nd/23rd he had won his DSO. He was responsible for improving and making wheel track crossings over the Wadi Zigzaou. He personally recconnoitered the two crossings under very heavy shell fire. He began work with the sappers at 2330 hours and stayed with them under heavy fire the whole time. At 0200 hours on March 23rd he was advised to stop working as he was in front of the attacking troops, but continued working when the attack did not materialise. Ordered to withdraw at 0400 hours, his work enabled tanks and carriers to be brought back without loss.

Always prepared to put himself at risk, he was not so fortunate on April 6th when Montgomery's forces lunged northwards, and he was killed in the attack on German positions at Wadi Akarit. John Blundell is buried in grave X111.A.6. Sfax War Cemetery (Tunisia).

On that same day of battle, another dalesman, this time from Reeth, fell on the battlefield at Wadi Akarit.

PRIVATE JOHN EVERILL SPENCE
NO. 4396428 7TH BATTALION GREEN HOWARDS
DIED APRIL 6TH 1943 AGED 28

Marrick Priory is in the background.
Left to right: Isabelle Spence, John Spence, Ada Alsopp

John's parents were John William and Everill Spence from South Shields. His father had been invalided out of the army in the Great War and couldn't work. He was advised to come to the dales for health reasons, arriving in 1917, first at Leyburn and soon afterwards at Reeth. John and his brother George had been born in South Shields, but at Reeth, Robert, Isabella, Everill and Sheila became additions to the family.

In 1921 their parents took a newsagents and shop at the bottom end of the village, with mother mainly running the business. John William's health deteriorated and they moved to live in the old police house.

At 14, John was employed as a farm labourer by John James Wilkinson at "The Hagg", on the road between Fremington and Marrick, and "lived in". His father died in 1937, his mother now had MS and, becoming ill himself, John left farming and came back to live with his mother, where he was able to look after her. Surprisingly, he passed his medical for the army and joined up in July 1940, being posted to the 7th Battalion Green Howards (Bobby enlisted into the Royal Artillery 1939, George into the RASC in 1940, Everill went to work in a fever hospital, whilst Isabella was already nursing).

John and the 7th Battalion were in North Africa by early 1943 and were involved in the later stages of the fighting in Tunisia, at Wadi Akarit. This obstacle formed a naturally strong defensive position for the German and Italian soldiers. Before dawn, on April 6th 1943, three infantry divisions, and with them the 7th Green Howards, supported by massed artillery, were launched against fierce opposition. The objectives were gained, but more fierce resistance was met when the enemy recovered from his surprise. It was later that day when John Spence was killed. A group of eight men, including John, were resting in a tent from the exertions of battle, when a shell exploded and all eight men were killed. His body was never recovered and his name is commemorated on Face 18 Medjez-El-Bab Memorial, 60 kilometres west of Tunis.

LIEUTENANT COLONEL GUY WORDSWORTH GIBSON NO. 21472
1ST BATTALION THE LOYAL REGIMENT (NORTH LANCASHIRE)
DIED APRIL 23RD 1943 AGED 43

Guy was born in Westmorland, the son of Daniel and Mary Gibson. He joined the army towards the end of the Great War and made the army his career, joining the 1st Battalion Loyal Regiment (North Lancashire). As a Lieutenant, he was involved in the fighting in Ireland during the troubles of the early 1920's. When war broke out in 1939 he was a Major, going out with the BEF to France and being evacuated from Dunkirk in June 1940.

He was already married by this stage and he brought his wife Betty to live in rented rooms at Cogden Hall, Grinton, near Reeth, which he visited when on leave. However, by early 1943 he had been promoted to Lieutenant Colonel and was in command of the 1st Battalion in Tunisia, North Africa. They had landed at Algiers on March 9th, in the later stages of Operation "Torch", the American and British landings in North Africa. Just 45 days later, Guy Gibson would be killed.

On April 23rd 1943 the 1st Battalion stormed the dominating high ground known as Gueriat el Atach, protected by wire and minefields, and defended by three German battalions. "A" Company were confronted by machine guns and mortars but the position was taken by storm and 40 prisoners taken. However, they encountered a minefield and suffered casualties. They failed to make headway in the face of mortar and machine gun fire. Forward Battalion HQ, who were advancing behind "A" Company, also ran into a minefield. Lieutenant Colonel Gibson was mortally wounded by the first mine to explode, as was Major Oclee by another, when he gallantly went to his CO's assistance. The remnants of Battalion HQ withdrew. Hearing Guy Gibson calling for help a few minutes later, Lieutenant

Hawkins recrossed the gulley and with the aid of a volunteer brought him back on a stretcher. Battalion HQ was again withdrawn and, despite the risk, Captain Dow, the Battalion's Medical Officer, crossed the intervening cornfield to attend to L/C Gibson, who, owing to some misunderstanding, had been left behind.

By the end of the day the Battalion had received 300 casualties. L/C Guy Gibson died from his wounds that day and is buried in grave II.K.8. Massicault War Cemetery, Tunisia.

By May 13th 1943, the war in Tunisia, and therefore North Africa, came to an end as the German and Italian forces surrendered. More Axis troops were captured at Tunis (250,000) than had been at Stalingrad on February 2nd 1943. Some historians have dismissed the Desert War as a sideshow. In terms of numbers it was, with only a handful of German divisions employed. Yet its importance in restoring British pride and giving the Americans battle experience, together with safeguarding communications with India and helping towards knocking Italy out of the war, has to be acknowledged.

PILOT OFFICER BASIL ARTHUR CURTIS (W.OP./AIR GUNNER) NO. 51673 196 SQUADRON RAF DIED APRIL 29TH 1943 AGED 22

Basil Curtis of Bolton Abbey

Basil was the youngest child of Arthur Clifford Curtis and Florence Amelia Curtis, the other offspring consisting of Gwen, Harold and Clifford. They lived at Endor Crescent, Burley in Wharfedale, from where their father worked as a traveller in lace work, though by now he was a widower.

Basil was educated at Ilkley Grammar School, but when Arthur became ill, they stayed for awhile at Bolton Abbey, at the home of his brother, who was head gardener for the Duke of Devonshire. It was to be on the Bolton Abbey War Memorial that Basil's name was commemorated after his death.

From his early days, Basil always wanted to fly (his books were all about flying) and his father got him into Cranwell College in 1938 at the age of 16, where he trained as a wireless operator and air gunner. He had been in the RAF for only a year when war was declared. Basil was put on operational duties with Bomber Command immediately.

He eventually completed 30 operational missions with 51 Squadron and was awarded the DFM for his bravery and devotion to duty, in October 1940 (in a raid over Berlin, when the rear gunner was wounded, Basil rendered first aid and then manned the gun himself). A very modest person, Basil would never talk about what he had done. The strain was telling however (when he came home on leave, his hands would be shaking a little) and he was taken off operational duties and sent to Lossiemouth as an instructor (he was a flight sergeant by now). He enjoyed his time in Scotland and recovered his fitness.

Whilst on leave, he announced that he had volunteered to go on operational duties again and it came as a shock to everyone. He was posted to 196 Squadron, RAF Leconfield in Yorkshire, flying Wellington bombers, and sadly completed just three trips before he was shot down and killed.

The five man crew of Wellington bomber HE395 took off at 2055 hours on April 28th for a "Gardening" operation (mine laying operation) in the Baltic Sea, near Denmark. They were shot down by a German night fighter and crashed at 0058 hours on April 29th. The crew of five were buried in Allied Military Plot Row 6 Collective grave 7 Aabenraa Cemetery, Denmark, on the SE Jutland coast, 25 kilometres north of the German border. On May 1st 1943 his commission as a pilot officer came through, but, of course, he never knew about this.

In 1947 his father received news that the Commonwealth War Graves Commission had located the place where the plane had crashed and an obelisk was to be raised to honour the crew. Arthur and his daughter Gwen were invited to attend the ceremony. They discovered that the local Danes had been taking flowers each week to place at the scene over all these years. They were warmly received by the Danish people and at the end of the week a dinner was given in honour of them.

FLIGHT LIEUTENANT WILLIAM ABBOTSON TETLEY (NAVIGATOR0 NO. 81378 35 SQUADRON RAF DIED MAY 30TH 1943 AGED 33

Bill was the second son of Harry and Isabella (Ella) Tetley and the family lived at Wisp Hill, Grassington. He was educated at Greshams School, at Holt in Norfolk, before joining the family business of Noil merchants (short wool combings) at Well Street, Bradford. Bill was a good sportsman and played rugby as a wing three quarter for Ilkley Rugby Club and hockey for Bradford.

Flight Lieutenant William Abbotson Tetley of Grassington and Bradford

In September 1939 he enlisted in the RAF and became a navigator, joining 78 Squadron at Dishforth, where he flew Whitley bombers, and then moved on to RAF Graveley and 35 Squadron on May 10th 1943 to take up the duties of Squadron Bombing Leader. Twenty days later he would be dead. At Graveley they flew the newly introduced Halifax bomber. Bill was awarded the DFC, partly for his work in helping to introduce the new bomber and for the many missions undertaken over the years.

On May 29th 1943 he was asked to stand in as a bomb aimer for a fellow airman and was killed on the mission on the 30th. At 2227 hours on May 29th Halifax bomber HR833 took off from Graveley for a raid on Wuppertal, in the industrial Ruhr. On that night over 700 bombers arrived over Wuppertal and sadly 35 Squadron lost four aircraft on the mission.

On its way to the target, Bill's plane was hit by flak, setting off the bomb load and it was finished off by a night fighter. It crashed at Hoogstraten, near Antwerp, Belgium. Five members of the crew were killed, the other two being taken prisoner. Bill Tetley was buried in grave II.G.3. Schoonselhof Cemetery, Antwerp.

MAJOR ARTHUR FRANKLIN SHELTON
NO. 45331 ROYAL ARMY SERVICE CORPS
DIED JULY 29TH 1943 AGED 55

I unfortunately know little about the service record of Major Shelton or his connection to Richmond, on whose war memorial his name is inscribed. His name is on Panel 4 at the Woking (St. John's) Crematorium in Surrey. It would appear that when he died of acute heart failure at the age of 55, he was living with his wife and daughter in officers' quarters at Feltham, near Hounslow and Twickenham, Middlesex. Arthur's father, Frederick, had been born at St. Neots, in Cambridgeshire, and married Isabella, a girl from Alnwick in Northumbria. He was employed on the railways and in 1901, the family, including 13 year old Arthur, the eldest son, was living in the western suburbs of Leeds, where Frederick was the local station master. Arthur had been born in the small town of Stanley, between Leeds and Wakefield, and I believe he would have served in the Great War, before making a career for himself in the regular army during the inter-war years.

FLIGHT SERGEANT WILLIAM THOMAS PEVERELL (PILOT U/T), NO. 1494705 RAFVR 23 FLYING SERVICE TRAINING SCHOOL RAF, DIED AUGUST 6TH 1943 AGED 27

Born in the Richmond district in 1916, William was the eldest son of Mary Jane Peverell and the late William Peverell, the family living first at 5 Ryders Wynd and later 2 Lombards Wynd. His father had been killed during the Great War. Arriving in Richmond, William attended Richmond Grammar School from 1929 to 1932, where he took an interest in amateur dramatics, for he played the part of Mary Stuart in the school production on Speech Day, 1931.

William Thomas Peverell of Richmond
Courtesy of the Darlington and Stockton Times

Leaving school, William went to Welwyn Garden City, where he took up radio as a profession, but returned to Richmond and was in the employ of Alderman A. Brand. Afterwards, he was in the Tynemouth Constabulary for 4 years and it was there that he married, and he and his wife, Elizabeth Patricia Peverell, lived at 96 Bamburgh Terrace, North Shields.

William's brother joined the Royal Engineers during the war, but he was accepted into the RAF. William Peverell was killed in a flying accident whilst serving with 23 Service Flying Training School, based near Bulawayo, in Rhodesia, Africa, and would shortly have gained his "wings". He is buried in grave 79 Bulawayo (Athlone) Cemetery.

DRIVER FRED LONGTHORNE
NO. T/155949 ROYAL ARMY SERVICE CORPS
DIED AUGUST 26TH 1943 AGED 25

Freddy's parents were Sam and Maude Annie Longthorne. Maude Ellis was a Skirethorns girl and after their marriage they settled down, first at Rose Bank

Cottage, Hebden, and then at Ferndene, near Hebden Post Office, where they raised three children, Vera, Fred and Jean. Sam worked in the boiler house at Grassington TB Sanatorium.

After leaving Hebden School at 14, Freddy first worked at Hebden Mill and then for T. and A. Stockdale, the farmers' provisions merchants at Hebden. It was a thriving business that employed quite a few people in the district.

During 1940 Freddy joined Hebden platoon of the Home Guard but he was soon called up and became a driver for the RASC. By this stage he had married Maude Kayley from Grassington. For a while he served in London during the Blitz but was then posted to Northern Ireland. It was there, whilst sleeping rough on concrete floors, that he contracted TB, was brought back to England and discharged from the Army. He died on August 26th 1943 and was buried in Linton Churchyard. (Freddy's elder sister, Vera, had married Arthur Walmsley from Grassington, who won the MM during the war, but lost his arm in the process).

Fred Longthorne from Hebden, Wharfedale

PRIVATE JOHN ROY PICKLES NO. 4392637 7TH BATTALION GREEN HOWARDS DIED SEPTEMBER 8TH 1943 AGED 24

John's father, Benjamin, was a Linton man working in Swinden Quarry, near Cracoe. He met his wife Maude, a girl from Richmond in Surrey, who was in service with a wealthy family from the south. The family, with Maude, used to travel north to Scotland for the shooting season and stopped over in Linton.

John Roy Pickles of Linton, near Grassington

Benjamin took up farming on a smallholding, before he became the tenant at Manor House Farm, Linton. John was the youngest in the family (Preston, Molly, Kathleen, Marjorie, Jean and Nellie). He left Threshfield School at 14 and began work on the farm with his father.

In December 1939, at the age of 20, John joined up and was at Dunkirk. He then went to North Africa as a driver in "C" Company 7th Battalion Green Howards, part of the Eighth Army. In June 1942 they were involved in the retreat to Egypt, as Rommel's forces powered forwards in their attempt to reach Cairo.

At the Battle of Mersa Matruh, June 28th/29th 1942, there was a bold holding action and it was here that John was captured. Later, he was transferred to Italy and incarcerated in an Italian POW Camp. John's mother was to receive the terrible news that he was missing, presumed dead and then came relief with a telegram that told her he was a POW.

Between September 3rd and 8th 1943, news came of the capitulation of Italy and its disengagament from the war. The Italian guards suddenly disappeared from the POW camps. Most Allied prisoners in the camps stayed where they were, believing they would simply wait for the arrival of Allied forces. However, within days, the Germans simply occupied the camps. A few POW's had attempted to escape in the interval and John was one of these. It is believed that on September 8th 1943, the day Italy officially announced its armistice with the Allies, John Pickles was shot by the Germans whilst escaping.

He has no known grave and is commemorated on Panel 6 of the Cassino Memorial, Italy. The shocking news of his death, after all the other traumas of the past year, caused his mother's hair to turn white within two weeks of receiving the news.

FLIGHT SERGEANT JOHN HENRY MURPHY
NO. 411356 RAF
DIED SEPTEMBER 19TH 1943 AGED 47

John was the son of Michael and Maria Murphy and husband of Bridget Murphy of Richmond.

He joined the RAF and rose to the rank of Flight Sergeant. In September 1943 he was serving with 4 Operational Training Unit, based at RAF Alness, on the banks of the Cromarty Firth, 4 miles west of Invergordan, 15 miles north of Inverness. On September 19th the aircraft crashed and John Murphy was killed, his body being returned home and buried in grave C.89 Richmond Cemetery.

PRIVATE ALLAN CHANDLER NO. 4399476
5TH BATTALION THE BUFFS (ROYAL EAST KENT REGIMENT)
DIED NOVEMBER 5TH 1943 AGED 20

Allan Chandler of Hudswell, near Richmond, Swaledale

Allan's maternal grandparents, Jack and Mary Johnson, were licensees of the George and Dragon Inn, Hudswell, after arriving from Lancashire, where his mother, Rachel, had worked in the Lancashire cotton mills.

Rachel Johnson met Arthur Chandler, a local man working as a butcher in nearby Richmond, and when they married they lived in a small cottage attached to the George and Dragon. Allan was the eldest of three children, his siblings being Mary and Thomas.

When the Johnsons retired from the pub they moved to Moor Cottage Farm, in the village. The Chandler family joined them, living in a small cottage at the farm, called South View. By this time there was no post office in Hudswell and Rachel Chandler became the post mistress, running the post office from a room in her cottage and delivering the mail around the parish.

When Allan Chandler left the village school he became apprenticed to George Ralph Wade, a Richmond joiner. War intervened, however, and Allan joined the local regiment, the Green Howards, but by the time that he arrived to fight the Axis forces in Italy, he had been transferred to the Royal East Kent Regiment, known as "The Buffs".

On September 3rd 1943 the Allies invaded the Italian mainland, coinciding with the armistice made by the Italians. By October 3rd the British had established a bridgehead at Termoli on the Adriatic coast and the 5th Buffs were involved, taking up positions on a wooded plateau and receiving serious casualties when being attacked by six tanks of the 16th Panzer Division. A further push was made by the 5th Buffs at 11p.m. on November 2nd, crossing the Trigno River. Intense mortar and machine gun fire was opened on the Battalion in the darkness as they made their way up the escarpment and serious casualties occurred.

By 10-30a.m. on November 3rd their objectives were being captured and they consolidated their position. At 12-30p.m. German tanks attacked. The Buff's position was smothered in mortar fire and under cover of this, infantry from the 64th Panzer Grenadiers came forward and snipers attempted to infiltrate. At 5p.m. a full scale enemy assault with infantry and tanks began and the 5th Buffs had to withdraw. 16 men were killed, 35 wounded and 14 were missing.

By the evening of November 4th it was clear, however, that the enemy was falling back along the whole front and the Allies began their advance towards the River Sangro on November 5th. However, Allan Chandler was one of those wounded during the fighting on November 3rd and died on November 5th. He is buried in grave II.C.14. Sangro River War Cemetery, Italy.

The final fatality amongst the dales servicemen for 1943 was a man from Richmond.

BOMBADIER HAROLD JOSEPH MORRIS
NO. 968644 23 FIELD REGIMENT ROYAL ARTILLERY
DIED DECEMBER 7TH 1943 AGED 28

Harold was the son of Thomas and Eva May Morris of Richmond, and he lived in the market town with his wife, Elsie Pat Morris. His father had been a Quarter Master Sergeant with the Yorkshire Regiment and in Chapter Three we have seen that he was killed in 1915. The two World Wars of the 20th Century would rob the Morris family of both father and son. Harold was on the staff of the Ministry of Labour at Richmond and later was with the Shell-Mex Company at Catterick Bridge Station. He joined the Royal Engineers in the signalling section.

The 23rd Field Regiment had taken part in Operation "Torch", landing in Algeria on January 3rd 1943 and helped bring about the defeat of the Afrika Korps.

They landed on the beaches of Salerno, in the Italian Campaign, on September 23rd 1943. By October 8th they were in prepared positions, ready for the Battle of the River Volturno, supporting the advance across the river. Twenty enemy planes raided their position on October 28th, resulting in seven people being killed and ten wounded. By the end of October the Allies were facing the German winter defensive position known as the Gustav Line and initial attempts to break it were unsuccessful.

On December 1st the Regiment took part in Operation "Konker", the objective of which was to take the Comino and Maggiore features, their role being a counter-battery one. They provided fire-power against enemy mortars, whilst on December 6th they supported 201 Guards Brigade as they attacked on Monte Difensa. Bombadier Harold Morris was killed by enemy shellfire on December 7th 1943 whilst on Monte Difensa. He is buried in grave II.K.17. Minturno War Cemetery, Italy, 78 kilometres north of Naples.

1944

At the beginning of 1944 the U-boats still menaced the Atlantic and Arctic sea lanes, whilst the embattled German economy was producing war materials at ever increasing rates, despite the ravages of Allied bombing. The war was far from a decision, especially as the Japanese were fighting tenaciously in the Far East theatre of war.

Despite this, the Axis Powers were now on the defensive. The eastern front in Russia was crumbling as Hitler's Russian gamble proved to be lost. Italy's capitulation had taken her forces out of the war, whilst North Africa had been cleared and the sea lanes in the Mediterranean were open. Above all, the burgeoning power of America was now coming to the fore.

The Allies held the priceless advantage of strategic interior lines as they looked across at Europe from their bridgehead in the British Isles. They could, in principle, attack Germany at any point. The invasion of Western Europe, code-named Operation" Overlord", would come in Normandy on June 6th 1944, whilst mean-while, the difficult assault on the mainland of Italy continued against a well-led and motivated German Army.

The ever-widening campaigns of 1944 witnessed the largest number of deaths of servicemen from these dales in any one year of the war. Twenty eight servicemen would pay the supreme sacrifice.

PILOT OFFICER SYDNEY DAGGETT (WIRELESS OPERATOR) NO. 169391 10 SQUADRON RAFVR DIED JANUARY 29TH 1944 AGED 29

Sydney was born in 1914, at Old North Cote, Kilnsey, the son of Aaron and Maud Daggett, who were farmers. A sister, Margaret and brothers Maurice, Alan and Norman completed the family. Sydney attended Conistone School before continuing his education at Ermysted's Grammar School in Skipton. Each day he cycled to Threshfield Station and travelled by train to Skipton.

He left the grammar school at 15 to farm with his father at North Cote and continued working for his mother when his father died. In 1933, he and his mother moved to Toppan House, a smaller farm at Cracoe (opposite the old Methodist Chapel , which is nowadays the Corncrake Restaurant). Sydney was very well liked in the district and played rugby for the Upper Wharfedale team.

As a farmer, Sydney was in a reserved occupation when war was declared. However, his mother retired from farming early in the war and Sydney volunteered for the RAF. During his training, Sydney married Doris Robinson, a farmer's daughter from Cracoe. He trained as a wireless operator and was eventually posted to 10 Squadron, based at Melbourne, near York, and flying Halifax bombers.

Pilot Officer Sydney Daggett of Cracoe

On the night of 28th/29th January 1944 Sydney Daggett's Halifax took off from Melbourne on the crew's 12th mission, a raid on Berlin by 677 aircraft. The aircraft was one of 42 shot down, for the Germans had concentrated many night fighters over the city that night.

The port wing tanks and the overload fuel tanks were set on fire as a Junkers 88 attacked, causing the hydraulics to be knocked out and the plane to go out of control. The Australian skipper, Bill Kilsby, ordered his crew to bale out, but for some reason, Sydney Daggett remained with the skipper. His body was found close to that of his skipper's in the burnt out plane. The rest of the crew were taken prisoner as they landed near Tempelhof Airport and were taken from Berlin Central Railway Station by armed guards, who had to protect them from the anger of the civilians gathered nearby. The mystery remains as to why Sydney did not bale out, since an unopened parachute was discovered in the wreckage.

Sydney Daggett is commemorated on Panel 211 Runnymede Memorial.

On that same raid over Berlin another dalesman died, this time one with Grinton connections.

Sydney Daggett and his crew.
Back row: Don Collumbell, Don Shipley, George Woods, Frank Capper.
Front row: Sydney Daggett, Bill Kilsby, Reg Davies

FLIGHT SERGEANT JOSEPH WILLIAM IVAN ROBINSON NO. 1082484 77 SQUADRON RAFVR DIED JANUARY 29TH 1944 AGED 22

The crew of Halifax bomber LK729 KNF on the runway at Elvington aerodrome, near York. Flight Sergeant Joseph Robinson stands second from the left

Joe was the eldest child of Thomas and Sarah Annie Robinson (sister Bessie and brother Lawrence completed the family). Thomas was a lead miner and small-holder at Hauxwell Head, St. Johns Chapel, Weardale, 15 miles east of Alston. Their father worked in the lead mine while Sarah looked after the smallholding. Times were hard in the 1930's and Thomas became bankrupt. All farm implements and stock, including their sheep dog, were sold.

During 1935-1936 Thomas became a shepherd on another remote Weardale farm, but by 1937 the family moved to the farming hamlet of Gammersgill, in Coverdale, where Thomas worked on a farm. It was here that Joe began farming, working for Mr. Guy at Horsehouse and "living in".

In 1938 the family moved once again, this time to Swaledale, where Thomas worked for Charlie Wood at Hagsgill Farm, Ellerton Abbey, and the family lived at Gate House Cottage, half a mile from the farm. Joe began working for Mr. Barker at Ellerton Farm, one mile down the valley, and had accommodation at the farm.

Joe volunteered for the RAF in 1940 and was accepted for training for Bomber

Command crew, being posted to 77 Squadron at RAF Elvington in Yorkshire in 1943, whilst his sister Bessie joined the WAAF's in 1942 and was a cook at RAF Leeming. Sarah joined the WVS and knitted garments for forces personnel, whilst also taking in an evacuee from Gateshead.

Between 1941 and 1942 Thomas moved with the rest of the family, first to near Ripon and then to Middleton Moor, Ilkley, before arriving for a short stay at Westfield Farm, Wensley. In 1943 they finally arrived at Hartforth Hall, near Gilling West, where Thomas became a shepherd on the estate of Major G.H. Craddock. Joe came home on leave that Christmas, with no one realising it would be his last visit before his death.

Between January and March 1944 Bomber Command concentrated on attacking Berlin. On the night of 29th January 1944 Joe's Squadron lost 4 planes, with 21 men killed and 7 men taken prisoner. Halifax bomber LK729 took off from Elvington at 2344 hours but was attacked by night fighters over Berlin and the plane crashed. Both air gunners are buried in Berlin but the other five crew members, including Joe Robinson, have no known graves, and Joe is commemorated on Panel 221 Runnymede Memorial. He is also named at St. Johns Chapel, Reeth and Gilling West.

Joe, Bessie and Lance Robinson in Coverdale, early 1930's

GUNNER HAROLD WELLER
NO. 1764932 ROYAL ARTILLERY
(ATTACHED TO 301 FIELD REGIMENT EAST AFRICAN ARTILLERY)
DIED FEBRUARY 12TH 1944 AGED 28

Harold was the third son of William and Cecilia Weller (nee Frank), and was born at Kirkbymoorside, on the southern fringes of the North York Moors. His father, William, never saw Harold for he was killed in action on the Western Front in 1916, before the birth of his third son. Eventually, Cecilia married John William Brown from Leyburn, the family moving to live in the village of Downholme, near Richmond.

John William Brown was a tree feller and dealer who travelled the country felling trees on large estates. Sadly, in 1928, he was badly injured and with his compensation he later bought a lorry and set up in business as "haulage contractors, furniture and cattle removers". When Harold left school he began work as a farm hand on the Maskell's farm, near Middleham, "living in", before working on a farm in Coverdale. In 1939 his step father died and Harold learned to drive. He returned to the family home at Downholme and became a partner in the haulage business, together with his brothers.

As the war progressed, however, Harold enlisted in the army and joined the Royal Artillery as a gunner. By the start of 1944, he was attached to 301 Field Regiment East African Artillery and was on the eastern seaboard of Africa, at Mombassa, waiting to join a convoy that would transport them to India and the fight against the Japanese. Sadly, Harold and many of his colleagues would not arrive at their destination.

Harold Weller of Downholme

On Sunday February 5th 1944, Convoy KR8 departed Mombassa, Kenya, and set sail for Colombo, Ceylon (Sri Lanka). There were 5 troop ships, the largest being the "Khedive Ismail", carrying the convoy commodore, a crew of 187 and 1,324 military personnel, including 80 Wrens and nurses. Also on board was Harry Weller. The convoy was escorted by the cruiser "Hawkins" and two destroyers, "Paladin" and "Petard".

Mid-day on February 12th saw a calm sea and a stifling heat. An Ensa concert was in full swing in the main lounge of the "Khedive Ismail", when, at 1430 hours the port lookout on HMS "Petard" sighted the periscope of a Japanese submarine and sailors raced to their action stations. All eyes were drawn to the "Khedive Ismail" where smoke and flames were coming from the stern quarters. Within three minutes the ship had completely disappeared. Among the survivors was a man who had left the concert party to answer the call of nature, to see, on returning, the entire audience disappear into the wrecked engine room below.

The destroyers attempted to rescue survivors, but the "Paladin" sighted the submarine and attempted to ram it. A collision occurred, resulting in the submergence of the submarine and a large hole appearing in the side of the destroyer. The captain of the "Petard" had to decide whether to save more survivors or sink the enemy submarine. He chose the latter course and many of the survivors in the water were killed in the devastating attack of patterned depth charges.

The submarine, I-27, captained by Captain Toshiaki Fukumura, was forced to the surface and finished off by torpedoes from the destroyer. There were no Japanese survivors. The convoy had scattered when the submarine struck and the destroyers eventually headed for Addic Atoll, in the Maldive Islands, the "Petard" towing the crippled "Paladin". It was here that the survivors were transferred to the cruiser "Hawkins" on February 13th and she left for Colombo on the 15th.

Of the 1511 passengers and crew on board the "Khedive Ismail", only 214 survived, including six women. Harold was not one of the survivors and his name is commemorated on Column 6 East Africa Memorial, in Nairobi War Cemetery, Kenya, and on the Downholme war memorial.

FLIGHT LIEUTENANT JOHN ALAN BROADLEY DSO, DFC, DFM, NO. 47690 NAVIGATOR 487 SQUADRON RAF DIED FEBRUARY 18TH 1944 AGED 23

John Alan Broadley, known to everyone as Alan, was born at Leyburn in 1921, the son of Thomas Broadley and wife Irene. Thomas and his brother John ran the family butchers shop in Leyburn, with Tom also attending their meat stall at Richmond on market days.

Shortly after Alan's birth, Irene died, and since Tom had difficulty in raising Alan and daughter Ann by himself, the two children lived with their grandmother. Aged 3, Alan, together with Ann, spent the next few years living with their aunt, Peggy Siddall, in Leyburn. Meanwhile Tom had remarried, to the landlady of the Fleece Hotel, in Richmond.

Alan was educated at Yorebridge Grammar School, Askrigg, but in 1934 he transferred to Richmond Grammar School when he went to live with his father. However, Alan spent the weekends in Leyburn, where his heart really belonged. In 1939, shortly after his 18th birthday, he left the Grammar School, and the girl he loved, farmer's daughter Kitty Ovesby, to volunteer for the RAF and was accepted in April of that year.

John Alan Broadley
of Leyburn and Richmond

To Alan's disappointment, he failed the selection for pilot but trained as an air observer and was posted to Navigation School. Between 1939 and 1944 Alan Broadley came to be recognised as one of the best and most skilful navigators in the RAF (winning the DSO, DFC and DFM), and in his partnership with pilot Percy Charles Pickard (Pick), their reputation and exploits were legendary (for a fuller account of their story, see "Wensleydale Remembered" by Keith Taylor).

After returning to the dales for Christmas leave, December 1943, Alan and Kitty announced their engagement but a few days later Alan was back with his Mosquito Squadron, No. 21, at RAF Hunsdon, preparing for a very special operation. 700 French Resistance workers were in Amiens Prison, France, in late 1943. With the forthcoming invasion of Normandy planned for 1944, it was vital that the French Resistance Movement could still operate its sabotage missions in conjunction with the invasion. Many of the prisoners were under sentence of death, with a deadline of February 19th 1944. Plans were therefore prepared for their release by means of a low level bombing raid attacking the prison walls. The man put in charge of the bombing plans in Operation "Jericho" was Charles Pickard.

Although Alan and Pickard were in 21 Squadron, they were to fly in the last aircraft of 464 Squadron, allowing Pickard to make an assessment of the results. 487 Squadron was to bomb the outer walls and German guardroom, whilst 464 Squadron was to breach the actual prison walls, thus allowing the prisoners to break free. 21 Squadron was held in reserve, ready to bomb the whole area if the breach had not been made.

On February 18th 1944, the 18 Mosquitoes took off to rendezvous with their Typhoon escort. The weather was better over the French coast, but the flak was accurate and a leading Mosquito was badly damaged, pulling clear and dropping its bombs in open countryside. The five remaining bombers of the first wave headed for the prison, with three bombing the walls, the other two coming in after the bombs had exploded, and dropped their bombs from 10 feet above the ground.

After the explosions, the four Mosquitoes of 464 Squadron came in low and fast. In the last of these planes were Charles Pickard and Alan Broadley. Alan released the bombs and the plane climbed sharply, but they saw the walls of the prison collapse. As the other Mosquitoes headed back, Pickard circled the area in order to make his assessment of the damage. Hundreds of people were running out of the broken down walls and he decided the mission had been successfully achieved. As he began his turn for home, Pickard saw a Mosquito in trouble, after being hit by flak. He went to investigate and saw the crippled plane crash land in a snow covered field.

Suddenly, two Focke Wulf 190 fighters of Adolf Galland's Squadron dived upon Alan's circling Mosquito from the advantage of height. The tail of the Mosquito was shot away, resulting in the aircraft cart wheeling and crashing into the ground a few kilometres from Amiens. Both air crew died in the wreckage of their plane.

The mission had been a success, for more than 250 Resistance workers survived, continuing their work against the Germans. News that Alan was reported missing arrived for his family and Kitty. At Easter, a sergeant from Alan's Squadron arrived to see Kitty, bringing with him the engagement ring bought by Alan for Kitty.

Alan Broadley was remembered on the war memorials at Leyburn and Richmond, at Richmond Grammar School and on his grave, 3.A.11. St. Pierre Cemetery, Amiens.

FLYING OFFICER (PILOT) THOMAS GEOFFREY DIXON
NO. 52613 547 SQUADRON RAF
DIED FEBRUARY 24TH 1944 AGED 26

Thomas Geoffrey Dixon of Halton East, near Bolton Abbey

Thomas was born at Malham in 1917, the son of Clarence and Mary Dixon. They farmed at Cherries Farm, near Gordale Scar, and young Thomas was educated at Malham School and Ermysted's Grammar School, Skipton.

He entered the army at the start of the war and was with the BEF in France and Belgium, before being evacuated at Dunkirk. He was living at "Lingstead", Cross Hills, between Keighley and Skipton, but brought his young wife, Constance Muriel Dixon and son to live at Rose Cottage, Halton East, on the Bolton Abbey Estate. There, another son was born during the war years.

Thomas joined the RAF in 1942, training at Cranwell, and eventually flying Whitley bombers with 58 Squadron, Coastal Command, in the north of Scotland. He then flew Wellingtons with 547 Squadron, Coastal Command, from St. Eval airfield, Cornwall, patrolling the waters of the Bay of Biscay. Here they were engaged on anti-submarine and anti-shipping operations, equipped with torpedoes.

On February 23rd 1944 the crew of nine set off on another anti-submarine patrol, but near their return on February 24th they were short of fuel and decided to make an emergency landing at St. Mary's on the Scilly Isles. The runway proved to be too short and the plane overshot, causing it to crash. All of the crew survived the crash except for Thomas. The port-side propeller broke off and crashed into the side of the plane, severing his leg and although he was rushed to the hospital on St. Mary's, he died soon after arrival. Thomas Geoffrey Dixon was brought back to Yorkshire, where he was buried in grave 5.8. Cononley (St. John) Churchyard. His name is also commemorated on the plaque in Bolton Priory.

The next two men to die were both from Richmond and were killed on the same day, one serving in Burma and the second whilst flying over Germany.

SERGEANT ALFRED DUNN
NO. 3603820 9TH BATTALION BORDER REGIMENT
DIED MARCH 15TH 1944 AGED 30

The fifth son of Alfred and Ruth Dunn of 38 Frenchgate, Richmond, Alfred junior was the husband of Alice Ethel Dunn, of 57 Market Place, Richmond. Alfred senior had worked on Lord Zetland's Aske Estate for 45 years and Alfred junior had also worked there, playing football for Aske in his spare time. Later, he worked at Catterick Camp. He enlisted on June 15th 1940 and was soon posted to the 9th Battalion Border Regiment.

Alfred Dunn of Richmond
Courtesy of the
Darlington and Stockton Times

Between February 7th 1941 and February 26th 1942 the Battalion was on coastal guard duty on the coastline between Berwick and Bamburgh, Northumberland. However, on May 31st 1942 they sailed on HMT "Orcades" from Glasgow, destination Bombay, which they reached on August 8th 1942, and then were based at Calcutta until July 1943.

In July 1943 they were sent to Assam as part of the 17th Indian Light Division, attached to General Slim's 14th Army. They were to take part in an incursion into the Arakan region of Burma, to clear it of the enemy and form a diversion to the main thrust by General Stilwell's American and Chinese Army.

Early in November 1943 they advanced down the Tiddim Road, to south of that town. Tiddim was set in a range of hills, with thick forests and scattered villages. A patrol of five miles might take ten hours or so. By December 9th they were stationed on Kennedy Peak and clashing with the enemy on patrols throughout January and February. On one occasion, a fighting patrol of 16 men surprised a party of 60 Japanese, who were walking along a hill side path. The patrol opened fire on them, and those Japanese who were not hit chose to leap down a steep hill side to escape.

On March 1st the enemy commenced shelling Kennedy Peak, causing great damage amongst the transport animals. From then on the shelling continued daily, for the enemy had artillery superiority. This shelling was the prelude to the Japanese assault to invade India. They followed up their main assault with a second strong attack across the Chindwin River and powerful thrusts up the Tiddim Road.

The 17th Indian Light Division was forced to withdraw on March 8th 1944, with the 9th Battalion moving to Tiddim as a rearguard. The enemy had by-passed Tiddim, infiltrating from the hills and jungle in order to cut off the Division. The position was therefore very serious and dangerous. Everyone in the rearguard Battalion were nervous and edgy because the Japanese seemed to be appearing from every quarter. By this stage Tiddim had been set on fire by the Battalion and the infrastructure destroyed.

On March 15th the 9th Battalion arrived at Milestone 144 and took up a perimeter guard, forming a defensive "box" to enclose Divisional HQ. However, at 9p.m. firing was heard and tracer seen coming from the direction of Milestone 142. This caused some consternation amongst the jittery soldiers in the "box", and when one of these men slid accidentally down a steep slope, it caused some of the others to start firing in the darkness. Sadly, it resulted in the deaths of two of their own men and the wounding of two others.

One of the men killed by "friendly fire" was Sergeant Alfred Dunn, who was burird at Milestone 144 on the Tiddim Road. His body was later recovered and buried in collective grave 16A.A.15-17. Taukkyan War Cemetery, Rangoon.

FLIGHT SERGEANT (FLIGHT ENGINEER) THOMAS ROY SHAW NO. 1039039 97 SQUADRON RAFVR (DFM) DIED MARCH 15TH 1944

Thomas was an old boy of Richmond Grammar School (1933 to 1937) and was connected to one of the chief builders in Richmond, George Shaw. When the war started he volunteered for the RAF. Eventually, he was promoted to Flight Engineer and was posted to 97 Squadron, flying Lancaster bombers from Bourne airfield in Cambridge-shire.

Thomas Roy Shaw

The seven men crew of Lancaster JB361 took off from Bourne at 1920 hours, their target, Stuttgart. It was intercepted by a night fighter and crashed at Zillhausen, 40 miles south of Stuttgart. All seven members of the crew were buried in collective grave 4.J.1-3. Durnbach War Cemetery, south of Munich. Although not unique, it was unusual that all seven men had received gallantry awards – four had the DFC, whilst Thomas Shaw and two others had the DFM.

Richmond Grammar School Rugby Team 1937/1938.
Thomas Roy Shaw, John Alan Broadley and Raisbeck Denis Bell
would all be killed in the Second World War whilst serving in the RAF.
Back row: J.A. Broadley, J.W. King, J.W. Sidebottom, P.J. Pendlebury, J.R. Cubberley, J.G. Rossor.
Next row: T.R. Shaw, G.W. Trott, J.N. Evans, F.H. Pedley (captain), R.D. Bell, J.S.E.R.R. McGregor, J.H. Gaine.
Front row: J.M. King, G. Glover, P.C. Williams

PRIVATE JOHN WILLIAM STANLEY WILKINSON
NO. 7591239 ROYAL ARMY ORDNANCE CORPS
DIED MARCH 21ST 1944 AGED 40

John, or Sandy as he was commonly known, was born on March 6th 1904, the son of Esther Isabel Wilkinson of Reeth. When John married, he and his wife, Evelyn Isabel Wilkinson, lived with their children, Derrick, Eileen and Joan, at East View, Reeth. He was a member of Grinton Parochial Church Council. Before the war he had worked for a short while in Jim Kendall's butchers shop at Reeth and at Downholme Quarry but he then became a lorry driver.

As a member of the Army Reserve, John Wilkinson was called up at the outbreak of war and due to his driving experience, he became a driver with the Royal Army Ordnance Corps. He served with the RAOC in France and went through the Dunkirk evacuation. However, he was discharged from the army due to ill-health and although he took up lorry driving again, whilst in the Sedgefield district he was taken ill and died of complications resulting from a chronic gastric ulcer. He was brought back to Reeth and was buried with full military honours in the new cemetery.

SERGEANT RONALD THORPE
NO. 1594817 (AIR GUNNER)
DIED MARCH 22ND 1944 AGED 29

Ronald was the son of Sydney and Florence Amelia Thorpe of Albert Square, off Hurgill Road, Richmond, and the husband of Louvaine Thorpe of Darlington. His father, Sydney, was a joiner who had his yard near Ryders Wynd. Two sisters, Peggy and Nancy Thorpe, completed the family.

Joining the RAF Volunteer Reserve, Ronald eventually became an air gunner and sergeant in Bomber Command. He was aboard Halifax bomber W7865 belonging to 1658 Heavy Conversion Unit No. 4 Group Bomber Command, which took off from RAF Riccall, 10 miles south of York, on 22nd March 1944, on a general training flight. Four of the eight man crew were Canadians, including the pilot. It crashed at 1757 hours near Cattal Station, just beyond the village of Kirk Hammerton on the York to Knaresborough railway line, just over 2 miles NNE from Marston Moor airfield. Five out of the eight crew members survived the crash, but air gunner Ronald Thorpe, Canadian pilot Bath and Flying Officer Cogbill (Flying Control Staff) were killed. Ronald's body was brought back to Richmond and he was buried in grave U.117 Richmond Cemetery. A RAF contingent was present, and because Ronald had been a member of the Rover Scouts, the Richmond Troop was represented.

SERGEANT ALAN WALTON SHERWOOD
(W.OP./AIR GUNNER) NO. 1088330 61 SQUADRON RAF
DIED MARCH 24TH 1944 AGED 20

Alan was the youngest son of Frederick and Mabel Theresa Sherwood of Gordon Crescent, Richmond. The family had arrived in Richmond from Pocklington, in the Yorkshire Wolds, where Alan had received his education. In Richmond, he joined the Air Training Cadets and became the first member of the Richmond flight to join the RAF, in September 1941.

Alan Sherwood of Richmond
Courtesy of the
Darlington and Stockton Times

Alan became a wireless operator and air gunner, being promoted to sergeant, and by March 1944 was serving with 61 Squadron, flying Lancaster bombers out of RAF Coningsby, in Lincolnshire.

The seven man crew of Lancaster DV397 took off from Coningsby at 1827 hours, their target being Berlin. The bombers took a northerly route over Denmark and into the Baltic before making landfall near Rostock and the final leg southward to Berlin. Ill luck beset the participants from the start. Incorrectly forecast wind strengths fragmented the bomber streams and by the time the capital was reached the main force was well and truly scattered.

The wind strength pushed them south at speed and dozens overshot the aiming point, only to find it almost impossible to turn about for a second try. Later, as they headed towards the west, many found to their cost that they were bracketed by flak from the Ruhr. Seventy four bombers were lost that night, including Alan Sherwood's plane, although they were shot down at Gehrden, eight miles SW of Hannover, on their journey home. Six crewmen, including Alan, were killed and one was taken prisoner. Alan Sherwood is buried in grave 6.H.9. Berlin 1939 –1945 War Cemetery.

LIEUTENANT JOHN BRIAN STURGEON
ROYAL NAVAL VOLUNTEER RESERVE (DSC)
HM MOTOR TORPEDO BOAT 242
DIED APRIL 3RD 1944 AGED 31

John was the eldest of the three sons of Robert and Dorothy Sturgeon, his brothers being Denis and Larry. The Sturgeons were not from the dales but arrived in Hebden, near Grassington, in 1932, when Robert and Dorothy began running a guest house at Jerry and Bens Cottage, at Hebden Ghyll. They also used Scar Top House to accommodate some of the guests.

John Brian Sturgeon of Hebden, a member of Ermysted's Grammar School, Skipton

John was born in 1912, his father being a mechanical engineer and patents agent. In 1920 they were living near Derby, but by 1923 the family had moved to Brighouse, between Halifax and Dewsbury, and John began attending Rastrick Grammar School. In September 1924, he and Denis were sent as boarders to Ermysted's Grammar School, Skipton, until they were taken away in 1928, when the family moved to Birmingham. John, who was now 16, began training in Yorkshire as an engineer in the woollen trade. By 1932, his parents, Robert and Dorothy, had arrived at Hebden Ghyll to set up their guest house and their youngest son, Larry, continued his education at Ermysted's.

By the start of the war John did not live with his parents at Hebden, although he was a regular visitor. He was a very good tennis player and between 1934 and 1939 he played at Wimbledon in the singles, men's doubles and mixed doubles. He did not have a great deal of success, being knocked out in either the first or second rounds, but in 1938 he reached the Quarter Finals of the Men's Doubles with his partner, Gwyn Tuckett, before being defeated by Franjo Kukuljevic and Josip Palada (3/6, 8/10, 4/6).

John volunteered for the Royal Navy when war began and by September 1943 was a Lieutenant, in command of Motor Torpedo Boat 242. He had already been awarded the Distinguished Service Cross for his bravery, having seen much service in the Mediterranean all through the North African and Italian Campaigns. By this time he was married to his wife, Vivienne, and she, together with their young daughter, were living at Cove in Dumbartonshire.

In Yugoslavia, Tito's Partisan forces controlled 40,000 square miles of his homeland, by 1943. With the surrender of the Italian Army to the Allies on September 3rd 1943, many of them in occupied Yugoslavia, Germany rushed as many troops as

Ermysted's Grammar School Rugby Team 1927/1928, Skipton.
(Brian Sturgeon was killed during the Second World War.)
Back row: J.W. Haslewood, L. Atkinson, W. Doherty, C.L. Frankland, T.A. Feather, J.B. Sturgeon, J.E. Frankland.
Next row: F. Hayton, F. Hurst, R.E. Harker (vice-captain), E. Pickles (captain), J.C. Smith, J. Dean.
Front row: T. Potts, S. Senior

they possibly could into that country and into the Dalmatian Islands, situated just off the coast. In late 1943 the Allies decided to throw their support behind Tito, instead of his rival guerrilla leader, General Mihajlovic, leader of the Chetniks.

Tito's headquarters for the next few months became the Dalmation island of Vis (the other islands of Brac, Korcula and Hvar were in German hands). From Italy, a large military build up on Vis was begun by the Allies. Fifty British commandos were sent to the island to cooperate, encourage and support what they could for the Partisan war effort. III Field Regiment RA was transported there and this British contingent, called Force 133, was told to help hold the island of Vis to the last man. A British naval detachment of Motor Torpedo Boats and Motor Gun Boats (mainly Canadians, but including John Sturgeon) was sent to Komiza, the main port on Vis, under the command of Lieutenant Commander Tommy Fuller of Ottawa, Canada (known as the "Pirate of the Adriatic").

The waters surrounding Vis were under constant German air and naval patrol and the island was subject to German bombing raids from the islands of Brac and Hvar. The Germans also used the surrounding waters as a merchant shipping lane to re-supply their troops on the mainland as well as other islands.

This British naval detachment was a constant thorn in the side of the German naval operations. A small German schooner was boarded and captured, containing a cargo of Bavarian ale, whilst the "Libecchio", a German 400 ton Brigantine re-supply ship under full sail was towed back to Komiza. The Allied sailors were greeted by a brass band and were invited to a dinner with Tito himself. The ship contained sauerkraut, goulash and ten tons of Danish butter. During the first week of April 1944 the British captured eight ships and sank three more.

A price was paid, however, for 41 British seamen died in the surrounding waters, trying to stave off the German invasion of Vis, and harassing the German maritime naval re-supply efforts. One of those who was killed was John Brian Sturgeon. On April 3rd, Motor Torpedo Boats 651 and 647 captured a German schooner off the island of Hvar, whilst off the north coast of the island Motor Torpedo Boats 242 and 81 had a gun action with an enemy ship. The enemy was damaged but escaped, whilst the only Allied casualty was John Brian Sturgeon. A monument has been erected on the mole in Komiza harbour in remembrance of those lost. It is also sad to mention that a number of British vessels were mistakenly sunk, with loss of life, by "friendly fire" during this period. John was buried on Vis but after the war his body was re-interred by the CWGC in grave 9.A.10. Belgrade War Cemetery.

It is interesting to note that after the war John's parents and brother started a fresh life as tobacco farmers in Southern Rhodesia (now part of Zimbabwe).

SERGEANT THOMAS GEORGE RUTTER
NO. 1439922 (W./OP./AIR GUNNER) 357 SQUADRON RAFVR
DIED APRIL 6TH 1944 AGED 21

Thomas George Rutter attending a course for wireless operators/air gunners. He is 3rd from the left on the front row

Tom was born at Sheffield, the youngest of five children of James and Edith Rutter. James had been born in Gunnerside, Swaledale, and after leaving the village school went into service and rose to become butler in the houses of several influential families. He met his wife, Edith, a Hungerford girl, whilst in service in London and they travelled to South Africa, in service in the household of a government official in the colony. It was there that their first child, Betty, was born.

Arriving back in England, James took up the position as butler at the Wortley Hall home of Earl Fitzwilliam, near Denby Dale, between Holmfirth and Barnsley, where Ruby, Daphne and Raymond were born. Finally they moved to Firth Park, Sheffield, where James entered the catering business. It was here that Tom was born.

Although away from Gunnerside, they visited the village regularly, spending many happy holidays with their grandmother.

Tom left school in Sheffield and joined the firm of Charles R. Lowen and Co., Accountants and Surveyors. He was a keen member of the 140th (St. Cuthbert's) Rover Scout Group, and, as a God fearing person, it was believed by the family that if he had survived the war he may have attempted to enter the ministry.

Thomas George Rutter on horseback in the hills of Assam, Northern India, taking a break from the arduous and hazardous operations of flying over and between the mountain ranges, Assam to China

When war broke out, Tom joined the Home Guard. In December 1940, during a severe raid on Sheffield, the Rutter family were extremely lucky to escape death or injury. Incendiaries and flares fell in the garden and the family entered their Anderson Shelter. An ARP man arrived to tell them that a landmine, on its parachute, had landed in the road but had not exploded.

Tom volunteered to join the RAF (Raymond had already joined the REME and would serve in North Africa and Italy). Training as a wireless operator and air gunner, Tom was assigned to Wellingtons and then to a Halifax bomber squadron at

Memorial service held at Yileang, China, on April 22nd 1944 in honour of the RAF crew of the Liberator aircraft who were killed when the plane crashed into a mountain side

Upper Heyford and Upper and Nether Wallop, flying on many missions over Europe, and once over Norway, spotting enemy shipping. He always said that his worst experience was flying over the railway marshalling yards at Hamm, in Germany.

In 1943 he was sent out to an aerodrome in Assam, Northern India, with 357 Squadron, as part of Force 136. Flying Liberator bombers, one of their jobs was to fly over "The Hump" (The Himalayas) between Jessore (Assam) and Kuming in China, dropping supplies to both the Chindits and regular army units in the Burmese jungle. It was a perilous operation that required great skill by pilot and navigator.

On his last mission, he was flying over the "Hump" with 12 other servicemen, some of them possibly ground crew acting as "handlers", ready to send the supplies falling from the aircraft. As they flew over China, near the end of their outward journey, they flew into a belt of thick mist and sadly they crashed into the high point on a Chinese mountain side at 5-30a.m. on April 6th 1944, near Yileang, in Hunnan Province. All 13 occupants were killed instantaneously.

On April 22nd 1944 the remains of the men were buried in oak coffins by the Chinese on the mountain side, with a Chinese Christian priest leading the service. After the war the bodies were taken from their resting place in what was then Communist China and re-interred in grave II.D.10. in Sai Wan War Cemetery, in the NE part of Hong Kong island. Thomas Rutter's name is also commemorated on the Gunnerside War Memorial, Swaledale.

SERGEANT IRVIN NEWBOULD (AIR GUNNER) NO. 1495896 70 OPERATIONAL TRAINING UNIT RAFVR DIED APRIL 12TH 1944 AGED 23

Irvin was the youngest son of George and Alice Newbould of Appletreewick, near Burnsall. They farmed at Laburnum Farm until they took over the Craven Arms Inn next door, running it as both an inn and a farm. It was here that young Irvin began work after leaving school, helping his father with the farmwork.

He joined up early in the war and became an air gunner in the RAF. By early 1944 Irvin was serving with No. 70 Operational Training Unit, flying Baltimore aircraft from Shandur airfield in Egypt. On April 12th 1944 his Baltimore aircraft left Shandur on a training flight, but crashed almost immediately in Little Bitter Lake, part of the Suez Canal, just one mile to the north. Irvin Newbould is buried in grave 2.D.7. Fayid War Cemetery, Egypt, 20 kilometres south of Ismailia.

Sergeant Irvine Newbould of Appletreewick

An Appletreewick School group of 1929, showing Irvine Newbould.
Back row: Leonard Horton, Irvine Newbould, Teacher Muriel Sanderson, Herbert Reynoldson, Gordon Holme, George Reynoldson, Tot Reynoldson, Ted Newbould, John Payley, Frank Rodwell, David Holme, Norman Webster, X, Mrs. Lumb.
Next row: Gladys Houseman, Rene Houseman, Margaret Hargreaves, Phyllis Lumb, Rene Newbould, Sally Wellock, Rhoda Ellison, Nora Hawley.
Next row: Hartley Spencer, Ena Horton, Marjorie Hargreaves, May Simpson, Peggy Reynoldson, Tim Horton.
Front row: Frank Holme, Bill Naylor

LANCE CORPORAL EDWARD GILBERT
NO. 4395171 (MM) 1ST BATTALION GREEN HOWARDS
DIED MAY 24th 1944 AGED 24

Edward lived with his parents, John Thomas (Jack) and Elizabeth Gilbert (nee Pratt), his elder sister, Ida, and younger brother, Richard, at Skirethorns, near Grassington. Jack Gilbert worked in the Skirethorns Quarry and Edward eventually began work there.

By January 1943, however, Edward was serving as a private with the 1st Battalion Green Howards in Tunisia, where he was awarded the Military Medal. Serving as a stretcher bearer with "C" Company, he time and again crossed and re-crossed the bullet swept ground, tending casualties in the open and carrying them back to the Regimental Aid Post. His devotion to duty and great fortitude in spite of fatigue, were magnificent.

On March 6th 1944 the 1st Battalion arrived off Anzio, to take part in the landing on the Italian coast. This spot was their base for the next three months, to which they returned after each tour of duty in the line. By mid May, the time was approaching for a general move forward towards Rome and General Mark Clark issued orders for the breakout from the Anzio beachhead to take place at 6-30a.m. on May 23rd.

The Green Howards were to make a diversionary attack before the main attack started, an assault crossing of the River Moletta. They fought so gallantly and against such fierce opposition, both on the Moletta and near Ardea a few days later, that their numbers were so reduced as to make reinforcements necessary.

Edward Gilbert of Threshfield.
Left to right: Edward (Teddy) Gilbert, Gwen Warhurst, Gordon Smith, Jack Tate

Many casualties were caused by a minefield they had to pass through. By daylight of May 24th they were firmly established on the south bank of the Moletta, but being subjected to shelling from light mortars and machine gun fire across the river. The enemy were German paratroopers and the bitter fighting resulted in grievous casualties. The Battalion gained their objective but because of lack of support being sent to them, were forced to retire back across the river and suffered further losses as they extricated themselves (162 casualties in all).

One of those killed on May 24th was Lance Corporal Edward Gilbert and he is buried in grave XVIII.C.10. Beach Head War Cemetery, Anzio.

Our attention now switches to Normandy, as British, Empire and American forces prepared themselves for the main invasion of Western Europe on June 6th and the opening of the Second Front. Sadly we shall find that eight servicemen from these dales would lose their lives during the Normandy landings, in the fighting on the beachhead or in the eventual breakout.

LANCE CORPORAL WILLIAM HENRY WALLBANK NO. 125537 (CROIX DE GUERRE) 629 FIELD SQUADRON ROYAL ENGINEERS DIED JUNE 6TH 1944 AGED 28

Harry, as he was known to family and friends, was born in 1917 and lived with his parents, Thomas Henry and Mary Wallbank (nee Winder), and siblings Mary, Maggie and John, at Hambleton Cottages, on the road between Bolton Abbey and Skipton. Thomas, a soldier from the Great War, worked at Skipton Rock Quarry, near Embsay, and it was there that he was killed in an accident in 1929.

Harry joined the army, becoming a member of the Royal Engineers. In December 1941, he married Catherine (Kay) Dalrymple from Sutton in Craven and whenever he was on leave he would return to this village. During late 1942 and early 1943 he was involved in Operation "Torch", the Allied landings in Algeria and Tunisia, and it was during the fighting in this part of North Africa that Harry was awarded the

Croix de Guerre by the Free French Forces for his bravery.

By early 1944 Harry was back in England, training with his unit, 629 Field Squadron RE, for their forthcoming role on the Normandy beaches on the first day of the invasion. Part of their job was to help clear the beach of obstacles and make the way clear for tanks and carriers. 629 Field Squadron landed with the first wave and came under shell, mortar and machine gun fire. Lance Corporal Harry Wallbank died at the water's edge, as the landing craft hit the beach, cut down before he could begin the job he had been training for during the previous months. Later he was buried in grave I.J.3. Hermanville War Cemetery, 13 kilometres north of Caen, in Normandy.

Harry Wallbank of Bolton Abbey

COLOUR SERGEANT THOMAS P. FERGUSON NO. 789185 6TH BATTALION GREEN HOWARDS DIED JUNE 11TH 1944 AGED 34

Thomas Ferguson had strong connections with Richmond and rose to the rank of Colour Sergeant in a local regiment, the 6th Battalion, Green Howards.

The Battalion disembarked from the "Empire Lance" into the landing crafts at 5a.m. on June 6th 1944, seven miles from the Normandy beaches. The last man waded ashore at 7-37a.m., though several were drowned. Enemy pill boxes were overcome but the men were held up when they reached the sea wall, for behind it, the Germans were lobbing grenades. Eventually the beach was cleared of small arms fire. Severe fighting took place as they pushed further inland and casualties were heavy.

On June 11th the Battalion was ordered to advance and occupy a position in the Oristot area. They moved off at 2-30p.m. and by 4p.m. had passed through Audrieu. By 6p.m. they came to grips with the Germans, who, waiting until the tanks had passed, opened up a withering fire on "B" Company, which sustained heavy casualties.

"C" Company on the left was also pinned down by extremely heavy Spandau fire from the orchards around Oristot. The Company Commander, Captain Chambers, C.S.M. Thomas Ferguson and Lieutenant Rynning (a Norwegian Officer) were killed. The Company was trapped in the middle of a cornfield, and in addition to the heavy crossfire from the orchards on the left, and from a group of farm buildings 200 yards in front, snipers in the trees surrounding the cornfield were taking a heavy toll. The latter were almost impossible to locate, as they wore mottled green blouses and used smokeless ammunition.

This Bocage countryside of cultivated fields, orchards, undergrowth and high sided hedgerows would prove to be a difficult landscape to fight in and would result in very high casualties occurring amongst the opposing sides. One of these casualties was Thomas Ferguson, who was buried in grave XI.K.24. Bayeux War Cemetery.

PRIVATE HAROLD KIPLING
NO. 14598287 12TH (10TH BATTALION GREEN HOWARDS) BATTALION PARACHUTE REGIMENT AAC
DIED JUNE 17TH 1944 AGED 32

Harold was a Richmond man, the second son of Frank and Isabella Kipling. Frank, one of 14 children, came from a long standing Richmond family, and he and Isabella lived at 23 Fontenay Road, where they raised Harold, Peter, Ernest and Walter. Sadly, both Harold and Walter would be killed in the war, within the space of four days of each other. Their father operated a haulage and coal delivery business from the bottom of Lombard Wynd and both sons eventually worked in the family business. Harold was married and he and his wife, Mary Mainland Kipling, and their two children, lived in the market town, in Maison Dieu. After the death of his father, Harold helped his mother run the family business.

He joined the local regiment in late 1942 and was posted to the 10th Battalion Green Howards, a coastal defence unit, which also provided drafts of men to other Green Howard battalions. In 1943, whilst on duty in Cornwall, volunteers were asked for to convert the Battalion into a Parachute Battalion (12th). The response was good, and included Harold Kipling. After the initial parachute training at Ringway, Manchester (8 long descents), about 250 men assembled at Larkhill in June 1943 to form the nucleus of 12th Battalion.

From June 1943 to May 1944 the Battalion took part in vigorous training for the invasion of Europe. Departing Keevil airfield, their destination Normandy, the Battalion dropped at 00-50 hours on June 6th. La Bas de Ranville was taken without many casualties. The Battalion held their position in protecting the river bridges against repeated attacks from Tiger tanks and motorised infantry. They were relieved on the evening of the 7th.

For the next few days they helped 4th Commando in operations at Longueval, receiving 51 casualties. On the evening of June 12th the Battalion was ordered to attack the village of Breville, at 22-30 hours and by midnight it was in Battalion hands. The opposition was stiff, however, and the casualties were 150 out of 260 who started the attack.

June 14th to 16th saw the Battalion back in their rest area at Ranville but three men were killed and ten wounded by enemy shell fire, including Harold Kipling, who was wounded and died on June 17th. He was buried in grave IIA.K.10. Ranville War Cemetery.

As if the terrible news of Harold's death was not enough for his family to bear, news reached them that Harold's younger brother, 19 year old Walter, had been killed four days later, fighting in the Italian Campaign.

FUSILIER WALTER C. KIPLING
NO. 14587439 2ND BATTALION LANCASHIRE FUSILIERS
DIED JUNE 21ST 1944 AGED 19

Walter Kipling was the youngest of the four sons of Frank and Isabella. At one time he was employed at the Richmond Cinema, but when Harold joined up, he decided to help his mother with the haulage business. When he enlisted, he joined the 2nd Battalion Lancashire Fusiliers and was sent to fight in the Italian Campaign, when he landed on the beaches of Anzio, in late January, 1944.

After Rome fell on June 4th 1944, the broken German armies under the leadership of Kesselring streamed northwards in disorder, closely pursued on land and harassed by continuous air attack. General Clark's 5th U.S. Army attacked along the coast towards Pisa whilst General Alexander's Eighth Army followed up along the River Tiber, towards Lake Trasimeno in the north.

Alexander was confident of breaking through the Appenine mountain range into the valley of the Po and beyond within a few months. However, he failed by a small margin due to the withdrawal of some of his best troops for Operation "Anvil", the landings in the south of France, and by the competence of his German adversary, Kesselring.

Kesselring delayed the British advance until he had reorganised his troops and occupied his next strong defensive position, the Gothic Line. He had to fight for time to complete and man it and to receive eight more divisions from northern Europe and Russia. After 10 days of pursuit the German resistance began to stiffen and the Eighth Army, including the 2nd Battalion Lancashire Fusiliers and Walter Kipling, came in for severe fighting to overcome strong positions on the shores of Lake Trasimeno. It was not until June 28th that the Germans retired and fell back on Arezzo.

Walter Kipling was killed on June 21st during the severe fighting around Lake Trasimeno and was buried in grave I.J.6. Orvieto War Cemetery, halfway between Rome and Trasimeno. Shortly after Walter's death, his mother received two telegrams on the same day, telling her the tragic news of the loss of two of her sons. Another son, Ernest, was serving in the Middle East at the time, but thankfully he survived the war.

PRIVATE WILLIAM CROUCH
NO. 4468464 10TH BATTALION DURHAM LIGHT INFANTRY
DIED JUNE 23RD 1944 AGED 20

William was the youngest son of James Walter and Lillie Crouch of 2 Temple View, Bargate, Richmond. He was formerly employed in the market gardens of Mr. Gibson, Market Place, Richmond.

On June 11th (D-Day +5), William Crouch and the 10th Battalion set sail from Newhaven, destination the Normandy beaches, and passed the "Mulberry" Harbour being towed across the Channel. They waded ashore on June 12th with no opposition and marched inland for six miles, along dusty roads full of military vehicles.

On the afternoon of June 16th patrols moved into the village of St. Pierre and found it empty, though they were sniped at from the hills and orchards beyond. The enemy proved troublesome and next day, the 18th, a Company attack was put in, making some progress but had to pull back. Next day another Company was successful.

For the next few days there was stalemate, during which both sides settled down to secure their positions and patrolled with vigour. There were frequent clashes on night patrols, for the Germans were expecting an Allied breakout and were extremely alert. Enemy sentries were posted about 25 yards apart. A Platoon of "A"

Company was involved in a lively action in which the enemy brought up some tanks, one of which fell victim to the Battalion anti-tank gunners. It was during these actions that William Crouch was wounded and he died on June 23rd. He is buried in grave VIII.E.4. Bayeux War Cemetery. Another son was reported missing in France, but the good news was received that he was a Prisoner of War.

SERGEANT HARRY KINCHIN
NO. 1596079 (AIR GUNNER) 17 OPERATIONAL TRAINING UNIT RAF
DIED JULY 8TH 1944 AGED 20

Harry was the youngest son of the seven children of Richmond joiner and undertaker, Allison Clark Kinchin and Laura Kinchin, of 11 Castle Hill. Allison had served in the Great War and seen his brother killed whilst serving in the same Battalion. Before the Second World War, Harry was working as a cobbler for Mr. Smith, the cobbler at Catterick Camp, mainly making and repairing officers' shoes, and had also been employed by Messrs. Mason of Shute Road, Catterick.

Harry Kinchin of Richmond

When war began, Harry and his father eventually joined Richmond Home Guard, with Allison serving as the Sergeant Major, and putting his Great War experiences to good practise, whilst Harry became a Sergeant. In October 1943 Harry joined the RAF as an air gunner.

On July 8th 1944 he was the rear gunner on a Liberator aircraft of No. 17 Operational Training Unit that was in a mid-air collision with another aircraft over Westbury, near Brackley, in Buckinghamshire. The two planes collided coming into the aerodrome and the entire crew were killed. Harry Kinchin's body was brought back to Richmond, where he was provided with a military funeral, and was laid to rest in Richmond Cemetery. The coffin was draped in the Union Jack and carried on a RAF wagon, with the Home Guard acting as bearers. The family's eldest son, Allison, was already a POW in Italy, whilst another son, Walter, was serving in a light A.A. Battery abroad. The two son-in-laws of their daughters were also POW's in Germany.

CORPORAL JOHN CRAVEN
NO. 7938920 13TH/18TH ROYAL HUSSARS ROYAL ARMOURED CORPS
DIED JULY 18TH 1944 AGED 21

John and his parents, Herbert and Delia Craven, had connections to Richmond, although his parents were living at Falsgrave, on the outskirts of Scarborough. His father had been a police inspector in Richmond until beeing posted to Scarborough in 1938. John was a pupil at Richmond Grammar School from 1934, although from 1938 he became a boarder, when his family moved away. John was a member of

Richmond Parish Church Choir and when he left the Grammar School he joined the staff of a bank at Northallerton.

When John enlisted in the army he joined the Royal Armoured Corps and in June 1944 he and the Royal Hussars were fighting in the difficult terrain of the Normandy bocage, not ideally suited to armoured warfare.

John Craven of Richmond as a grammar school boy

On July 18th, Montgomery launched his general offensive, Operation "Goodwood", with the aim of enlarging the bridgeheads and carrying them well beyond the River Orne. It began with a large scale attack by British bombers on enemy locations east of the River Orne. The Regiment was in the assembly area at Herouvillette, near Ranville and Caen.

At 7-45a.m. "C" Squadron began mopping up enemy weapon pits and prisoners started coming out in batches of 10. The fight for Touffreville continued all that morning, with considerable trouble coming from enemy artillery encountered on the Butte de la Hogue and mortars also concentrated at Escoville and Herouvillette.

At 14-00 hours, mortar fire in Escoville killed Captain Lyon-Clark and another soldier, as well as wounding others. "C" Squadron sent No. 2 Troop forward and were fired on by dug-in enemy tanks, which knocked out four tanks of the Royal Hussars, killing John Craven at the same time. At 23-00 hours there was a heavy enemy air attack on the area and damage was done to vehicles. Losses in the Royal Hussars mounted to four officers and 90 other ranks. John Craven's body was eventually buried in grave IVA.C.9. Ranville War Cemetery.

The next casualty from the dales was also from Richmond and fell close to John Craven on the next day of the battle.

PRIVATE FRANCIS HENRY LE MINEUR
NO. 4399427 5TH BATTALION EAST YORKSHIRE REGIMENT
DIED JULY 19TH 1944 AGED 22

Francis was the youngest son of John Francis Marie Le Mineur and Marcella Le Mineur of 24 Whitcliffe Place, Reeth Road, Richmond. He joined the East Yorkshire Regiment and was with them in the Middle East when he was wounded. He made a good recovery and in 1944 his Battalion was back in England, preparing to take part in the Normandy fighting.

He was with the 5th Battalion East Yorks when they landed on "Red King" beach on D-Day and as they made their way inland on the 6th June they were badly mauled. Some 85 men were killed on the beach alone. However, Francis had survived.

Progress through the bocage was disappointingly slow and costly and the Germans had caught their second wind. Panzer Group West barred the British advance. Montgomery made some progress, finally taking Caen on July 13th and then, as we have seen, he launched his next offensive, Operation "Goodwood" on

July 18th. As the 5th Battalion East Yorkshire Regiment pushed forward against the Germans in the woods and villages around Tilly, they came up against strong opposition and in the fighting Francis Henry Le Mineur was fatally wounded and died shortly afterwards, on July 19th. His parents received a cheery letter from him, dated the day before he died. He lies buried close to his colleague, John Craven, in grave VII.A.13. Hottot-Les-Bagues War Cemetery, SE of Bayeux.

DRIVER HORACE MALLINSON
NO. 2122721 79 ASSAULT SQUADRON ROYAL ENGINEERS
DIED JULY 25TH 1944 AGED 34

Horace was the youngest son of William (Billy) and Ruth Mallinson. At one stage William was landlord of the Fox and Hounds at Starbotton, before moving to Manningham House, Kettlewell, which Ruth ran as a "Bed and Breakfast". Horace began work as a stone mason for Barrie Calvert, builder and contractor at Kettlewell, and in his spare time played football for Kettlewell. Eventually, Horace married the assistant school-mistress of Kettlewell School, Doris Wilson, a girl from near Penrith, and he and his wife settled down to married life in the village, with their daughter Margharite.

Horace Mallinson of Kettlewell with Starbotton

The war had begun and when Horace enlisted he joined the Royal Engineers, becoming a driver for 79 Assault Squadron by the time of the Normandy landings. In the planning of the invasion, specialised engineers led the assault, breaching the sea wall and opening routes inland. On July 25th 1944, in the latter stages of Operation "Goodwood", the Canadian and British forces made an attack from Caen down the Falaise road, which was effectively opposed by four Panzer divisions. It was on this day that Horace Mallinson was killed, the news eventually reaching his wife who was living with her relatives at Kirby Thore, near Penrith. Horace Mallinson was buried in grave VIII.B.6. La Delivrande War Cemetery, Douvres, 14 kilometres north of Caen.

FLYING OFFICER FREDERICK ELLIS SPINK
NO. 151832 (DFC) 489 SQUADRON RAF
DIED AUGUST 8TH 1944 AGED 24

Known as Ellis to his family and friends in the dale and Freddy by his RAF pals, he was the youngest son of Thomas Frederick and Elizabeth Spink of Conistone, their other child being Aubrey. Thomas had married Elizabeth Fawcett from Hebden, and, in the tiny village of Conistone she ran the post office whilst Thomas farmed at Town Head Farm. He was also a butcher, with his own small slaughter house and in the 1930's travelled the dale in his butcher's van.

Ellis won a scholarship to Ermystedd's Grammar School, Skipton, and went on to study art at Skipton Art School, planning later to study at the Royal College of Art in London. This was not to be, as the war intervened. He joined the RAF and did his training as a navigator in Canada, before joining 489 Squadron at RAF Leuchars in Fife, Scotland.

Flying Officer Frederick Ellis Spink of Conistone

They had been flying Hampden aircraft on anti-submarine patrols but now they were re-equipped with Beaufighters and specialised in anti-shipping attacks, the most dangerous of all RAF roles. They moved to RAF Langham in Norfolk, to be closer to the invasion taking place across the English Channel. It was at this time that Ellis became the navigator for Squadron Leader Peter Hughes and he received the DFC for the accuracy of his navigation and the many sorties he undertook.

On August 4th and 6th they had flown operations against German E-boats, in support of the invasion of Normandy, but on August 8th most of 489 Squadron joined other Squadrons at RAF North Cotes, south of Grimsby, to attack a convoy off Egersund, south of Stavanger, Southern Norway. 45 Beaufighters, escorted by 48 Mustangs from American Squadrons, took off from North Cotes and three Mustangs and three Beaufighters would not return.

The convoy was near enough to shore to be protected by the fire from shore batteries, but the convoy escorts also sent up heavy flak. Two Beaufighters had already been shot down when Peter Hughes attacked a trawler acting as a flak ship, firing his cannons and then turning over land and giving the vessel another burst of fire, resulting in the death of 11 sailors on board.

It seems clear, however, that their plane had been hit by flak, for Ellis called out to Peter that there was a fire in the port engine and the pilot took action to close it down, but the flames spread to the cockpit. Peter ordered Ellis to bale out but it appears that he failed to clip on his parachute before jettisoning the perspex cupola and was sucked out without it, falling to his death on the hard surface of the sea.

Peter Hughes was also sucked out but his parachute and dinghy were strapped on and he survived the ordeal, landing in the sea some 10 miles from the coast. He paddled for 12 hours, landing that night, and was arrested by German troops the next morning. In 1988, survivors of the Squadron organised a visit to Norway as guests of the Norwegian Air Force. Peter and other members were taken by helicopter to drop a wreath on the sea, near the spot where Ellis died.

The body of Ellis was never recovered and he is commemorated on the RAF Memorial at Runnymede and on a Squadron plaque in the church at Langham, Norfolk.

PRIVATE REGINALD DOUTHWAITE
NO. 14253358 1ST BATTALION SUFFOLK REGIMENT
DIED AUGUST 28TH 1944 AGED 28

Known to his family and friends as Reggie, he was born in Westmorland in 1916, the son of Reginald and Mary Douthwaite, with a daughter Hilda completing the family. Reggie's father was the gardener to a Canon in Westmorland and moved with his employer, eventually settling on Main Street, Grassington, in 1926. Reggie began working at the local quarry and was a member of Linton Church Sunday School, a member of the choir, a server and crucifer and a good friend of the priest and Rector, Frederick Arnold Mosby. A new start began when he left the village in 1937 to serve as a police constable in the West Riding Constabulary, being stationed near Doncaster.

Reginald Douthwaite of Grassington

In 1942 he joined the army as a Military Policeman and was posted to an Anti-Aircraft Regiment RA. However, in early 1944 he became an infantryman, serving in the 1st Battalion Suffolk Regiment and preparing for the invasion of France. In July 1944 the Battalion was involved in Operation "Goodwood", beginning July 18th and in the push by the Canadians and British from Caen towards Falaise. The fighting was ferocious in difficult, dangerous terrain and against a determined Panzer Army Group. Casualties were high in the bocage countryside near Falaise, and one of those who was severely wounded was Reggie Douthwaite.

He was brought back to England and entered St. Margaret's Hospital, Swindon, but his parents were informed that he died on August 28th. Reginald Douthwaite was brought back home and buried in Linton churchyard on Friday September 1st 1944.

FLYING OFFICER DAVID HENRY ATKINSON (BA)
AIR BOMBER NO. 133788 570 SQUADRON RAFVR
DIED SEPTEMBER 23RD 1944 AGED 23

David was the younger of the two sons of Charles and Dorothy Lee Atkinson of Marske, a village situated between Richmond and Reeth, with Ronald being the eldest son. Charles worked at times on odd jobs on local farms, whilst his wife, Dorothy, was the headmistress of Marske village school, which consisted of around 40 pupils taught in one room by two teachers. She retired from the position in 1947, after 25 years at the school. The Atkinson family lived first in a cottage in the village and then in rooms at Skelton Hall, nearby.

David was educated at his mother's school and then became a boarder at Richmond Grammar School, where he excelled at English and the Arts. In 1938 he was a school prefect and in 1939 won Half Cricket and Full Rugby Colours for the school. In that same year he won a County Major Scholarship that allowed him to go on to Durham University. In the Richmond School Year Book, "The Compostellan", for 1937, a poem of David's was printed that provides, in its own way, an evocative picture of those dangerous years of the late 1930's.

Politics

"The paper world is printing it,
The paper boys are hinting it.
There's really awful, dreadful News!
There've been some bad incendencies –
Just minor Fascist tendencies.
There's been some kind of ghastly row
In Haya Wangsi and Kow Chow.
The Japs have taken Kowchungtee –
Oh, please pronounce it, BBC!
Up Hitler's sleeve there lies a trick,
Or why with Rome is he so thick?
The Bolsheviks must mind their backs,
Berlin and Rome are on their tracks.
Then Franco's done so well in Spain
That Mussolini's good again.
Suicides, murders, bombs in flats,
Earthquakes, smashes, new fashions in hats!
On all of these the Press expound.
Oh dear, oh dear, bad words all round!
And after reading all this news,
Of rumours, wars, and murdered Jews,
I'll need a tonic made by Schweppes
(Pronunciation as in "steppes.")
Here's news! Here's news! Here's better news!
Last night, at six, Sir Jeremy Perks
Strangled himself with physical jerks.
A billiard's player swallowed his cue –
"He bit off more than he could chew."
A babe in bath has swallowed the soap –
Doctors and nurses sigh "No hope!"
Devouring soap and blowing bubbles
Is more to me than national troubles.
Though Politics may vital be,
That, oh, Press, is the news for me."

Sadly, those national and international troubles did impinge on David's life. In 1941 he took his BA Degree, and, already a member of the University Air Squadron, he joined the RAF in that same year and trained for a period in South Africa. David would be killed in 1944 (his older brother Ronald also served in the RAF, but on the ground crew).

By mid 1944 David was a Flying Officer serving with 570 Squadron RAF and

David Atkinson of Marske, Swaledale, as a Richmond Grammar School boy

operating Stirling aircraft. The Squadron had formed in November 1943 at Hurn, one mile north of Bournemouth, as an airborne force unit in No. 38 Group. Equipped with Albemaries, it took part in training exercises and in February 1944 began supply dropping missions to resistance forces in occupied Europe. On D-Day the Squadron contributed 22 aircraft for the initial airborne landings, 20 more following during the day. In July 1944 they converted to Stirling aircraft.

As the Germans were forced out of France and retired through Belgium and Holland, plans were put into operation to attempt to capture certain bridges over the Rhine, including the one at Arnhem, in Holland. It was here that the British 1st Airborne Division made a successful drop on September 17th 1944, but found that the German forces were stronger than expected. As German reinforcements arrived, the paratroopers were forced into an ever smaller perimeter between September 17th and 26th. Bad weather prevented the flying in of reinforcements but RAF planes attempted to drop supplies to the beleaguered force. 570 Squadron carried out 22 glider-towing sorties to Arnhem and 58 re-supply missions followed. During this period, eleven aircraft were lost, including the one on which David Atkinson was on board.

David Atkinson of Marske in RAF uniform
Courtesy of the Darlington and Stockton Times

Eight men were on board Stirling aircraft LJ883, carrying supplies to the Airborne forces at Arnhem, on September 23rd, when it was hit by flak over Holland. Despite the efforts of the two pilots, David Atkinson and 20 year old Flying Officer Brown, the plane crashed near the town of Ede, 15 miles NW of Arnhem, resulting in the death of six members of the crew. The two survivors were Flight Sergeant Wood and Despatcher S. Badham of the Royal Army Service Corps. David Atkinson was buried in grave 4.A.15. Arnhem Oosterbeek War Cemetery.

***** On a Grammar School rugby photograph from 1937-1938, showing David Atkinson, two other team mates were Dennis Bell and Peter Squires and they too would be killed whilst serving in the RAF.

FLIGHT LIEUTENANT (PILOT) RAISBECK DENNIS BELL
NO. 63454 51 SQUADRON RAFVR
DIED OCTOBER 6TH 1944 AGED 24

Dennis Bell's father was Raisbeck Bell, head master at Bellerby School, near Leyburn. Dennis attended Richmond Grammar School at the same time as Alan

Broadley. He was a fine cricketer, both he and his father playing for Bellerby and Hawes. It was in Richmond that Dennis met his future wife, Margaret Hilda Metcalfe, a Richmond girl. They settled down to married life and a daughter was born.

Having joined the RAF, Dennis trained in Canada and eventually returned to join 51 Squadron at Snaith, in Yorkshire, flying Halifax bombers. On April 9th 1944 a plan was approved to begin systematic attacks on the German synthetic fuel industry. It was on one of these missions that Dennis Bell lost his life.

At 2-39p.m. on October 6th 1944 the Halifax carrying Dennis Bell departed Snaith airfield, its destination Sterkrade-Holten, an oil production target in the Ruhr. The plane was shot down by flak and all seven crew on board were killed. Dennis Bell is buried in grave 8.A.8. in the Reichswald Forest War Cemetery, near Kleve, in Germany.

Dennis R. Bell (Bellerby)

SERGEANT (FLIGHT ENGINEER) PETER SQUIRES
NO. 1096448 83 SQUADRON RAFVR
DIED AUGUST 25TH 1942 AGED 20

Peter was the son of William and Rhoda Squires, and together with his brother David, they lived at Hipswell, where William was the village head master between 1927 and 1948. Peter was educated at Richmond Grammar School, until just before the war started. Leaving school, he was involved in helping a building contractor at Richmond, before being accepted into the RAF. He trained as a Flight Engineer, and by August 1942 was serving with 83 Squadron, based at RAF Wyton, near Huntingdon, Cambridgeshire.

Peter Squires of Hipswell

The Squadron had just become part of the newly formed Path Finder Force, used to pinpoint enemy targets by dropping flares and so enabling the rest of the bomber force to drop their bombs more accurately.

Lancaster bomber R5610 took off from Wyton at 2051 hours on August 24th 1942, its destination Frankfurt. A few hours later, at 0215 hours on August 25th, it was intercepted on its homeward journey by a Messerschmitt night fighter, piloted by Walter Barte and shot down over the Belgian village of Morkhoven, 20 miles east of Antwerp. It was the first Pathfinder to be shot down on Belgian soil. Sixteen planes were lost that night and two of them came from 83 Squadron.

Peter was killed, together with three other crew

members, whilst two others were captured and the pilot, Oliver Matheson, managed to escape with the help of a local resistance man. The four men were buried in the local cemetery in Morkhoven and their graves have been tended by the local villagers since that day. In 1946, the Squires family travelled to visit the grave and in November 2005, his brother David and his family were able to attend a special commemoration in the village.

LEADING AIRCRAFTMAN JOHN THOMAS GATES
NO. 1783116 BASE SIGNAL RADAR UNIT RAFVR
DIED NOVEMBER 7TH 1944 AGED 21

John was the only son of William and Gertrude Gates, a Roman Catholic family living at 24 Newbiggin, Richmond. His late father was a licensee at Gilling West for nine years and the family had lived in Richmond for the past 13 years. John was an altar boy at Richmond Roman Catholic Church for 13 years and a member of the Catholic Boys Club. By the time of his death, he was engaged to Miss Bamber of St. Annes, Blackpool.

John Thomas Gates of Richmond
Courtesy of the Darlington and Stockton Times

John joined the RAF in February 1942, before which he was employed by builder George Wade and was a member of Richmond Home Guard. He became a Leading Aircraftman in the RAF during the war and by 1944 was part of the ground crew dealing with a radar unit. By November 1944 the unit was close up to the forward lines, in the vicinity of Antwerp, Belgium, which had been captured on September 4th.

Antwerp was of no use as a port, however, without control of the Scheldt Estuary. Between October 1st and November 8th, therefore, the battle for South Beveland and Walcheren Island took place. There were furious British assaults against the German 1st Parachute Army, plus amphibious attacks, which eventually took the peninsular after both sides suffered heavy losses. Walcheren Island fell on November 8th, following the flooding of the defences by Allied air bombing of the sea dykes. It was on this same day that John Thomas Gates was killed as a result of enemy action at sea and he is buried in grave 9.2.34. Oostende New Communal Cemetery.

The last fatality of a serviceman from these dales in 1944 came in Italy and was the misfortune of another Richmond man.

PRIVATE FREDERICK COCKERILL
NO. 4468870 16TH BATTALION DURHAM LIGHT INFANTRY
DIED NOVEMBER 16TH 1944 AGED 22

Frederick Cockerill, a married man, was the only son of Mrs. J. Earl of 51 Market Place, Richmond, although when he died his wife, Gladys, was living at 72

Ayresome Street, Middlesborough.

In late October 1944, Frederick's 16th Battalion DLI were just north of San Marino in Italy, with the Allied advance stalled as winter set in and the Germans dug in to a number of key defensive positions.

On the night of 14th/15th November the Battalion moved up to S. Varano and a position was taken on the Villa Grappa road, next to the Lazarro River. The morning of the 15th saw a successful crossing with the aid of tanks and the taking of 10 prisoners, although 3 casualties resulted. By nightfall, they were established on the line of the Bolzanino River, with "A" Company creating a diversion by defensive patrolling and fire, enabling a Bailey bridge to be built.

During November 16th ,"A" and "C" Companies moved forward to reach the line of the River Cosina, but a strong counter-attack forced "A" Company to pull back and "C" Company only made little headway. During the evening "C" Company's patrol was fired upon and a recce was not carried out. It was during this day's actions that Frederick Cockerill was killed and his body buried in grave I.B.26. Meldola War Cemetery.

1945

During the winter and spring of 1945 British forces continued their advance towards the River Rhine and across the mighty river defences into the heart of Germany, whilst Bomber Command aircrews maintained the pressure on German industry as they pounded what was left of the cities and towns. The German Reich would surrender at midnight on May 8th/9th 1945 and the following day the parishes throughout the dales were able to bring out the bunting, ring the church bells and light bonfires to celebrate VE Day. Out in the Far East, however, despite the celebrations in Britain for the end of the conflict in Europe, British forces (the so called "Forgotten Army") would continue the desperate fight against the Japanese in Burma, Malaya and elsewhere, until the surrender of Japan on September 2nd. Throughout these months of 1945 the dales would lose a further eleven servicemen.

SAPPER JOHN WILSON
NO. 1921516 241 FIELD COMPANY ROYAL ENGINEERS
DIED JANUARY 7TH 1945 AGED 35

John was the son of George and Elizabeth Wilson of Intake Farm, on the Bolton Abbey Estate. As a boy he had been a member of the church choir. George was a gamekeeper on the estate, whilst his son, John, worked as a woodman and was known as a daring and venturesome climber.

John had entered Europe with 241 Field Company Royal Engineers and during the severe winter weather of early January 1945 the Allies faced the Germans across the border rivers separating Holland and Germany. Preparations were in hand for an advance to be made by the British and Americans on January 17th towards the German border and the Field Companies of the Royal Engineers were busy on the dangerous task of clearing paths through the German minefields.

During this period, 50 men of the Royal Engineers, including John Wilson, were killed by the explosion of the mines they were removing. Their bodies lie in joint graves in Brunssum War Cemetery, Netherlands, close to the German border, 35 kilometres NE of Maastricht. John lies in joint grave V.208 - 209.

SERGEANT (FLIGHT ENGINEER) FRANCIS ALDERSON KENDALL NO. 1676293 106 SQUADRON RAFVR DIED JANUARY 14TH 1945 AGED 20

His father, Oliver Kendall, although a farmer's son, was more interested in things mechanical. He was employed in driving a lorry and married Lizzie Sunter from Robson House, Whitaside, Swaledale. By the start of the Second World War, they and their children, Mary and Francis, had moved to the old Kendall family farm at Low Whita, between Healaugh and Low Row, since Oliver's brother, Mark, had left farming because of ill-health.

Francis Alderson Kendall of Low Whita, near Healaugh, Swaledale

After leaving Reeth School, Francis worked for his father on the farm, although he too was not really interested in farming. Like his father, he was mechanically minded and loved to ride his motor bike through the dale. Francis, who passionately wanted to join the RAF, was accepted for that service in late 1943, whilst his sister Mary worked on the farm.

Francis qualified as a sergeant, flight engineer, with 106 Squadron, flying Lancaster bombers out of RAF Metheringham in Lincolnshire. When Mary married on Boxing Day 1944, her brother Francis could not attend because his plane had come down somewhere in Scotland, due to mechanical problems. Shortly before this, he had been home on leave and loved the chance to once again ride through the dale on his motor bike. He also took the opportunity to attend the dance in Keld village hall and enjoyed the occasion. A few weeks later he would be dead.

The seven man crew of Lancaster PB122 took off from Metheringham at 16-10 hours on January 14th 1945 to bomb a synthetic oil plant at Leuna, eighteen miles west of Leipzig, Germany. It was homeward bound and damaged by flak, when, at 23-59 hours, the Lancaster crashed into the ground at an acute angle near Vignacourt on the Somme, in France, a few miles NW of Amiens. All seven crew-men were killed and were first buried at Amiens, before later being moved to St. Sever Cemetery Extension at Rouen, where Francis is buried in grave S.1.N.1. The average age of the crew was 22, with their skipper being the oldest at 31.

MAJOR ALBANY KENNETT CHARLESWORTH NO. 59123 (MC) 3RD CARABINIERS (PRINCE OF WALES'S DRAGOON GUARDS) ROYAL ARMOURED CORPS DIED FEBRUARY 1ST 1945 AGED 52

Albany Charlesworth, known as "Bany" to his friends, was the only son of the late Colonel Albany Charlesworth of Chapelthorpe Hall, near Wakefield, and part of the family known as "The Yorkshire Coal Kings", due to their ownership of numerous collieries.

He was educated at Eton and Christ Church, Oxford, and in the Great War had won the Military Cross whilst serving with the 3rd Dragoon Guards. Albany became Chairman of J. and J. Charlesworth Ltd., colliery proprieters, Wakefield, and was a director of the Yorkshire Conservative Newspaper Co., proprietors of the "Yorkshire Post". In 1923 he married Diana Beckett and lived at Virginia Water, Surrey.

Albany Kennett Charlesworth of Grinton, near Reeth

Albany owned the Grinton Estate, near Reeth, with large shooting rights over Grinton, Harkerside and Whitaside Moors. He regularly stayed at Grinton Lodge during the season, from where he entertained his shooting parties. He was President of Reeth Agricultural Society for many years, regularly attending the Show there, as well as being President of Grinton Literary Institute and Reeth and District Nursing Association. He was interested in country pursuits and was at home on a horse, or with a gun.

Albany Charlesworth was Aide de Camp to Field Marshall Sir Alan Brooke from the days of Dunkirk (Commander in Chief Home Forces 1940 - 1941, Chief of the Imperial General Staff 1941 - 1946 and one of the greatest military intellects of his generation). In his job he was in France on two occasions in the desperate days of May/June 1940, once departing from Dunkirk and soon afterwards leaving by way of St. Malo.

For February 1945 it was arranged that Churchill, Roosevelt and Stalin should meet at Yalta, in the Crimea, to review the whole shape and structure of post-war Europe. Each leader would need to take with him a large delegation of advisors, both military and political. One of Churchill's delegation was Albany Charlesworth. Churchill's party would fly out to the island of Malta by January 31st, whilst Roosevelt would arrive by ship on February 2nd, before departing for Yalta and their meeting with Stalin.

Winston Churchill and the official party left Northolt aerodrome on January 29th. The rest of his personal staff and officials travelled in two other planes. Churchill's plane landed safely just before dawn on the 30th, but he was told that one of the other planes had crashed near the Italian island of Pantelleria. The plane, a York, was one of Britain's latest air liners and 15 members of Churchill's staff were killed and five others wounded in the crash. Major Albany Charlesworth was severely wounded and died in hospital on the island of Malta on February 1st.

Albany Kennett Charlesworth was buried in joint grave 1.1C.6. Imtarfa Military Cemetery, Malta. It is sad to report that Albany Charlesworth's son, David, who was serving as a Lieutenant out in Palestine during the troubles of 1947/1948 was killed. With double death duties to pay, the Charlesworth family was forced to sell off the Grinton Estate.

PRIVATE SIMON ALLEN MUDD
NO. 4395944 5TH BATTALION GREEN HOWARDS
DIED FEBRUARY 2ND 1945 AGED 32

Simon was the son of Mr. and Mrs. T. Mudd of 3 Whitcliffe Place, Reeth Road, Richmond. His father was a builder and when Simon left school, he joined the family business. Early in the war he became a member of the 5th Battalion Green Howards Regiment, whilst his brother Harry was in the Royal Army Medical Corps and by late 1941 they were both serving in North Africa. At Christmas 1941 they met unexpectedly, opening their Christmas parcels together and sharing their contents.

Simon Mudd of Richmond
Courtesy of the
Darlington and Stockton Times

In late May, 1942, however, Simon Mudd was in the Western Desert, fighting for his life as Rommel's forces threatened to sweep towards the Egyptian border. The Battalion found itself in the killing ground known as "Knightsbridge Box", one of the main British defensive positions, but after a gallant defence, it was overrun by armoured units of the Afrika Korps, and Simon Mudd was one of many British soldiers taken prisoner by the Italians (we have already seen that another Richmond man, John Hetherington of the 4th Battalion Green Howards, was killed during this battle). Simon was transported across the Mediterranean to Italy and spent some time in POW camp PG66, just north of Naples before being transferred to POW camp PG73, between Modena and Reggio.

When Italy capitulated in September 1943, the Germans took over the camps and as they were forced to retire northwards, the prisoners were also taken north. Simon Mudd found himself in Stalag XVIIIC at Spittal-Drau, in southern Austria. Allied forces liberated the camp in late January 1945 but sadly his parents were informed that he had died at sea, in transit to this country, on February 2nd 1945. His body was buried at sea and Simon Mudd's name is commemorated on Panel 60 Alamein Memorial.

PRIVATE HARVEY CHARLES TODD NO. 14700447
2ND BATTALION KING'S OWN SCOTTISH BORDERERS
DIED FEBRUARY 24TH 1945 AGED 18

Harvey was the youngest child of Charles and Ada Todd, their other children being Harry, Thomas and Rowena. Charles, a Richmond man, had married Ada Gates, also from Richmond, and they lived at 76 Frenchgate, where they ran a green grocers shop. They also had a small market garden on a large piece of ground by the side of Lombard Wynd. Here, on the terraced ground overlooking the River Swale, they had greenhouses and vegetable plots and kept pigs and chickens.

When Harvey left school he eventually began working as a lorry driver for the haulage and coal merchant, Frank Kipling, who, together with his sons, Harold and Walter, ran his business from the bottom of Lombard Wynd. Harvey was a popular, devil may care lad, and was the best of pals with Walter Kipling. We have already seen that brothers Harold and Walter Kipling were killed during June 1944.

Harvey Todd became a member of Richmond Home Guard, but in 1944, both he and Walter Kipling enlisted in the army, and went their separate ways, Harvey joining the 2nd Battalion King's Own Scottish Borderers and was sent to fight the Japanese in Burma.

Harvey Charles Todd of Richmond

General Slim, leader of the 14th Army, planned three assaults across the Irrawaddy River in early 1945, with the 2nd Battalion involved in one of these. The Battalion left Kohima on December 28th 1944, marching southwards with 50 mules added to their transport, whilst being supplied on a regular basis from air drops by Dakota aircraft. The column steadily pushed on for 168 miles, fording streams and toiling up and down the switchback tracks over the hills, until they reached Yozayat on January 29th 1945, fifteen miles from the Irrawaddy.

On February 14th the assault across the Irrawaddy was made under extreme machine gun fire, with "B" Company detailed for Beachmaster duties in the assault and the whole Battalion was across by February 16th. The job of the 2nd Battalion was now to mop up Japanese positions along the banks of the Irrawaddy and on February 23rd they attacked the village of Nakyo-Aing, in an area of cactus hedges and small creeks.

The Japanese defended it from numerous bunkers manned by machine gun teams. On February 24th the village was shelled. Supported by Sherman tanks, the Borderers moved into the attack at 8-45a.m., "A" Company leading. Heavy Japanese machine gun fire inflicted casualties.

Nakyo-Aing was now in flames and the enemy tried to escape. Forty of them made a dash for it and ran into heavy fire from the tanks, whilst the rest of the garrison remained to fight. A combined attack was made on the village and by 1p.m. "C" Company had made firm contact with "A" Company. The Borderers fought on through the afternoon and the evening to clear the village. The well hidden bunkers held determined Japanese who took a toll of the attackers. Three officers were killed, four wounded, whilst nine other ranks were killed and twenty six wounded.

One of those killed was 18 year old Harvey Todd. He was laid to rest near where he died, but shortly after the war's end he was reburied in grave 21.B.20. Taukkyan War Cemetery, just outside Rangoon.

Nine days later, another man from Richmond was killed whilst taking part in the third and final crossing of the River Irrawaddy.

MAJOR JOHN MCKENZIE SINCLAIR BAIN NO. 137904
1ST BATTALION QUEENS OWN CAMERON HIGHLANDERS
DIED FEBRUARY 25TH 1945 AGED 26

We have already seen that John Bain's brother, Charles, had been killed in 1942 whilst serving in Bomber Command. John was the eldest son and like his brothers, he was educated at Richmond Grammar School, leaving in 1936 to attend

Edinburgh University.

He joined the Cameron Highlanders, his father's old regiment, whilst still at University, rising to the rank of Second Lieutenant in 1940 and was the first to receive an Honours degree in Edinburgh while on active service. In September 1940 he married Erika, the daughter of the retired County Clerk for Midlothian and by the time of his death she was living with their young son in Edinburgh.

By late 1944, having risen to the rank of Major, he was to be found deep in the jungles of Burma. During the summer he had been wounded, as was his brother, Captain Finlay Bain of the 8th Gurkha Rifles.

John Bain of Richmond as a grammar school boy

In early 1945 it was decided that General Slim's 14th Army would advance against the main enemy body west of Mandalay and subsequently advance on Rangoon. To do this they needed to cross the River Irrawaddy. The 19th Division seized a bridgehead across the river 40 miles north of Mandalay in late January 1945, on 13th February the 20th Division (including Harvey Todd) crossed lower down and on 23rd/24th February they were joined by the 2nd Division (including the Cameron Highlanders and John Bain, the CO of "A" Company), as they too crossed the mighty river.

At 21-30 hours on February 23rd the leading companies of the Cameron Highlanders slipped their assault boats into the water and paddled into the darkness ("A" Company and John Bain were to cross the next morning). With 300 yards to go they were spotted. "D" Company made the bank with only three casualties but "C" Company received serious casualties, including one boat that disappeared and was never heard of again. Thankfully, though, a small bridgehead was made.

John Bain of Richmond in army uniform

Throughout the night, repeated efforts were made to find the hidden Japanese machine gun which was causing such losses on the beach and jeopardising the reinforcement, but without success. Early the following morning the reinforcements made the crossing and most of the remainder of the Battalion crossed safely. However, the whole of "A" Company HQ, including the Company Commander, Major Bain, was lost, with the exception of one man.

John Bain was buried close to where he died, but after the war his body was brought to Taukkyan War Cemetery and buried in grave 19.D.16., close to that of his Richmond compatriot, Harvey Todd.

MAJOR JOHN HOLDSWORTH (MC)
NO. 117672 2ND BATTALION KING'S ROYAL RIFLE CORPS
DIED MARCH 2ND 1945 AGED 24

The Holdsworth family of Scargill House, near Kettlewell, had already suffered in the war, when, in February 1942, Michael Holdsworth had died in his Swordfish aircraft whilst serving in the Fleet Air Arm in the Mediterranean.

John Holdsworth of Kettlewell, Wharfedale

John, his older brother, had been a Territorial soldier before the war and at its outset served with the 2nd Battalion KRRC, rising to the rank of Major. Whilst serving with his regiment in the Western Desert he won the Military Cross for his bravery in action and in the process received a severe wound to the face, part of it being blown away. He returned to England and was in hospital for a long time, his face being permanently disfigured, and then recuperated later at Scargill House. He was there in October 1942 when his father, George Bertram Holdsworth died. The coffin was borne from Scargill to Kettlewell Church on a lorry, on which it rested on a bed of heather taken from his grouse moors at Conistone. The grave was also lined with heather and six tenants and employees on his estate acted as bearers.

As the war began to edge towards its conclusion, John Holdsworth was desperate to be in there at the end. He should never normally have been allowed to go back, considering his injuries and the splendid effort he had already put into the war effort, but the Regiment gave him special dispensation to go back to his old Battalion, knowing that the war was coming to an end.

Between February 8th and March 10th 1945 the clearing of the Rhineland began, in the region of the Reichswald Forest. A pincer move was made by Montgomery's forces between the River Maas (Meuse) and the Rhine and by March 3rd the pincers met at Geldern. German resistance began collapsing. However, on March 2nd, during the battle, John Holdsworth was killed.

A few days prior to his death, the Battalion had played its part in capturing the German town of Udem, 30 miles NW of Duisberg and Essen. After a brief respite, however, the 2nd Battalion came back into the attack

The attack at 13-30 hours on March 1st was to be against the Schleiffen defence line of fire trenches, anti-tank ditches, mine-fields and machine gun posts. Though the opposition was extremely fierce it was still believed that a breakthrough of the Line was possible and so it was planned on March 2nd that "B" Company, led by John , would pass through "A" and "C" Companies at 14-00 hours and make a frontal attack against and through the Schlieffen Line up to Brovenhof, 1000 yards further east.

At that hour No. 7 Platoon went down the road while Nos. 6 and 8 Platoons went through the woods on the right, with some of "B" Squadron's tanks giving close support. No. 7 Platoon took the next farmhouse beyond the ditch, but not without casualties. It was at this moment that John Holdsworth led his men against the next house where there was a very troublesome German with a Spandau machine gun. John was mortally wounded, and though Sergeant Flanagan brought him in and made him comfortable he died shortly afterwards. The next morning, after being relieved, stock was taken and a special funeral service was held by Leslie Morrison, the Padre, for Johnny Holdsworth.

Later in the war he was buried in grave 46.B.5. Reichswald Forest War Cemetery. In the 1950's two stained glass windows were commissioned for Kettlewell Church, one commemorating Michael and the other, John Holdsworth. However, these were kept in crates for many years until they were installed in the early 1970's.

The next two casualties in 1945 came from Richmond and both were part of the same air crew of an aircraft that was brought down on April 24th 1945 in the waters off Southern Norway.

SERGEANT ALLEN DOUGLAS BLAKEY
NO. 1055959 (W. OP./AIR GUNNER) 58 SQUADRON RAFVR
DIED APRIL 24TH 1945 AGED 24

Allen was the son of Beatrice Blakey of Tynemouth, Northumberland, but he had strong connections with Richmond, living at Newbiggin. He trained as a wireless operator and air gunner and in 1945 was serving with 58 Squadron of Coastal Command, operating Halifax bombers out of RAF St. Davids, on the northern shore of the Firth of Forth.

AND
FLIGHT SERGEANT GEORGE WILLIAM RAMSAY
NO. 1558928 (W.OP./AIR GUNNER) 58 SQUADRON RAFVR
DIED APRIL 24TH 1945 AGED 24

Coronation Place, Richmond, was the home of John and Annie Ramsay and their son George. He, too, volunteered for the RAF and trained to become a wireless operator and air gunner, finding himself in the same Squadron as his Richmond colleague, Allen Blakey, and even more amazingly, flying in the same aircraft. They had met by chance at a Training School in the United States and continued flying together.

Both airmen were killed on April 24th 1945 when their heavy bomber, Halifax JP299, went missing while on Anti-Shipping Patrol in the Skaggerak and Kattegat sea area, between Denmark and Southern Norway.

Allen Douglas Blakey's name is commemorated on Panel 273 Runnymede Memorial, whilst George William Ramsay's name is on Panel 272.

The sadness felt by their families would be great, but happiness of a kind came to most dales people with the news that the German Reich would surrender at midnight on May 8th/9th and the following day, Victory in Europe Day (VE Day), celebrations in all the parishes began. In Grassington and Linton a service was held in the church and chapel, whilst bonfires and beacons blazed out.

Skipton's observance of VE Day was in the nature of thanksgiving rather than jollification and it was not until late evening that the lights came on again in High Street and the war memorial and parish church were floodlit, the first time since September 1939 that the town really let itself go for a few hours. A crowd gathered in High Street and loudspeakers broadcast music that the people danced to. A bonfire blazed on waste ground and the town was bedecked with the colours of the Allied nations. For the children, there was the good news that schools would be closed for two days.

At Cracoe, festoons of streamers were draped about and across the main street, in addition to many flags. The children gathered material for a bonfire, until a huge pile, capped by a "Hitler", was built in Mr. Haighton's croft, opposite the Devonshire Arms, where there was much jubilation, including the setting off of home made fireworks. Earlier that evening, a well attended service of thanksgiving was held at Rylstone Church by Reverend Rees.

Church bells rang out in Richmond as a Service of Thanksgiving took place, whilst the Band of the Green Howards played in the Friary Gardens and the townspeople began to dance. There was dancing in the Castle Grounds and large crowds flocked up Hurgill Road to the High Moor where the beacon was set alight, after the National Anthem was sung.

As darkness fell, electric lamps gleamed from the trees in Queen's Road, whilst Greyfriars Tower was floodlit and 1940's music was played, as people danced until 1a.m.

A house decorated for VE Day on The Green, Richmond

Next day, the celebrations continued with sports for the children in the Castle Grounds. A flag sent by the children of Richmond in Tasmania in 1910 was flown from Trinity Tower. In the days that followed, tea parties and street sports were held. A Victory tea party for 90 children was held in Coronation Place and another

VE Day street party on Tower Street, Richmond

was held on The Green, together with sports and a competition for the most suitably decorated house. The Dunn family won first prize. On Thanksgiving Sunday Richmond Parish Church was packed, with Lord Zetland taking the salute as a great parade marched past him, whilst a repatriated POW stood on either side of him.

At Reeth and Grinton a United Thanksgiving Service was held in Reeth Methodist Chapel in the afternoon and Grinton Church in the evening, when the congregation was augmented by troops from Reeth Battle School, under Major Parry. Houses were decorated with flags and streamers, some being floodlit during the evening, whilst a bonfire was set alight on the Green, when an effigy of Hitler was burned.

Meanwhile, despite the relief that the war in Europe had come to an end, the fight against the Japanese continued in the Far East, with many dales' servicemen involved. It was at home in England, however, that the next serviceman died.

AIRCRAFTMAN 2ND CLASS PERCY EARL
NO. 1689955 RAFVR
DIED MAY 17TH 1945 AGED 40

Percy Earl was from Richmond, a younger son of George and Margaret and husband of Kathleen Earl. His parents were both born in Richmond, with George employed in 1901 as a gas stoker at the town's gas works. One branch of the Earl family in Richmond were fellmongers, agents for collecting the carcasses of animals and their hides. When Percy married, he lived with his wife at 53 Newbiggin, Richmond, and joined the RAF during the war, serving as an Aircraftman Second Class. However, he was discharged from the RAF on a pension, due to ill-health, and resumed work as a general labourer. However, his illness worsened and he died at home from Pulmonary Tuberculosis on May 17th 1945. Percy Earl was buried in grave N54, Richmond Cemetery.

The final death of a serviceman from these dales during the Second World War took place far away in India and involved a man from the village of Hudswell, near Richmond.

STAFF SERGEANT JAMES E. ATKINSON
NO. 4389441 ROYAL ELECTRICAL AND MECHANICAL ENGINEERS
DIED JUNE 7TH 1945 AGED 24

Jimmy Atkinson was the second eldest child of Arthur and Florence (two sisters and a brother completed the family). Arthur was from the village of Cockfield, between Barnard Castle and Bishop Auckland, whilst his wife was from London. He was a bricklayer, de-mobbed after the Great War, and Catterick Camp was "crying out" for builders and associate trades. Arthur and his wife arrived in the nearby village of Hudswell.

Jimmy left Hudswell School at 14 and became an apprentice mechanic on Catterick Camp. He joined the Territorial Army before the war and was called up when war was declared. With Jimmy's work background, it was no surprise that he was posted to the Royal Electrical and Mechanical Engineers and by 1944 was in India, helping in the fight against the Japanese attempt to enter that country.

Hudswell School 1932.
Back row: Joseph Brohee, Dennis Hunt, James Atkinson, Frank Stephenson, Ronald Stephenson, George Stephenson, Hanry Lazell.
Next row: Teacher Miss Copes, Annie Brunskill, Doreen Stephenson, Peggy Collinson, Martha Brunskill, May Blenkiron, Elizabeth Brunskill, Mary Brunskill, Daisy Wilson, Headmistress Miss Bramall.
Next row: Florence Stephenson, Annie Collinson, Margaret Brunskill, Mary Atkinson, Edna Stephenson, Bessie Collinson, Doris Pearson, Eunice Watt, Mary Chandler, Elsie Mattison.
Front row: Arthur Atkinson, Jack Birstall, Robert Walker, William Harrison, Ronald Brown, Albert Hustwick, Dennis Parnaby, Allan Chandler, Arthur Hustwick, Richard Brunskill.
James Atkinson and Allan Chandler would both die whilst serving with the army in the Second World War. Joseph Brohee's father was a wounded Belgian soldier from the Great War who remained in England as a gardener at Hudswell Vicarage and married a local girl working at the vicarage.

It was, however, in an accident in India, that James Atkinson died, on June 7th 1945. He was buried in grave I.E.9. Kirkee War Cemetery, near Poona, India.

The surrender of the Japanese on September 2nd 1945, resulting mainly from the dropping of atomic bombs on Hiroshima and Nagasaki in August, brought the Second World War to a conclusion. Although the celebrations were a little more muted than on VE Day, Victory over Japan Day witnessed the relief and thanksgiving of people in the dales.

Celebrations at Skipton were on similar lines to those of VE Day and on Wednesday morning there were long queues at the bread shops. On VJ Day at Grassington there was a tea party for the children at Church House. A bonfire was lit on Beacon Hill in the evening and there was a dance, with the company being entertained by the local glee club.

At Kettlewell the flag of St. George flew from a flagpole on the tower of the parish church and many flags and bunting were strewn from the houses. A thanksgiving service was conducted on Wednesday by Reverend A. Marchant and on Thursday the children enjoyed a tea and games at the village hall and later there was a "social".

A combined service was held in St. Peter's Church in the village of Hebden. A dance was held in the schoolroom and a happy crowd danced to the music supplied by Mr. Whip Parker's accordion and a friend on the piano. On Thursday evening, the villagers assembled on the street to sing and dance and Mrs. Simpson had her piano brought out into the road to provide music. At nearby Linton, the children's sports on Wednesday were postponed because of the bad weather and were held on Thursday on the village green.

At Burnsall there was a tea and games for the children on Thursday, with a whist drive and social following in the evening. On Saturday night there was a firework display in Old School Yard.

Twenty two children enjoyed a party held in Arncliffe Village Hall on the Saturday. Cakes, difficult to produce in any case, and with the position being aggravated by the two day holiday, miraculously appeared for the children. Tea was followed by games. A photograph of parents and children was taken to commemorate the event. On Friday night there had been a well attended dance in the village hall. Some 200 people from a wide area patronised the event, giving it all the elements of a real victory celebration. The Midnight Follies Dance Band supplied the music.

Children's parties were held all over Richmond. 80 children from Darlington Road, Anchorage Hill, Maison Dieu and The Terrace held celebrations in the grounds of St. Nicholas. In the Parish Room there was a party for 100 children from Frenchgate, Pottergate and Lombard's Wynd, whilst 200 children from Victoria Road, Quaker Lane, Hurgill Road, Westfields, etc., had their party in Joplings Field.

Japan's surrender brought to a conclusion the participation of Swaledale, Arkengarthdale, Wharfedale, Langstrothdale and Littondale in the Second World War. As the servicemen and women began their return to civilian life during 1946 and 1947, they readjusted to the novel experience of being back with their loved ones and looked forward to a return to peacetime conditions.

For the families of the 98 servicemen who had died in the war there was sadness. Yet even with an end to the conflict, it was not to be the end of the story of the men whose names are commemorated on the village war memorials. Between 1946 and 1947, four more servicemen died and had their names inscribed.

WARRANT OFFICER CLASS II (CSM) ALFRED STUBBS
NO. 1865137 ROYAL ENGINEERS
DIED MAY 21ST 1946 AGED 42

Alfred was born in Grassington, the second son of James Stubbs, and after leaving school he worked in the local quarries. In 1929 he decided to join the regular army and went to Aldershot, where he became a member of a mounted section of the Royal Engineers. Although based at Aldershot throughout his army career, he came home regularly to Grassington, and married May Longstaffe, a local girl.

Alfred Stubbs of Grassington

By 1938 they were living in Aldershot and it was there that their sons, James and Harold, were born. However, in these pre-war years, Alfred was often away serving abroad, mainly in Egypt and Palestine. He served with the BEF in France and Belgium and was evacuated from Dunkirk. He spent a great deal of the rest of the war years in Egypt, helping in training the new arrivals and being involved in the fighting in the Western Desert.

Alfred survived the war and continued serving in the army. However, in the Spring of 1946, he was taken ill and admitted to the Cambridge Hospital at Aldershot, with suspected double pneumonia brought on by his work in the army. It was discovered, however, that he also had lung cancer and after nine weeks of illness Alfred died on May 21st 1946, at the age of 42. His body was brought back to Grassington by road by an officer and eight members of the Royal Engineers and he was buried in Linton churchyard with full military honours. The cortege left the Black Horse Hotel, Grassington, on Monday May 27th for internment at 2-30p.m. The family returned to live in Grassington and Alfred's name was inscribed on Linton War Memorial.

CRAFTSMAN EDWIN HARKER
NO. 10592739 ROYAL ELECTRICAL AND MECHANICAL ENGINEERS
DIED NOVEMBER 7TH 1946 AGED 30

The son of Mr. and Mrs. Edwin Harker of Grassington, Edwin worked for Messrs. G.H.. Mason and Sons, a firm of painters and plumbers, at No. 54 High Street, Skipton. Edwin was a popular member of the Devonshire Institute and Congregational Church. He enlisted during the war and joined the Royal Electrical and Mechanical Engineers. He married and he and his wife, Alice Edna Harker, lived at Sylvadene, Grassington, where their son was born in 1942.

However, in 1944 Edwin contracted tuberculosis whilst serving in the army and received treatment for the illness. He died, at the age of 30, in Middleton Sanatorium on November 7th 1946, leaving a young widow and four year old son. His coffin was draped in the Union Jack when he was buried in grave S.31. Grassington Independent Chapel Yard.

GUNNER NEVILLE LITTLE
NO. 781532 16TH FIELD REGIMENT ROYAL ARTILLERY
DIED MAY 27TH 1947 AGED 37

Neville was born in Leeds, the son of John and Mary Little. In civilian life he became a crane driver but by 1930 was serving in the regular army as a farrier with the Royal Artillery, and later as a gunner. He arrived in the Richmond area, at Catterick

Above: Neville Little in Burma, sitting on the extreme right

Right: Neville Little of Richmond

Camp, and in 1932 he met and married a Richmond girl, Muriel Jane Kipling (she was related to Walter and Harold Kipling, who had been killed within days of each other, in June 1944). Children were born and the family lived at 9 Hurgill Road.

When war broke out in 1939, Neville was on paid reserve and was called back straight away, going out with the BEF to France and returning to Richmond from Dunkirk in a very bedraggled state. By 1942 he was in the Far East, fighting the Japanese on the north east border of India and later in Burma, with the 2nd Division. He was involved in actions near Kohima, and in the fighting at Imphal and Tiddim, but during later actions he was wounded when the jeep he was travelling in received a direct hit from a Japanese shell. It was some time before he was attended to and he contracted malaria.

Neville was transferred to hospital in India and was then brought back to England, still suffering from malaria. Although his wounds healed, it was not realised that a blood clot had formed as a result of the injuries, and on May 27th 1947 he died, aged 37. He is buried in grave N.52. Richmond Cemetery.

Richard Gilbert as a child at Threshfield School

PRIVATE RICHARD GILBERT
NO. 5885509 NORTHAMPTONSHIRE REGIMENT
DIED JULY 12TH 1947 AGED 25

Richard was the son of Thomas and Elizabeth Gilbert of Threshfield, near Grassington, and the younger brother of Edward, who, we have seen, won the Military Medal during the war and was killed in Italy in 1944. Richard, who lived with his wife, Elsie Laura Gilbert, at South View, Threshfield, worked as a limestone quarry labourer and was in the army during the later stages of the war. However, he contracted tuberculosis and in 1947 he was admitted to Middleton Sanatorium,

Aireborough, Wharfedale. He died from Tuberculous meningitis, pulmonary tuberculosis and TB of the spine at the Sanatorium on July 12th 1947 and is commemorated in St. Michael's Churchyard, Linton.

The stories of the lives and deaths of servicemen from the dales, whose names are inscribed on the parish war memorials, is now complete, with the exception of two. Sadly, I have been unable to find any details about **Private A. Brand of the Middlesex Regiment**, whose name is commemorated on the Richmond War Memorial (he may be connected to the Brand family who ran a garage and bus company in Queen's Road). **Captain John Michael Sharp**, whose name appears on the Reeth Memorial, has also proved something of an enigma. I do know that during the latter part of the war he brought his wife and children to live at High Fremington, in a cottage behind Draycott Hall. One resident of Fremington from those times remembered his weeping wife being led back to her cottage from Draycott Hall, after receiving news of her husband's death from Mrs. Radcliffe, the owner of the hall. Another resident remembers, as a young girl, having the responsibility of taking the two sons to Fremington School for a short while, before the family left the Reeth area. As with the seven servicemen from the Great War, whose stories I was unable to tell, Private Brand and Captain Sharp are remembered with honour in "Swaledale and Wharfedale Remembered".

The Second World War had finally come to an end, and with it, the dales' participation in five and a half years of dreadful conflict. The many parishes throughout Swaledale, Arkengarthdale, Littondale, Langstrothdale and Wharfedale had experienced the closeness of war with the activities of the local ARP, Fire Brigade, Home Guard and the arrival of the regular army, together with that of the evacuees from the threatened urban areas, during the anxious days of 1940/1941.

Bringing the horrors of war even closer to many people in the dales was the involvement of family members and friends in combat with the enemy in different theatres of war and the loss of 102 people from these parishes whilst serving their country. For those who returned home safely to the dales, there was relief and joy, but for 102 families and their relations, there was much sadness.

Born just after the conclusion of the Second World War, I have lived through 60 years of relative peace in these islands, without the necessity of being called to fight for "Queen and Country". It is my sincere belief that this is partly due to the sacrifice made by people such as those whose stories are told within the pages of this book, and to those who fought alongside them and thankfully survived. This book is dedicated in honour of the men from these dales who did not return. They will be remembered.

Index